International Economic Association Series

More information about this series at
http://www.springernature.com/series/13991

INSTITUTIONS AND COMPARATIVE ECONOMIC DEVELOPMENT
Edited by Franklin Allen, Masahiko Aoki, Nobuhiro Kiyotaki, Roger Gordon, Joseph E. Stiglitz and Jean-Paul Fitoussi

COMPLEXITY AND INSTITUTIONS: MARKETS, NORMS AND CORPORATIONS
Edited by Masahiko Aoki, Kenneth Binmore, Simon Deakin and Herbert Gintis

CORPORATE SOCIAL RESPONSIBILITY AND CORPORATE GOVERNANCE
The Contribution of Economic Theory and Related Disciplines
Edited by Lorenzo Sacconi, Margaret Blair, R. Edward Freeman and Alessandro Vercelli

IS ECONOMIC GROWTH SUSTAINABLE?
Edited by Geoffrey Heal

KEYNE'S GENERAL THEORY AFTER SEVENTY YEARS
Edited by Robert Diman, Robert Mundell and Alessandro Vercelli

CORRUPTION, DEVELOPMENT AND INSTITUTIONAL DESIGN
Edited by János Kornai, László Mátyás and Gérard Roland

MARKET AND SOCIALISM
In the Light of the Experience of China and Vietnam
Edited by János Kornai and Yingyi Quian

INSTITUTIONAL CHANGE AND ECONOMIC BEHAVIOUR
Edited by János Kornai, László Mátyás and Gérard Roland

INTERGENERATIONAL EQUITY AND SUSTAINABILITY
Edited by John E. Roemer and Kotaro Suzumura

PSYCHOLOGY, RATIONALITY AND ECONOMIC BEHAVIOUR
Challenging Standard Assumptions
Edited by Bina Agarwal and Alessandro Vercelli

MULTINATIONALS AND FOREIGN INVESTMENT IN ECONOMIC DEVELOPMENT
Edited by Edward M. Graham

POST-CONFLICT ECONOMIES IN AFRICA
Edited by Paul Collier and Augustin Kwasi Fosu

STRUCTURAL REFORM AND MACROECONOMIC POLICY
Edited by Robert M. Solow

THE PAST, PRESENT AND FUTURE OF THE EUROPEAN UNION
Edited by Alan V. Deardorff

LATIN AMERICAN ECONOMIC CRISES
Trade and Labour
Edited by Enrique Bour, Daniel Heymann and Fernando Navajas

ADVANCES IN MACROECONOMIC THEORY
Edited by Jacques H. Drèze

EXPLAINING GROWTH
A Global Research Project
Edited by Gary McMahon and Lyn Squire

TRADE, INVESTMENT, MIGRATION AND LABOUR MARKET ADJUSTMENT
Edited by David Greenaway, Richard Upward and Katherine Wakelin

INEQUALITY AROUND THE WORLD
Edited by Richard B. Freeman

MONETARY THEORY AND POLICY EXPERIENCE
Edited by Axel Leijonhufvud

MONETARY THEORY AS A BASIS FOR MONETARY POLICY
Edited by Axel Leijonhufvud

ECONOMIC DEVELOPMENT IN SUBSAHARAN AFRICA
Proceedings of the Eleventh World Congress of the International Economic Association, Tunis
Edited by Ibrahim Elbadawi and Beno Ndula

International Economics Association
Series Standing Order ISBN 978-0-3337-1242-9 (Hardback)
978-0-3338-0330-1 (Paperback)
(*outside North America only*)

You can receive future titles in this series as they are published by placing a standing order. Please contact your bookseller or, in case of difficulty, write to us at the address below with your name and address, the title of the series and one of the ISBNs quoted above.

Customer Services Department, Macmillan Distribution Ltd, Houndmills, Basingstoke, Hampshire RG21 6XS, England

Kaushik Basu • Tito Cordella
Editors

Institutions, Governance and the Control of Corruption

palgrave
macmillan

Editors
Kaushik Basu
The World Bank
Washington, DC, USA

Tito Cordella
The World Bank
Washington, DC, USA

International Economic Association Series
ISBN 978-3-319-73822-2   ISBN 978-3-319-65684-7   (eBook)
https://doi.org/10.1007/978-3-319-65684-7

Library of Congress Control Number: 2017955820

Printed on acid-free paper

This Palgrave Macmillan imprint is published by Springer Nature
The registered company is Springer International Publishing AG
The registered company address is: Gewerbestrasse 11, 6330 Cham, Switzerland

The promotion of shared prosperity and the battle against poverty require interventions to reach out to the poor and the disadvantaged. Yet time and again we have seen such effort foiled or diminished by corruption and leakage. The creation of good governance and institutions and structures to combat corruption require determination and passion but also intricate design rooted in data, analysis, and research. In this book, leading researchers from around the world bring to the table some of the best available ideas to help create better governance structures, design laws for corruption control, and nurture good institutions.

Contents

Contributors

Pranab Bardhan is professor of Graduate School in the Economics Department of the University of California at Berkeley. He was educated in Presidency College, Calcutta, and Cambridge University, UK. Before joining Berkeley he had been on the faculty of MIT, Indian Statistical Institute and Delhi School of Economics. He was the Chief Editor of the *Journal of Development Economics* for 18 years. He is the author of 14 books and more than 150 journal articles, and the editor of 12 books.

Timothy Besley is School Professor of Economics and Political Science and W. Arthur Lewis Professor of Development Economics at the London School of Economics and Political Science and a Fellow of All Souls College, Oxford. From September 2006 to August 2009, he served as an external member of the Bank of England Monetary Policy Committee and since 2015 was appointed as a founding commissioner of the UK's National Infrastructure Commission. He is the President of the *International Economic Association* and served as the President of the *European Economic Association* in 2010. In 2018, he will serve as President of the *Econometric Society*. He is a past co-editor of the *American Economic Review* and winner of the 2005 Yrjo Jahnsson Award.

Laura Chioda is a Senior Economist in the Office of the Chief Economist of the Latin America and Caribbean Region and in the Office of the Chief Economist for Equitable Growth, Finance, and Institutions at the World Bank. She received her PhD in Economics from the University of California, Berkeley. Prior to joining the World Bank, Laura was an Assistant Professor of Economics at Princeton University. Her research interests range from theoretical econometric issues of identification, limits of experiments, and weak identification to behavioral economics, intra-household decisions, and crime and violence. She is the author of the Regional Study on crime and violence prevention titled *Stop the Violence in Latin America: A Look at Prevention from Cradle to Adulthood*, and of another Regional Study on gender and labor markets titled *Work and Family: Latin American and Caribbean Women in Search of a New Balance*. She has also co-authored the World Bank report "Making Brazilians Safer: Analyzing the Dynamics of Violent Crime." Her research includes published and ongoing work on the impacts of conditional cash transfers on crime and violence in Brazil, and on the human and economic costs of violence induced by Mexico's "kingpin" strategy. As a member of the World Bank's Development Impact Evaluation Initiative (DIME), Laura co-leads DIME's Program on Fragility, Conflict, and Crime and Violence.

João Manoel Pinho Mello After receiving his PhD in Economics from Stanford University in 2005, Joao Manoel Pinho De Mello joined the faculty of the Economics Department at the Catholic University in Rio de Janeiro (PUC-Rio). He is a Professor of Economics at Insper (on leave) and the Deputy Minister for Microeconomic Reforms at the Ministry of Finance, Brazil. His work has been published in prestigious international academic journals and books, such as the *Review of Economic Studies;* the *Review of Economics and Statistics;* the *Economic Journal;* the *Journal of Money, Credit, and Banking;* the *Journal of Economic Behavior and Organization;* the *Economics of Education Review* and *Review of Finance*. He is a researcher of the Brazilian National Counsel of Scientific and Technological Development (CNPq) and was a member of the Brazilian Academy of Sciences (2012–2016). He was a founder and a co-head of the America Latina Crime and Policy Network – LACEA (AL CAPONE). De Mello was also a regular Op-Ed columnist for *Folha de São Paulo*, the most important Brazilian newspaper (2016–2017).

Shantayanan Devarajan is the Chief Economist of the World Bank's Middle East and North Africa Region. Since joining the World Bank in 1991, he has been a Principal Economist and Research Manager for Public Economics in the Development Research Group, and the Chief Economist of the Human Development Network, South Asia and Africa Region. He was the Director of the *World Development Report 2004, Making Services Work for Poor People*.

Before 1991, he was on the faculty of Harvard University's John F. Kennedy School of Government. The author or co-author of over 100 publications, Mr.

Devarajan's research covers public economics, trade policy, natural resources and the environment, and general equilibrium modeling of developing countries. Born in Sri Lanka, Mr. Devarajan received his Bachelor's degree in Mathematics from Princeton University and his PhD in Economics from the University of California, Berkeley.

Avinash Dixit is Sherrerd University Professor of Economics, Emeritus, at Princeton University. He previously held faculty positions at Berkeley, Oxford, and Warwick Universities, and visiting scholar positions at the World Bank, IMF, and the Russell Sage Foundation. He was President of the Econometric Society (2001) and of the American Economic Association (2008). He was elected to the American Academy of Arts and Sciences in 1992 and the National Academy of Sciences in 2005, the American Philosophical Society in 2010, and a Corresponding (Foreign) Fellowship of the British Academy in 2006. His awards include the Padma Vibhushan from the President of India (2016) and honorary doctorates from the Norwegian School of Economics and Business Administration (1996), Warwick University, UK (2007), and Stockholm University (2009). His research interests have included microeconomic theory, game theory, international trade, industrial organization, growth and development theories, public economics, political economy, and the new institutional economics. His book publications include Theory of International Trade (with Victor Norman), Thinking Strategically (with Barry Nalebuff), Investment Under Uncertainty (with Robert Pindyck), The Making of Economic Policy: A Transaction Cost Politics Perspective, Games of Strategy (with Susan Skeath), Lawlessness and Economics, and Microeconomics: A Very Short Introduction. He has also published numerous articles in professional journals and collective volumes.

Juan Dubra is a Professor of Economics at Universidad de Montevideo. His fields of study are decision theory, applied economic theory, and political economy. His recent focus in his theoretical work has been in overconfidence and in attitude polarization. His studies in political economy include the analyses of why do good cops defend bad cops, and why some countries punish more than others. He holds a Bachelor's degree in Economics from Uruguay, and Master's and PhD degrees from New York University. Although he has lived in Uruguay since graduation, he has been a visiting professor at Yale, Carnegie Mellon and New York University.

Claudio Ferraz is the Itaú-Unibanco Associate Professor of Development Economics at the Pontifícia Universidade Católica do Rio de Janeiro (PUC-Rio). He is a co-director of LACEA's Network of Political Economy, a research fellow of the Bureau for Research in Economic Analysis of Development (BREAD), a research fellow of the IGC and a member of the Jameel Poverty Action Lab (JPAL) at MIT. He holds a PhD in Agricultural and Resource Economics from UC-Berkeley and has been a visiting professor at LSE, MIT and Stanford University.

Frederico Finan is a jointly appointed associate professor in the Department of Economics and the Haas School of Business, at UC-Berkeley. He is a co-director of Berkeley's Center for Economics and Politics, a research associate at the National Bureau of Economic Research, a research fellow of the Bureau for Research in Economic Analysis of Development, and a member of the Jameel Poverty Action Lab at MIT. In 2013, Finan was an Alfred P. Sloan Research Fellow. He holds a PhD in Agricultural and Resource Economics from UC-Berkeley and has held faculty positions at UCLA and Stanford GSB.

Francis Fukuyama is a Senior Fellow at Stanford and Director of its Center on Democracy, Development and the Rule of Law. He is the author of *Political Order and Political Decay: From the Industrial Revolution to the Globalization of Democracy* (Profile Books 2014).

Diego Gambetta is Professor of Social Theory at the European University Institute, in Florence, Italy. Born in Turin, Italy, he received his PhD in Social and Political Sciences from the University of Cambridge, UK, in 1983. From 1984 to 1991, he was Research Fellow at King's College, Cambridge. Since 1992 he has been at the University of Oxford. He has been visiting professor at the University of Chicago, Columbia University, EHT in Zurich, Stanford University, Science Po and the Collège de France in Paris. His interests are trust, signaling theory and its applications, organized crime and violent extremists. He is the author of *The Sicilian Mafia* (1993), *Streetwise* (2005), *Codes of the Underworld* (2009) and *Engineers of Jihad* (2016). In 2000 he was made a Fellow of the British Academy.

Nona Karalashvili is an Economist at the Enterprise Analysis Unit of the World Bank. Her research interests span the fields of economics, psychology and anthropology, with the main focus on institutional economics. She received her PhD in Economics from the University of Maryland, College Park.

Stuti Khemani is a Senior Economist in the Development Research Group of the World Bank. She joined through the Young Professionals Program after obtaining a PhD in Economics from the Massachusetts Institute of Technology. Her area of research is the political economy of public policy choices, and institutional reforms for development. Her work is published in economics and political science journals, such as the *American Economic Journal, Journal of Development Economics* and *American Political Science Review*. She is the lead author of the Policy Research Report *Making Politics Work for Development: Harnessing Transparency and Citizen Engagement*. She is examining how policy actors can design governance and transparency interventions to build state capacity and strengthen behavioral norms in the public sector. Her research and advisory work spans a diverse range of countries, including Benin, China, India, the Philippines, Nigeria, Tanzania and Uganda.

Stephen Knack is a Lead Economist in the Development Research Group (Macro and Growth Team). His research on aid effectiveness, public sector governance, and social capital has been widely published in leading economics and political science journals. Prior to joining the World Bank in 1999, Knack was a research associate at the University of Maryland's IRIS Center, and assistant professor in the School of Public Affairs at American University. He received a PhD in Economics from the University of Maryland in 1991.

Aart Kraay is an Economist in the Development Research Group at the World Bank. He joined the World Bank in 1995 after earning a PhD in Economics from Harvard University (1995), and a Bachelor's degree in Economics from the University of Toronto (1990). His research interests include international capital movements, growth and inequality, governance, and the Chinese economy. His research on these topics has been published in scholarly journals such as the *Quarterly Journal of Economics*, the *Review of Economics and Statistics*, the *Economic Journal*, the *Journal of Monetary Economics*, the *Journal of International Economics*, and the *Journal of the European Economic Association*. He is an Associate Editor of the *Journal of Development Economics*, and co-editor of the *World Bank Economic Review*. He has also held visiting positions at the International Monetary Fund and the Sloan School of Management at MIT and has taught at the School of Advanced International Studies at Johns Hopkins University.

Hannes Mueller is a Ramon y Cajal Researcher at the Institute for Economic Analysis (IAE, CSIC). He is affiliated with the Barcelona GSE, MOVE and CEPR. Hannes completed his PhD in Economics at the London School of Economics (LSE). He holds Master's degree in Economics from the LSE and a diploma in Economics from the University of Mannheim. His research interests are political economy, development economics and conflict studies. He has worked on the economic costs of armed conflict in several research projects and published policy reports at the International Growth Centre (IGC) and the World Bank.

Peter Murrell is the Mancur Olson Professor of Economics at the University of Maryland, College Park. He received both his Bachelor's and Master's degrees in Economics from the London School of Economics and his PhD from the University of Pennsylvania. He has written over 70 peer-reviewed journal articles, 19 book chapters, two books, and one edited collection. His research interests in the transition economies of Eastern Europe and the successor states of the USSR included field work—surveying firms—in Mongolia, Russia and Romania. This research raised the question of the accuracy of survey-based estimates of corruption, which provided the stimulus for the work investigating the underestimation of corruption.

Santiago Levy is the Vice-President for Sectors and Knowledge at the Inter-American Development Bank, and previously Chief Economist. Previously, he was General Director at the Mexican Social Security Institute (IMSS) from December 2000 to October 2005.

From 1994 to 2000, Levy served as the Deputy Minister at the Ministry of Finance and Public Credit of Mexico, becoming the main architect of the renowned social program *Progresa-Oportunidades* that benefits the poor.

He holds a PhD in Economics and a Master's degree in Political Economy from Boston University. He was a post-doctoral fellow at Cambridge University. Mr. Levy has advised several governments and international organizations and has held several teaching positions, including faculty positions at the Instituto Tecnológico Autónomo of Mexico and Boston University, where he was associate professor and Director of the Institute for Economic Development.

He is the author of at least 80 articles, monographs and book chapters on such diverse subjects as poverty reduction, competitiveness, foreign exchange policy, export imbalances, pricing, microeconomics and energy. His paper *Poverty in Mexico* won the 1992 National Research Prize in Economics awarded by the Bank of Mexico. His recent published books are *No Growth without Equity? Inequality, Interests and Competition in Mexico* (edited with Michael Walton), Palgrave-Macmillan and the World Bank, 2009; *Good Intentions, Bad Outcomes: Social Policy, Informality, and Economic Growth in Mexico*, Brookings Institution Press, 2008; *Progress Against Poverty: Sustaining Mexico's Progresa-Oportunidades Program*, Brookings Institution Press, 2006; *Sin Herencia de Pobreza*, Editorial Planeta, 2005 (with Evelyne Rodríguez); and *Ensayos sobre el Desarrollo Económico y Social de México*, Fondo de Cultura Económica, Mexico, 2004.

Luis F. Lopez-Calva is the Practice Manager for Europe and Central Asia in the Poverty and Equity Global Practice at the World Bank. Previously, he was co-director of the World Development Report 2017: Governance and the Law. He has been Lead Economist and Regional Poverty Advisor in the Europe and Central Asia region, and until 2013 was Lead Economist in the Poverty, Equity and Gender Unit in the Latin America and Caribbean PREM Directorate at the World Bank. He also served as Chief Economist for Latin America and the Caribbean at the United Nations Development Program (UNDP) from 2007 to 2010. He has been an Ivy League Exchange Scholar in the Economics Department at Harvard University, as well as Visiting Scholar at the Center for International Development at Stanford University and the World Institute for Development Economics Research (WIDER). In Mexico, he was a member of the National System of Researchers (SNI), Associate Professor and Chair of the Masters in Public Economics at Tecnológico de Monterrey, Mexico City Campus, and he also taught at Universidad de las Américas Puebla and El Colegio de México. He holds a Master's degree and PhD in Economics from Cornell University and a Master's degree in Economics from Boston University. His publications and research interests focus on labor markets, poverty and inequality, institutions and development economics.

Bonnie J. Palifka is an associate professor at the Tecnologico de Monterrey, Campus Monterrey, in Mexico, where she has taught a course on corruption since 2004; she has taught a similar course since 2011 at Yale University. She has spoken on corruption at conferences internationally and collaborated on projects for the UNODC and Transparency International. Dr. Palifka is co-author of *Corruption and Government: Causes, Consequences, and Reform* (Second edition).

Martin Rama is the Chief Economist for the South Asia region of the World Bank, based in Delhi. Before that he was the Director of the World Development Report (WDR) 2013, on *Jobs*. Previously, for eight years, he was the Lead Economist for Vietnam, based in Hanoi. Prior to moving to operations, he spent ten years with the research department of the World Bank. Martin Rama gained his degree in Economics from the Universidad de la República (Uruguay) in 1981 and his PhD in Macroeconomics from the Université de Paris I (France) in 1985. Back to his home country, Uruguay, he worked in CINVE, the country's largest think tank. In parallel with his World Bank duties, he was visiting professor at the graduate program in Development Economics at the Université de Paris I until 2005.

Francesca Recanatini is a Senior Economist at the World Bank. Her work and research interests focus on integrating governance issues and institution building in development and economic growth. She has published several papers on indicators, corruption and governance, contributing recently to *Anticorruption Policy: Can International Actors Play a Role?* edited by Susan Rose-Ackerman and Paul Carrington (September 2013). She is working on institution building, anti-corruption and performance indicators in high-income countries and fragile environments.

Susan Rose-Ackerman is Henry R. Luce Professor of Jurisprudence (Law and Political Science), Yale University. She has published widely in the fields of law, economics, public policy, and corruption. She is the author, most recently, of *Corruption and Government Causes, Consequences and Reform* (second edition with Bonnie Palifka, 2016); *Due Process of Lawmaking: The United States, South Africa, Germany, and the European Union* (with Stefanie Egidy and James Fowkes, 2015); *From Elections to Democracy: Building Accountable Government in Hungary and Poland* (2005); *Comparative Administrative Law* (second edition, edited with Peter Lindseth and Blake Emerson, 2017). She holds a PhD in Economics from Yale University and has held fellowships at the Wissenschaftskolleg zu Berlin, at the Center for Advanced Study in the Behavioral Sciences in Palo Alto, at Collegium Budapest, and from the Guggenheim Foundation and the Fulbright Commission. Her research interests include comparative regulatory law and policy, the political economy of corruption, public policy and administrative law, and law and economics.

Ernesto Schargrodsky received his PhD in Economics from Harvard University in 1998. He is the President of Universidad Torcuato Di Tella in Buenos Aires, Argentina. Previously, he was the Dean of Di Tella Business School. He has been the Edward Laroque Tinker Visiting Professor at Stanford University and the De Fortabat Visiting Scholar at Harvard University. His research includes studies of the impact of police deployment on crime, the effect of the privatization of water companies on child mortality, the analysis of popular support for privatizations, the relationship between bureaucratic wages and corruption, the effect of mandatory military service on crime, the impact on recidivism of the use of electronic monitoring devices instead of incarceration, and the effects of awarding land titles to squatters. His work has been published at the *American Economic Review, Journal of Political Economy, Quarterly Journal of Economics, American Economic Journal: Applied Economics, Journal of Law and Economics, Journal of Public Economics,* and *Journal of Development Economics,* inter alia, and has been discussed at *The Economist, Financial Times* and *Wall Street Journal.* He has received the 2009 Houssay Award for Researcher in the Social Sciences of the Ministry of Science and Technology of Argentina, the 2005

Houssay Award for Young Researcher in the Social Sciences of the Ministry of Education of Argentina, and the 2008 *Premio Consagración* from the National Academy of Economic Sciences of Argentina. He has been awarded fellowships, grants and prizes from Harvard University, Stanford University, Inter-American Development Bank, World Bank, United Nations, Tinker Foundation, International Finance Corporation, Financial Times, PREAL, CONICET of Argentina, Corporación Andina de Fomento, Ronald Coase Institute, Lincoln Institute, and the Global Development Network. He has worked as a consultant for Telefónica de Argentina, Movicom, Münchener Ruck, CICOMRA, NERA, Banco Río, Procuradoría General del Estado of Ecuador, and Procuración General del Tesoro, Ministerio de Economía and Comisión Nacional de Defensa de la Competencia of Argentina.

1

Introduction

Kaushik Basu and Tito Cordella

This book is the outcome of a roundtable organized by us and held in Montevideo, Uruguay, on May 26–27, 2016. It is an ambitious project because of the breadth of its reach. There is increasing recognition, albeit with a long history of forays into this, from the time of Karl Polanyi (1944), through the writings of Mark Granovetter (1985), to the emergence of new institutional economics (see North 1990; Williamson 2000), that economics cannot be viewed in isolation. It is a discipline embedded in institutions, politics, and the law and, if we are to be more effective in terms of the impact of economic policy, we have to recognize this embeddedness and design our interventions with this in mind.[1]

K. Basu (✉) • T. Cordella
The World Bank, Washington, DC, USA
e-mail: kb40@cornell.edu; tcordella@worldbank.org

© The Author(s) 2018
K. Basu, T. Cordella (eds.), *Institutions, Governance and the Control of Corruption*, International Economic Association Series,
https://doi.org/10.1007/978-3-319-65684-7_1

1

Further, the perpetrators of corruption often work, hand in hand, with the functionaries of government, who, ironically, are supposed to enforce the law (see, for instance, Kugler et al. 2005). The World Bank's most-recent **World Development Report on Governance and the Law** (World Bank 2017) is a recognition of the significance of these perspectives. And our roundtable assembled some of the finest minds that have contributed to this multidisciplinary venture to do a stocktaking of the best ideas and how they can be put to action on the ground. It was an engaging two days of discussion and debate.

The breadth, ambition, and excitement of the project, however, comes with a concomitant challenge—that of organizing what we analyzed and discussed into a cogent statement. This book is an attempt at that. While we do not attempt one comprehensive statement or chapter that collects the entire proceedings, we worked with the authors and organized the book to make it as readable, consistent, and cogent as possible. It is organized so as to begin with some of the broadest questions, rooted in history and institutions to more focused micro-analytic topics, such as corruption and the law.

The book opens with Avinash Dixit's chapter on *"Anti-Corruption Institutions: Some History and Theory,"* where he argues that, despite the importance of broad common principles of economics, each country needs to find its own way to improve governance. Indeed, the one lesson he can draw from history is that no universal solution exists. For instance, to prevent corruption, during the late Middle Ages, small city states in Italy decided to outsource the exercise of power to a "foreign" city manager, the *podestà*, offering him an incentive compatible contract—based on a security deposit and a management fee. In the twentieth century, small city states in East Asia, such as Singapore and Hong Kong, quickly became "clean," thanks to a reform effort backed by a leadership that felt the need to react swiftly to some big corruption scandals. In the US, instead, the reduction in corruption was quite a long process, spanning over half a century (late nineteenth–early twentieth century), and it was made possible by the alliance of business interests and the progressive movement, an alliance that was aided by the emergence of a free press.

The fact that each country should find its own way to grow out of corruption, however, does not mean that no general lessons can be learned from history. History indeed suggests that all successful transitions to good governance have required a change in norms such that, at the end of the process, a large majority of citizens found it in their best interest to abide by the rule of law. This could be the outcome of a coordination effort that transformed a Prisoner's Dilemma type situation to a game where cooperation is feasible, and the emergence, for a number of different reasons, of a new focal point that allowed agents to move to a Pareto superior equilibrium—as in the classical Stag-Hunt Game.

A good example of a (bottom up) coordination solution that has the potential to improve governance in mafia-plagued Sicily is *Addiopizzo*, a movement of Sicilian businesses that challenged mafia rackets by agreeing publicly not to pay the *pizzo* (protection money extorted by the mafia). Such a pledge may increase substantially the cost for the mafia to retaliate against those who refuse to pay, as retaliation would be against the entire association and not the individual shop owner. Thus, *Addiopizzo* could help coordinate businesses so as to get to the good equilibrium where if others do not pay the *pizzo*, no one has an interest in unilaterally paying, and the *mafiosi* refrain from asking it.

The problem is that, when we start looking at coordination problems, then there is no such thing as a "good" policy. In addition, fighting corruption by itself does not necessarily bring good governance. The reason, as Francis Fukuyama argues in his chapter on "*Corruption as a Political Phenomenon*", is that good governance also requires state capacity so that anti-corruption efforts may be fruitless absent state capacity and proper incentives. This may explain why the first generation of anti-corruption policies, aimed at reforming civil services in the Weberian tradition, failed: corrupt bureaucracies do not police themselves.

The failure of such a (top down) approach led the developmental community to focus on transparency and accountability measures aimed at mobilizing civil society. However, lacking collective action mechanisms that allow the society to move to a new equilibrium, the disruption of an existing system of clientelism or patronage may end up deterring investments. This, for instance, is the case when property rights are not clearly defined and contract enforcement is weak. This brings us back to the importance of state capacity above and beyond the control of corruption. China is a good example of a country that, thanks to a long lasting tradition of ample state capacity, has been able to grow fast despite relatively high levels of corruption.[2]

The link between corruption and organized crime is the focus of Susan Rose-Ackerman and Bonnie J. Palifka's chapter on *"Corruption, Organized Crime, and Money Laundering."* The starting point of their analysis is that a culture of corruption creates opportunities for organized crime to flourish and to expand its control over both licit and illicit activities. This, in turn, makes it easier for organized crime to capture whole sectors, creating a vicious circle that can be difficult to break. In such situations, ambitious anti-corruption reforms may be challenging to implement, as those who are in charge of executing them (public officials, police, judges) may be controlled by the same organized crime they are expected to fight.

Starting from this premise, Rose-Ackerman and Palifka suggest that the fight against organized crime should focus on smart policies aimed at reducing organized crime's rents and thus its ability to control enforcement agencies. Among the interventions that can create such a virtuous cycle, the authors call attention to anti-money laundering policies. In their view, this is perhaps the most effective way to tax illicit activities and thus to reduce the power of organized crime. Of course, the success of anti-money laundering depends on international cooperation and this may be the area where multilateral institutions, like the World Bank, have an edge over other players (and a consequent responsibility) in contributing to the governance agenda, both national and international.

Anti-money laundering activities may act as an effective tax on illicit activities. Such a tax, by reducing the rents that criminal groups can secure, diminishes their ability to "buy" enforcement agencies. Extending such a logic, one may wonder whether other reforms that reduce rents, such as those promoting economic and political liberalization, are also likely to decrease corruption and foster a virtuous cycle of economic dynamism and increase in state capacity. Pranab Bardhan in his chapter on *"Reflections on Corruption in the Context of Political and Economic*

Liberalization" challenges such a blanket extension and hints at more complex dynamics between liberalization and governance that may lead to possible unforeseen consequences.

For instance, economic liberalization usually starts in the product market. When this is the case, then (relative) rents in primary factor markets and, more generally, in the non-tradable sectors necessarily increase. Since those are the sectors more subject to political allocations, corruption opportunities may thus also increase. The case is even worse when economic liberalization entails a privatization process that too often ends up transferring resources from state monopolies to crony oligarchs. This not only creates new opportunities for grand corruption but it also changes the nature of corruption from bribing, that is, bending the rules to lobbying, to changing the rules. Such a phenomenon could be reinforced by political liberalization, especially when electoral competition is costly. If politicians need money to be elected and sectors subject to regulations have the resources, the likelihood of state capture by powerful individuals or lobbies necessarily increases.

In addition, Bardhan suggests that political competitions, by disenfranchising certain sector of societies (e.g., lower castes in India) that cannot rely on a well-established network of relations to obtain favors, may foster outright corruption. Of course, this does not make the system necessarily worse, but it substitutes tacit quid pro quo agreements, which could have even complied with the letter of the law, with bribe payments. Moreover, since powerful groups may be able to shape legislation in their own favor, what is accepted practice or legal in one country may be illegal in others. For instance, lobbies' contributions to Political Action Committees are legal in the US but not elsewhere. Finally, the fact that "legal" corruption, as it is often called, may not be any better than the "illegal" one, and that only illegal payments are usually captured in corruption measures,[3] implies that it is very difficult to compare corruption measures across countries.

This brings us to Diego Gambetta's provocative chapter on *"Why Is Italy Disproportionally Corrupt?: A Conjecture"*. If control of corruption and development go hand in hand, one ends up wondering how such a developed country can be so corrupt, and, conversely, how such a corrupt country can be so developed. Leaving aside that poor governance and poor contract enforcement mechanisms may have indeed contributed to Italy's poor economic performance in the new millennium, Gambetta's story hints at the complex dynamics of sharing compromising information.[4]

The logic is as follows. One of the reasons widespread corruption hinders investment and growth is that, in corrupt societies, the rule of law cannot be trusted to enforce contracts. This, in turn, implies that, in such societies, agents should rely on personal relations and networks; among such networks, the strongest are those whose members are partners in some form of crime. When this is the case, every member can blackmail, and be blackmailed by, everybody else. This creates trust and, as strange as it may sound, the more pervasive such networks are, the larger is the scope for economic activity. The next question that arises is: how many "partners in crime" should exist in Italy to explain the level of economic development? Probably many more than one may suspect. This may partly reflect weak moral norms but, according to Gambetta, to a great extent it reflects the myriad of existing laws and regulation. They often contradict one another so that, in Italy, breaking some law, knowingly but often unknowingly, is the rule rather than the exception. The next essential piece of the Italian puzzle is the presence of an overburdened and "mostly incorruptible" judiciary that, because of being overburdened, only starts an investigation if a crime is reported, but because of being incorruptible always does it if presented with evidence. This means that criminal behaviors are not prosecuted unless someone breaks the *omertà*. However, any potential reporter of crime has probably also broken some rule or law, and, would therefore be concerned about retaliation, and so will be unlikely to violate *omertà* to start with. That is how Italy could "square the puzzling circle of corruption *cum* development:" in the *bel paese* the widespread violation of some law may end up being the ultimate source of trust.[5]

The fact that the relation between institutions and economic development is complex is also the focus of Timothy Besley and Hannes Mueller's chapter on "*Cohesive Institutions and the Distribution of Political Rents: Theory and Evidence.*" Besley and Mueller's starting point is that we should unbundle institutions and explicitly distinguish between those that regulate access to, and those that regulate the use of, power. Their view is that the international community has focused too much on the former, implicitly assuming that free elections could insure inclusive societies. However, the fact that, nowadays, most governments have been elected in increasingly free elections has not implied that civil society, or the respect for minority rights, strengthened *pari passu*.

Besley and Mueller develop a normative model showing that under a veil of ignorance there would be an agreement in selecting a more inclusive society and thus higher constraints on the executive. Of course, there would also be an agreement for a more open society with a fair distribution of political control. However, once we abandon the veil of ignorance, minority groups have nothing to gain from an increase in openness—they will remain minorities. This means that openness does not provide any guarantee against political exclusion. This may well be the reason why attempts to encourage elections where executive constraints are weak are prone to failure (for instance, in Afghanistan, Egypt, and Iraq).

In order to bring the theory to the data, they then look at measures of exclusion and assess to which extent these correlates with constraints on the executive and/or electoral openness. Their main finding is that, in a large panel of countries, between group inequality[6] is negatively correlated with standard measures of executive constraints (e.g., Polity IV), while political openness does not have significant explanatory power. They also show that, within countries, political exclusion negatively affects a group's income, and that the effect is stronger where executive constraints are weak.

The recognition that inclusive institutions do not appear overnight, but require coordination between individuals with different objectives, creates new challenges and opportunities for the developmental community. In their thought provoking chapter entitled "*If Politics Is the Problem, How Can External Actors Be Part of the Solution?*", Shanta Devarajan and Stuti Khemani argue that the traditional model of delivering aid was based on the implicit assumption that development was hindered by market failures and that the interests of all actors, donors, government, and general public, were aligned. Under such an assumption, it made a lot of sense to bundle financial and technical assistance as the latter would provide valuable information to all stakeholders on how to use resources in the most effective way.

However, one should recognize that the track record of such a model of assistance is at best mixed. The reason, according to the authors, is that, in too many instances, the problem was not one of market failure but of political failure—mainly due to incentive problems in the public sector—exacerbated by the fact that well-intentioned reforms were undermined and emptied by powerful groups whose interests were threatened. If the incentives of the different stakeholders in aid-receiving countries are not aligned, the developmental community should start thinking on how to redress the political failures arising from the principal-agent problems between citizens, politicians, policymakers, and service providers.

In order to increase the accountability of policymakers and service providers, Devarajan and Khemani suggest completely delinking financial assistance from knowledge assistance. The former should be provided to governments that should be left free to use the resources as they wish. But governments should be accountable, too. This is where unbundled knowledge assistance may play a key role. If knowledge assistance is provided to increase transparency about the specific outcomes of government actions, then citizens could use such information to sanction political leaders, and political leaders to sanction service providers. This would help address some of the critical principal-agent problems that undermine aid effectiveness, and has been the cause of much debate and soul-searching.

The idea that transparency may improve incentives and be an effective way to deter corruption is also discussed in Claudio Ferraz and Federico Finan's chapter entitled *"Fighting Political Corruption: Evidence from Brazil."* The chapter reviews how Brazil's federal random audits of local governments have affected the use (and misuse) of federal funds. The evidence presented suggests that voters did use audits' information to punish corrupt politicians; this was particularly the case where the presence of local media helped disseminating the findings of the audits.[7] Since the program started in 2003, it is now possible to distinguish between the extents of corruption in municipalities that have already been audited versus those municipalities that have not yet been. This allows to get a better understanding of whether the audits and their release helped reducing corruption. Looking at this specific issue, Avis et al. (2016) show a significant reduction, of the order of 8 percent, in the incidence of corruption; they also show that such a reduction was larger in the more corrupt municipalities.[8]

But what are the channels through which the audits have led to less corrupt administration? Was it through the selection of better politicians by voters? Or was it by increasing politicians' awareness of the possibility of either being prosecuted (discipline effect) or of losing election (reputation effect)? Alternatively, audits may have improved the pool of candidates running for election (political selection). Structural estimates show that two-thirds of the reduction in corruption is imputable to the discipline effect, and one third to the reputation effect. The effect on political selection, however, is negligible.

The findings above provide new insights into how increased accountability may improve public administration's effectiveness. However, they also show that accountability, by itself, is not likely to improve the quality of politicians running for office, at least in the short run. This is worrisome as a new political class is needed everywhere, and most emphatically in countries experiencing high corruption.

If political participation depend upon citizens' perception of the quality of government, Nancy Birdsall, Charles Kenny, and Anna Diofasi's chapter on *"What Drives Citizen Perceptions of Government Corruption? National Income, Petty Bribe Payments and the Unknown"* provides new insights into the sources of trust in governments. Using data from the Global Corruption Barometer, they analyze factors that are correlated with citizens' perceptions of corruption, both across sectors within countries, and across countries. The analysis shows that the perception of political corruption varies significantly between high- and low-income countries; it is much higher in the latter. Such perceptions are also affected by age, education, and income.

Interestingly enough, there is a striking difference between how education and income affect the perception of corruption in high- and low-income countries. In high-income countries, the wealthier and more educated have lower perceptions of corruption and the opposite is true in low-income countries. This, to a large extent, may reflect the fact that demand for bribes is "regressive" (with the exception of grand, political bribes) in richer countries, and "progressive" in poorer ones, but the insights of the chapter remains puzzling, and deserves more analysis and research in the future.

Interestingly the authors find that, aside from GDP per capita, and the actual experience of paying a bribe, nothing else is correlated with corruption perceptions (such as other governance indexes, sectoral performance, and so on). This raises the chicken-egg question of whether it is growth that leads to better governance or good governance that leads to faster growth and higher levels of GDP. Leaving this big question (which was one of the main areas of concern for the conference) aside, the other important message of the chapter is that reducing exposure to bribes (no matter how small they are) is an effective instrument to reduce the perception of how corrupt a country is. This means that reducing tolerance of petty bribes, even if not too important in itself, could help increase trust in government and ultimately contribute to creating a better political class at the helm.

If perception surveys looking at actual experiences with paying a bribe are keys to evaluate the success of anti-corruption reforms, Aart Kraay and his co-authors, Nona Karalashvili and Peter Murrell, in their chapter on *"Doing the Survey Two-Step: The Effects of Reticence on Estimates of Corruption in Two-Stage Survey Question"* raise some doubts about the reliability of perception surveys since individuals are prone to underreport corruption. The fact that respondents may be reticent in answering surveys creates serious problems when one makes comparisons both across countries and across time. For instance, one can imagine that since the rule of law is weaker in highly corrupt countries, respondents are more worried about the confidentiality of the surveys, and they are thus more prone to underreport corruption. This not only means that in cross-country comparisons countries with a stronger rule of law tend to perform relatively worse than countries with a weaker one, but also that, across time, the effect of improvements in the rule of law on corruption tends to be underestimated.

To address such a problem, the chapter develops a structural methodology to estimate the rate of false answers and to control for the different degree of reticence of survey respondents. The methodology relies on the use of both conventional questions (e.g., did you pay a bribe last year?) and forced-response random-response questions (e.g., toss a coin, and answer yes if either the coin comes up heads or you paid a bribe last year), exploiting differences in the characteristics of responses to these questions. It applies this methodology to two-part conventional questions about corruption (e.g., did you receive a visit from a government official, and if so did you pay that official a bribe?), where the respondent faces a choice of whether to lie on the first part in order to avoid answering the second part. Under specific assumptions on the correlation between the degrees of respondents' reticence in the two kind of questions, the authors are able to estimate reticence-corrected corruption measures. Applying such a methodology to the last round of World Bank Enterprise surveys, they show that, after controlling for reticence, corruption rankings across countries change significantly. This has important implications for the developmental community that often links aid allocations to such rankings.

As will be evident by now, it is a broad set of inter-related topics that this monograph investigates. We do not come out with a uniform set of guidelines for all countries. Indeed, as the opening chapter makes amply clear, it is not evident we ought to even try to do so. What we hope the volume accomplishes is to present the policymaker (and also future researchers) with some rigorous research results, findings from carefully designed analysis and ingredients for devising better governance and development policy, and more effective control of corruption. In an area where there is so much hand-waving and so little substance, it is hoped that this book will serve as a useful manual for attending to matters of governance, institutions, and the control of corruption, subjects of immense importance in today's world.

Notes

1. See Basu (2000) for an analysis of how to situate economics within sociology and politics.
2. It is arguable that the (high) predictability and the (contained) size of bribes may have also played a role. In addition, China has used a strategy of

asymmetric punishment which may have contributed to keeping corruption within limits (Berlin and Spagnolo 2015).
3. An emblematic case is Singapore that fares extremely high both in anti-corruption and in crony capitalism indexes.
4. See Schelling (1980).
5. A less benign interpretation is that in Italy prosecution is mandatory but because of the malfunctioning of the judiciary indictment is random. This would sustain the same set of equilibria with a less favorable view of the judiciary.
6. Measured by difference in the luminosity per capita in the homelands of the different ethnic groups, using both Alesina et al. (2016), and the Grow^{up} dataset from Girardin et al. (2015).
7. See Ferraz and Finan (2008).
8. More precisely, they compare the outcome of municipalities that have been audited twice versus those that have only been audited once.

References

Alesina, Alberto, Stelios Michalopoulos, and Elias Papaioannou. 2016. Ethnic Inequality. *Journal of Political Economy* 124: 428–488.

Avis, Eric, Claudio Ferraz, and Frederico Finan. 2016. *Do Government Audits Reduce Corruption? Estimating the Impacts of Exposing Corrupt Politicians.* Working Paper, w22443. National Bureau of Economic Research.

Basu, Kaushik. 2000. *Prelude to Political Economy: A Study of the Social and Political Foundations of Economics.* Oxford: OUP.

Berlin, Maria Perrotta, and Giancarlo Spagnolo. 2015. *Leniency, Asymmetric Punishment and Corruption. Evidence from China.* Working Paper No. 34. Stockholm Institute of Transition Economics. Stockholm School of Economics.

Ferraz, Claudio, and Frederico Finan. 2008. Exposing Corrupt Politicians: The Effects of Brazil's Publicly Released Audits on Electoral Outcomes. *The Quarterly Journal of Economics* 123: 703–745.

Girardin, Luc, Philipp Hunziker, Lars-Erik Cederman, Nils-Christian Bormann, and Manuel Vog. 2015. *GROWup–Geographical Research on War, Unified Platform.* Zurich: ETH Zurich.

Granovetter, Mark. 1985. Economic Action and Social Structure: The Problem of Embeddedness. *American Journal of Sociology* 91: 481–510.

Kugler, Maurice, Thierry Verdier, and Yves Zenou. 2005. Organized Crime, Corruption and Punishment. *Journal of Public Economics* 89: 1639–1663.

North, Douglass C. 1990. *Institutions, Institutional Change and Economic Performance*. Cambridge: Cambridge University Press.

Polanyi, K. 1944. *The Great Transformation*. Boston: Beacon Press.

Schelling, Thomas C. 1980. *The Strategy of Conflict*. Cambridge, MA: Harvard University Press.

Williamson, Oliver E. 2000. The 'New Institutional Economics': Taking Stock, Looking Ahead. *Journal of Economic Literature* 38 (3): 595–613.

World Bank. 2017. *World Development Report: Governance and the Law*. Washington: World Bank.

2

Anti-corruption Institutions: Some History and Theory

Avinash Dixit

Introduction

Corruption is a complex, multidimensional problem. Even its definition is elusive and a matter of disagreement among those studying it. Many attempts to define it yield some variant of "use of public office for personal gain." I will broadly follow this usage in this paper.[1]

This is a revision of a paper delivered at the International Economic Association Roundtable on Institutions, Governance and Corruption, Montevideo, Uruguay, May 26–27, 2016. I thank my discussant Stuti Khemani, other participants in the conference, Karla Hoff, and Chiara Superti for valuable comments and suggestions. The first draft of the paper was written during a very pleasant term as Sanjaya Lall Visiting Senior Research Fellow at Green Templeton College and the Department of Economics, Oxford. I thank the College and department colleagues for their generous hospitality and useful discussions.

A. Dixit (✉)
Princeton University, Princeton, NJ, USA
e-mail: dixitak@princeton.edu

© The Author(s) 2018
K. Basu, T. Cordella (eds.), *Institutions, Governance and the Control of Corruption*, International Economic Association Series,
https://doi.org/10.1007/978-3-319-65684-7_2

15

Corruption comprises a range of such malfeasance. Start with petty bribery, which can take two forms. The first entails extorting money or other favors as a price for some good or service (such as rationed food or medical care under a national health service) or a document or permit (such as a passport or driving license), to which the citizen is entitled for free or at a low price. Variants of this include delaying delivery of the good or document unless the bribe is paid. The second form of petty bribery involves extracting money to convey a favor for which the applicant does not qualify; for example a customs officer waiving import duty in exchange for a payment or kickback. And there is a spectrum spanning these categories where the qualification is a matter of discretion or judgment; for example, an inspector's decision as to whether a restaurant meets sanitary standards that are not precisely quantitatively measurable. Corruption also includes larger deals, where in exchange for bribes or kickbacks, politicians or bureaucrats award government contracts for supply or construction, overpay providers of public services, give public property including land and the airwave spectrum for free or at a low price, and grant waivers or exemptions from regulations. Finally, there is grand corruption: contributions tantamount to purchase of politicians in order to secure monopolies or laws that create private profit. Some definitions also include politicians' and officials' use of inside information about future public projects to make private profit by acquiring lands or businesses that stand to benefit from the projects, but when this is not explicitly prohibited by law, others call it "legal corruption" or "honest graft." All these forms of corruption are facilitated if the judiciary is also corrupt, for example if judges are complicit in violation of property rights or let off any prosecuted officials or politicians lightly.

Some or all of these forms of corruption have existed in most countries and throughout history.[2] Perhaps the earliest mention is in Kautilya (also known as Chanakya) in his *Arthashastra,* which was written more than 2000 years ago. The following is noteworthy: "Just as it is impossible not to taste the honey or the poison on the tip of the tongue, so it is impossible for a government servant not to eat up at least part of the king's revenue. Just as a fish moving under water cannot possibly be found out either as drinking or not drinking water, so servants employed in government work cannot be found out while taking money for themselves." See Rangarajan (1992, chapter IX). This nicely captures both the temptation of officials who have the power to create or distribute economic rents, and the difficulty of detecting their corrupt actions.

Actually many of Kautilya's remarks pertain to embezzlement from the state treasury, which we may or may not regard as corruption. Mungiu-Pippidi (2015, p. 63) observes the same about Europe in the middle ages under feudalism and monarchy. Her explanation is as follows. Most modern societies profess ethical universalism—application of the same impersonal and impartial rules to everyone—and practice it to varying degrees. In pre-modern Europe, "since no one … even aspired to the norm of ethical universalism, one could hardly speak of corruption in the modern sense." When all allocation is at the ruler's whim, creation and misappropriation of rents by his officials is at worst a principal-agent problem between those parties.

To the extent that corruption acts like a tax on business, it deters production, investment, and innovation. Worse, to the extent that it is a tax levied at arbitrary rates at the whim of a politician or official, it creates uncertainty, which has particularly harmful effects on investment and growth.[3] The economic costs of corruption have been well documented in the literature and need not be recounted here. It is sometimes argued that bribery enables firms to get around bad rules and regulations and thereby reduces the distortionary costs of these.[4] But this is at best a "second-best" argument; it would be better to get rid of the bad rules.

Corruption being complex and multidimensional, anti-corruption policies and strategies need to tackle its many different aspects. At its broadest, the whole culture of a society needs to change, from regarding corruption as a way of life to thinking it to be unacceptable and shameful or even evil.[5] Each such culture is sustained by its own set of beliefs, expectations, and actions. Therefore the desired change entails shifting from one equilibrium to another. There is no clear game-theoretic prescription for doing so. In this paper I examine a small selection of such attempts in history. They are varied, with an equally varied record of successes and failures. They suggest a few necessary conditions, but not a clear set of sufficient conditions, for shifting away from a corruption-ridden equilibrium. Then I briefly touch on some related theory. In the concluding section I draw on the history and the theory to offer some tentative suggestions and lessons for current and future anti-corruption efforts.

Europe and the United States

Mungiu-Pippidi (2015, chapter 3) gives a good account of corruption in pre-modern Europe and the different routes by which different countries reduced it. Especially instructive is the case of many Italian city-states, which took elaborate steps to design their governance systems to prevent corruption. They "opted for … a city manager, a professional … It was mandatory for this manager, or *podestà,* to come from a different city so that no local candidates could be favored. He brought his own staff with him, including law enforcers, clerks, and magistrates. He paid a security deposit at the beginning of his term and after his final management report was accepted, he received his money back along with his fees, less any fines incurred. He was usually appointed for a one-year term." He was confined to a (luxurious) palace in order to insulate him from being influenced by local families. "[N]either [he] nor [his] staff were allowed to perform any activity other than [the management] service. … Continuous controlling and auditing were regular features of government. … Many services provided by the state to its citizens were funded by fees that passed directly from the consumer to the provider, without actually circulating in the treasury." All this points to "the Italians' understanding that conflicts of interest are ubiquitous." (Mungiu-Pippidi 2015, p. 65.) Some of these practices were copied by cities and republics of northern Europe, especially if they had trade relations with Italy. However, "[b]y a gradual diminution of power, and by inter-city conquest, the office gradually disappeared" (Born 1927, p. 869). The underlying reasons are not clear; were there any basic defects in the system or did better governance institutions evolve?

Nor is it clear how and why the system was developed and sustained.[6] Mungiu-Pippidi (2015, pp. 66–67) argues that three important features underlay the governance system of these city-states: participation in public affairs by a high proportion of the citizenry; the concept that public office was not a privilege but a civic duty; and equality before the law.

In some countries the road to combating corruption passed through a crisis. In Denmark, a major military defeat in 1658 was a crisis that forced the nobles to transfer power and privileges to a king. He consolidated his position by replacing aristocratic administrators with bureaucrats hired from the bourgeoisie. These had to swear loyalty directly to the king, and having no private fortunes, were also reliant on their positions for their incomes. Gradually this service became more professional, with meritocratic appointments based on objective criteria of education. Other military defeats also led Denmark, Britain, and France to move away from selling officers' commissions in the armed forces. (Mungiu-Pippidi 2015, pp. 69–72.) The historical accounts do not explain why the reaction to the crises and the subsequent developments took this path, rather than some other path that might have led to some worse authoritarian rule with its own, perhaps worse, form of corruption. In any case, one hesitates to recommend defeat in war as a way to improve governance!

In Britain and France, many reforms in the appointment and functioning of public administration followed revolutions: the Glorious Revolution of 1688 in the former and the bloodier one in France a century later. However, the process lasted many decades. Britain in mid- and late eighteenth century was regarded as highly corrupt, both by British thinkers and by American fighters for independence and framers of the constitution (Teachout 2014, chapter 2). The path of revolution is too risky and too slow to serve as an anti-corruption policy, hardly to be recommended to today's Asian, African, and Latin American countries.

In the United States, corruption was widespread in mid-nineteenth century. The economy and the role of government were both expanding rapidly; that created opportunities and incentives for all forms of corruption. But it declined in some quite rapid spurts from 1870 to 1920. How did this happen, and does it hold any lessons for today's anti-corruption efforts? We find useful descriptions and analyses in a book edited by Glaeser and Goldin (2006).[7] They identify, not one definitive answer, but several actions and movements that contributed to the outcome.

They recognize three distinct theories of institutional change. First, a social welfare maximizing person or party or coalition come into power and enact and enforce the necessary reforms. Second, powerful special interests find it to their benefit to reduce corruption and influence policymakers to bring this about. Third, political entrepreneurs manipulate public opinion and tools of government toward reform. They find instances where each of the three played a part.

The rise of an independent press and investigative journalism proved very important. This in turn was linked to rising standards of literacy in the population, and to the decrease in the costs of communication and transport following the spread of the telegraph and of railways. Newspapers could be delivered promptly to much larger readerships. The resulting economies of scale made it possible for the press to be free of the need to placate politicians and seek patronage. These changes also interacted positively with the rise of the Progressive Movement in politics.

Producer interests have often captured the regulatory process and agencies under various pretexts of appealing to consumer interests. This may have happened in workplace safety regulations, which were supported by large manufacturing firms to raise the costs and deter smaller firms. When opportunities to deregulate arose, a by-product was their role as anticorruption weapons. For example, reduction in chartering requirements of New York banks in the late 1830s increased competition.

Corruption in the provision of public relief, welfare, and unemployment compensation took the form of clientelism practiced by local political party machines. Moving these functions to the federal level and basing benefits on objective criteria reduced this problem, especially because the Roosevelt administration needed to acquire and maintain a reputation for efficiency and credibility in the face of political opposition that would have exploited any evidence of corruption. This observation runs counter to the belief frequently asserted that "empowerment," placing the handling of projects and benefits in the hands of local governments, will reduce corruption.

Political competition helped, but corrupt politicians were often able to remain in power on the basis of ethnic or other factional support. A notorious case in point was James Michael Curley, who remained mayor of Boston for many years by appealing to Irish-Catholic jingoism. He was defeated only when political challengers emerged with a clean image but the same Hibernianism.

Thus the decline of corruption in the United States had multiple causes. Some were top-down, others bottom-up. Some were explicitly targeted to combat corruption; others were a part or an incidental aspect of movements aiming to clean up other dimensions of the society and the economy. There was undoubtedly some synergy between the multiple forces acting toward the same goal, but there does not seem to have been much explicit coalition-building or coordination between them. It is not clear that the interests of the emerging newspaper industry would be aligned in exposing corruption. Investigative journalists probably benefited from doing so, but owners might have been on the side of the status quo. Thus the reduction in corruption seems to have been a fortuitous combination of synergy of reforming forces and good luck.

Even with all the forces of improving education and technology, the press, political movements and competition operating in the right direction, it took several decades for corruption in the United States to fall to relatively low levels. And even now the country does not rank very highly for being corruption-free among the world's advanced economies; see Table 2.1. This is a cautionary lesson for developing countries and transition economies in the twenty-first century that are trying to reduce corruption much more rapidly.

Table 2.1 Cross-country comparisons of corruption

Country	WB-WGI-CC 2014	TI-CPI 2015
Singapore	97.12	85
Hong Kong	92.31	75
Denmark	99.52	91
Germany	94.71	81
United Kingdom	92.79	81
United States	89.42	76
Italy	55.29	44

Sources: World Bank, Transparency International

Hong Kong and Singapore

A more optimistic perspective comes from Singapore and Hong Kong, both of which had high levels of corruption and a culture that accepted it as a fact of life, and turned this around rapidly and thoroughly. Today both countries rank very high, better than many western countries. Table 2.1 shows some such comparisons. The second column shows the World Bank's 2014 World Governance Indicators for "Control of corruption" (labeled WB-WGI-CC 2014 in the table), and the third column shows Transparency International's 2015 "Corruption perception index" (TI-CPI 2015). In each case 100 is best and 0 would be worst. No country attains 100, but it is amusing to note how things have changed since Shakespeare's time—now almost nothing is rotten in the state of Denmark.

How was this turnaround achieved? In each case, the wake-up call resulted from a big scandal. Thereafter the two took somewhat different approaches but the ultimate and explicit aim was to change the whole equilibrium.

Corruption was prevalent in Singapore's administration and police force for almost a century of British colonial administration; attempts to counter it were weak and ineffective.[8] The situation became even worse during the Japanese occupation in World War II. The big scandal came in 1951, when the police force was found to be involved in an opium hijacking operation. This led to the establishment of a Corrupt Practices Investigation Bureau (CPIB), which was independent of the police force. It got effective backing from the top. Its powers were increased after self-government in 1959 when Lee Kwan-Yew became Prime Minister; in fact the CPIB came to be located directly in his office and answerable only to him (Quah 2007, p. 23). The strategy was "to minimize or remove the conditions of both the incentives and opportunities that make individual corrupt behavior irresistible" (Quah 2007, p. 17).

The strategy on the incentive side seems to have consisted of improving the detection process and imposing much stricter penalties upon conviction (Quah 2007, pp. 20–21). As the economy grew, civil service salaries were improved substantially, creating one more weapon on the incentive side, namely efficiency wages (Quah 2007, pp. 27–29). As for opportunities, the government's general pro-market economic policies may have reduced the magnitude of rents available.

Except for speeches and statements by the Prime Minister emphasizing the importance of being free from corruption, this strategy does not seem to have been backed up by much educational or publicity efforts; in fact surveys point to this as one weakness of the CPIB (Quah 2007, pp. 33–34). However, over time the strict and impartial enforcement seems to have sufficed to change the public perception and culture to the point where corruption is regarded as unacceptable.

Hong Kong shows some similarities but also important differences.[9] The British colonial and Japanese occupation histories were similar, and rapid economic changes and low civil service salaries after World War II sustained much corruption and its acceptance through the 1960s. There was an anti-corruption unit in the police force, but it was itself a partner in the crimes. The jolt to this prevailing culture again came from a big scandal. A British senior police officer Peter Godber, who had amassed a fortune of 4.3 million Hong Kong dollars, came under investigation in 1973 and fled to the UK. (He was later extradited back, tried, and convicted.) The public outcry led to the establishment of the Independent Commission Against Corruption (ICAC). It had strong backing from a new Governor, Murray MacLehose, and was answerable directly to him. Its strategies combined whistleblower-protection, amnesties and forced retirements for smaller offenses, and some prominent trials and sentences for bigger ones. It gradually achieved a reputation for being clean and effective. Today it has a staff of more than 1000 dedicated professionals. Along the way, it had to overcome strong resistance (including physical confrontations and punch-ups!) from corrupt elements in the police force. It also had to ensure its own integrity, quickly tackling any scandals within ICAC, even ones unrelated to corruption. Its activities were helped by some policies such as legalization of off-track betting, which reduced the scope for corruption.

The ICAC combines these enforcement strategies with ones focusing on public relations and education. Its officers actively reach out to companies and organizations to help them put into place systems and procedures to prevent corrupt practices taking hold. It also conducts publicity, and education starting at the kindergarten level: children are told stories and shown films where characters face ethical dilemmas and the honest ones win. To quote from the CNN news story cited in footnote 9 above: "We don't teach them about laws but we teach them about values," said Monica Yu, executive director of the Hong Kong Ethics Development Centre, an ICAC division.

Hong Kong enjoys one other advantage: its largely free and open economy creates much less rent at the disposal of officials, thereby reducing the temptation for corruption. Legalization of off-track betting was an important step in this direction. However, land sales and public housing are exceptions to the general rule, and corruption scandals in these do erupt from time to time despite the ICAC's strong enforcement efforts.

Both Hong Kong and Singapore had the advantage of being small city-states where power was effectively centralized, and getting strong backing from the top for the drive to eliminate corruption. In Singapore this seems to have sufficed; in Hong Kong a broader effort to change the society's culture helped the process.

One further remark of caution should be added to this account. Although these states get high ratings for freedom from bribery in their public administration, they are far from being open access societies: insiders get favored treatment and access to rents, without explicit quid pro quo bribes. In *The Economist*'s index of crony capitalism Singapore stands very poorly at No. 4 (the ranking goes from worst to best), China (which includes Hong Kong in this index) is not much better, at No. 11.[10] Using the broad definition advocated by Teachout (2014) or the concept of grand corruption, perhaps they should rank lower in the corruption indexes, and their transformations regarded as much less successful.

Italy Today

Substantial corruption of all kinds persists in modern Italy. Its score and ranking in Table 2.1 are very poor in comparison with the other European countries, Hong Kong and Singapore. In another unfavorable comparison, Transparency International gives Italy the same score as Lesotho, Senegal, and South Africa. But this section is about a somewhat different form of corruption, namely extortion by the Sicilian mafia from local businesses. This is not strictly within the definition of corruption as the mafia does not hold a public office that it exploits for private gain. But the difference is only of degree, not kind, between extortion under a threat of burning down a store and extortion under a threat of denying the owner some license or certification crucial for staying in business. Also, perhaps the difference between official and private extortion is minor in this context because the mafia has enjoyed close political connections. The bigger difference is that the drive to combat extortion in this instance is almost entirely a bottom-up social movement.

Pizzo is the name for protection money the mafia extorts from local businesses; this was believed to involve 160,000 businesses and to yield the mafia more than 10 billion euros per year (Superti 2009). Battisti et al. (2015, p. 3) report that the extortion payments may reach 40% of Sicilian firms' gross profits.

In 2004 an initially anonymous group of young people started a movement they called *Addiopizzo* to fight the mafia's extortion.[11] They began by plastering all over Palermo small stickers that read "un intero popolo che paga il pizzo e' un popolo senza dignitá" ("an entire population that pays the pizzo is a population without dignity"). This was a clever "counter-hijacking" of the concept of "dignity," which the Mafia had previously hijacked to connote conforming to the Mafia's rules and to its code of silence (Vaccaro and Palazzo 2015, pp. 1079, 1083.)

A year later the group shed its anonymity and launched a three-fold drive. First, they recruit businesses that promise not to pay *pizzo;* these get certificates and banners to post on their storefronts. They investigate members who might have secretly paid *pizzo,* and have expelled a few such "double-game" players. (Battisti et al. 2015, p. 7.) Second, they seek to convince consumers to patronize only those businesses that participate in this venture. They also organize public events and education programs in schools to discuss the Mafia and the harm it causes. (Vaccaro and Palazzo 2015, p. 1080.) More recently they have started ventures like *pizzo*-free tourism, organized tours that use only *Addiopizzo*-certified hotels, restaurants, and travel (Superti 2009, p. 9).

In 2012 "Addiopizzo could count on the support of 56 activists, 10,143 consumers, 154 schools, 29 local associations (e.g., the Sicilian branch of Confindustria, the highly influential Confederation of Italian Industry), and more than 700 affiliated firms (over 10% of the entrepreneurs in the Province of Palermo)." (Vaccaro and Palazzo 2015, p. 1080.) This is a small but significant dent in the power of the Mafia. It is all the more remarkable because the movement has not had much support, let alone leadership, from the political elite. However, it has benefited from some support from the police, at least the chief and other high-level officials (Superti 2009, p. 7).

Superti (2009, pp. 4–5) identifies resisting the Mafia as a collective action problem. An individual firm or store is helpless when the Mafia demands *pizzo;* the business would be burned down, or the proprietor killed. But collectively the victims have power.[12] "Retaliation would … have the potential to create unrest in the population. … Moreover, by attacking representatives of a popular grassroots movement the criminal organization might transform the victims into new popular heroes, further fertilizing the environment for a general uprising. Active discontent among Palermitans would damage the Mafia's interests more than the current decrease in profit from Addiopizzo's campaign." (Superti 2009, p. 5.) To reinforce this, the movement keeps the names of its leaders and member businesses public and visible: "Since media coverage of an attack on Addiopizzo would be as great as the organization's current popularity and would bring the situation to the forefront of the entire population's mind. This is not in the interests of the Mafia." (Superti, p. 8.) Indeed, secret interceptions of telephone conversations have shown Mafiosi ranting against *Addiopizzo*, but they have generally refrained from violence against volunteers of the movement or businesses adopting the credo. "Cosa Nostra chiefs appear to understand that with public opinion solidly behind the group, targeting its volunteers could backfire disastrously."[13]

Addiopizzo has thus used good strategies in mobilizing public opinion, building coalitions, and starting collective action among businesses and consumers. However, it is far too soon to declare victory. The movement must overcome many difficulties if it is to maintain and expand its foothold. Its system of detecting and expelling "double-gamers" who pledge not to pay *pizzo* but do so in secret needs to be improved. It has yet to demonstrate whether and how it can survive a retaliatory lashing out by the Mafia. Superti (2009, p. 9) identifies some other weaknesses. The movement has so far relied on idealism, and a Manichean dichotomy between good and evil. It is not clear whether this can scale up beyond the limited context of Sicily. Nor is it clear whether the movement can include police and political elites in its broad social alliance.

Finally, it has to overcome understandable hesitance to join on part of businesses. Battisti et al. (2015) conduct a statistical analysis of firms' decisions in this matter. They find several correlates that make intuitive sense. Older firms, and firms with more physical assets, are less likely to join; they have more to lose from any Mafia retaliation. Also, they may have greater need for credit, and banks seem to restrict credit to *Addiopizzo* members, perceiving higher risks (Battisti et al. 2015, p. 7). Firms with more employees and ones with higher levels of human capital, and ones located in districts with higher levels of socio-economic development (including higher education levels), are more likely to join; they are probably more influenced by the social coalition that the movement has built. This points to a hopeful future; as economic development proceeds in Sicily, perhaps itself assisted by *Addiopizzo*'s initial success, it may set in motion a virtuous circle of higher education, human capital, socio-economic development, and entry of new firms, leading to greater participation in *Addiopizzo*, and in turn further accelerating growth.

And if a privately organized societal coalition can notch up some success against the Sicilian Mafia, similar collective action should be able to face up to mere bureaucrats and politicians!

Anti-corruption Agencies Across Countries

Many countries have established anti-corruption agencies (ACAs) in various forms, given them differing mandates and powers, and obtained equally mixed results. Recanatini (2011) offers a good summary of this cross-country evidence, and some initial policy recommendations.

She starts by listing "the four traditional anti-corruption functions" and the proportions of ACAs assigned to cover these: "prevention, including education and public awareness (82 percent); investigation of corruption cases (78 percent); prosecution of corruption cases (58 percent); and policy, research and coordination (52 percent)." As most ACAs do not have sole or comprehensive responsibilities for all four, they must coordinate with other public institutions: "[those] responsible for investigation and prosecution . . . , the audit authority, the ombudsman, the financial intelligence unit, tax authorities, regulatory authorities, ministries and agencies across the public sector." Proper coordination requires a clear mandate for the ACA, and well-specified enabling legislation.

Many ACAs face serious budgetary and staffing problems; in some cases politicians cut their budgets during high-profile investigations. Politicians can also affect the independence and impartiality of the work of ACAs through their powers of appointing and reappointing their leadership.

The best ACAs maintain good communication and information links with the public through their media and web strategies, and establish partnerships with public sector and civil society organizations. Almost all of them are required to issue annual reports listing investigations conducted and concluded.

Thus we see some factors that determine an ACA's effectiveness: (1) political support from the country's leadership, especially in appointing good heads for the agency and giving them secure terms of tenure, (2) a clear and comprehensive framework of legislation that delineates its powers and relationships with other policy agencies, (3) guarantee of adequate resources and independence, and (4) accountability and relationship with the citizenry and the media.

A public policy research program at Princeton University conducted a comparative case study of ACAs in eight countries, Botswana, Croatia, Ghana, Indonesia, Latvia, Lithuania, Mauritius, and Slovenia (Innovations for Successful Societies (ISS), 2014). The different circumstances in these countries, the different strategies pursued by the agencies, and their different degrees of success, have yielded some useful suggestive insights, even though there are too many variables and too few data points for any definitive statistically significant conclusions.[14] The study emphasized four "key lessons":

1. Strong internal controls and accountability mechanisms play important roles in preserving integrity and protecting ACAs from being subverted or discredited.
2. ACAs often can outflank their antagonists by building alliances with citizens, state institutions, media, civil society, and international actors.
3. Preventive efforts that disrupt corruption networks, together with educational efforts that reshape public norms and expectations, can enable an ACA to make long-term gains without triggering overwhelming pushback.
4. Under certain conditions, ACAs pursuing high-level corruption can overcome retaliation by carefully managing timing, resources, and external support.

Observe that all four pertain to the need for ACAs to deter, counter, and overcome opposition from the beneficiaries of corruption. The opposition's tactics range from maligning ACA personnel, to behind-the-scenes lobbying, to open legislative battles. To counter this, ACAs have to deploy multiple strategies and balance some tradeoffs across these strategies.

First, ACAs should strive not to leave themselves open to valid criticisms. They should ideally have highly qualified and competent staff with top integrity, cohesion, and morale. When starting from scratch, this requires time to build, and in the meantime the agency can be criticized for doing nothing, as happened to the one in Indonesia. If the agency rushes to recruit and start with some high-profile cases to show its activism, that can create its own internal problems and scandals, as happened to the one in Latvia. If and when such criticisms hit home, it is essential to improve the procedures and recover from the setback quickly, as both did.

The high-profile strategy galvanizes public opinion, but also attracts strong political opposition. The low-profile strategy mutes such opposition, but may also render the public apathetic toward the anti-corruption movement, and lull the corrupt officials into a true sense of security!

To counter the powerful elite who strategize to weaken ACAs, the agencies must build coalitions with media, civil society, and the international community, as well as sympathetic elements in political parties and other administrative agencies. Indonesia's Corruption Eradication Commission (Komisi Pemberantasan Korupsi or KPK) did this well; when the government tried to reduce its powers and arrest its commissioners, their allies in citizens' movements held mass protests and foreign diplomats lobbied behind the scenes on their behalf. Such support is best won by acquiring a reputation for boldness, impartiality, and competence, but should be enhanced by good communication and public relations. The ACAs of Mauritius and Lithuania failed to cultivate journalists and civil society groups; they suffered from public misperceptions and distrust despite objectively reasonable performance at their tasks. If the country does not have anti-corruption civil society groups, the ACA can itself foster their development, as the one in Ghana did.

Two later ISS case studies (2015a, b) also illustrate the value of maintaining good public relations. In Slovakia, an open data initiative was having some success until a change of government in 2012, when it lost support of the new Prime Minister's office. By working with NGO activists, the office in charge of the initiative was able to continue and even expand its scope. In El Salvador, integrity pacts served to focus collaboration between the government, the private sector, and civil society, and counter some internal opposition from the bureaucracy, to reduce corruption and improve the culture at the Ministry of Public Works.

The ACA's procedures should also be designed to minimize the risk of false accusations and public distrust. Transparency is important, as are clear guidelines and prompt and full handling of complaints. As a former commissioner of Hong Kong's ICAC said: "If a citizen has screwed up his courage to come and tell you something, if you treat him or his complaint as insignificant, he will never come to you again. You've lost him, and you've probably lost all his friends as well."

Preventive and educational efforts, by the ACAs themselves or in alliance with other social organizations, are very helpful, and also hard for opponents to oppose openly. High-profile investigations and low-profile education have proved complementary in changing public perceptions and culture.

Some agencies publicly ranked government offices; "No head . . . would want their ministry to be labeled as the most corrupt ministry," said Rose Seretse, head of Botswana's Directorate on Corruption and Economic Crime (DCEC). In the next section I suggest a similar ranking scheme on the "supply side" of corruption, to rate firms by their clean practices in this regard.

In contrast to the relatively optimistic conclusions of the ISS report, Heeks and Mathisen (2012) flatly declare: "Most anti-corruption initiatives in developing countries fail." They attribute this to a large gap between design and reality, i.e. a big mismatch between expectations built into the design and realities of ground-level context of implementation. They recommend "a move away from grand designs developed by technocrats to a focus on interventions that have local fit and strategic fit."

The key difficulty they identify is the same as that emphasized by the ISS report: "few if anyone in a position of power and benefiting from corruption would like to see the opportunities for extraction reduced." The strategy and tactics of the opposition depend on their local power and context, and leaders of anti-corruption initiatives must counter-strategize accordingly.[15] The ISS report offers a somewhat selective sample of ACAs that successfully did this; Heeks and Mathisen look at several others that did not.

In her discussion of Heeks and Mathisen, Mungiu-Pippidi (2015, pp. 208–9) suggests a more fundamental difference of philosophies. She argues that many Western scholars and donors take a purist line: corruption is a disease or social pathology, and the only solution is to cure it. Therefore they regard partial progress as essentially no progress. She believes this zero-tolerance approach is mistaken: "in developing countries corruption is not a deviation, but rather the norm." The task is then to change beliefs and the norms, which entails changing the whole equilibrium. This is always a slow process, and partial success should not be dismissed.

Some Theory: Prisoner's Dilemma or Assurance Game?

Prime Minister Lee Kuan Yew in Singapore and Governor Murray MacLehose in Hong Kong provided strong leadership and backing for anti-corruption laws, agencies, and actions in those countries. But we cannot generally expect politicians and bureaucrats to do so; after all, they are the main beneficiaries in a corrupt system. Rather, we should expect them to pass laws that are weak and have loopholes, to enforce them as slowly and feebly as possible, and to obstruct the workings of any independent ACA they may have been compelled to create. Coalitions of the victims of corruption, like the *Addiopizzo* movement, have stronger incentives to fight it. Their main problem is organizing collective action, and game-theoretic analysis can help us understand the issues.

For the business community as a whole, most forms of corruption create a game of prisoner's dilemma. In bidding for government contracts or licenses, each firm stands to get a better deal by offering a higher bribe. But when they all do this, they are merely transferring more of their profits to the bureaucrats or politicians who have the power to award these favors, so in the aggregate they lose. Worse, to the extent that corruption acts like a tax, and worse because it is often levied at uncertain and arbitrary rates, it dampens incentives to invest and innovate, so the dynamic losses exceed the pure static transfer costs. This situation, where pursuit of individual incentives leads to a collectively bad outcome, is the classic Prisoner's Dilemma game.

Some argue that business will simply pass on such a tax to consumers through higher prices. But such recovery will in general be much less than full. If the bribe is for a permit to operate the business per se, that is a fixed cost, and does not alter the pricing decision. Any market power would already have been exercised to the same extent and reflected in prices even without the existence of a bribe, so the bribe is a pure subtraction from profit. A bribe that raises marginal cost will impact prices. But if the original price was optimally chosen to maximize profit, the added cost of the bribe can only lower the net profit. In some unusual circumstances, higher cost can act as a collusion-facilitating device for oligopolists; see Seade (1983) and Dixit (1986). But such an industry can surely find simpler and more legal ways to raise its costs than corruption! For example, it can support regulation that requires all firms in the industry to spend to achieve some generally agreed socially desirable goal such as reducing pollution or carbon emissions.

There are forms of grand corruption where business can collude with politicians or regulators to create monopolies for their mutual benefit at the expense of the public, and the following analysis does not apply to these. However, if other forms of corruption are tackled, that can contribute to changes in overall culture and attitudes, which in turn make this form of corruption difficult to sustain.

Game theory has yielded several ways the parties to a prisoner's dilemma can resolve it. The two most pertinent in our context are (1) repeated interaction and (2) multiple interactions involving different issues. If members of the business community need to deal with one another over time on several matters such as supply, subcontracting, trade credit, finance, and marketing, then they can create a system of rewards for cooperative behavior and penalties for selfish deviations. To combat corruption, the community should establish a norm that no member shall obtain an advantage by bribery in matters of government licenses or contracts. In matters of deals among themselves, each member should give preference to those who are known to adhere to the norm, and avoid dealing with those who are known to have violated it. A firm that is known to be an egregious briber will be ostracized by others, and thereby effectively put out of business. Since it is almost impossible for a firm to operate without any business deals with others in any moderately complex economy, the prospect of such ostracism should suffice to ensure adherence to the norm.

Such self-governing institutions based on norms and sanctions have operated in several business communities to achieve adherence to contracts among members. Avner Greif's study of a group of Jewish traders in North Africa nearly 1000 years ago (Greif 1993), and Lisa Bernstein's studies of contemporary diamond merchants and cotton traders (Bernstein 1992, 2001) are well known. Dixit (2004) constructs mathematical models to explicate their working.

Kingston (2008) and Dixit (2015a, b) develop similar models of community-based anti-corruption institutions. Of course the rigorous analysis reveals several conditions necessary for success of the scheme. The community must have an accurate mechanism for detecting violations of the norm, and must be careful to catch, deter, and punish false accusations. It needs some support from the formal state apparatus in that verdicts of its adjudication forum should be accepted and not double-guessed by courts in the same way that those of arbitration tribunals are. It must not become an insiders' clique that cartelizes the industry and deters new and innovative entry. It needs to get some large and highly respected businesses as launch or anchor members to attract attention and by example induce others to join. It must maintain good relations and build alliances with broader social groups, NGOs, and media. Dixit (2015a, b) discusses such issues in detail.

Dixit (2015b) finds that a business community institution of this kind is complementary or synergistic to any anti-corruption efforts the government may undertake: the two together are more effective than the sum of the effects of each on its own.

Other theoretical, empirical, and experimental work has clarified the requirements for sustaining cooperation in a prisoner's dilemma. Perhaps the most important one is that members of the group should be willing to participate in the prescribed punishment of a cheater. If the cheater is being ostracized, he may offer an extra tempting reward to any firm that breaks the ban and deals with him. However, how would this firm know that the cheater would not cheat it also? In fact, the cheater is already ostracized and other firms are not dealing with him, so he has nothing worse to fear. A firm that deals with him would have to give him a greater share of the rent to keep him honest in an ongoing relationship. Therefore it is actually more costly to deal with an ostracized cheater than to deal with a firm that has a clean history. Greif (1993, p. 535) gives a formal proof of this in Proposition 2.

Willingness to participate in punishment of a cheater to sustain a good social outcome, even at a private cost to oneself, also exists. Evidence has mounted for such "altruistic punishment" (Fehr and Gächter 2002), and it has been found to be ingrained in some basic neural circuitry of the brain (De Quervain et al. 2004). Of course we also need the members to understand that others have this willingness to punish, and the common understanding created by the society's culture can help.

A recent working paper by Transparency International (2016) suggests an even more promising avenue for the business community institution to combat corruption.[16] It argues that today's young people want the economy to have good governance and to be corruption-free. They, especially the smartest among them, prefer to work for firms that are good and clean in this respect. A firm that credibly pledges and acts in an ethical manner will find it easier to attract and retain such workers, and keep them happy in their work. Therefore it will enjoy higher productivity and lower labor turnover rates. Customers will favor it; indeed we already see this in the success of some firms like Patagonia. Therefore being more ethical is also becoming conducive to being more profitable.

Of course if most firms are corrupt, being a rare ethical standout does not do much because such a firm will lose out in most aspects of treatment by bureaucrats and politicians. But once enough firms start to be ethical, the relative advantage will tip in favor of good behavior.

In other words, the game may not be a prisoner's dilemma, but one called "assurance," like driving on the left versus right. If other cars drive on the left, it is in your own best interest to drive on the left, but if other cars drive on the right, it is best for you to do likewise. Similarly, if other firms are corrupt it pays you to be corrupt, but if others are good and clean, then it is best for you to be likewise.

Thus assurance games have two equilibria; which one prevails depends on what common knowledge and expectations of others' actions the players have. Such knowledge and expectations can be created and sustained by the overall culture of the society in which the players live; see Footnote 5 above.

In the driving example it may not matter much which of the two equilibria prevails, but in the case of business conduct the equilibrium with good behavior is better for everyone. The question is how the business community can move from a prevailing bad equilibrium to the good one.

This is not easy, but it is easier than resolving a prisoner's dilemma. To get the process started, reliable information about the identity of good and clean firms should be made available, so the smart young people can seek work at these firms and can support them as customers. As this starts to happen, other firms will recognize the advantages of being good and clean, and will strive to improve their behavior. Once this virtuous circle gathers momentum, the eventual outcome will be the preferred equilibrium. In other words, the whole social culture will change from one where corruption is expected and accepted to one where it is against the norms of behavior and unacceptable.

Think of the information-creating system by analogy with the Michelin star ratings for restaurants. There are one, two, and three star restaurants. Owners and chefs try very hard to earn and keep stars; losing a star is a disgrace. The idea is to create a similar rating system for companies, with the difference that in the eventual equilibrium almost every firm will have at least one star, whereas most restaurants never get any Michelin stars.

Of course it is crucial for the rating machinery itself to be entirely above-board and free from corruption. For that, it should be under continuous scrutiny of an independent oversight committee consisting of representatives from different kinds and sizes of companies, highly respected elders in society, some academics, and so on.

Lessons for the Future

The historical examples as well as the theory reviewed above suggest several approaches to combating corruption. Some try to design the rules and operation of politics and administration so that opportunities and incentives for corruption are minimized. Others focus on enforcement, to detect and punish the corrupt, using independent ACAs or similar bodies. Some are top-down; others are bottom-up. This variety of methods produces an equal variety of degrees of success, and the historical accounts do not give much guidance about the deeper underlying structures that can explain or predict success. But taken together, the examples and the theory do have some common themes and offer some tentative suggestions—strategies to adopt and mistakes to avoid.

First, we see the importance of leadership, or at any rate support, from among the topmost tiers of government: the elite in the city-states in Italy who participated in launching and sustaining the podestà system, the king of Denmark who got rid of the corrupt bureaucrats, Lee Kuan Yew who led the transformation of Singapore, and so on. Purely citizen-led bottom-up coalitions, like the *Addiopizzo* movement in Italy, can achieve success, but it will be limited. Lack of support from the top may be the biggest obstacle anti-corruption activists in many LDCs will face.

Next, in many instances different groups and strategies appear to be mutual complements: together they accomplish more than the sum of their individual effects. The most successful campaigns, like the one in Hong Kong, combine support from the top and good coalitions at the bottom. Case studies of ACAs in several countries show that their efforts have to balance and combine different strategies, and choose the right level of aggressiveness, taking proper account of the political and social context.

Many episodes of anti-corruption action started with a crisis. Although the path from the crisis to the change in the culture of corruption was not always the same and often not very clear even in hindsight, anti-corruption activists should be alert for such opportunities. They should keep in mind the famous saying of Rahm Emanuel (President Obama's first Chief of Staff and later Mayor of Chicago): "Never let a serious crisis go to waste. And what I mean by that its an opportunity to do things you think you could not do before."

The main obstacle facing a group that seeks to fight corruption—whether a government agency or a private movement—will be opposition from entrenched interests that are gaining from the corrupt system. They will look for and exploit all errors and weaknesses of the anti-corruption group. Therefore it is especially important for these groups to avoid any taint of corruption within themselves, or indeed any other scandals that can be used by the opponents to discredit them.

In the modern age, coalitions for anti-corruption action must include the media, including social media, schools, and related networks of information and communication. The anti-corruption groups should actively present themselves to the public, using modern publicity methods, clever slogans, and so on. They should develop and maintain good relations with the media, which will then treat discrediting allegations from opponents of these groups with skepticism, and in doubtful cases give the groups the benefit of the doubt.

Whether the movement is led from the top or the bottom, it has to work to change social norms and culture. The experience of Hong Kong demonstrates the value of education, especially at the early school level, for this.

Many of the examples I reviewed demonstrate the importance of contingency (as does so much of history more generally); therefore even good strategies need to be supported by good luck.[17] Just as Louis Pasteur said in matters of scientific observation, "chance favors the prepared mind," in fighting corruption chance is likely to favor the prepared alliance. Even then, as the historical episodes sketched above show, progress is likely to be slow, and success much short of 100%. Activists and critics alike should not disdain partial success, or criticize attempts at reform because they do not yield a perfect outcome; waiting for perfection merely ensures the status quo, which amounts to 0% success.

Comments by Stuti Khemani,[18] The World Bank, September, 2016

The paper by Avinash Dixit argues that persistent and systemic corruption should be understood in a game-theoretic framework as the equilibrium of a Prisoner's Dilemma. Although it would be beneficial for society as a whole to reduce corruption, society is instead stuck at high corruption levels because individuals believe that engaging in corruption is the best they can do given how others are behaving. For example, bureaucrats ask for bribes in order to provide public services, and citizens pay these bribes because they believe that most others engage in bribery; if you refuse to pay the bribe, you will get nothing, or worse, you may suffer retribution. Combatting corruption when it is entrenched and pervasive requires collective action and coordinated effort to escape the Prisoner's Dilemma. The paper provides examples from the history of different countries of how such collective action has come about through different pathways and policy choices. The main contrast offered is between the top-down processes followed by powerful national leaders to create professional and accountable bureaucracies, as in the case of Hong Kong and Singapore; and the bottom-up process by which civil society groups organize a social movement, as in the case of the *addiopizzo* in Italy to resist extortion by the Sicilian Mafia. Dixit distills general lessons for different actors who aspire to tackle corruption by placing these examples within the game-theoretic problem of collective action.

The big lesson nestled within the concluding section deserves greater prominence than it receives in this thoughtful and instructive paper by an intellectual giant of our times. Leaders matter crucially. In most of the examples—such as the creation of professional bureaucracies by the King in Denmark and an autocrat in Singapore—powerful national leaders take deliberate steps to set up the institutions needed to change incentives to engage in corruption. Even the success of the bottom-up social movement of the *addiopizzo* in Italy depends ultimately on whether it will be supported by local and national government leaders and the state institutions over which they exercise power (Daniele and Geys 2015). Leaders may need to include initiatives to support bottom-up change in social norms, such as through ethics education in Hong Kong, but bottom-up approaches on their own cannot succeed in reducing corruption without the support of leaders. Effective civil society leaders need to emerge even to organize bottom-up social change. Where do leaders come from, and what meta-initiatives or institutional arrangements might make it more likely for good leaders to emerge who have the capacity to pursue the public interest? It would be valuable to probe the rich examples offered in this paper for some suggestive answers, and guidance for future research concentrated on this question.

Each of the rich examples in the paper intertwines two very different institutional features to combat corruption—the proximate institutions that shape principal-agent problems of government, and the underlying meta-incentives of leaders to take up better proximate institutions that would reduce incentives and opportunities for corruption. Dixit provides a wonderful description of various proximate institutions—such as the

Podestà system in Italian city-states—that reduce the principal-agent problem between the leaders of the city-state (the principal) and the city manager (the agent). But it is not clear what prompted the political leaders of these city-states, those who wield power over the decision to select and enforce the Podestà system, to establish these effective institutions.

Others have argued that inclusive political institutions, which enabled the participation of a large proportion of citizens in selecting and sanctioning leaders, explain why the leaders of Italian city-states were held accountable for responsible management of public resources (Mungiu-Pippidi 2015, is cited in the paper, and World Bank 2016 reviews a larger body of work examining the effects of these political institutions). Indeed, regions in Italy that belonged to the erstwhile "free states," and thereby had a longer history of participatory democracy than other regions, still today experience greater social capital and more "civic" voting in elections whereby corruption is lower and transgressors are more likely to lose office. A strand of literature examining regional differences in the quality of government and social norms within Italy, between the center-north and the south, ultimately attributes better performance to earlier experience with participatory democracy, dating back to the twelfth century (Putnam et al. 1993; Guiso et al. 2006; Alesina and Giuliano 2015). The inclusiveness of political institutions triggered a set of cultural traits (civic and cooperative behavior) whose effects persist today. Regions that were not free cities in the twelfth century but that currently have the same institutions of local democracy are argued to suffer from "uncivic" voting, which allows corruption by political leaders to go unpunished (Nannicini et al. 2013). This series of arguments on variation in governance outcomes within Italy supports the notion that political norms (e.g. whether to punish transgression or not) develop through the experience of political engagement over time. The earlier experience with democratic institutions, and greater accumulation of such experience over time, is the underlying source of differences in governance within Italy today (World Bank 2016).

On the other hand, arguments about the inclusiveness of political institutions are challenged by the success of more authoritarian institutions in East Asia, such as those in China and Singapore. Another paper in this volume, by Francis Fukuyama, argues that some authoritarian regimes can build effective state capacity to deliver public services and promote economic growth, without similar success in controlling corruption. A new book on the Chinese experience further argues that national leaders gave incentives to bureaucratic cadres to invest in business ventures to fuel economic growth; bureaucrats in turn invested public resources through their social networks (Ang 2016). This appears to be an extraordinary case where crony capitalism—channeling public investments into the private business networks of public office holders—not only resulted in corruption (personal gain from holding public office) but at the same time delivered broader benefits of economic growth.

The literature really does not provide a sufficient explanation for why some authoritarian regimes perform well (in delivering services, and facilitating economic growth, even if they allow some corruption) while others are disastrous all around. Besley and Kudamatsu (2008) model the conditions under which autocracies can produce better outcomes than democracies. Their main argument is that if an autocracy is governed by a selectorate (that is, a group of presumably elite citizens with the power to select the leader), and if the selectorate exercises control to discipline poor performance, then the autocracy will promote good policies. Societies in which elites do not have norms and capacity to sanction leaders, or where elites benefit from leaders staying in office despite poor performance, would not satisfy the criteria for successful autocracies. Empirically, the authors characterize successful autocracies as those that had a growth rate above the 80th percentile of the distribution. Consistent with their theoretical explanation, they show that autocracies that are successful according to their definition of high growth are associated with more leadership turnover.

A common thread in the literature that applies to both democratic and autocratic institutional arrangements, is whether leaders are selected and sanctioned on the basis of performance (World Bank 2016). Besley and Kudamatsu (2008) show how the performance of both democracies and autocracies depends upon the political environment within which each system of government is implemented. They show that although a successful autocracy performs better than a polarized democracy in which elections do not reward public interest policies, the autocracy is in turn outperformed by a well-functioning democracy in which public interest policies are politically salient. The worst of all systems in their model are autocracies in which leaders are able to maintain their grip on power despite bad performance. Consistent with their model and with other work (Rodrik 2000; Mobarak 2005), they document a high degree of variance of growth under autocracies compared with democracies. While the cross-country correlation between democracy and economic growth is much debated, recent research reports a robust positive association (Acemoglu et al. 2014). On average, this evidence suggests that more inclusive political institutions lead to better development outcomes.

Dixit also hints at how the threat of revolution (a highly inclusive type of political engagement!), or the aftermath of an actual revolution, such as the Glorious Revolution of 1688 in England and the French Revolution a century later, creates incentives for leaders to placate citizens by improving the provision of public goods. Yet, Dixit writes: "The path of revolution is too risky and too slow to serve as an anti-corruption policy, hardly to be recommended to today's Asian, African and Latin American countries" (page 6). But a slow, or less turbulent, revolution may already be underway in today's developing countries. It consists of vigorous participation in electoral institutions, not just as voters, but perhaps even more importantly, as contenders for leadership at multiple levels of local government (even where national political systems are more authoritarian and thwart competition). The conditions resemble those of the Progressive Era in the United States and the nineteenth century reforms in the UK after the Industrial Revolution, of widespread political engagement, supported by mass media (cheap, "muckraking" newspapers that report on corruption scandals).

But, as Dixit notes, in the case of the Progressive Era in the US there was another ingredient in the mix—and that was a rise in demand for common interest public goods which brought together a critical coalition of elite business interests and civil society leaders. This probably allowed political engagement to unfold in healthy ways—with leaders being selected and sanctioned on the basis of performance in delivering public goods. The problem with political engagement in the poor world today is that it can revolve around the extraction of private benefits—such as cash in exchange for votes; or ethnic favoritism in dispensing government jobs—at the expense of public goods (World Bank 2016). Corrupt leaders can gain and remain in office despite condoning and even promoting corruption, because they share the spoils with their constituents.

This brings us full circle to Dixit's conclusion that both good leaders and bottom-up social movements are needed to transition out of the Prisoner's Dilemma equilibrium of high corruption. What is not spelt out in Dixit's paper, but is explicit in World Bank (2016) is the interaction between the two. Bottom-up or widespread social movements need to focus not just on collective action against bribery and extortion in the economic realm, but also in the political realm, urging citizens to select and sanction leaders on the basis of public good performance, not in exchange for private benefits. Mass media is a powerful instrument because it can go beyond addressing information asymmetries to persuading citizens to shift their demands or preferences for public goods, and emphasize performance in delivering public goods when evaluating leaders (Keefer and Khemani 2016). Mass media is powerful also because it can serve as a coordination device for citizens. Whether mass media indeed serves this role by enabling coordination on public good platforms is another question. It may instead coordinate tragic actions such as a genocide (Yanagizawa-Drott 2014); it may disseminate "fake news"; and it may create echo-chambers that confirm the prior ideological views of citizens, allowing them to effectively avoid information. Well-intentioned practitioners who want to promote better outcomes have to contend with these opposing forces in the messiness of politics. Unhealthy politics may be difficult to tackle, but it cannot be bypassed with technical and technological solutions. Even when the technology works, it can be sabotaged; even when the reforms work, they can be repealed (World Bank 2016).

For well-intentioned practitioners who want to learn from research about what they might do to reduce corruption, the message in Dixit's paper and this accompanying set of comments (drawn on the basis of the analysis in World Bank 2016) is to go beyond the setting-up of formal anti-corruption institutions, to changing political norms, an especially important subset of social norms pertaining to the selection and sanctioning of leaders. Policy efforts to establish formal institutions and change formal rules to reduce corruption will not work if the political norms for selecting and sanctioning leaders condones corruption. Efforts to improve political norms are necessary complements to anything else practitioners may choose to do to reduce corruption. They may not be sufficient; unhealthy political norms may persist, but there is no side-stepping it. Political norms to select good leaders, and give them incentives to provide public goods, can serve as a meta-institution to support all other anti-corruption institutions. Future research would do well to examine the nature of political norms, and how to measure them, with an eye toward informing initiatives to reduce corruption and promote public goods.

Notes

1. There can be similar misuse of authority in private enterprise; for example, a firm's purchasing manager may overpay in exchange for a kickback from the supplier. Firms attempt to deter such behavior using efficiency wages and similar strategies, and presumably they do so to an optimal extent trading off costs of detection and benefits of deterrence. This is basically a principal-agent problem in corporate governance. Therefore I will leave it aside and focus on corruption in exercise of public authority.
2. The recent leak of Panama Papers shows how much corruption at high political levels persists, even in advanced and supposedly squeaky-clean countries.
3. See for example Dixit and Pindyck (1994).
4. Findings of some recent research on Russia (Mironov and Zhuravskaya 2016) contradict this "greasing the gears of bureaucracy" hypothesis.
5. The concept of culture is even more complex than corruption! The Merriam-Webster dictionary defines it in several parts: (*a*) the integrated pattern of human knowledge, belief, and behavior that depends upon the capacity for learning and transmitting knowledge to succeeding generations; (*b*) the customary beliefs, social forms, and material traits of a racial, religious, or social group; *also* the characteristic features of everyday existence (as diversions or a way of life) shared by people in a place or time; (*c*) the set of shared attitudes, values, goals, and practices that characterizes an institution or organization; (*d*) the set of values, conventions, or social practices

associated with a particular field, activity, or societal characteristic. (http://www.merriam-webster.com/dictionary/culture, accessed May 13, 2016.) For my purpose here, the key feature is the sharing of values, practices, and so on. This creates the common knowledge—everyone knows, everyone knows that everyone knows, and so on—that helps sustain equilibria in games.

6. Ancient China had a somewhat similar system of "guest" officials with supervisory role (Parker 1903, p. 234). And Paul Romer's idea of "charter cities" (see e.g. Fuller and Romer 2012) has some parallels with the podestà system. Therefore a better understanding of that system can have broader use and application.

7. For a narrative account over a longer span of time, together with an argument for a broad definition of corruption, namely systemic use of public power to serve private ends instead of the public good, see Teachout (2014).

8. My account is based on Quah (2007).

9. The ICAC web site http://www.icac.org.hk/en/about_icac/bh/ gives a good account. See also the Wikipedia article: https://en.wikipedia.org/wiki/Independent_Commission_Against_Corruption_%28Hong_Kong%29 Some recent developments are recounted in a news article http://www.cnn.com/2013/10/15/world/asia/china-hong-kong-corruption/.

10. "The party winds down," *The Economist*, May 7, 2016.

11. The first scholarly study of *Addiopizzo* published in English known to me is Superti (2009). More recent and more detailed quantitative and sociological studies include Battisti et al. (2015) and Vaccaro and Palazzo (2015).

12. A similar philosophy motivates India's "zero-rupee note" movement to combat petty bribery. When a cop or official asks for 100 or 500 rupees, offering this note instead of merely refusing "shows a person's affiliation with a larger movement." ("Small change," *The Economist*, December 7, 2013.)

13. See http://www.newsweek.com/2014/09/26/addiopizzo-grassroots-campaign-making-life-hell-sicilian-mafia-271064.html.

14. One problem with the study is that all eight ACAs in the sample "were considered by experts to perform well relative to peer agencies." Understanding determinants of success requires a sample with sufficiently many and varied instances of failure!

15. Unfortunately anti-corruption movements and their leaders are often driven purely by idealism and enthusiasm; they lack organizational and strategic

skills. Anna Hazare's Lokpal (ombudsman) movement and Arvind Kejriwal's Aam Aadmi Party in India are good examples of this.

16. Discussions with some prominent Indian businesspeople at a recent conference organized by the World Bank confirm Transparency International's claims about the private benefit of to corporations from being non-corrupt. Experimental research of Grant (2008) also finds that intrinsic pro-social motivation has positive effect on job performance and productivity.

17. See Dixit (2007) for more on the theme that "strategic complementarities plus luck" is the broadly valid recipe for development success.

18. The World Bank, Author's views do not necessarily coincide with those of the institution she is affiliated with.

References

Acemoglu, Daron., Suresh Naidu, Pascual Restrepo, and James A. Robinson. 2014. *Democracy Does Cause Growth*. NBER Working Paper 20004, National Bureau of Economic Research, Cambridge, MA.

Alesina, Alberto, and Paola Giuliano. 2015. Culture and Institutions. *Journal of Economic Literature* 53: 898–944.

Ang, Yuen Yuen. 2016. How China Escaped the Poverty Trap. In *Cornell Studies in Political Economy*, 19. Ithaca, NY: Cornell University Press.

Battisti, Michele, Andrea Mario Lavezzi, Lucio Masserini and Monica Pratesi. 2015. *Resisting the Extortion Racket: An Empirical Analysis*. Discussion Paper 206, University of Pisa, Department of Economics and Management.

Bernstein, Lisa. 1992. Opting Out of the Legal System: Extralegal Contractual Relations in the Diamond Industry. *The Journal of Legal Studies* 21 (1): 115–157.

———. 2001. Private Commercial Law in the Cotton Industry: Creating Cooperation Through Rules, Norms, and Institutions. *Michigan Law Review* 99: 1724–1788.

Besley, T., and M. Kudamatsu. 2008. Making Autocracy Work. In *Institutions and Economic Performance*, ed. E. Helpman. Cambridge, MA: Harvard University Press.

Born, Lester K. 1927. What is a *Podestà? American Political Science Review* 21: 863–871.

Daniele, Gianmarco, and Benny Geys. 2015. Organised Crime, Institutions and Political Quality: Empirical Evidence from Italian Municipalities. *Economic Journal* 125: F233–F255.

De Quervain, Dominique, J.F., Urs Fischbacher, Valerie Treyer, Melanie Schell-hammer, Ulrich Schnyder, Alfred Buck, and Ernst Fehr. 2004. The Neural Basis of Altruistic Punishment. *Science* 305: 1254.

Dixit, Avinash. 1986. Comparative Statics for Oligopoly. *International Economic Review* 27: 107–122.

———. 2004. *Lawlessness and Economics: Alternative Modes of Governance*. Princeton, NJ: Princeton University Press.

———. 2007. Evaluating Recipes for Development Success. *World Bank Research Observer* 22: 131–157.

———. 2015a. Corruption: Supply-Side and Demand-Side Solutions. In *Development in India: Micro and Macro Perspectives*, ed. S. Mahendra Dev and P.G. Babu, 57–68. New Delhi: Springer.

———. 2015b. How Business Community Institutions Can Help Fight Corruption. *World Bank Economic Review* 29: S25–S47.

Dixit, Avinash, and Robert Pindyck. 1994. *Investment Under Uncertainty*. Princeton, NJ: Princeton University Press.

Fehr, Ernst, and Simon Gächter. 2002. Altruistic Punishment in Humans. *Nature* 415: 137–140.

Fuller, Brandon, and Paul Romer. 2012. *Success and the City: How Charter Cities Could Transform the Developing World*. Ottawa, Canada: Macdonald-Laurier Institute.

Glaeser, Edward, and Claudia Goldin, eds. 2006. *Corruption and Reform: Lessons from America's Economic History*. Chicago, IL: University of Chicago Press.

Grant, Adam M. 2008. Does Intrinsic Motivation Fuel the Prosocial Fire? Motivational Synergy in Predicting Persistence, Performance, and Productivity. *Journal of Applied Psychology* 93: 48–58.

Greif, Avner. 1993. Contract Enforceability and Economic Institutions in Early Trade: The Maghribi Traders Coalition. *American Economic Review* 83: 525–548.

Guiso, Luigi, Paola Sapienza, and Luigi Zingales. 2006. Does Culture Affect Economic Outcomes? *Journal of Economic Perspectives* 20: 23–48.

Heeks, Richard, and Harald Mathisen. 2012. Understanding Success and Failure of Anti-corruption Initiatives. *Crime, Law and Social Change* 58: 533–549.

Innovations for Successful Societies. 2014. *From Underdogs to Watch Dogs: How Anti-corruption Agencies Can Hold Off Potent Adversaries*. Princeton University. https://www.princeton.edu/successfulsocieties

———. 2015a. *Bringing Government Data into the Light: Slovakia's Open Data Initiative, 2011–2015*. Princeton University. https://www.princeton.edu/successfulsocieties

————. 2015b. *A Blueprint for Transparency: Integrity Pacts for Public Works, El Salvador, 2009–2014.* Princeton University. https://www.princeton.edu/successfulsocieties

Keefer, Philip, and Stuti Khemani. 2016. *Media's Influence on Citizen Demand for Public Goods, Revised Version of "Radios Impact on Preferences for Patronage Benefits.* Policy Research Working Paper 6932, World Bank, Washington, DC.

Kingston, Christopher. 2008. Social Structure and Cultures of Corruption. *Journal of Economic Behavior and Organization* 67: 90–102.

Mironov, Maxim, and Ekaterina Zhuravskaya. 2016. Corruption in Procurement and the Political Cycle in Tunneling: Evidence from Financial Transactions Data. *American Economic Journal: Economic Policy* 8: 287–321.

Mobarak, A.M. 2005. Democracy, Volatility, and Economic Development. *Review of Economics and Statistics 87*: 348–361.

Mungiu-Pippidi, Alina. 2015. *The Quest for Good Governance: How Societies Develop Control of Corruption.* Cambridge: Cambridge University Press.

Nannicini, Tommaso, Andrea Stella, Guido Tabellini, and Ugo Troiano. 2013. Social Capital and Political Accountability. *American Economic Journal: Economic Policy* 5: 222–250.

Parker, Edward H. 1903. *China, Past and Present.* London: Chapman and Hall.

Putnam, R., R. Leonardi, and R.Y. Nanetti. 1993. *Making Democracy Work.* Princeton, NJ: Princeton University Press.

Quah, Jon S.T. 2007. Combating Corruption Singapore-Style: Lessons for Other Asian Countries. *Maryland Series in Contemporary Asian Studies* 2007: 1.

Rangarajan, L.N., ed. 1992. *The Arthashastra.* New Delhi: Penguin Books India.

Recanatini, Francesca. 2011. Anti-corruption Authorities: An effective Tool to Curb Corruption? In *International Handbook on the Economics of Corruption*, ed. Susan Rose-Akerman and Tina Soreide, 528–570. Cheltenham, UK: Edward Elgar. Chapter 19.

Rodrik, Dani. 2000. Institutions for High-Quality Growth: What They Are and How to Acquire Them. *Studies in Comparative International Development* 35: 3–31.

Seade, Jesús K. 1983. Prices, Profits and Taxes in Oligopoly. Research Paper in Economics No. 260, University of Warwick, UK.

Superti, Chiara. 2009. Addiopizzo: Can a Label Defeat the Mafia? *Journal of International Policy Solutions* 11: 3–11.

Teachout, Zephyr. 2014. *Corruption in America: From Benjamin Franklin's Snuff Box to Citizens United.* Cambridge, MA: Harvard University Press.

Transparency International. 2016. *The Benefits of Anti-corruption and Corporate Transparency.* Working Paper #01. Transparency International, Berlin.

Vaccaro, Antonio, and Guido Palazzo. 2015. Values Against Violence: Institutional Change in Societies Dominated by Organized Crime. *Academy of Management Journal* 58: 1075–1101.

World Bank. 2016. *Making Politics Work for Development: Harnessing Transparency and Citizen Engagement.* Policy Research Report. Washington, DC: World Bank.

Yanagizawa-Drott, David. 2014. Propaganda and Conflict: Evidence from the Rwandan Genocide. *The Quarterly Journal of Economics* 129: 1947–1994.

3

Corruption as a Political Phenomenon

Francis Fukuyama

Corruption has in many ways become the defining issue of the twenty-first century, just as the twentieth century was characterized by large ideological struggles between democracy, fascism, and communism. Today, a majority of the world's nations accept the legitimacy of democracy, and at least pretend to hold competitive elections. What really distinguishes political systems from one another is the degree to which the elites ruling them seek to use their power in the service of a broad public interest, or to simply enrich themselves, their friends, and their families. Countries from Russia and Venezuela to Afghanistan and Nigeria all hold elections that produce leaders with some degree of democratic legitimacy. What distinguishes them from Norway, Japan, or Britain is not so much democracy as the quality of government, which in turn is greatly affected by levels of corruption.

F. Fukuyama (✉)
Stanford University, Stanford, CA, USA
e-mail: ffukuyam@stanford.edu

© The Author(s) 2018
K. Basu, T. Cordella (eds.), *Institutions, Governance and the Control of Corruption*, International Economic Association Series,
https://doi.org/10.1007/978-3-319-65684-7_3

Corruption hurts life outcomes in a wide variety of ways. Economically, it diverts resources away from their most productive uses, and acts like a regressive tax that supports the lifestyles of elites at the expense of everyone else. Corruption incentivizes the best and the brightest to spend their time gaming the system rather than innovating or creating new wealth. Politically, corruption undermines the legitimacy of political systems by giving elites alternative ways of holding on to power other than genuine democratic choice. It hurts the prospects of democracy when people perceive authoritarian governments performing better than corrupt democratic ones, and undermines the reality of democratic choice.

However, the phenomenon labeled corruption comprises a wide range of behaviors whose economic and political effects vary greatly. It is remarkable that for all of the academic effort put into the study of corruption, there is still no broadly accepted vocabulary for distinguishing between its different forms. Before we can tackle corruption, we need some conceptual clarity as to what it is, and how it relates to the broader problem of good government.

Corruption as a Modern Phenomenon

Corruption can exist in many contexts, from bribery in a sports organization to a secretary stealing from the office pool. I am here going to focus on political corruption, which concerns the abuse of public office for private gain.[1]

The first point to note is that corruption is a modern phenomenon. The very terms public and private did not always exist in earlier historical times. In the European Medieval era, virtually all regimes were what Max Weber labeled "patrimonial": that is, political authority was regarded as a species of private property which could be handed down to descendants as part of their patrimony. In dynastic times, a king could give away an entire province with all of its inhabitants to his son or daughter as a wedding present, along with all of the inhabitants living there, since he regarded his domain as a private possession. Under these circumstances it made no sense to talk about public corruption.[2]

The concept that rulers did not simply own their domains but were custodians of a broader public interest was one that emerged gradually in the sixteenth and seventeenth centuries. Theorists like Hugo Grotius, Jean Bodin, Thomas Hobbes, and Samuel Pufendorf began to argue that a ruler could be legitimately sovereign not by right of ownership, but out of a kind of social contract by which he or she protected public interest, above all the common interest in peace and security. The very notion that there was a difference and potential conflict between public and private interest thus emerged historically with the rise of modern European states. In this respect, China beat Europe to the punch by nearly 1800 years, having been one of the earliest civilizations to develop a concept of an impersonal state that was the guardian of a collective public interest.

Today, no ruler dares assert publicly that they "own" the territories over which they exercise authority; even traditional monarchs like those in the Arab world claim to be serving a broader public interest. Hence we have the phenomenon that political scientists label "neo-patrimonialism," in which political pretend to be modern servants of the common good, in political systems with modern outward trappings like parliaments, ministers, and bureaucracies. But the reality is that elites enter politics to extract rents or resources and enrich themselves and their families at the expense of everyone else.

The fact of the matter is that a modern state, which seeks to promote public welfare and treats its citizens impersonally, is not just a recent modern phenomenon, but also one that is difficult to achieve and inherently fragile. The reason has to do with human nature. Human beings are social creatures by nature, but their sociability takes very specific forms. The biological phenomenon of kin selection or inclusive fitness means that people will behave altruistically toward genetic relatives in proportion to the number of genes they share. Reciprocal altruism is also rooted in biology and is built around the exchange of favors between non-relatives. Human beings, in other words, tend to favor family and friends; such favoritism extends across all known human cultures and historical times. It is not a learned behavior, but the default form of sociability to which humans revert when not otherwise incentivized. The demand that we treat people on an impersonal basis, or hire a stranger who is qualified rather than a relative or a friend, is not something that comes naturally to human beings. Modern political systems set up incentive systems and try to socialize people into different forms of behavior, but because favoritism toward friends and family is a natural instinct, there is a constant danger of relapsing into this kind of behavior—something I have elsewhere labeled "repatrimonialization."[3]

People who live in rich, developed countries often look down at countries pervaded by systemic corruption as if they are somehow deviant cases, bearers of a mysterious disease that prevents them from being a normal healthy, modern state. But the truth of the matter is that, up until a few centuries ago, there were virtually no modern, "uncorrupt" states. Making the transition from a patrimonial or neo-patrimonial state to a modern-impersonal one is a difficult and historically fraught process, much more difficult in most respects than making the transition from an authoritarian political system to a democratic one. Corruption and poor government performance are the Achilles Heel of many new democracies around the world, from India and Brazil to Romania and Bulgaria.[4]

But if most countries in most of human history were patrimonial or neo-patrimonial, there were still large differences between them with regard to the quality of government. So we need to make some finer distinctions between types and levels of corruption.

Types of Corruption

There are two separate phenomena related to corruption but are not identical to it. The first is the creation and extraction of rents, and the second is what is alternatively referred to as patronage or clientelism.

In economics, a rent is technically defined as the difference between the cost of keeping a good or service in production, and its price. One of the most important sources of rents is scarcity: natural resource rents exist because the selling price of oil far exceeds the cost of pumping it out of the ground.

Rents can also be artificially generated by governments. Many of the most common forms of corruption revolve around the government's ability to create artificial scarcities through licensing or regulation. Placing tariffs on imports restricts imports and generates rents for the government; one of the most widespread forms of corruption around the world lies in customs agencies where the customs agent will take a bribe in order to either reduce the duties charged, or expedite the clearance process so that the importer will have his or her goods on time.

The ease with which governments can create rents through their taxation or regulatory power has led many economists to denounce rents in general as distortions of efficient resource allocation by markets, and to see rent creation and distribution as virtually synonymous with corruption. The ability of governments to generate rents means that many ambitious people will choose politics rather than entrepreneurship or the private sector as a route to wealth.

But while rents can and are abused in the fashion described, they also have perfectly legitimate uses which complicate any blanket denunciation of them. The most obvious type of a "good" rent is a patent or copyright, by which the government gives the creator of an idea or creative work the exclusive right to any resulting revenues for some defined period of time. Economist Mushtaq Khan points out that many Asian governments have promoted industrialization by allowing favored firms to generate excess profits, provided they were plowed back into new investment. While this opened the door to considerable corruption and abuse, it also worked as a means of stimulating rapid growth at a rate possibly higher than market forces on their own would have produced.[5]

All government regulatory functions, from protecting wetlands, to requiring disclosure in initial public offerings of stocks, to certifying drugs as safe and effective, create artificial scarcities and therefore rents. But while we can argue about the appropriate extent of regulation, few people would like to see these functions abandoned simply because they produce rents. The creation and distribution of rents by governments have a high degree of overlap with corruption, but are not simply the same phenomenon. One must look at the purpose of the rent, and judge whether it is generating a purely private good that is being appropriated by the government official, or whether it is actually serving a broader public purpose.

A second phenomenon that is often identified with corruption is that of patronage or clientelism. A patronage relationship is a reciprocal exchange of favors between two individuals of different status and power, usually involving favors given by the patron to the client in exchange for the client's loyalty and political support. The favor given to the client must be a good that can be individually appropriated, like a job in the post office, or a Christmas turkey, or a get-out-of-jail card for a relative, rather than a public good or policy that applies to a broad class of people.[6]

Patronage is sometimes distinguished from clientelism by scale; patronage relationships are typically face-to-face ones between patrons and clients and exist in all regimes whether authoritarian or democratic, while clientelism involves larger scale exchanges of favors between patrons and clients, often requiring a hierarchy of intermediaries.[7] Clientelism thus exists primarily in democratic countries where large numbers of voters need to be mobilized.[8]

Clientelism is considered a bad thing and a deviation from good democratic practice in several respects. In a modern democracy, citizens are supposed to vote for politicians based on the politician's promises of broad public policies, or a "programmatic" agenda. Such choices are supposed to reflect general views of what is good for the political community as a whole, and not just what is good for one individual voter. Of course, voters in advanced democracies cast their ballots according to their self-interest, whether that is lower taxes or particular social programs.

Moreover, targeted programs must apply impartially not to individuals but to broad classes of people. A politician is in particular not supposed to give a benefit to specific individuals based on whether they supported him or her.

Targeted benefits to individuals are bad from the standpoint of social justice. Redistributive programs that are supposed to help all poor people, for example, end up benefiting only those poor people who support a particular politician in clientelistic systems. This weakens support for effective universal policies, and preserves existing social inequalities.

Nonetheless, there is reason to think that clientelism is actually an early form of democratic participation; in the United States and other countries, it was a way of mobilizing poor voters and therefore encouraging them to participate in a democratic political system. It was suboptimal when compared to programmatic voting, yet provided a degree of accountability insofar as the politician still felt obligated to provide some benefits in return for political support. In that respect clientelism is quite different from a more destructive form of corruption in which a politician simply steals from the public treasury for the benefit of his family, without any obligation to provide a public service in return. The problem with clientelism is that it usually does not remain a mechanism for getting out the vote, but morphs into more destructive forms of misappropriation.

A final conceptual distinction that needs to be made is between corruption and low state capacity. "Anti-corruption and good governance" have become an often-repeated slogan in the development policy community, and some people treat good governance and absence of corruption as equivalents. And yet they are very different: a squeaky-clean bureaucracy can still be incompetent or ineffective in doing its job, while corrupt ones can nonetheless provide good services.[9] Beyond low levels of corruption, good governance requires state capacity, that is, the human, material, and organizational resources necessary for governments to effectively and efficiently carry out their mandates. It is linked to the skills and knowledge of public officials, and whether they are given sufficient autonomy and authority to carry out their tasks. Corruption of course tends to undermine state capacity (e.g., by replacing qualified officials with political patronage appointees); conversely, highly professional bureaucracies tend to be less subject to bribery and theft. Low levels of corruption and high state capacity therefore tend to be correlated around the world. But getting to good governance is a much larger task than simply fighting corruption.

The distinction between corruption and low state capacity then allows us to better understand differences between the effects of corruption in different countries around the world. In the World Bank Institute's Worldwide Governance Indicators, China ranks in the 47th percentile with respect to control of corruption, behind Ghana and just ahead of Romania. On the other hand, China has a great deal of state capacity; in the government effectiveness category it is in the 66th percentile while Romania is in the 55th while Ghana is in the 44th. This validates the common perception that the Chinese government has a great deal of capacity to achieve the ends it sets, despite strong perceptions of pervasive corruption. The predictability and levels of corruption levels is also important; if a business owner expects to pay 10% of the transaction value in bribes, he or she can regard that as a kind of tax, which is less damaging to investment than a bribery level of 75%, or one that varies arbitrarily from year to year.

Overcoming Corruption

The first generation of anti-corruption measures taken from the mid-1990s on by development finance institutions involved ambitious efforts to overhaul civil service systems along Weberian lines, incentivizing officials by increasing wage dispersion and setting formal recruitment and promotion criteria. These measures had very little effect; the problem lay in the fact that corrupt governments were expected to police themselves, and to implement bureaucratic systems developed over the years in rich countries with very different histories. More recent efforts have focused on fighting corruption through transparency and accountability measures, that is, increasing the monitoring of agent behavior and creating positive and negative incentives for better behavior. This has taken a variety of forms, from cameras placed in classrooms to ensure that teachers are showing up for work, to participatory budgeting where citizens are given direct voice in budgeting decisions, to websites where citizens can report government officials taking bribes. Since governments could not be trusted to police themselves, civil society has often been enlisted in a watchdog role, and mobilized to demand accountability. Other mechanisms of horizontal accountability like anti-corruption commissions and special prosecutors, if given enough autonomy, have also shown some success in countries like Indonesia and Romania.

These later efforts have also met with uneven success.[10] In particular, transparency initiatives by themselves do not guarantee changes in government behavior. For example, in countries where clientelism is organized along ethnic lines, co-ethnics are frequently tolerant of leaders who steal. Citizens may be outraged by news of corruption, but then have no clear way of holding individual politicians or bureaucrats accountable. In other cases, successes in punishing individual politicians are not sufficient to shift the normative framework, in which virtually everyone in the political class expects to profit from office. Finally, anti-corruption campaigns may disrupt informal understandings and personal relationships that underpin investment and trade; lacking a working formal system of property rights and contract enforcement under a system of independent courts, the paradoxical effect of prosecuting corrupt officials may be to deter new investment and thereby lower growth.

There is a single truth underlying the indifferent success of existing transparency and accountability measures to control corruption, which is that the sources of corruption are deeply political, and that without a political strategy for overcoming the problem, any given solution will fail. That is, corruption in its various forms—patronage, clientelism, rent-seeking, and outright theft—all benefit existing stakeholders in the political system, who by and large are very powerful players. Lecturing them about good government or setting up formal systems deigned to work in modern political systems will not affect their incentives, and therefore will have little transformative effect. That is why transparency initiatives on their own often fail: citizens may be outraged by news about corruption, but without collective action mechanisms to bring about change, nothing will happen. The mere existence of a democratic political system is no guarantee that citizen anger will be translated into action; they need leadership and a strategy for displacing entrenched stakeholders from power. Outside pressure, in the form of loan conditionality, technical assistance, or moral pressure, is almost never sufficient to do the job. Anti-corruption commission and special prosecutors who have had success in jailing corrupt officials have done so only because they receive strong, grassroots political backing from citizens.

The American Experience

The political nature of corruption, and the necessarily political nature of the reform process, can be illustrated by the experience of the United States in the nineteenth century.[11] American politics in that period was not too different from politics in contemporary developing democratic countries like India, Brazil, or Indonesia. Beginning in the 1820s, American states began expanding the franchise to include all white males, vastly expanding the voter base and presenting politicians with the challenge of mobilizing relatively poor and poorly educated voters. The solution, which appeared particularly after the 1828 presidential election that brought Andrew Jackson to power, was the creation of a vast clientelistic system by which elected politicians appointed their supporters to positions in the bureaucracy or rewarded them with individual payoffs like Christmas turkeys or bottles of bourbon. This system, known as the spoils or patronage system, characterized American government for the next century, from the highest federal offices down to local postmasters in every American town or city. As with other clientelistic systems, patronage led to astonishing levels of corruption, particularly in eastern cities like New York, Boston, or Chicago where machine politicians ruled for generations.

This system began to change only in the 1880s, as a consequence of economic development. The country at that point was being transformed by new technologies like the railroads from a primarily agrarian society into an urban industrial one. There were increasing demands both on the part of business leaders and from a newly emerging civil society for a different, more modern form of government that would prioritize merit and knowledge over political connections. Following the assassination of the newly elected President James A. Garfield in 1883 by a would-be office seeker, Congress was embarrassed into voting for the Pendleton Act, which for the first time established a US Civil Service Commission and the principle that public officials should be chosen on the basis of merit. Even so, expanding the number of classified (i.e., merit-based) officials met strong resistance, and did not become widespread until after the First World War. Individual municipal political machines, like Tammany Hall in New York, were not dismantled completely until the middle of the twentieth century.

The American experience illustrates a number of features of both corruption and reform of corrupt systems. In the first place, the incentives that led to the creation of the clientelistic system in the first place were deeply political: politicians got into office via their ability to distribute patronage; they had no incentive to vote in favor of something like the Pendleton Act that would take away those privileges. The only reason it passed was a tragic exogenous event, the Garfield assassination, which mobilized public opinion in favor of a more modern governmental system. Second, reform of the system was similarly political. The Progressive Era saw the emergence of a vast reform coalition, made up of progressive business leaders, urban reformers, farmers, and ordinary citizens who were fed up with the existing patronage system. It required good leadership from politicians like Theodore Roosevelt (who was himself head of the US Civil Service Commission) or Gifford Pinchot, head of the US Forest Service. And it required a clear reform agenda pointing toward modern government, one that was formulated by intellectuals like Frank Goodnow, Dorman Eaton, and Woodrow Wilson himself. Finally, reform was helped along by economic development. Industrialization in the US produced new social groups, like business leaders who needed efficient government services, a broad and better-educated middle class who could mobilize for reform, and grassroots organization of civil society groups. It was only the creation of a Progressive reform coalition under strong leadership that succeeded in bringing about the political changes necessary to overcome resistance from the older generation of patronage politicians.

Anti-corruption Agencies

That overcoming corruption is a political process is evident as well in the more recent experience of anti-corruption agencies (ACAs). Since the 1980s, there has been a proliferation of over 60 ACAs, mandated by a number of international agreements like the UN Convention Against Corruption or the Inter-American Convention Against Corruption.[12] And yet, while certain ACAs like those in Hong Kong or Indonesia have seen successes prosecuting high-level offenders, the vast majority have not been seen as effective.[13]

Much of the analysis of what separates successful ACAs from their ineffective peers has revolved around their legal powers and institutional design. For example, some agencies have only limited investigative power but no power to initiate prosecutions of corrupt officials. Many have to rely on other agencies like police or prosecutors which are themselves corrupt or potential targets for investigation. In some countries, even a criminal indictment is no guarantee that justice will be done, since the court system is itself corrupt or subject to political pressure. In other cases, commissions are dependent on presidential appointment, or else require budget appropriations from legislatures for their continued operations. Even ACAs that have been initially successful at prosecuting high officials become targets of payback at a later date, with their own staff or commissioners being charged with corruption or crimes by other agencies.

All of these design issues are critical, of course. Take the case of Indonesia's ACA, the Corruption Eradication Commission or KPK that was established in 2003. Based on the experience of Bernard de Speville and the Hong Kong Independent Commission Against Corruption, the KPK's founding statute gave it the ability to carefully select personnel from other agencies and to protect them from rival power centers. The KPK had the power to conduct its own investigations, could launch prosecutions, and did not have to cooperate with the police or Attorney General's office. Due to the Indonesian judiciary's reputation for corruption, the KPK law established a new Anti-Corruption Court (TIPIKOR) to exclusively handle cases arising out of KPK investigations. Three of the five judges on this court were selected from outside the regular judiciary, so as not to be subject to the latter's control. The KPK was given a substantial budget, and was allowed to pay its staff substantial premiums over the pay of other civil servants.

All of these powers and design characteristics were critical in allowing the KPK to achieve some early successes, like the prosecution and conviction of Aceh governor Abdullah Puteh. Between 2004 and 2009, the KPK successfully convicted 86 high-ranking Indonesian officials. But this record of success begs the question of what political conditions give rise to such institutions in the first place, since most other countries ACAs were deliberately crippled in their powers and could provide only the appearance of effective enforcement. The answer is that it was the product of the immediate aftermath of the ouster of President Suharto and the democratic transition that occurred in Indonesia after 1999. There was a broad societal consensus on the need to completely renovate the country's institutions. As in the case of the Georgian police reform after the Rose Revolution in 2004, Indonesian civil society was highly mobilized to support anti-corruption efforts, and ordinary citizens voted for politicians like Susilo Bambang Yudhoyono who was elected president in 2004 on an anti-corruption platform.

The political support provided by Indonesian civil society proved critical to the KPK's later survival. In September 2009 two KPK commissioners were charged with corruption and the chairman arrested on murder charges. These charges were politically motivated efforts on the part of the police to discredit the KPK, and provoked a furious reaction by Indonesian civil society which came out in large numbers to demonstrate in favor of the agency. The police had to back down in the face of a presidential commission that revealed, among other things, the existence of a police conspiracy.

Conflict with the police continued in 2015 when a new president, Joko "Jokowi" Widodo, appointed Gen. Budi Gunawan as National Police chief as a result of pressure from his party, the Indonesian Democratice Party of Struggle, or PDI-P. Gunawan was charged by the KPK with corruption, provoking the police to charge three KPK commissioners in what was widely perceived as a retaliatory move. This once again provoked a large outcry from Indonesian civil society which interpreted the police moves as an effort to undermine "their" commission. Jokowi was eventually forced to back down and KPK's independence was for the moment protected.

The case of the KPK demonstrates the completely political nature of ACA powers. The body would not have been established in 2009 with extensive powers absent the political momentum stemming from Indonesia's democratic transition. Those same statutes were not sufficient to protect it from the efforts of the police and other corrupt bodies to undermine it in 2008 and 2015, but for the rapid mobilization of Indonesian civil society and the media on its behalf. Conversely, the weakness of ACAs in other countries like the Philippines or Sierra Leone stem from the absence of a supportive coalition of political actors demanding accountability from corrupt officials. These struggles may be played out through legal institutions, but they are fundamentally political ones over power and privilege.

Conclusions

The American experience is suggestive of how progress in the fight against corruption may be waged in contemporary societies suffering from it like Brazil or India. Reform is always a political matter that will require formation of a broad coalition of groups opposed to an existing system of corrupt politicians. Grassroots activism in favor of reform may emerge spontaneously, but such sentiments will not be translated into real change until it receives good leadership and organization. Reform also has a socio-economic basis: economic growth often produces new classes and groups that want a different, more modern political system. The growth of the middle class and a modern business sector were critical to the American transformation during the Progressive Era.

The term "political will" is often used to describe the ingredient necessary to bring about serious reform. This term is very misleading insofar as it suggests an analogy to individual will, a psychological characteristic. In fact, political will is nothing other than a metaphor for the creation of a coalition of political actors sufficient to overcome entrenched incumbents and bring about policy change. What politicians from time immemorial have done is to generate political power by forming coalitions through negotiation, persuasion, rhetoric, and occasionally bribery and intimidation. Overcoming systemic corruption, whether during the Progressive Era in the United States or in contemporary Indonesia, means creating a sufficiently large coalition to defend modern institutions like the US Civil Service Commission or the KPK against attempts to repatrimonialize it.

The American experience points to another feature of anti-corruption efforts as well. The control of corruption was very much bound up with efforts to increase state capacity. The period that saw the emergence of an industrial economy was also characterized by huge increases in levels of education, and particularly higher education that produced an entirely new class of professionals who worked for both private businesses and the government. One of the first US government agencies to be modernized in the late nineteenth century was the US Department of Agriculture, which benefited from an entire generation of professional agronomists that had been trained in the numerous land-grant universities that had sprung up around the United States. The latter in turn were the product of the Morrill Act, a far-seeing piece of legislation passed at the beginning of the Civil War that sought to provide higher education to among other things increase agricultural productivity. Gifford Pinchot, head of the US Forest Service, personally founded the Yale School of Forestry at his alma mater. It would not have been possible to reform the old patronage-based bureaucracy without access to the human capital represented by this entire generation of university-educated officials. Every important reform effort undertaken to create modern state bureaucracies—in Germany, Britain, France, Japan, and elsewhere—was accompanied by parallel efforts to modernize the higher education system in ways that would benefit public administration. Today, development finance institutions focus on helping to provide universal primary and secondary education to poor countries, and have largely given up on supporting elite education. The reasons for this are understandable, but do not correspond to the historical experience of state modernization in countries that became rich in earlier eras.

State capacity was also critical to the success of Indonesia's KPK. Erry Hardjapemekas, one of the founding commissioners, was a former corporate CEO who recognized the importance of having a highly professional and moral staff. He invested considerable effort in building the KPK's investigative capacity, and in ensuring that it had sufficient resources to remunerate its staff adequately. Its professional credibility was critical to the legitimacy it was eventually awarded by Indonesian civil society.

These general observations about historical efforts to build modern, uncorrupt administrations suggest that the process will be a very long and extended one, characterized by prolonged political struggle. Fortunately, having a modern bureaucracy is not a sine qua non of economic development—no existing rich country had a squeaky-clean government in its early stages of economic growth—not Britain or the United States in the nineteenth century, nor China today. Corruption and weak governance are obstacles to economic growth, but economic growth can happen also in poorly governed societies, and will produce, over time, social conditions and resources that will make government reform more feasible. This is perhaps a pessimistic conclusion, given the fact that rentier states and kleptocratic governments are the source of international conflict and instability in today's world. But it is also a realistic assessment coming out of the historical record.

Comments by Luis F. Lopez-Calva

Francis Fukuyama's "Corruption as a Political Phenomenon" underscores the importance of thinking about "eradicating corruption" more broadly in terms of the transition of a society from a deals-based to a rules-based equilibrium. This is consistent with recent views in literature, such as in Mungiu-Pippidi (2015). It is critical for the development community to move away from a perspective that views corruption as a virus that "invades" the system and which can be eradicated through technical interventions. Rather, as Fukuyama eloquently explains, we need to recognize that since the beginning of human history corruption has existed as means to sustain social order—and thus the notion of corruption as such is a "modern phenomenon."

Moving from a Deals-Based to a Rules-Based Equilibrium

Moving to a rules-based equilibrium has advantages in terms of growth, legitimacy, and equity. To date, the effects of corruption have mainly been analyzed by economists in terms of growth, such as in the classic Mauro (1995) paper on "Corruption and Growth." However, Fukuyama's analysis introduces other important elements which matter for development progress, such as the role corruption plays in undermining political legitimacy which can make the equilibrium very persistent. While the paper briefly acknowledges the impact of corruption on equity, I want to call further attention to this area. By definition, a deals-based equilibrium makes those who have less control over resources more vulnerable and the system less responsive to their interests. As the bargaining power of those at the bottom is weakened, this can lead to growing perceptions of unfairness in the system and result in a more fragmented social contract. As Fukuyama notes, corruption "acts like a regressive tax that supports the lifestyles of elites at the expense of everyone else." Frustrations reflecting this type of breakdown in social cooperation have erupted in events such as 2013 protests in Brazil and the 2011 uprisings in the Arab world.

The incidence of both types of corruption described by the paper, namely rent-seeking and patronage-clientelism, characterize all types of political systems—ranging from patrimonial (though as he argues, no system is really openly patrimonial today), to neo-patrimonial (think of Mexico's education system where public bureaucratic positions as teachers could be inherited, until the reform introduced in 2013), to modern-impersonal states. Thus, in order to make progress in improving control of corruption, we need to move our focus beyond the form of institutions: interventions such as redesigning civil service systems, introducing transparency initiatives, or instating ACAs. More fundamentally, we need a better understanding of the conditions under which societies can transit to an equilibrium in which the rules are credibly and impersonally applied.

The Rule of Law and State Capacity

I want to emphasize two important elements of the transition to a rules-based equilibrium which the paper discusses and which are explored in the 2017 World Development Report (WDR) on *Governance and the Law*—namely the rule of law and state capacity.

As Fukuyama pointed out in his 2010 article on "Transitions to the Rule of Law" in the *Journal of Democracy*, there is a vast literature on transitions to democracy (i.e., to electoral democracy) and much less on transitions to rule of law. This is surprising, as it is in fact the latter which is the defining characteristic of impersonal states, and a doorstep condition for states to transition to "open access orders"—in the language of North et al. (2009). One way to think about the transition to the rule of law is to understand better the different "roles of law" and what makes law effective. The WDR 2017 identifies three key roles that law plays. First, law is an instrument to order power; for example by imposing limits on the exercise of power and by delegating authority and responsibilities. Second, law is an instrument to order contestation by challenging decisions and authority. In this role, law becomes a key mechanism for adaptation to new circumstances. Third, law is an instrument to order behavior by serving as a "focal point" to coordinate people's beliefs and credibly induce compliance (McAdams 2015; Basu 2015). Understanding how to strengthen the effectiveness of these different roles of law could help us think about how to move toward a stronger rule of law.

A key element in this transition is the underlying role of state capacity—as low levels of state capacity can undermine the commitment to make the different roles of law effective. For example, Fukuyama explains how investing in state capacity was a critical factor behind the success of Indonesia's Corruption Eradication Commission. However, and this is part of the persistence of certain equilibria, the WDR 2017 argues that capacity is overtime a function of power. Where to invest in building a stock of capacity –and where to use that capacity—is a decision made by those actors in society with higher bargaining power. The example provided by Fukuyama in his work, about the US in the nineteenth century is an excellent illustration of how broad coalitions of actors can re-balance the distribution of power and effectively change the incentives of politicians.

Another compelling example took place very recently. In May 2016, the Inter-American Commission of Human Rights (CIDH) announced that it will be unable to continue fulfilling its mandate to monitor human rights violations in the region due to a lack of resources. The Commission did not even have sufficient resources to cover 40% of its payroll. Interestingly enough, the same countries that are supposed to contribute to finance the CIDH have contributed very generously in past years to finance the International Court of Justice at The Hague –which is far less likely to get involved in the type of human rights cases present in Latin America. Indeed, where to invest in capacity is a decision mediated by the interests of those in power. From this perspective, the emphasis of the development community on drawing lessons from how "pockets of effectiveness" or "islands of excellence" emerged in one country to build capacity somewhere else is actually questionable. The more common thread that holds true across contexts, is that elites choose to invest in capacity in certain areas, and not others, in an effort to gain legitimacy and reinforce their power. Thus, in order to promote change we need to understand under which conditions elites may actually make decisions which limit their own power.

Change Takes Time: Inclusive Growth, Collective Action, and the Demand for Better Governance

These dynamics, as Fukuyama explains, are the reason why change is very difficult and slow. While shocks can become opportunities for more rapid progress, as they change the incentives and reduce the veto power of certain actors, more incremental changes play a very important role in long-term dynamics. Fukuyama's points about collective action and economic growth –particularly if it is inclusive—as forces that can lead to change in the equilibrium, are very important. Recent public reactions about corruption cases in Chile, Brazil, and other countries in Latin America show a potential change in the public tolerance toward corruption. Politically and economically powerful people have been brought to court. Collective action initiatives, also in Chile and Brazil, and I would mention Mexico's citizen initiative 3de3, are also positive signs, which could bring a less pessimistic perspective to the prospects for breaking out of a persistent cycle.

The apparent change in people's tolerance toward a deals-based system and growing demand for a more impersonal application of the rules in Latin America coincides with a period of sustained growth, economic mobility, and an unprecedented change in the educational profile of the population. As Fukuyama explains in the case of the reform of the American system, as the economy develops new actors such as business leaders and the middle class become key constituencies in the demand for better enforcement of the rules and better quality of services and public good provision. In particular, a growing middle class can play a critical role in the demand for better governance. As households move out of poverty and begin contributing more to taxes, they may also begin to shift their expectations of what the government should provide in return; in particular related to the provision of education and health services and access to economic opportunities. As Fig. 3.1 illustrates, evidence

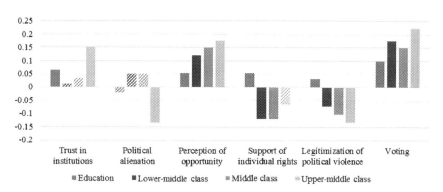

Fig. 3.1 Class associations with political values in selected Latin American Countries. Source: Adapted from Lopez-Calva and others (2012). Note: Striped columns are statistically insignificant at the 10% level. Effects are all expressed in terms of the values' standard deviation. Education is multiplied by its standard deviation. Class dummies refer to the difference from the poor (0–4$ a day). Lower-middle class: 4–10$ a day; Middle class: 10–20$ a day; Upper-middle class: 20–50$ a day. Countries analyzed include Brazil, Chile, Colombia, Mexico, and Peru

from perception surveys in Latin America corroborates the notion that income levels are associated with different political values such as trust in institutions, perception of opportunities, and the likelihood of voting (Lopez-Calva et al. 2012).

This is one way to think about how equitable growth may feed back into demand for better governance. As countries develop, the incentives and relative bargaining power of actors change, generating new demands for the redistribution of power and resources—as Hirschman proposed long time ago. Whether governance systems can effectively respond and adapt to these demands will determine how countries progress. In some cases, a lack of capacity to adapt may result in certain groups in society choosing to "exit," and manifest in challenges such as violent dispute resolution, high informality, or low tax-compliance. In other cases, it can be seen as an opportunity to strengthen the social contract, enhance state legitimacy, and induce broader voluntary compliance with the law. But again, as Fukuyama says, it will be difficult to judge in the short run.

Notes

1. Johnston (2005: p. 11).
2. An important exception to this was the republican tradition which started in Greece and Rome, and was carried by numerous city states in Italy, the Netherlands, and elsewhere. The very term "republic" comes from the Latin *res publica*, or "public thing," denoting that the political order was representative of a larger public good.
3. See Fukuyama (2011).
4. See Fukuyama (2015).
5. Khan and Sundaram Jomo (2000).
6. Eisenstadt and Roniger (1984).
7. Thus Scott (1972) describes a patronage system in pre-democratic Thailand and a clientelistic system in Ghana and India.
8. See the definition given in Piattoni (2001).
9. A classic case was the French foreign minister Tallyrand, who was a highly corrupt individual who was nonetheless a very talented diplomat who helped negotiate the settlement at the Congress of Vienna.
10. See for example: Kolstad and Wiig (2009), Mauro (2004).
11. For more detail on the history of this period, see Chaps. 9–11 in Fukuyama (2014).
12. Recanantini (2011).
13. See for example: Alan Doig et al. (2007), Heilbrunn (2004).

References

Basu, Kaushik. 2015. *The Republic of Beliefs: A New Approach to 'Law and Economics'*. Policy Research Working Paper 7259. Washington, DC: World Bank.

Doig, Alan, David Watt, and Robert Williams. 2007. Why Do Developing Country Anti-corruption Commissions Fail to Deal with Corruption? Understanding the Three Dilemmas of Organisational Development, Performance Expectation, and Donor and Government Cycles. *Public Administration and Development* 27 (3): 251–259.

Eisenstadt, Shmuel Noah, and Luis Roniger. 1984. *Patrons, Clients and Friends: Interpersonal Relations and the Structure of Trust in Society*. Cambridge, UK: Cambridge University Press.

Fukuyama, Francis. 2011. *The Origins of Political Order: From Prehuman Times to the French Revolution*. London: Macmillan.

———. 2015. Why is Democracy Performing So Poorly? *Journal of Democracy* 26: 11–20.

———. 2014. *Political Order and Political Decay: From the Industrial Revolution to the Globalization of Democracy*. London: Macmillan.

Heilbrunn, John R. 2004. *Anti-corruption Commissions: Panacea or Real Medicine to Fight Corruption*. Washington, DC: World Bank Institute. The Many Faces of Corruption.

Johnston, Michael. 2005. *Syndromes of Corruption: Wealth, Power, and Democracy*. Cambridge, UK: Cambridge University Press.

Khan, Mushtaq H., and Kwame Sundaram Jomo. 2000. *Rents, Rent-Seeking and Economic Development: Theory and Evidence in Asia*. Cambridge, UK: Cambridge University Press.

Kolstad, Ivar, and Arne Wiig. 2009. Is Transparency the Key to Reducing Corruption in Resource-Rich Countries? *World Development* 37 (3): 521–532.

López-Calva, Luis-Felipe, Jamele Rigolini, and Florencia Torche. 2012. Is There Such Thing as Middle Class Values? Class Differences, Values and Political Orientations in Latin America. Discussion Papers 6292. Institute for the Study of Labor (IZA), Bonn.

Mauro, Paulo. 1995. Corruption and Growth. *The Quarterly Journal of Economics* 110: 681–712.

Mauro, Paolo. 2004. The Persistence of Corruption and Slow Economic Growth. *IMF Staff Papers* 51: 1–18.

McAdams, R. 2015. *The Expressive Powers of Law: Theories and Limits*. Cambridge, MA: Harvard University Press.

Mungiu-Pippidi, A. 2015. *The Quest for Good Governance: How Societies Develop Control of Corruption*. Cambridge, UK: Cambridge University Press.

North, Douglass C., John J. Wallis, and Barry R. Weingast. 2009. *Violence and Social Orders: A Conceptual Framework for Interpreting Recorded Human History*. New York: Cambridge University Press.

Piattoni, Simona. 2001. *Clientelism, Interests, and Democratic Representation: The European Experience in Historical and Comparative Perspective*. Cambridge, UK: Cambridge University Press.

Recanantini, Francesca. 2011. *Effectiveness of Anti-Corruption Authorities (ACAs): Selected Emerging Lessons*. Washington, DC: World Bank.

Scott, James C. 1972. Patron-Client Politics and Political Change in Southeast Asia. *American Political Science Review* 66 (1): 91–113.

World Bank. 2017. *World Development Report 2017: Governance and the Law*. Washington, DC: World Bank. Forthcoming.

4

Corruption, Organized Crime, and Money Laundering

Susan Rose-Ackerman and Bonnie J. Palifka

Introduction

The relationship between private wealth and public power frames the discussion of corruption and embraces not only explicit quid pro quo deals but also lobbying, campaign donations, and other forms of pressure exerted by both private individuals and businesses. Some use the term "corruption" to cover all the ways that concentrated wealth influences political choice (Johnston 2005; Lessig 2011). We are sympathetic to such concerns but are not convinced that extending the corruption label to all these issues is the most productive route to understanding and reform.

S. Rose-Ackerman (✉)
Yale Law School, New Haven, CT, USA
e-mail: susan.rose-ackerman@yale.edu

B.J. Palifka
ITESM, Campus Monterrey, Monterrey, Mexico
e-mail: bonnie@itesm.mx

© The Author(s) 2018
K. Basu, T. Cordella (eds.), *Institutions, Governance and the Control of Corruption*, International Economic Association Series,
https://doi.org/10.1007/978-3-319-65684-7_4

Our own work has concentrated on quid pro quo trades that violate legal or institutional rules and where the benefits from making a payoff are concrete and specific (Rose-Ackerman 1978, 1999; Rose-Ackerman and Palifka 2016). Once one understands such situations, the debate can move to gray areas that are not per se corrupt in that sense but that can slide into outright illegality and that, in any case, can undermine public institutions. Of course, different legal systems and cultural norms draw the lines between acceptable and unacceptable influence in different ways. However, even payoffs that are entrenched and routine may be deeply destructive of human development and political legitimacy.

Corruption highlights underlying problems at the state/society inter-face. Decisions that officials should make on the grounds of efficiency, equity, or citizen accountability are instead influenced by benefits pro-vided directly to public officials and their kin, or perhaps to their political parties and allies. Targeted quid pro quos substitute for actions that are officially required of those accepting or extorting the payoff. Even if the recipient of the payoff follows the rules on allocating public benefits and costs, the payoff itself ought to be categorized as corrupt. Of course, in some cases paying for a government benefit may be the best way of allocating a scarce public service, but then the payments should be legal and public, and the funds should go into the government treasury.

Some forms of corruption are well studied, and reasonable reform proposals can constrain the underlying incentives for corruption. These include low-level payoffs by households and small businesses to obtain scarce government benefits, to qualify for benefits or licenses, and to lower the costs of taxes and fines. Reforms focus on eliminating rules that serve little purpose beyond generating payoffs, permitting the legal sale of scarce benefits, streamlining programs to reduce official discretion (perhaps through e-government), plus a range of monitoring and transparency initiatives open to the victims of corruption. Anti-corruption measures must balance limits on official discretion to deter bribes and kick-backs against legitimate demands for individualized treatment. Similarly, "grand" corruption in procurement, privatization, and the allocation of concessions arises because deals are complex and opaque and involve those at the top of the state. They cannot be controlled without the help of those in positions of domestic power or possessing external leverage. One response is to streamline procedures and to benchmark behavior against outside measures. Programs that make government more transparent and accountable can help in both cases, but there are few strong tests of the best ways to structure such reforms. Of course, the criminal law of bribery stands in the background, but it is not sufficient taken by itself. The structural changes and oversight initiatives that we stress in our recent book remain, in our view, the keys to successful reform (Rose-Ackerman and Palifka 2016).

But sometimes corruption permeates whole institutions or even entire states so that partial reforms are ineffective. The most vexing problem for those seeking systemic reform is deciding where to begin. Insiders point to a "culture of corruption," often despairing of the possibility of change. Vicious cycles are common where widespread corruption feeds on itself to produce a downward spiral. But cultural norms do change for both better and worse, and the task for reformers is to figure out what policies might succeed and which could provoke a backlash that exacerbates the situation. In some cases a self-reinforcing spiral of corruption occurs when organized crime has deeply infiltrated state institutions, such as the police, the judiciary, and law enforcement. In such cases, especially if political leaders are extracting large-scale private benefits, the global financial system may facilitate grand corruption by easing the cross-border flow of funds and by supporting financial havens, both on small islands and in global money centers. To highlight these links, this chapter concentrates on the interface between corruption, organized crime, and money laundering.

Organized Crime[1]

Corruption and organized crime often go together. Organized crime dominates illegal businesses, but it may also infiltrate legal businesses to gain monopoly profits and launder illicit profits. Research finds that organized crime can have important economic effects: limiting foreign investment, reducing economic activity, squeezing profits, and increasing the cost and availability of credit.[2] Large-scale illegal businesses or mafia infiltration of legal activities are both likely to have a corrupting influence on government, including law enforcement and border control, and to distort the use of public funds (Di Gennaro and La Spina 2016). Corrupt rulers and illegal businessmen feed on each other. Bribes reduce the cost of illegal business ventures and help them raise capital, fueling their growth and generating more corrupt arrangements. If a strong symbiotic relationship exists, anti-corruption policy needs to target organized crime. Otherwise it will ignore a key root of the problem.

Unfortunately, when organized crime permeates economics and politics, those in political power may be unwilling to undertake true anti-corruption reform. In such states, anti-corruption agencies have little power and insufficient resources. Laws may be strong on the books but in practice be rarely enforced, or enforced only against the powerless, while the powerful enjoy impunity.[3] Anti-corruption campaigns tend to target opposition politicians, and anti-organized crime efforts focus only on certain groups, while protecting others. Political parties may forge alliances with specific organized crime groups (OCGs).

An OCG "has some permanence, commits serious crimes for profit, uses violence, corrupts officials, launders criminal proceeds and reinvests in the licit economy" (Buscaglia and van Dijk 2003: 5). The credible threat of violence is a mafia tool, but violence is a costly strategy so actual violence may be low when mafias are firmly in control. They may have so intimidated the public, local businesses, and law enforcement, that they do not need to commit violent crimes. Thus, in critiquing data on Italian mafias, Di Gennaro and La Spina (2016: 6) claim that " … in a given area we could find none or very few complaints not because mafia-type associations were absent, but on the contrary because they are very powerful and much feared."

The European Police Office (Europol 2013: 6) has identified approximately 3600 OCGs operating in the European Union, many connected via the drug trade and human smuggling to other regions. Due to globalization and the internet, many groups are international in membership, crimes, products, markets, and routes (Center for the Study of Democracy 2010; Europol 2013). Historical, societal, and cultural factors influenced the emergence and persistence of organized crime (McIllwain 1999; Varese 2015). Its prevalence is often traceable to a time when some groups were underrepresented or disenfranchised, such as during foreign occupation, civil war, or mass immigration. In these circumstances, political groups employed criminals to advance their agenda, and OCGs used the political system to advance theirs or infiltrated or replaced weak state institutions (Center for the Study of Democracy 2010; Beare 1997; Feldab-Brown 2011; Gambetta 1993; Schneider and Schneider 2005).

Buscaglia and van Dijk (2003) found that high levels of organized crime were associated with a weak state, high tax evasion, an ineffective customs service, protectionism, high financial risk ratings, lack of democracy, a poorly functioning judicial system, politicization of the civil service, and state capture. Where organized crime is stronger, there tend to be more police and prosecutors, yet fewer arrests for drugs and lower conviction rates overall. Ineffective law enforcement encourages organized crime, as ordinary people distrust formal institutions, turning, instead, to "illegal organizations, such as mafia-type groups, to deal with minor crimes" (ibid.: 10). Likewise, when the banking system fails to serve the needs of citizens, they turn to underground options for loans. A weak state is ill-prepared to resist infiltration by organized crime, but organized crime can also undermine the effectiveness of the state. In such situations corruption is likely to be endemic even if organized crime has not infiltrated legal and illegal markets. As OCGs mature and become intertwined with civil society and the state, they may engage in state capture, manipulating the law to favor their business (Johnston 2014). This includes customs duties, (de)regulation of mafia-dominated sectors, and laws regarding the illegality of certain activities or statutes of limitations (Beare 1997). In the extreme, the result is a mafia-dominated state (Rose-Ackerman and Palifka 2016: 287–288).

In Italy whenever an investigation into either corruption or organized crime is undertaken, it leads to the other (Center for the Study of Democracy 2010: 18). In Mexico drug cartels use *plata o plomo* (bribe or bullet) techniques to corrupt the police, judges, politicians, prison guards, and bureaucrats in many parts of the country. In an effort to override corrupt local officials, the military and federal police have been moved from one hotspot to another. This policy, which effectively reduced the impact of the mafia in the United States during the twentieth century, has proven less effective in Mexico (Feldab-Brown 2011). When law enforcement targets one area, the cartels move their operations elsewhere in what is known locally as the "cockroach effect" (Wainwright 2016). The result has been the spillover of cartel violence into large parts of Mexico and Central America (Organization of American States 2013a).

Although organized criminal groups operate on the margin of formal markets and outside legal norms, they behave very much like business firms, often operating like franchises loosely linked to a central organization. They produce where costs are lowest and sell where the return is highest. Instead of paying taxes, they make direct payments to government representatives in the form of bribes.[4] OCGs face competition, but their methods are often based on threats of violence, rather than on advertising and creative marketing (Reuter 1987). Because they operate in fast-changing business environments, they must be entrepreneurial, adapting to develop new and better products and delivery methods. For example, in response to the 2008–2011 economic crisis, organized crime in Europe shifted toward increased trafficking in counterfeit and substandard consumer goods (Europol 2013: 11). As marijuana moves toward widespread legalization in the United States, one can expect that Latin American OCGs will shift to other drugs and products.

Di Gennaro (2016: 28–29) argues that Italian OCGs have adapted their organizational structures both to their location and to changing demands. Thus, the traditional Cosa Nostra groups in Sicily are organized hierarchically, so that those in the lower ranks often cannot identify their superiors. Others, such as the Camorra in Campania in and around Naples, have had a more decentralized structure (Center for the Study of Democracy 2010; Di Gennaro 2016; Thoumi 2003: 80). The difference reflected their business model—the drug trade in Sicily, and extortion and usury in Campania. However, as OCGs in Campania moved into smuggling cigarettes and other goods and then into drug trafficking, they too have become more formally organized (Di Gennaro 2016: 28–29).

If OCGs have infiltrated, corrupted, and undermined the state, this opens up profit-making opportunities that build on the state's inability to enforce the law. One very lucrative activity is extortion. Legal businesses that benefit from prime urban locations are especially at risk in countries with weak or corrupted police forces. This includes restaurants and shops serving tourists and business travelers. Manufacturers can hide in remote locations (Webster and Charap 1993), but service businesses cannot "go underground."[5] If the police are bought off or unreliable, criminal groups may demand protection money where the funds are, in part, protecting the business from attacks by the group itself (De Melo et al. 1995; Webster 1993; Webster and Charap 1993).[6] In Northern Mexico, due to violence-backed demands for payment (called *piso*, literally "floor" but implying the right to occupy the space), many businesses closed and many entrepreneurs moved to the United States or less affected parts of Mexico, rather than pay or risk kidnapping or execution.[7] In Italy mafias collect a *pizzo* from businesses in some parts of the country, with as many as 70% to 80% of firms paying this "tax" in some parts of Sicily (Di Gennaro and La Spina 2016: 3). In contrast to such periodic payments levied on established businesses, the construction industry is especially vulnerable to one-off extortion that buys the developer freedom from on-going harassment once it starts a project (ibid.: 7, Di Gennaro 2016: 34).[8]

A second option is to engage in legitimate business backed by the threat of violence to discourage competition and by payoffs to public officials to look the other way. Even in developed countries some legitimate businesses are especially vulnerable to criminal infiltration. Diego Gambetta and Peter Reuter provide a list of the factors supporting the emergence of mafia-controlled cartels (Gambetta and Reuter 1995: 128). In the most favorable cases for OCGs, product differentiation and barriers to entry are low; technology is unsophisticated and labor, unskilled; demand is inelastic, and the industry consists of a large number of small firms. In other words, cartelization would not be possible without the threat of violence as a backup. Private garbage collection provides a good example. Entry is straightforward and inexpensive—one need only purchase a truck. However, because garbage trucks operate alone on the public streets, it is relatively easy to intimidate unwanted rivals by attacking their trucks without attracting police attention. To minimize their risks, the mafia pays the police to look the other way (Reuter 1987).

Third, OCGs may take over the sale of legal but pirated goods—for example, unauthorized copies of music, movies, and other products. OCGs maintain these businesses and limit competition by bribing public officials, such as the police and other inspectors. They can then reinvest the profits, earned without paying taxes, in legitimate business and in obtaining public contracts via payoffs (Gambetta 1993; Varese 1994).

Fourth, OCGs can become government contractors, using their criminal muscle to win tenders. Businesses, such as road repair and building construction, which do a heavy business with the state, are prime candidates for organized crime influence. If organized criminals have corrupted public officials to protect their illegal businesses, it may be a relatively short step to make payoffs to obtain public contracts. For example, drug cartels in Mexico have used both extortion and campaign funding to obtain government contracts on very profitable terms.[9] In the extreme, OCGs manage cartels that share contracts and pay off public officials to buy their complicity or at least their silence. In Southern Italy, for example, a 1990s survey of small- and medium-sized businesses found that over half reported that they had withdrawn from a public tender after pressure from criminal groups or their political allies.[10]

Finally, disasters, civil war, and regime transformation create opportunities for organized crime. A natural disaster, such as a major earthquake, risks OCG infiltration of the relief effort because urgency and institutional breakdown undermine the usual checks. This apparently occurred in Naples in the 1980s after a major earthquake (Di Gennaro 2016: 28). The post-conflict situation in Iraq and Afghanistan is riddled with both corruption and organized crime.[11]

Even peaceful regime transformations are periods of high risk. Thus, when the Soviet Union collapsed, the benefits to both legitimate investors and OCGs were extremely high as the entire wealth of the state was up for grabs. In some cases, organized crime managed to create an atmosphere of uncertainty and the threat of violence that drove competitors away, leaving the criminal groups with a free field (Shelley 1994). The weakness of state institutions created an environment ripe for the development of organized crime and allowed them to use corruption to infiltrate government and business. In Georgia, for example, in spite of success in limiting corruption in some parts of the bureaucracy, organized crime took advantage of a voucher program—designed to enable citizens to participate in the privatization process—to obtain privatized assets

(Kukhianidze 2009). As the Center for the Study of Democracy (2010: 40) concludes, "[i]n its most advanced form, organized crime is so thoroughly integrated into the economic, political, and social institutions of legitimate society that it may no longer be recognizable as a criminal enterprise."[12] According to Europol (2013: 15) "Social tolerance towards certain crimes reduces risks for OCGs and increases public demand for illicit commodities." In coca-, poppy-, or marijuana-producing countries, the criminalization of traditional activities calls into doubt the legitimacy of the state and further marginalizes indigenous groups (OAS 2013a: 25). If the production of traditional crops is criminalized and prosecuted while more powerful criminals or corrupt economic and political actors operate with impunity, the populace loses faith in the government as an advocate for the people (Organization of American States 2013a: 82).

Organized crime also corrupts private businesses into facilitating their illicit production or smuggling operations. For example, OCGs might collude with employees of cigarette, clothing, or medicine manufacturers to produce after-hours; pay truck drivers to smuggle illicit goods or people; and tip the employees of restaurants, night clubs, bars, and retail stores to allow the sale of counterfeit or contraband cigarettes, alcohol, and drugs (Center for the Study of Democracy 2010: 113–116).[13] Alternatively, OCGs may take advantage of other widely accepted illegal activities. For example, in Colombia, drug trafficking organizations used existing contraband networks to launder their drug proceeds (Thoumi 2003: 85). As private businesses cross the line into illegitimate activity, and the public welcomes access to these goods (low-cost contraband or new psychotropic substances, for example), the law becomes less relevant.

In short, vicious cycles are pervasive. Corruption enables organized crime, but organized crime also feeds corruption. OCGs often actively try to corrupt customs officials, immigration authorities, law enforcement, the judiciary, procurement officials, and those with access to sensitive information. The OCGs seek not only immunity from prosecution for themselves but also assurance of monopoly power in the illegal market. Banks with restrictive lending policies may push small businesses into the hands of mafia-controlled money lenders who use threats of violence to collect debts and finance underworld activities (Di Gennaro and La Spina 2016: 3). In many parts of Italy, OCGs control local politics and, by extension, police forces (Center for the Study of Democracy 2010: 90). Mexican cartels reportedly have more public officials on the payroll than rank-and-file traffickers or foot soldiers: information from confiscated ledgers indicates that a single *plaza* (controlled area) in Mexico may have 1–600 "employees" but 109–1000 officials on the payroll (Organization of American States 2013b: 24–25). Thus, OCGs corrupt low-level bureaucrats, law enforcement, and politicians alike, as they extend their reach and debilitate institutions (Organization of American States 2013a).

As some parts of government become corrupt, transparency becomes increasingly difficult, thus enabling more corruption in other sectors and feeding a vicious spiral (Organization of American States 2013a: 56). In the extreme, organized crime members may become "vote collectors, capable of winning electoral support, political support for party leaders or parties in exchange for contract management, [and] public services … " (Di Gennaro 2016: 28, referring to the Camorra in Italy). If organized crime has a strong foothold, many standard reform proposals will have only minor effects. Deeper changes are needed to shift from a vicious cycle to a virtuous cycle where the relative lack of corruption reduces the impunity of OCGs, leading to arrests and prosecutions that further reduce the reach of organized crime, and so forth.

Studies of Italy suggest one promising approach: citizen and business organizations that challenge mafia extortion by banding together to refuse payoff demands, called "*Addiopizzo*" (Di Gennaro and La Spina 2016: 12; Di Gennaro 2016: 35; Scaglione 2016: 62). Of course, that strategy does nothing to limit illegal businesses, such as drugs and human trafficking, and it could backfire in other contexts if the mafias are strong enough to take revenge on those who resist. However, collective action, under the right conditions and with support from law enforcement, can open a space for legitimate retail and wholesale businesses to become stronger and more competitive. This initiative is similar to anti-corruption measures involving private sector firms that sign integrity pacts promising to abstain from using corruption to obtain public contracts.

Money Laundering[14]

Both public officials' corrupt proceeds and the profits of organized crime eventually end up in the legitimate economy, either deposited in financial institutions or invested in real estate or business ventures. Much of it flows across national borders into assets and financial institutions located in money centers in wealthy countries or in so-called financial paradises. Legitimate financial institutions engage in money laundering, but OCGs can also be directly involved, as a way either to export their own profits or to facilitate others' illegal actions (Scaglione 2016: 62, 69). Hence, the international control of money laundering and of investment vehicles with opaque ownership would make corruption and criminal enterprise more expensive and troublesome even if domestic law enforcement is weak.

Money laundering is the process by which illicitly gained funds are made to look legitimate—facilitating illicit activity by hiding it. The magnitude of money laundering, like all secretive activity, is difficult to measure. Kar and Spanjers (2014) estimate that illicit financial outflows from developing countries totaled US $991.2 billion in 2012, over ten times the official development assistance received by these countries; over the period 2003–2012, nearly US $6.6 trillion left these countries illicitly. The flow of illicit funds increased by 9.4% per year in this period, faster than the growth of these economies. The United Nations Office on Drugs and Crime (UNODC) (2011) estimated that 2.7% of global GDP is "available" for laundering, including 1.5% of global GDP laundered in connection with drug trafficking and organized crime. Peter Reuter (2013) argues, however, that it is not only impossible to measure money laundering but also useless because money laundering itself has not been shown to cause significant damage on a macroeconomic scale. The real damage, according to Reuter, is perpetrated by the crimes that money laundering supports, such as drug trafficking. But tracking down, arresting, and prosecuting criminals successfully is difficult, so anti-money laundering (AML) efforts offer a trail and a means to apply justice that may be more cost-effective than seeking out the predicate offenses. The OAS (2013b: 32) argues, in contrast to Reuter, that money laundering itself causes economic damage, including price distortion, unfair competition, speculative bubbles and crises, and considerable movements in the value of currencies, leading to either "Dutch disease" (that is, currency appreciation in offshore financial centers) or rapid devaluation. Unfortunately, however, definitive evidence is lacking.

The traditional model of money laundering involves three steps: placement, layering, and integration. The entire process may absorb some 15% of the value of the funds laundered (Organization of American States 2013b: 27). In the placement phase, illicit funds are introduced into the financial system. Funds may be deposited (in cash) in a bank or invested in another financial institution, or transferred from one account to another. AML efforts have identified certain red flags and persuaded some countries to place a limit on the size of transfers permitted without providing identification or filling out additional paperwork. To escape scrutiny, the launderer may make many small deposits and employ a third party, rather than make large deposits directly. During layering, the funds move between multiple—often offshore—accounts, sometimes using shell companies or fake NGOs to create the illusion of payment for services. This helps to obscure the source of illicit funds. With integration, the funds flow to the final beneficiary in a form that seems perfectly legitimate. Even if the financial industry has not broken any laws, it facilitates the underlying crime, be it the illegal drug trade or bribery, by allowing individuals to establish firms or open accounts without identification of the owners (Platt 2015).[15]

Offshore banks are responsible for large volumes of laundered money. So-called financial havens are countries that do not tax interest on deposits, have low or nil corporate taxes, and have minimal controls on financial flows. In many cases, the owners of the accounts or companies registered in these districts need not even identify themselves. The Cayman Islands, the British Virgin Islands, and the Bahamas are well-known examples. Dubai is also an important money laundering and tax fraud center (Europol 2013: 13).[16] Even within the United States, certain states, such as Delaware and Nevada, offer corporate registration and tax options that are attractive to both legitimate businesses and criminal elements (Platt 2015: 58).[17] One common practice is to establish a shell company in a favorable district; to make payments to the shell company for "services rendered," and to instruct the shell company to make payments to politically exposed persons (PEPs) or others.[18] Incorporation creates the illusion of distance between the responsible parties and the money.

The large commercial banks of the United States and Europe are also involved in money laundering. Indeed, many critics in developing countries argue that the wealthy countries are responsible for both generating bribes and laundering the funds (Levi et al. 2007: 407). For example, ill-gotten funds deposited in a subsidiary in Mexico can be moved to an account in New York. Conversely, funds could be deposited in the United States, and then transferred to accounts in Mexico to pay for drugs delivered. In the wake of a major money laundering scandal involving London bank HSBC in Mexico (HBMX), it was alleged that HBMX was responsible for 60–70% of laundered funds in Mexico (Platt 2015: 16). Between 2005 and 2007, US bank Wachovia reportedly transferred US $14 billion in cash from Mexico to US branches on behalf of foreign exchange houses "and other foreign correspondent bulk cash customers"; HSBC's Mexican subsidiary laundered $881 million or more from Mexican and Colombian drug cartels (Platt 2015: 75–76).

Although organized crime profits are a major source of laundered funds, in many small developing countries corruption may be the most important source (Chaikin and Sharman 2009: 27). Some laundered funds are profits that were made possible by bribes paid to government officials. Both the bribes themselves and the illicit gains they generated may be laundered through money center banks with severe consequences for the states subject to these illicit outflows. Corruption, organized crime profits, and money laundering feed on each other and need to be attacked simultaneously. As Chaikin and Sharman (2009: 151) state, " . . . the proceeds of grand corruption end up in international financial centers, such as New York, London, Zurich, and Geneva." Under their own names or those of associates or shell companies, corrupt high-ranking officials or PEPs open accounts in these banks and receive deposits via wire transfer. Procurement officers, police chiefs, members of the legislature, and heads of state have the potential to receive large quantities of cash and other "gifts" in return for their influence. For instance, in the early 1990s, Citibank transferred $100 million in "questionable funds" for Raul Salinas, the brother of then-president of Mexico, using shell companies (van der Does de Willebois 2011: 37).[19] A former governor of the Mexican state of Quintana Roo pled guilty in a US court to charges of money laundering. He had apparently accepted bribes from the Juárez drug cartel and laundered them through Lehman Brothers (Platt 2015: 69). Teodoro Nguema Obiang Mangue ("Teodorin"), the son of Equatorial Guinea's president and a high-ranking member of the government, amassed a fortune in overseas real estate and other assets with the assistance of estate managers and lawyers, who helped him set up shell companies and bank accounts (van der Does de Willebois 2011: 28–29; Platt 2015: 84–95). It may not be necessary for the PEPs to launder the funds themselves. In a study of twenty-one (not necessarily representative) cases from around the world, Gordon (2011: 5, italics in original) finds that in the majority, "...the proceeds of corruption had already been laundered *before they were received by the PEP.*"

Organized crime often owns the institutions used to launder funds in the "layering" phase and supports informal international money transfer systems. Money launderers in the Middle East use *hawala* networks (informal money transfer systems) to make payments internationally (Varese 2015); heroin traffickers based in Afghanistan have used these to circumvent an international financial blockade (Platt 2015: 70). The system itself is neither illegal nor corrupt, but it can be a route for the transfer of illicit funds.

In the formal sector, casinos offer an especially attractive option for OCG ownership because cash transactions are large and common, hence accounts are easy to manipulate. Where gambling is illegal, OCGs work to change the laws and legalize gambling. In some cases, OCG members actually run for elected positions to change the laws from the inside. (Center for the Study of Democracy 2010; Johnson 2002). In order to guarantee returns from gambling on sports, OCGs corrupt professional and amateur athletes, as well as sports officials, persuading them to engage in match-fixing (Europol 2013); these funds may need to be laundered. Money laundering also leads to corruption in private businesses, as the launderers bribe employees to turn a blind eye to their unusual practices (Center for the Study of Democracy 2010: 17).

Domestic and International Efforts

International initiatives historically have focused on only one or two of the three phenomena—corruption, organized crime, and money laundering. National bodies (often created to comply with one international convention or another) still tend to concentrate on only one of the three. Yet combining efforts could lead to economies of scale, higher conviction rates, and more funds recovered that could further future law enforcement efforts. Countries and international organizations have begun to acknowledge these connections, but they should do more to encourage interagency cooperation by training the members of all agencies in anti-corruption, AML, and anti-organized crime laws and procedures. Judges and prosecutors should be aware of the links, and laws should reflect the connections—enabling prosecutors not only to convict the guilty but also to recover the corrupt or criminal funds to compensate victims or fund public programs.

Strengthened legislation is necessary, but not sufficient. If the judiciary is corrupt or otherwise ineffective, no amount of legislation or policing will reduce illicit activity. It is essential, therefore, to ensure professionalism and trustworthiness in the judiciary, prosecutors, and law enforcement, and to improve the transparency of judicial proceedings. A professional police force, trained in all three areas, will be better prepared to collect evidence that the prosecution can use. In short, many anti-corruption strategies will also serve to combat money laundering and organized crime. Likewise, knowledge of AML and anti-organized crime protocols will enable the law more effectively to detect, arrest, prosecute, and convict those guilty of corruption.

The United States pioneered AML and has pushed the AML agenda globally. Under US leadership, the Financial Action Task Force (FATF) was founded in 1989 and in 1990 published a list of "40 Recommendations" for dealing with drug-related money laundering. As terrorism gained priority in the early 2000s, nine additional recommendations were added. The "40+9 Recommendations" now cover money laundering linked to organized crime, terrorism, and corruption, and efforts to combat the illicit flow of funds are referred to as "AML/CFT" (anti-money laundering/counter financing of terrorism).[20] However, these guidelines are recommendations only; the enforcement mechanism is peer review among member countries. The UN Convention against Corruption (UNCAC),[21] signed in 2003, goes a step further, requiring signatories to criminalize a wide variety of corrupt acts and the laundering of corrupt funds, as well as to freeze and repatriate corruptly obtained assets. These two initiatives, and a set of regional initiatives that complement them, have led many countries to criminalize corruption and money laundering, but implementation has been uneven.

At present, at least eight international and regional initiatives or conventions seek to limit money laundering, sometimes under an anti-corruption umbrella.[22] Unfortunately, there is little solid evidence of the success or failure of these initiatives, in part due to the difficulty of measuring the amount of money laundered at any given time. In one cross-country study, Buscaglia and van Dijk (2003) found that organized crime (measured by an index that they created) was significantly higher in countries with low AML regimes versus strong AML regulation. However, they have not measured the marginal effects of recent efforts, and many legal changes have been made since their study was published.

Although it is difficult to demonstrate that AML policies have prevented the transfer of illicit funds, there have been notable—although insufficient—successes in repatriating corrupt funds ex post. Even the notoriously secretive Swiss have frozen questionable assets of deposed rulers and have transferred them to incumbents who claim that the funds belong to the state. General Sani Abacha reportedly stole approximately $4 billion from Nigeria; Switzerland froze some $660 million in Swiss bank accounts, and the Federal Supreme Court ruled in 2005 that $505.5 million of that total should be repatriated to Nigeria—the first such case of an African country receiving repatriated funds. Similarly, Switzerland and the US repatriated $100.7 million to Peru in relation to the corruption of Vladimir Montesinos, former top advisor to President Fujimori who was imprisoned for taking defense contract kickbacks (Levi et al. 2007: 400, 403). However, there is some reluctance to repatriate funds to countries with persistently high levels of corruption for fear that the funds would simply be embezzled by the new leaders. There are other limitations to AML, as well. For starters, the onus of detection is on financial institutions and others in the private sector, and AML legislation is not necessarily backed up with enforcement, leaving the firms to turn a blind eye in the interest of profit (Levi et al. 2007). Indeed, Financial Intelligence Units (FIUs) are rarely responsible for bringing money laundering cases to light. Banks may even find paying the non-compliance fines to be an optimal response, rather than playing an active AML role, so that the level of scrutiny applied is inversely related to the profitability of the client, rather than vice-versa. Even when banks apply due diligence, they will not necessarily discover the launderers. For example, the UN Oil-for-Food investigation of Saddam Hussein's Iraq concluded that "the banks had used acceptable levels of due diligence in vetting the oil contracts they financed and did not have access to information that would have shown that some of these contracts involved bribes." (Levi et al. 2007: 411). Indeed, Cuéllar (2003) finds that in the US, AML laws have not led to many more convictions, but have mainly produced higher penalties when the predicate crime is linked to money laundering. In other words, the AML laws in the United States have not been implemented as intended. Very few people are convicted for money laundering alone.

The existence of enabling jurisdictions makes AML efforts more difficult. It is not enough to keep most developed countries pure. At issue is both the ease with which corrupt officials in one country can hide their gains in another, and the possibility that money laundering activities can undermine the credibility of a country's financial structure (Scott 1995). To further complicate matters, the traditional model of money laundering, outlined above, does not apply to all techniques, rendering the "red flags" next to useless in those cases. Platt (2015: 79–83) describes a scheme in which clients who want to launder large quantities of cash are matched with others who would like to withdraw funds from their overseas stashes without drawing attention to themselves. The broker shifts the cash from the one to the other, all the while keeping the older funds in the same bank account and merely making a bookkeeping transaction to show that the funds have changed hands.

Even as the various governments and organizations seek to limit money laundering, new methods emerge. At present the development of electronic payment systems and virtual currencies like bitcoins provide another way for funds to move across borders without the involvement of conventional financial institutions that must comply with national and international rules.[23] Virtual currencies offer anonymity, which is invaluable when illicit transactions are involved. The FATF has only just begun to address the risks involved, issuing a report and guidelines in 2014, five years after bitcoins were launched in 2009 as the world's first convertible virtual currency.[24] US authorities have prosecuted several cases successfully, including Liberty Reserve, a virtual money transfer "bank" which operated out of Costa Rica; Silk Road, an online black market that used encrypting and virtual currencies to ensure anonymity; and Western Express, an identity theft clearinghouse that operated out of Manhattan.[25]

The control of money laundering and the fight against organized crime require international cooperation along several dimensions. First, many countries now share investigative capacity and results under Mutual Legal Assistance treaties. In 2006, for example, under a bilateral treaty, Switzerland shared financial information with the corresponding authorities in the US, enabling the prosecution of a US citizen who had acted as an intermediary in corrupt oil deals in Kazakhstan.[26] Second, in order to prosecute a foreign individual or a national who is in a foreign country, a government must request that the foreign government extradite the defendant. Many countries now have signed bilateral extradition agreements.

Another area for fruitful cooperation is sharing information. Cross-debarment could work for countries, as well as International Financial Institutions: when one government debars a firm, it would be debarred from working with any government. Coordinated investigation of cases that cross borders is essential, as are procedures to make other countries' authorities aware of firms and individuals who are under investigation for corruption. Foreign governments should also be able to obtain the list of PEPs that governments must provide to banks.

International cooperation and the laws that support it allow the United States and the European countries to fill an important lacuna when other governments are unable or unwilling to pursue the corrupt. Where corrupt politicians enjoy prosecutorial immunity, they can be prosecuted through money laundering charges. Where civil servants take or extort bribes from multinational firms, the S.E.C. or an equivalent body can lead the prosecution; if the civil servants launder their bribes using dollar-based instruments, the money laundering laws in the US also apply to them. Where local law enforcement is subject to "*plata o plomo*" demands, extradition to the United States is a more credible threat.

New international precedents have recently been set. In Guatemala, in the context of growing organized crime violence and human rights violations, the government called on the United Nations for help in 2002. After much debate and an early effort that the Supreme Court declared unconstitutional, the Guatemalan government and the UN signed a convention in 2006, which gave the UN a mandate to set up the International Commission against Impunity in Guatemala (*Comisión Internacional contra la Impunidad en Guatemala* or CICIG) in 2007. Funded entirely by donations, the CICIG operates under Guatemalan law, in cooperation with Guatemalan authorities, but by its nature it is entirely independent of the government in power and the local political parties. In addition to proposing new policies, the CICIG conducts investigations of especially sensitive cases and may act as, or in conjunction with, the prosecution. Its primary focus is organized crime and militant groups, but it mandate extends to links between such bodies and government officials.[27] The CICIG has been a party to over twenty cases, leading to the conviction of dozens of defendants on a variety of organized crime, corruption, and money laundering charges (CICIG 2013). In 2015, based on CICIG investigations, Guatemala's president, vice-president, house speaker, and at least thirty other officials were arrested on charges ranging from customs fraud to procurement kickbacks to petty extortion.[28] Although detractors call the CICIG a foreign imposition, according to a public survey, 97% of Guatemalans support the work of the CICIG and want its mandate renewed in 2017.[29] Somewhat less dramatically, the UN also participates in a trust that oversees pharmaceutical purchases by hospitals in Honduras.[30] In both of these examples, weak state institutions were incapable of dealing with corruption and related offenses, so the UN was entrusted to fill this lacuna.

The World Bank and the UN also have internal anti-corruption controls (Rose-Ackerman and Palifka 2016: 481–484). For example, at the World Bank the Integrity Vice Presidency investigates and adjudicates instances of fraud and corruption inside Bank projects. It can debar firms from Bank projects for a period of time and has cross-debarment arrangements with several other International Financial Institutions (IFIs). To date, however, over 80% of cases have involved fraud, with only 18% arising from allegations of corruption, in part, because of the greater difficulty of collecting evidence for corruption.[31]

One role for international organizations and for law enforcement agencies in developed countries is the compilation of information on questionable transactions, combined with the prosecution of individuals and organizations based in developed countries that do business in developing countries. The most well-known international effort is the OECD Convention against Corruption that generalizes the US Foreign Corrupt Practices Act. Those nations that are party to the Convention must make it an offense for their firms to pay bribes to public officials to do business abroad.[32] International AML agreements also fill this need, as we discuss below, but more could be done. Cross-border efforts to control illegal businesses are a second important option that complements the anti-corruption instruments. If corruption facilitates organized crime, the problem for international aid organizations is especially difficult. If the entire state is permeated with crime, the only entry point for the international community may be constraints on money laundering that make it difficult for perpetrators to enjoy their gains outside of their domestic sphere. In less extreme cases, the experience of developed countries in fighting organized crime may be useful. In developing countries, unused to confronting organized crime, a combination of training and law reform is a useful first step. But such reforms are unlikely to be sufficient unless the economy is strong and competitive and provides decent jobs to those entering the labor force. The state may need to make more direct efforts to reduce the excess profits available to criminal entrepreneurs in legitimate business. One strategy is to promote the entry of well-capitalized legitimate businesses that, with some state help on the law enforcement side, can compete with mob-dominated firms. The corruption generated by the illegal drug trade is one argument in favor of legalization so as to produce a more competitive and less corrupt market (Global Commission on Drug Policy 2011).

In addition to the FATF, several other international organizations play an important role in promoting AML globally. The World Bank is one of the leaders. According to its own documents, it "is the only multilateral technical assistance provider on 'illicit flows' that has a specific focus on developing countries. It is also the lone provider with the expertise and skills to cover the whole range of issues at stake in AML/CFT..." (World Bank 2012: 3). The World Bank participates in two programs: the Financial Market Integrity (FMI) unit, founded in 2001 with a mandate to help developing countries establish AML mechanisms and legislation, and the Stolen Asset Recovery (StAR) Initiative, which aims to help countries recover illicitly appropriated assets, a difficult task.[33] These two programs help countries diagnose their AML/CFT programs, develop more effective AML/CFT policies, and train personnel so that the policies are implemented properly. They have helped establish Financial Intelligence Units in more than twenty countries and reform policy in more than sixty. (Ibid.)

The StAR Initiative is a joint World Bank-UNODC effort that began in 2007, but the Initiative works with other international organizations—such as the United Nations Development Program (UNDP), the Organization for Economic Cooperation and Development (OECD), the FATF, the G20, Transparency International, and Global Witness—as well as with individual countries. (Ibid.) Thus, it is an impressive example of international and interagency cooperation. Its primary mandate is to help countries comply with the UNCAC, especially regarding asset recovery. (Ibid.) The FMI also partners with other entities on a bilateral basis. "The training and capacity-building provided by FMI helps sustain national efforts to strengthen the governance and anti-corruption agenda." (Ibid.)

StAR has a set of searchable databases corresponding to Asset Recovery, "Puppet Masters," and Settlements.[34] For example, a search of all three databases for "Sani Abacha" reveals eight on-going cases and six completed, yielding $199 million repatriated from Jersey, $234 million from Liechtenstein, $700 million from Switzerland, and $1.5 billion from the UK. A similar search for "Halliburton" yields two results related to a single case: a completed settlement between Halliburton and the Nigerian government, in which Halliburton agreed to pay $35 million, and $135 million frozen in Switzerland, the status of which is unknown; the legal basis for recovery is "unspecified" because recovery is part of the plea bargain between Halliburton and Nigeria. Information on Asset Recovery is drawn from a variety of published sources, and much of the information seems to be provided by the public via an open request for updates. As of June 21, 2016, 109 cases are listed as "completed."

The Puppet Masters database was assembled in preparation for a StAR report (van der Does de Willebois 2011), and the World Bank does not appear to have updated it since. This effort collected 150 cases of grand corruption from around the world. A search of the Puppet Masters database for "United States" yields only eight cases. This should be updated as it has great potential as a source of information. The report provides insight into the methods and vehicles used in these cases and makes substantial recommendations to improve AML efforts.

The International Monetary Fund (IMF) also offers technical assistance, upon request from an IMF member, in AML/CFT compliance. The roles filled by the IMF are similar to those of the FMI: diagnosis and risk assessment, assistance in drafting legislation, and training in implementation. In addition, the IMF conducts regional workshops on various aspects of AML/CFT.[35]

Another example of international cooperation is the Egmont Group, founded in 1995. This is an organization of (currently 151) Financial Intelligence Units (FIUs) that meet to exchange knowledge and expertise. The FATF recommends that countries join the Egmont Group. In addition to providing training, the Egmont Group has established the Egmont Secure Web (ESW) to enhance international information exchange among FIUs.[36] The ESW is administered by FinCEN (US) "as an extraordinary voluntary contribution" (Egmont Group 2015: 22). The Egmont Group also works closely with the FATF, StAR, and FMI.

Despite these international initiatives, many jurisdictions still have very weak controls over AML/CFT. The Basel Institute on Governance evaluates AML/CFT laws and other risk factors, and publishes the Basel AML Index annually since 2012. Countries are scored from 0 (low risk) to 10 (high risk). In the 2015 AML Index, 110 of 152 countries score 5 or above; the scores range from 2.53 (Finland) to 8.59 (Iran). The United States received a score of 5.18, quite close to Barbados (5.19) and Mexico (5.24). Encouragingly, all regions are represented in the group of countries that score below 5 (Basel Institute on Governance 2016: 2). The publication of the Basel AML Index may exert pressure on countries in the same way that the Transparency International Corruption Perceptions Index (CPI) has done with respect to corruption. The Basel Institute, a non-profit organization associated with the University of Basel, also provides training on asset recovery and guidance for better governance.[37]

Conclusions

Vicious spirals enable organized crime to get a foothold and propagate by means of corruption and threats. Once some police, legislators, court clerks, and judges are "for sale," members of organized criminal groups will take advantage of this weakness in the rule of law, and such activity will escalate in a feedback loop. Some of the mafias' most lucrative businesses will be illegal—such as trafficking of drugs and people. Others may be legal with high profits (running casinos or "winning" public tenders) or provide opportunities to launder others' ill-gotten gains. The danger is that, rather than being a stage of development that will wither away over time, criminal activity may become so intertwined with corrupt politics and legitimate business, that it is difficult to tell them apart.

Specific anti-corruption policies are necessary but not sufficient in highly corrupt sectors, industries, and countries. Anti-corruption policies need to remove the background incentives for payoffs that arise from poorly designed and monitored public programs. They need to limit the opportunities for bureaucrats, judges, and elected officials to seek personal financial gain. However, large, specialized infrastructure projects or defense contracts cannot be converted into pure competitive bidding processes, and many organized crime activities cannot simply be legalized as an anti-corruption strategy. Anti-corruption proponents need to confront the global nature of both big business and organized crime, with their corresponding roles in corruption.

Hence, anti-corruption reformers need to confront organized crime networks. Some policies will be infeasible if those who pay bribes are members of OCGs and if public officials have become their collaborators. However, marginal progress may still be possible through limits on money laundering. This indirect approach targets neither corruption nor illegal business directly but rather concentrates on a factor that makes each one profitable—the ability to transfer funds across borders and to invest illicit gains in global financial markets. One aspect of this practice is the relative ease with which individuals and firms can create shell companies in both developing and developed countries (including many US states) without having to disclose the beneficial owner or, indeed, much else (Findley et al. 2014).

Individual governments, especially in low-income states, can seldom deal with these interlinked issues alone. In response, the World Bank and the IMF, as well as other aid and lending organizations, are seeking to limit corruption and to improve governance in beneficiary countries. They have policies directed at money laundering through reporting requirements and their support of global transparency initiatives such as the Extractive Industries Transparency Initiative and the work of Transparency International. However, as reflected in their own data, organized crime has not been front and center for development banks. The World Bank prepares Country Policy and Institutional Assessments (CPIA) that draw on extensive cross-country data. The Bank publishes the data for low-income countries that borrow at concessionary rates, but not for other countries.[38] The data, however, do not include material on crime levels except for homicides per 100,000. Thus, the published data are not helpful for comparing corruption and organized crime across countries. The World Bank's Enterprise Survey,[39] which is incorporated into the CPIA, has a few clues. Firm managers are asked about "gifts/informal payments" to get electricity connections and water services, to obtain permits and licenses, and in dealing with tax inspectors. They are also asked, in general, if corruption is an obstacle to "your business." Of course, bribery may be entirely unrelated to organized crime, and one cannot tell if mafias are available to smooth relations with the state. The surveys ask how much firms pay for security as a percent of sales or as an annual cost. This data could indicate the prevalence of extortion although, of course, it conflates mafia payoffs and high security costs arising from a disorganized, opportunistic level of criminality. Hence, the publicly available data from the World Bank do not permit one to assess the linked problems of organized crime and corruption or to understand how efforts to limit money laundering might feed back into the economics and politics of low- and middle-income countries. A first step for the IFIs and other development institutions would be better information about the constraints that OCGs impose on economic and social development.

As we have argued, corruption is often intertwined with international organized crime and is facilitated by money laundering; cooperation among countries, IFIs, and enforcement agencies is essential. Otherwise, the proceeds of corruption and organized crime will be hidden abroad or in cyberspace. Too many countries still have lax financial regulations or limited enforcement, and there is not enough cross-country investigative sharing and extradition of accused criminals. Coordinated efforts that link anti-corruption, organized crime investigations, and AML are likely to yield better results than each operating in isolation. Because anti-corruption agencies are often under-funded and under-staffed (Recanatini 2011), drawing on other agencies for support is one way to maximize their effectiveness. At the international level, several initiatives already recognize these interconnections and include two or three of these concerns.

How should the governance reform and anti-corruption programs of the World Bank and the other IFIs take account of the organized crime/money laundering nexus? These institutions ought to take a systemic, long-term view of the problem that goes beyond short-term crackdowns. Dramatic corruption scandals spotlight particular instances of corruption, and they can lead to aggressive prosecutions, but this response often neglects both the systemic factors that produced the scandal in the first place and other types of corruption that are entrenched and less dramatic. The IFIs need to help countries to concentrate institutional reforms on the most harmful ways that corruption undermines growth and delegitimizes government. They also need to support international efforts to control money laundering and to undermine the power of organized crime. These are difficult issues for IFIs to take on, but especially when OCGs have undermined portions of the state apparatus, only an outsider, such as the World Bank, may have the leverage to push for an end to the impunity of those who pay and accept payoffs and other types of illicit enrichment.

Comments by Ernesto Schargrodsky (UTDT)[40]

In this chapter, Susan Rose-Ackerman and Bonnie Palifka discuss extensively the relationship between corruption, organized crime, and money laundering. They build on their previous work on corruption and begin by characterizing it as quid pro quo trades that infringe legal or institutional rules where private individuals and businesses benefit from making a payoff to exert their influence on public officials. In a corrupt environment, decisions that should be made on grounds of efficiency, equity, or citizen accountability are nevertheless influenced by benefits provided directly to public officials (or their kin, or their political parties). As described by the authors, these problems in the state/society interface can seriously impair human development and political legitimacy.

Although the literature is relatively scarce considering the relevance of this topic, some forms of corruption have been studied, and some interventions have been able to constrain corruption incentives (see, for example, Shleifer and Vishny 1993; Di Tella and Schargrodsky 2003; Fisman and Wei 2004; Olken 2007; Yang 2008; Avis et al. 2016, *inter alia*). Reforms have aimed at eliminating rules that serve little purpose beyond generating payoffs, permitting the legal sale of a scarce benefit, streamlining programs to reduce official discretion, and providing monitoring and transparency tools to those harmed by corruption.

However, this chapter dwells on situations in which whole institutions or states are so permeated by corruption that partial interventions are unfeasible or ineffective. In these situations, corruption allows for the development of organized crime, while criminal organizations corrupt and/or threaten public officers and authorities through *plata* or *plomo* (bribe or bullet) threats (see Dal Bó et al. 2006). Corrupt officers and illegal businessmen feed on each other. As the authors explain, "Corruption enables organized crime, but organized crime also feeds corruption."

In those situations, organized crime dominates illegal businesses, but it may also control legal businesses to gain monopoly profits. In particular, organized crime blocks political interventions that threaten its activities. In turn, the process of money laundering provides a safe shelter for resources from illegal activities.

This article presents a rich description of the interactions between corruption, organized crime, and money laundering. The main image that emerges, and the authors consciously stress, is that of vicious cycles. In terms of a theoretical model, these vicious cycles reflect the existence of multiple equilibria in societies, where some societies get locked in a "culture of corruption." As the authors explain, rather than being a stage of development that will wither away over time, organized crime can deeply permeate state institutions (police, judicial, and law enforcement agencies), and become intertwined with politics and legal business, impeding development.

A paramount question is how societies can move from a "bad" to a "good" equilibrium avoiding a trap where corruption and organized crime feed on each other from the public and private sectors. Unfortunately, few experiences ended in success and we know little about them. A leading but exceptional example were the reforms in the United States in the Progressive Era, including political reforms, the deepening of democracy (including women's suffrage), modernization, and the media exposure of corruption (see, for example, Glaeser and Goldin 2007).

The authors finish by discussing how multilateral institutions could contribute to governance reform and anti-corruption programs in developing countries. They argue that these institutions ought to adopt an integral, long-term stand to the problem that exceeds short-term crackdowns. The international financial institutions should aid countries in their efforts to concentrate institutional reforms on the most pernicious and detrimental ways in which corruption undermines growth and delegitimizes government. They also ought to back international intents to control money laundering and to undermine the power of organized crime.

I agree that external help might be key to achieve success. And that an outsider, such as the World Bank, may have the upper hand to promote and ensure an end to the impunity of those who pay and accept payoffs and other types of illicit enrichment. In particular, international aid is crucial in the fight against money laundering, that no country can control by itself. However, long-term progress to break these vicious cycles needs, of course, strong local forces fighting against corruption and crime. The danger of international forces taking the lead in these interventions is that, for the most part, organized crime organizations are intertwined with local political forces that can exploit the external intervention as a nationalistic argument to radicalize the public opinion. These anti-imperialistic ideas can easily grow and spread in developing countries. An exceptional and successful experience in Latin America combining support of the majority of the society with external help (through military support and extraditions) was the progress made in Colombia in the fight against the drug cartels and their State infiltration.

A further contribution of the chapter is that it abounds in the description of money laundering as a complement to corruption and organized crime. As corrupt states typically lack safe institutions to protect savings and suffer from macroeconomic instability, most corrupt proceeds eventually end up in the legitimate global economy. The global financial system may indeed facilitate grand corruption and organized crime by easing the cross-border flow of funds and by supporting financial havens. The numbers are huge. The authors mention estimates that the illicit financial funds flowing from developing countries to developed centers can reach US$ 6.6 trillion over the 2003–2012 period. The phenomenon of money laundering might add an additional argument to explain the Lucas' paradox (Lucas 1990, see also for example, Prasad et al. 2007; Gourinchas and Jeanne 2013) on why capital flows from developing countries to developed economies, contradicting basic economic theory.

Notes

1. This section is a condensed version of Chap. 9 of Rose-Ackerman and Palifka (2016).
2. Di Gennaro and La Spina (2016: 2–8) review the literature on the topic.
3. In Mexico, for example, only 1–2% of violent crimes are prosecuted successfully (Feldab-Brown 2011).

4. For an excellent analysis of drug organizations as entrepreneurial, profit-maximizing firms that seek to develop brand loyalty see Wainwright (2016). The Organization of American States (2013a: 81) also argues that illegal drug providers seek profits, much like ordinary firms, but concludes (contradicting Wainwright) " . . . that they obey the dictates of money alone. They do not feel the need to maintain the prestige of a brand name, to promote their product in society, or to respect their clients. Their sole purpose and direction is to make a profit at any cost." However, it is not obvious that such behavior would hurt profits; after all, it is commonplace among legal business firms.

5. In a study of thirty-one Latin American countries, the World Bank (2014) found that crime and security issues are more costly to businesses in large cities than in small cities; Amin (2010) found a similar result in Eastern Europe and Central Asia.

6. Olken and Barron (2009) document that Indonesian truckers either pay organized crime to allow them safe passage, or pay to travel in convoys protected by the military or the police.

7. See, for example, Feldab-Brown (2011). In Russia the same type of extortion payment is called a "roof" or "krysha" (Varese 2001).

8. Frazzica et al. (2016: 53–54) estimate that the Camorra in Southern Italy take 3–5% of the value of work, including both extortion and purchase of over-priced inputs.

9. "Entran los narcos a construir en el Sur," *El Norte* October 13, 2012.

10. "Still Crooked," *The Economist* February 5, 1994.

11. Consult the websites of the Special Inspectors Generals for Iraq and Afghanistan: www.SIGIR.mil; www.SIGAR.mil (accessed June 25, 2016).

12. As Beare (1997: 158) writes: " . . . at the most sophisticated integrated level, the ability to corrupt enables one to control the definitions of what is or is not defined as corruption."

13. In Afghanistan, for example, organized criminals have used bribery and kidnapping of customs officials to enable their smuggling activities. See Special Inspector General for Afghanistan Reconstruction (2014).

14. Some of the material in this section is derived from Rose-Ackerman and Palifka (2016), Chaps. 9 and 15.

15. Platt (2015) provides step-by-step examples of laundering schemes. He challenges the traditional model, arguing that it is too narrow, and proposes instead a non-linear ("enable, distance, and disguise") model in which

money laundering allows "disconnects" between the criminal and the crime, the crime and the property, or the criminal and the property. In either model, the financial sector may or may not play a prominent role.

16. Until recently, Switzerland did not require identification to deposit or access funds and was a popular destination for corrupt funds paid to or embezzled by the political leaders of various countries. Also in Europe, the island of Jersey has been the subject of criticism.

17. Note, for example, that the Panamanian firm Mossack Fonseca had a branch in Nevada. See Kirk Semple, Azam Ahmed, and Eric Lipton. "Panama Papers Leak Casts Light on a Law Firm Founded on Secrecy," *New York Times*, April 6, 2016, http://www.nytimes.com/2016/04/07/ world/americas/panama-papers-leak-casts-light-on-a-law-firm-founded-on-secrecy.html?emc=edit_th_20160407&nl=todaysheadlines&nlid= 22635279&_r=0 (accessed April 12, 2016). For a specific example of Delaware-registered shell companies used in an international money laundering scheme, see Chaikin and Sharman (2009: 75–77). Several US states offer discreet banking options; "...the U.S. is one of the few places left where advisers are actively promoting accounts that will remain secret from overseas authorities." Jesse Drucker. "The World's Favorite New Tax Haven Is the Unites States," *Bloomberg Businessweek* January 26, 2016, http://www.bloomberg.com/news/articles/2016-01-27/the-world-s-favorite-new-tax-haven-is-the-united-states (accessed January 27, 2016).

18. The Financial Action Task Force (2012: 119–120) defines PEPs as "... individuals who are or have been entrusted with prominent public functions..., for example, Heads of State or of government, senior politicians, senior government, judicial or military officials, senior executives of state owned corporations, important political party officials"— not lower- or intermediary-level state employees. Financial institutions are required to monitor the accounts of PEPs for suspicious activity. Some countries require domestic PEPs to make public statements regarding their assets and income. Under Proclamation 7750 (Bush 2004), foreign PEPs may be denied visas for entry into the United States and are subject to having their assets frozen if they have engaged in corruption that interferes with US national (political or economic) interests. The *Global Magnitsky Human Rights Accountability Act* (https://www.hrw.org/news/2017/09/13/us-global-magnitsky-act; https://www.gpo.gov/fdsys/pkg/PLAW-114publ328/html/ PLAW-114publ328.htm) signed into law on December 23, 2106, expands the ability of the President to deny entry and freeze assets, but requires a (mostly unclassified) yearly report to Congress on those targeted under the act.

19. A shell company is an inactive company that has been established sometime in the past, and can be acquired in order to create the appearance of longevity or to obviate the sometimes onerous requirements involved in setting up a new company. See van der Does de Willebois (2011: 37–39).
20. See FATF 2012, *International Standards on Combating Money Laundering and the Financing of Terrorism & Proliferation: The FATF Recommendations*, http://www.fatf-gafi.org/media/fatf/documents/recommendations/pdfs/FATF_Recommendations.pdf.
21. The UNCAC is available at http://www.unodc.org/unodc/en/treaties/CAC/.
22. A summary of these efforts and their history is in Rose-Ackerman and Palifka (2016: 505–518).
23. Nathaniel Popper, "Can Bitcoin Conquer Argentina?" *The New York Times* April 29, 2015, http://www.nytimes.com/2015/05/03/magazine/how-bitcoin-is-disrupting-argentinas-economy.html.
24. FATF, "Virtual Currencies: Key Definitions and Potential AML/CFT Risks," June 2014, http://www.fatf-gafi.org/media/fatf/documents/reports/Virtual-currency-key-definitions-and-potential-aml-cft-risks.pdf and FATF, "Virtual Currencies: Guidance for a Risk-based Approach," June 2015, http://www.fatf-gafi.org/media/fatf/documents/reports/Guidance-RBA-Virtual-Currencies.pdf.
25. Ibid., 32–35.
26. Ron Stodghill, "Oil, Cash and Corruption," *New York Times* November 5, 2006, http://www.nytimes.com/2006/11/05/business/yourmoney/05giffen.html.
27. *Comisión Internacional contra la Impunidad en Guatemala* (CICIG), http://www.cicig.org/; UN, 2008, "Ten stories the world should hear more about," http://www.un.org/en/events/tenstories/08/justice.shtml (accessed June 19, 2016).
28. Thabata Molina, "Why It Took a UN Commission to Bring Down Corruption in Guatemala," *PanAm Post*, November 5, 2015, http://panampost.com/thabata-molina/2015/11/05/why-it-took-a-un-commission-to-bring-down-corruption-in-guatemala/ (accessed November 5, 2015).
29. CICIG, "En Vigencia Extensión de Prórroga del Mandato de la CICIG." http://www.cicig.org/index.php?page=NOT_059_20170904.
30. Transparency International. 2014. "Exposing health sector corruption saves lives in Honduras." March 28, 2014. http://www.transparency.org/

news/feature/exposing_health_sector_corruption_saves_lives_in_honduras (accessed June 19, 2016).

31. Consult the World Bank's Office of Suspension and Debarment (2015) for a review of the office's work.

32. Convention on Combating Bribery of Foreign Public Officials in International Business Transactions, 1997: http://www.oecd.org/corruption/oecdantibriberyconvention.htm (accessed June 25, 2016). The US Foreign Corrupt Practices Act is at: https://www.justice.gov/criminal-fraud/foreign-corrupt-practices-act.

33. The web site is: http://www1.worldbank.org/publicsector/star_site/. See Dubois and Nowlan (2013).

34. StAR Corruption Cases Search Center, http://star.worldbank.org/corruption-cases/assetrecovery/ (accessed June 19, 2016).

35. IMF, 2011, "Technical Assistance on AML/CFT," http://www.imf.org/external/np/leg/amlcft/eng/aml3.htm (accessed June 21, 2016).

36. "The Egmont Group of Financial Intelligence Units," http://www.egmontgroup.org/about (accessed June 21, 2016).

37. Basel Institute on Governance, https://www.baselgovernance.org/ (accessed June 21, 2016).

38. The data are available at http://datatopics.worldbank.org/cpia/cluster/public-sector-management-and-institutions (accessed June 28, 2016).

39. Available at http://www.enterprisesurveys.org/ (accessed June 28, 2016).

40. Ernesto Schargrodsky, Universidad Torcuato Di Tella, Av. Figueroa Alcorta 7350, (C1428BIJ) Buenos Aires, Argentina, eschargr@utdt.edu.

References

Amin, Mohammad. 2010. Crime and Security in the Eastern Europe and Central Asia Region. World Bank Enterprise Note No. 15. http://www.enterprisesurveys.org/~/media/GIAWB/EnterpriseSurveys/Documents/EnterpriseNotes/Crime-15.pdf. Accessed 20 June 2016.

Avis, Eric, Claudio Ferraz, and Frederico Finan. 2016. *Do Government Audits Reduce Corruption? Estimating the Impacts of Exposing Corrupt Politicians.* NBER Working Paper 22443. National Bureau of Economic Research, Cambridge, MA.

Basel Institute on Governance. 2016. *Basel AML Index 2015 Report.* Basel, Switzerland: Basel Institute on Governance.

Beare, Margaret E. 1997. Corruption and Organized Crime: Lessons from History. *Crime, Law & Social Change* 28: 155–172.

Buscaglia, Edgardo, and Jan van Dijk. 2003. Controlling Organized Crime and Corruption in the Public Sector. *Forum on Crime and Society* 3: 3–34.

Bush, George W. 2004. Proclamation 7750—To Suspend Entry as Immigrants or Nonimmigrants of Persons Engaged in or Benefiting from Corruption. http://www.presidency.ucsb.edu/ws/?pid=62035. Signed January 12, 2004. Accessed 19 June 2016.

Center for the Study of Democracy. 2010. *Examining the Links Between Organized Crime and Corruption*. European Commission. http://ec.europa.eu/dgs/home-affairs/doc_centre/crime/docs/study_on_links_between_organised_crime_and_corruption_en.pdf. Accessed 15 July 2014.

Chaikin, David, and J.C. Sharman. 2009. *Corruption and Money Laundering: A Symbiotic Relationship*. New York: Palgrave Macmillan.

CICIG. 2013. Sentencias condenatorias en procesos que apoya la CICIG. http://www.cicig.org/uploads/documents/2013/SENT-20131018-01-ES.pdf. Accessed 19 June 2016.

Cuéllar, Mariano-Florentino. 2003. The Tenuous Relationship Between the Fight Against Money Laundering and the Disruption of Criminal Finance. *Journal of Criminal Law and Criminology* 93: 311–465.

Dal Bó, Ernesto, Pedro Dal Bó, and Rafael Di Tella. 2006. Plata o Plomo? Bribe and Punishment in a Theory of Political Influence. *American Political Science Review* 100: 41–53.

De Melo, Martha, Gur Ofer, and Olga Sandler. 1995. Pioneers for Profit: St. Petersburg Entrepreneurs in Services. *World Bank Economic Review* 9: 425–450.

Di Gennaro, Giacomo. 2016. Racketeering in Campania; How Clans Have Adapted and How the Extortion Phenomenon is Perceived. *Global Crime* 17: 21–47.

Di Gennaro, Giacomo, and Antonio La Spina. 2016. The Costs of Illegality: A Research Programme. *Global Crime* 17: 1–20.

Di Tella, Rafael, and Ernesto Schargrodsky. 2003. The Role of Wages and Auditing During a Crackdown on Corruption in the City of Buenos Aires. *Journal of Law and Economics* 46: 269–292.

Dubois, Pascale Hélène, and Aileen Elizabeth Nowlan. 2013. Global Administrative Law and the Legitimacy of Sanctions Regimes in International Law. In *Anti-corruption Policy: Can International Actors Play a Constructive Role?*

ed. Susan Rose-Ackerman and Paul Carrington, 201–214. Durham, NC: Carolina Academic Press.

Egmont Group of Financial Intelligence Units. 2015. 2014–2015 Annual Report. http://www.egmontgroup.org/library/download/426. Accessed 21 June 2016.

Europol [European Police Office]. 2013. *SOCTA 2013: EU Serious and Organised Crime Threat Assessment.* The Netherlands: Van Deventer. https://www.europol.europa.eu/sites/default/files/publications/socta2013.pdf.

FATF. 2012. *The Fatf Recommendations: International Standards on Combating Money Laundering and the Financing of Terrorism & Proliferation.* Paris, France: Financial action task force. http://www.fatf-gafi.org/publications/fatfrecommendations/documents/fatf-recommendations.html. Accessed 20 June 2016.

Feldab-Brown, Vanda. 2011. Calderon's Caldron: Lessons from Mexico's Battle Against Organized Crime and Drug Trafficking in Tijuana, Ciudad Juarez, and Michoacán. Latin America Initiative at Brookings. http://www.brookings.edu/~/media/Files/rc/papers/2011/09_calderon_felbab_brown/09_calderon_felbab_brown.pdf

Findley, Michael G., Daniel L. Nielson, and J.C. Sharman. 2014. *Global Shell Games: Experiments in Transnational Relations, Crime, and Terrorism.* Cambridge, UK: Cambridge University Press.

Fisman, Raymond, and Shang-Jin Wei. 2004. Tax Rates and Tax Evasion: Evidence from 'Missing Imports' in China. *Journal of Political Economy* 112: 471–496.

Frazzica, Giovanni, Maurizio Lisciandra, Valentina Punzo, and Attilio Scaglione. 2016. The Camorra and Protection Rackets: The Cost for Business. *Global Crime* 17: 48–59.

Gambetta, Diego. 1993. *The Sicilian Mafia.* Cambridge, MA: Harvard University Press.

Gambetta, Diego, and Peter Reuter. 1995. The Mafia in Legitimate Industries. In *The Economics of Organised Crime*, ed. Gianluca Fiorentini and Sam Peltzman, 116–139. Cambridge, UK: Cambridge University Press.

Glaeser, Edward, and Claudia Goldin, eds. 2007. *Corruption and Reform: Lessons from America's Economic History.* Chicago, IL: University of Chicago Press.

Global Commission on Drug Policy. 2011. War on Drugs: Report of the Global Commission on Drug Policy. http://www.globalcommissionondrugs.org/wp-content/themes/gcdp_v1/pdf/Global_Commission_Report_English.pdf

Gordon, Richard K. 2011. *Laundering the Proceeds of Public Sector Corruption.* Working Paper 09–10, Case Western Reserve School of Law. http://papers.ssrn.com/sol3/papers.cfm?abstract_id=1371711

Gourinchas, Pierre, and Olivier Jeanne. 2013. The Allocation Puzzle. *Review of Economic Studies* 80: 1484–1515.

Johnson, Nelson. 2002. *Boardwalk Empire.* Medford, NJ: Medford Press.

Johnston, Michael. 2005. *Syndromes of Corruption.* Cambridge, UK: Cambridge University Press.

———. 2014. *Corruption Contention and Reform: The Power of Deep Democratization.* Cambridge, UK: Cambridge University Press.

Kar, Dev and Joseph Spanjers. 2014. Illicit Financial Flows from Developing Countries: 2003–2012. Global Financial Integrity. http://www.gfintegrity.org/report/2014-global-report-illicit-financial-flows-from-developing-countries-2003-2012/. Accessed 15 Oct 2015.

Kukhianidze, Alexandre. 2009. Corruption and Organized Crime in Georgia Before and after the 'Rose Revolution'. *Central Asian Survey* 28: 215–234.

Lessig, Larry. 2011. *Republic Lost: How Money Corrupts Congress—And a Plan to Stop It.* New York: Grand Central Publishing.

Levi, Michael, Maria Dakolias, and Theodore S. Greenberg. 2007. Money Laundering and Corruption. In The Many Faces of Corruption: Tracking Vulnerabilities at the Sector Level, ed. J. Edgardo Campos and Sanjay Pradhan, 389–426. Washington, DC: The World Bank.

Lucas, Robert. 1990. Why Doesn't Capital Flow from Rich to Poor Countries? *American Economic Review* 80: 92–96.

McIllwain, Jeffrey Scott. 1999. Organized Crime: A Social Network Approach. *Crime, Law & Social Change* 32: 301–323.

Olken, Benjamin A. 2007. Monitoring Corruption: Evidence from a Field Experiment in Indonesia. *Journal of Political Economy* 115 (2): 200–249.

——— and Patrick Barron. 2009. The Simple Economics of Extortion: Evidence from Trucking in Aceh. *Journal of Political Economy* 117: 417–452.

Organization of American States (OAS). 2013a. *The Drug Problem in the Americas.* Analytical Report. Washington, DC: Organization of American States. http://www.oas.org/documents/eng/press/Introduction_and_Analytical_Report.pdf

——— 2013b. *El Problema de drogas en las Américas: Estudios. La economía del Narcotráfico.* Washington, DC: Organization of American States. http://www.cicad.oas.org/drogas/elinforme/informeDrogas2013/laEconomicaNarcotrafico_ESP.pdf

Platt, Stephen. 2015. *Criminal Capital: How the Finance Industry Facilitates Crime.* New York: Palgrave Macmillan.

Prasad, Eswar, Raghuram Rajan, and Arvind Subramanian. 2007. Foreign Capital and Economic Growth. *Brookings Papers on Economic Activity* 1: 153–230.

Recanatini, Francesca. 2011. Anti-corruption Authorities: An Effective Tool to Curb Corruption? In *International Handbook on the Economics of Corruption*, ed. Susan Rose-Ackerman and Tina Soreide. vol. 2, 528–569. Cheltenham, UK and Northampton, MA: Edward Elgar.

Reuter, Peter. 1987. *Racketeering in Legitimate Industries: A Study in the Economics of Intimidation*. Santa Monica, CA: RAND Corporation.

———. 2013. Are Estimates of the Volume of Money Laundering Either Feasible or Useful? In *Research Handbook on Money Laundering*, ed. Brigitte Unger and Daan van der Linde, 224–231. Cheltanham, UK: Edward Elgar.

Rose-Ackerman, Susan. 1978. *Corruption: A Study in Political Economy*. New York: Academic Press.

———. 1999. *Corruption and Government: Causes, Consequences, and Reform*. Cambridge, UK: Cambridge University Press.

Rose-Ackerman, Susan, and Bonnie J. Palifka. 2016. *Corruption and Government: Causes, Consequences, and Reform*. Cambridge, UK: Cambridge University Press.

Scaglione, Attilio. 2016. Cosa Nostra and Camorra: Illegal Activities and Organisational Structures. *Global Crime* 17: 60–78.

Schneider, Jane, and Peter Schneider. 2005. The Sack of Two Cities: Organized Crime and Political Corruption in Youngstown and Palermo. In *Corruption: Anthropological Perspectives*, ed. Dieter Haller and Cris Shore, 29–46. London and Ann Arbor: Pluto.

Scott, David. 1995. Money Laundering and International Efforts to Fight It. *Viewpoints*, No. 48. Financial Sector Development Department, Vice Presidency for Finance and Private Sector Development, World Bank, Washington.

Shelley, Louise. 1994. Post-Soviet Organized Crime. *Demokratizatsiya* 2: 341–358.

Shleifer, Andrei, and Robert Vishny. 1993. Corruption. *Quarterly Journal of Economics* 108: 599–617.

Special Inspector General for Afghanistan Reconstruction. 2014. Afghan Customs: U.S. Programs Have Had Some Successes, but Challenges Will Limit Customs Revenue as a Sustainable Source of Income for Afghanistan (SIGAR 14-47 Audit Report). http://www.sigar.mil/pdf/audits/SIGAR-14-47-AR.pdf

Thoumi, Francisco E. 2003. *Illegal Drugs, Economy, and Society in the Andes*. Baltimore and London: The Johns Hopkins University Press.

United Nations Office on Drugs and Crime (UNODC). 2011. Estimating Illicit Financial Flows Resulting from Drug Trafficking and other Transnational

Organized Crimes: Research Report. http://www.unodc.org/documents/data-and analysis/Studies/Illicit_financial_flows_2011_web.pdf

Van der Does de Willebois, Emile, Emily M. Halter, Robert A. Harrison, Ji Won Park, and J.C. Sharman. 2011. *The Puppet Masters: How the Corrupt Use Legal Structures to Hide Stolen Assets and What to Do About It*. Washington, DC: Stolen Asset Recovery Initiative (The World Bank and UNODC). http://star.worldbank.org/star/sites/star/files/puppetmastersv1.pdf. Accessed 19 June 2016.

Varese, Federico. 1994. Is Sicily the Future of Russia? Private Protection and the Rise of the Russian Mafia. *Archives of European Sociology* 35: 224–258.

Varese, Frederico. 2001. *The Russian Mafia: Private Protection in a New Market Economy*. Oxford, UK: Oxford University Press.

———. 2015. Underground Banking and Corruption. In *Greed, Corruption, and the Modern State: Essays in Political Economy*, ed. Susan Rose-Ackerman and Peter Lindseth, 336–350. Cheltenham, MA: Edward Elgar.

Wainwright, Tom. 2016. *Narconomics: How to Run a Drug Cartel*. New York: Public Affairs.

Webster, Leila M. 1993. *The Emergence of Private Sector Manufacturing in Hungary*. Technical Paper 229, World Bank, Washington, DC.

Webster, Leila M., and Joshua Charap. 1993. The Emergence of Private Sector Manufacturing in St. Petersburg. Technical Paper 228, World Bank.

World Bank. 2012. Fighting 'Dirty Money' and Illicit Flows to Reduce Poverty: Helping Countries Establish Transparent Financial Systems and Robust Mechanisms for Asset Recovery. World Bank Document 93589. http://www-wds.worldbank.org/external/default/WDSContentServer/WDSP/IB/2015/05/18/090224b082e94c04/1_0/Rendered/PDF/Fighting00dirt0s0for0asset0recovery.pdf. Accessed 21 June 2016.

———. 2014. Avoiding Crime in Latin America and the Caribbean. Latin America and the Caribbean Series Note No. 7. http://www.enterprisesurveys.org/~/media/GIAWB/EnterpriseSurveys/Documents/Topic-Analysis/Avoiding-Crime-LAC.pdf. Accessed 20 June 2016.

World Bank, Office of Suspension and Debarment. 2015. *Report on Functions, Data and Lessons Learned, 2007–2015*. 2nd ed. Washington, DC: World Bank. http://siteresources.worldbank.org/EXTOFFEVASUS/Resources/OSD_Report_Second_Edition.pdf. Accessed 24 June 2016.

Yang, Dean. 2008. Integrity for Hire: An Analysis of a Widespread Customs Reform. *Journal of Law and Economics* 51: 25–57.

5

Reflections on Corruption in the Context of Political and Economic Liberalization

Pranab Bardhan

I

First some definitional issues to indicate the kinds of corruption I will be primarily concerned with in this paper.

I will take the usual definition of corruption as 'use of public office for private gain'.

This, of course, leaves out most of private-sector corruption (like financial scam or embezzlement), which often involves fraud. The public sector is sometimes indirectly involved in such private fraud by its laxity in enforcing regulations.

Holders of 'public office' include both politicians and bureaucrats. While some part of the literature associates bureaucratic corruption with 'petty' corruption and political corruption as 'grand' corruption, quite often bureaucrats and politicians are both parts of a collusive network.

P. Bardhan (✉)
University of California at Berkeley, Berkeley, CA, USA
e-mail: bardhan@econ.berkeley.edu

© The Author(s) 2018
K. Basu, T. Cordella (eds.), *Institutions, Governance and the Control of Corruption*, International Economic Association Series,
https://doi.org/10.1007/978-3-319-65684-7_5

In democracies the need for raising election finance is often the root cause of political corruption. Politicians can, as in India, keep even bureaucrats with job security in a tight leash through controlling the mechanisms of their transfers and promotion; nevertheless, there is plenty of evidence of two-way collusion between them.

The literature usually distinguishes between two types of corruption, 'facilitative' and 'collusive'.

* *Facilitative corruption*—the standard kind where you pay an official to speed up your case/file, you pay him to do what he is supposed to do anyway (Russians call this *mzdoimstvo*)
* *Collusive corruption*—where you pay an official to do what he is not supposed to do (Russians call this *likhoimstvo*).

Facilitative corruption can sometimes be administratively handled by legalizing speed money (like charging for 'express post' or 'fast track'). This also reduces somewhat the need for middlemen or touts in government offices who prey on customers' lack of information and uncertainty about where, whom and how much to bribe.

Collusive corruption is more insidious and difficult to erase. Examples of such corruption: the official connives at or looks the other way when

* goods are smuggled or over-invoiced
* taxes are evaded
* income or property value is under-assessed
* driver's license or targeted ration card is issued to unqualified people
* bids in public auctions are rigged
* lower-quality materials are substituted in government procurement

These cases involve collusion between the bribe-giver and the bribe-taker to evade laws, and both parties gain, thus neither is likely to report this to investigators. Middlemen sometimes play a coordinating role in arranging such collusion.

There is a third kind of corruption which I am not going to discuss much here; it involves pure harassment or extortion, when you do not want the official to do anything for you (except to simply go away). A system of rewarding enforcement officials for reporting violations of law may encourage such cases. This kind of corruption is called 'framing' in Polinsky and Shavell (2001).

Misuse of public office need not be always illegal. Laws are different in different countries (for example, large and secretive corporate donations to political campaigns are often legal in the US, but not in many other countries).

With the mixing up of corrupt with illegal, as is usually done in the reported data, inter-country comparisons and rankings in corruption are particularly problematic.

Dodgy rentier income in politically connected firms in 'rent-thick' sectors (like, land, natural resources, defense, finance, construction, telecommunication, etc.) is often legal and not counted as corrupt. In most international rankings of corruption Singapore comes out as one of the cleanest. But in *The Economist* magazine ranking of 22 countries of the world in terms of billionaire wealth from crony rent-thick sectors, Singapore is no. 4 in the crony-capitalism index, only after Russia, Malaysia and the Philippines, and worse than even Ukraine or Mexico.

Reported corruption data do not also usually include non-monetary forms of corruption:

* when connections, not direct bribes, are used to land a job or a contract (these connections are sustained by social forms of 'gift exchange')
* when a politician does you a favor not in exchange of money, but, say, political support
* when an official steals not your money but time, through absenteeism or shirking

II

With the definitional issues in the background, let us now turn to the impact of economic and political liberalization on the incidence of corruption. Since liberalization is about having more competition in some form or other, the general presumption is that open competition should help in reducing corruption.

Political liberalization in the form of democratic accountability mechanisms (including checks and balances and the disciplining effects of reelection prospects) should, controlling for other things, tend to clean up murky corrupt economic transactions. For example, across countries it has been noted by Treisman (2000) that in cross-country regressions a long exposure to democracy reduces corruption. Similarly, there is a positive correlation between the Economist Intelligence Unit data on the democracy index of a country and the corruption index data reported by Transparency International. But such correlation exercises are subject to serious endogeneity problems (apart from the usual subjectivity problems of corruption perception data).

Economic liberalization in the form of deregulation and opening to global competition should keep fewer matters for official discretion and hence opportunity for malfeasance. Ades and di Tella (1999), for example, estimate that almost a third of the corruption gap between Italy and Austria may be explained by Italy's lower exposure to foreign competition. Svensson (2003) shows from data in Uganda the significant relationship between intrusive business regulations and incidence of corruption across industries.

The relation between both types of liberalization and corruption is, of course, more complex than what one may surmise from such simple correlations, and in this paper we explore some aspects of this complexity.

Let us first take economic liberalization. One of the arguments in favor of such reform was that it will reduce corruption. Yet in some countries—for example, India—corruption is perceived to have gone up in recent post-reform decades.

Some attempts at partial explanation of this paradox bring out the complexities:

* Reform (de-licensing of investment as well as trade liberalization) has been much more in the product markets, less in the primary factor markets (land, labor, credit, energy, natural resources, etc.). With economic growth, partly fueled by those product-market reforms, land and natural resources in particular, have become more valuable than before, their essentially political allocation generating more rent

and hence more corruption opportunities. This is consistent with the general theory of the second-best: opening up some markets may not necessarily improve things, and may sometimes have an opposite effect.

* With more privatization, diversion of more able people to higher-paying jobs in the growing private sector after reform, has adverse effects on the composition and quality of public sector officials.
* The process of privatization itself has generated (particularly in the early years of transition economies) a great deal of corruption in terms of transfer of wealth from a public monopoly to a private monopoly run by crony 'oligarchs'.
* With a larger role of the private sector, regulatory agencies in different fields become more important—but often weak and non-transparent regulations, and more scope for post-retirement officers employed in sectors formerly regulated by them (called *amakudari* in Japan, 'revolving doors' in US), open the door for corruption.
* With economic growth, officials find out that there is more money to be made in large infrastructure contracts than in the delivery of routine public services to the poor.
* Post-reform public–private partnerships are often the preferred mode in infrastructure building, where collusion between business and politicians allow for rampant cost overruns and renegotiation of terms long after the bid has been closed (amounting in effect to bid-rigging).
* With economic growth leading to more commercial disputes, courts become more clogged and normal contract enforcement more difficult, leading to judicial corruption and more settlement outside courts.
* With economic development, firms, as they accumulate more capital, sometimes graduate from bribing ('bending the rules') to lobbying ('changing the rules'). Lobbying, of course, is usually legal, has more long-lasting effects, and often not firm-specific, hence it requires more resources and collective action.

Harstad and Svensson (2011) model this process: as bribe-taking officials cannot commit to not asking for larger bribes as the firm grows, after a point lobbying becomes more attractive to the firm. They cite evidence from firm survey data that small firms are more likely to bribe, large firms to lobby.

The boundary between non-corrupt and corrupt lobbying is rather murky. The former type of lobbying is usually the case when its function is mainly information-providing. But the cases of lobbying like in the US more often involve corruption, as lobbyists contribute staggeringly large sums to Political Action Committees of elected politicians and even give a hand in drafting the industry-friendly laws, and there is a 'revolving door' of people between jobs as Congressmen's aides and as employees of lobbying firms.

In most developing country democracies, laws are not as openly for sale as in the US, but the difference is only one of degree, and it is more than made up by the impunity with which commercial interests can breach the law. (There is an Italian saying, "Fatta la legge, trovato l'inganno"—no sooner is a law passed than someone finds a way to dodge it).

* With economic liberalization, government monopoly over the media declines, but often the concentration of private corporate ownership of media hinders the watchdog role of free media on investigation and reporting of collusive corruption in which business is involved.
* Mounting election expenses with a growing electorate and economy (we will come back to this).

III

In this section we will reflect on the relationship between political liberalization and corruption. Political liberalization sometimes refers to the phenomenon of democratic transition from autocratic regimes, as happened in several countries in recent decades. This transition sometimes increases corruption as regulatory institutions are yet to take shape, while dual markets multiply illicit arbitrage opportunities. We shall, however, show that even with an already established coherent democratic framework for quite some time (like in India), in developing countries with weakly institutionalized democracies, the effects of political liberalization in the form of increasing political competition on corruption may not be quite straight-forward.

* While in analogy with market competition political competition is usually assumed to be a good thing, there are cases when competition can lead to a race to the bottom. [This is related to the proposition in Persson and Tabellini (2009) that separation of powers can make citizens worse off by creating a common-pool problem in public decision-making.] Political competition in Indian elections, for example, often encourages competitive populism, in which incumbent politicians try to distribute private or 'club' goods at state expense, and voters sometimes reciprocate by electing the incumbent (this is like the benefit incumbent American senators get by 'bringing the pork home'). The incumbent's political rivals try to counter by promising public goods (like free electricity or water) in the future, and, if elected, end up depleting the treasury.

* In some cases the political leaders can work out a clientelistic system for dispensing selective benefits at least to a group of swing voters to win elections—anecdotes on this are easy to find, but for theoretical and empirical analyses of such systems, see Bardhan and Mookherjee (2012), and Robinson and Verdier (2013). In a household survey in rural West Bengal, Bardhan et al. (2009) find evidence that voting behavior is significantly influenced more by recurring benefits arranged by local governments (like subsidized credit or agricultural inputs, employment on public works, help in personal emergencies, etc.) than by even large one-time benefits (like land reforms, or provision of houses and latrines), suggesting political clientelism.

Also, in situations of social and ethnic heterogeneity where vote mobilization gets organized on sectarian lines, there may be more selective patronage distribution and less political interest in investing in general-purpose public goods. Wantchekon (2003) conducted a field experiment in Benin in which political candidates were persuaded to randomly vary their electoral platforms between a clientelistic program providing cash to specific ethnic groups and a developmental local public good oriented program—the former platform ended up generating higher votes. Such political clientelism, even while helping some poor people, can harm the cause of general pro-poor public investments. Fujiwara and

Wantchekon (2013) cite some experimental evidence from Benin that shows how informed public deliberation in town hall meetings can reduce clientelism.

The incidence of clientelism may in general depend on the stage of development. As incomes rise and markets develop, the need for political connections for jobs or personalized help may decline (though rather slowly, as many cases in southern Italy suggest even now). With the spread of education and information, the importance of the local vote mobilizer who provides selective benefits (the proverbial ward captain in Chicago precincts) diminishes, herding of voters by ethnicity or regional affinity may also decline. With the development of transport and communication, the reduction of territorial insulation allows for supra-local affinities which may diminish the importance of the local patron.

* As elections are becoming frightfully expensive, in democracies where there is no significant public financing of elections nor any effective independent auditing of party funds, mobilizing election finance (usually from the corporate sector, which, of course, expects a *quid pro quo* in terms of business-friendly laws and selective relaxation of regulations) is often a large root cause of corruption. In India the political parties have successfully resisted even being under the purview of the Right to Information Act.

   The Association of Democratic Reforms in India reported that, in 2014, 70% of the income of India's six major political parties came from undocumented sources.

   Min and Golden (2014) examine electoral cycles in electricity theft in India. Drawing upon geographically disaggregated data for the period 2000–2009 in Uttar Pradesh, they document that electricity losses from public distribution utilities tend to increase in periods immediately prior to state assembly elections. Sukhtankar (2012) finds evidence of electoral cycles in input prices paid for sugarcane among politically controlled sugar mills in Maharashtra. Kapur and Vaishnav (2015) link an electoral cycle in cement consumption by builders moving with exigencies of state elections, how competitive the elections are, etc.

The sorry fate of PT(Workers' Party) in Brazil shows how in trying to build a large political machine with enough funds for winning elections and for post-election horse-trading in the legislature, even an ideologically anchored, once grassroots-based, party gets inescapably mired in massive corruption.

⁂ Specific forms of the democratic set-up matters.

- As Rose-Ackerman (1999) points out, much depends on the particular electoral and legislative systems, party structures, etc. She also mentions that for the democratic framework to function efficiently, "politicians must seek reelection and must feel insecure about their prospects, but not too insecure". From Brazilian municipal audit reports, Ferraz and Finan (2011) estimate that mayors with reelection incentives misappropriated 27% less resources than those without reelection incentives. Ferraz and Finan (2008) show that dissemination of corruption information from audit reports before municipal elections significantly affects incumbents' election prospects.

  But from the data on the timing of audit reports for municipal governments in Puerto Rico, the findings of Bobonis et al. (2015) seem to suggest that, over time, information contained in the audits helps voters select competent but opportunistic politicians, rather than honest or virtuous ones.

- If the authority structure involves 'multiple veto powers', corruption becomes particularly dysfunctional, as even after bribing an official, you are never sure if the job will get done.

This is also related to the issue of centralization vs decentralization of the bribe collection machinery discussed in the literature—particularly in Shleifer and Vishny (1993) and Bardhan (1997). This is particularly the case when the different items procured through bribes are complementary to one another.

In centralized bribe-taking, the bribee can internalize some of the distortionary effects of corruption. Evidence of positive effects of centralized bribery is discussed for South Korea in Kang (2002) and Indonesia under Suharto by MacIntyre (2001).

In fragmented, anarchic systems of bribery, even after you have bribed an official, that itself may stimulate the entry of other bribe-collectors—free entry allows officials to 'overfish' in the 'commons' of rent collection.

In some cases of democratic transition, there are many stories of corruption *increasing* with liberalization and deregulation on account of the authority structure passing from an authoritarian centralized and thus predictable system of bribery ('one-stop shopping') to a more dispersed decentralized system.

– Centralization of the political machine also makes it possible to have a system approximating 'lump-sum' corruption, which like lump-sum taxation does not distort allocation decisions at the margin.

   However, the ability of the politicians to credibly commit to keeping the collection lump-sum is a feature of an effective state missing in some democratic developing countries.

   But authoritarianism is neither necessary nor sufficient for such credible commitment.

– As suggested by Rose-Ackerman (1978), in some cases competition among service providing agencies may reduce corruption. For example, there is a lot of corruption in India when any agency has the monopoly power to issue government certificates (relating to birth, marriage, death, caste, land title, below-poverty-line status, passport, etc.).

This corruption is now declining in some areas as the state has started outsourcing some of these services to competing authorized private agencies, with centrally computerized verification.

A related issue, discussed in Rose-Ackerman (1994), is of how overlapping jurisdictions of federal, state and city authorities helped in curbing narcotic-related corruption in NYPD (New York Police Department). This is particularly important in cases of collusive corruption.

* In some cases of collusive corruption, competition among officials may, however, have ambiguous effects. Drugov (2010) shows that in cases where some bureaucrats are honest and some are not, competition may give increased incentive to the applicant to invest

in the requisite qualification (learning to drive in the case of driver's license or carrying out pollution abatement in the case of a firm to be inspected). But if the applicant remains unqualified, competition among bureaucrats may increase the chance of the applicant meeting an appropriately dishonest bureaucrat.

– In ethnically divided and heterogeneous societies like in India, Nigeria or Indonesia, the widening of democracy can exacerbate some forms of corruption.

In India, for example, the upper castes having been in positions of power and privilege for centuries have well-developed and well-oiled networks which their members can utilize in fixing problems or getting jobs and contracts for their relatives and friends. By and large the lower castes lack such networks.

As democracy facilitated social mobility, it is quite possible that an upwardly mobile lower-caste person may now try to use money as a substitute for (the missing) network in getting things done.

The latter will be called corruption, but the upper-caste use of connections instead of money for similar objectives is often not described as corruption. That is why in section I, we have referred to such non-monetary forms of corruption which should be admissible in the definition of corruption.

Lack of network may also mean that corrupt low-caste people get caught more often than equally dishonest but more protected upper-caste people.

Moreover, for ethnic groups long subject to social humiliation, it may be quite understandable that dignity politics often trump good governance.

So it is often seen that a low-caste leader widely known as corrupt gets elected by his fellow caste members election after election, because these leaders in other ways have uplifted the self-esteem and dignity of whole groups of people.

The leaders' corruption may even be looked upon with an indulgent eye: all these years the upper castes have looted public money, maybe it is now 'our turn'.

Such symbolic group self-assertion in politics is quite prevalent in north India. In a survey of politician corruption in 102 legislative jurisdictions in north Indian state of UP, where caste-based polarization in voting behavior increased between 1980 and 1996, Banerjee and Pande (2009) show a decline in the quality (in terms of competence and honesty) of the politicians who win. They find clear evidence of a trade-off between caste loyalty and quality of politicians.

Thus in this paper we have tried to reflect on some of the complexities in the relationship between economic and political liberalization and the incidence of corruption. A proper appreciation of these complexities may deflate the simplistic view about some exaggerated positive consequences of liberalization for corruption.

Comments by Martin Rama, Chief Economist for South Asia, World Bank

The link between the practice of corruption and the existence of rents is at the center of the paper "Reflections on Corruption in the Context of Political and Economic Liberalization", by Pranab Bardhan. Based on this presumed link, the key hypothesis assessed—and challenged—by the paper is that reforms which increase competition and contestability should help in reducing the prevalence of corruption.

The paper considers two major types of reforms: economic liberalization and political liberalization. In the words of the author:

> Economic liberalization in the form of deregulation and opening to global competition should keep fewer matters for official discretion and hence opportunity for malfeasance. Political liberalization in the form of democratic accountability mechanisms (including checks and balances and the disciplining effects of reelection prospects) should, controlling for other things, tend to clean up murky corrupt economic transactions.

In exploring this key hypothesis, Pranab Bardhan positions the paper at the core of important development policy debates. Advocates for economic liberalization, and in particular for trade liberalization, often argued their case invoking resource misallocation and efficiency losses. Yet, static efficiency losses (Harberger triangles) are rarely large, while uniform tariffs are unlikely to be optimal when the elasticities of demand differ across imported products (Ramsey rule). Any practitioner knew that the real case for liberalization was related to the fact that protection encourages rent seeking and corruption over innovation and management. Similarly, political liberalization is often justified on the basis of individual freedoms and human rights considerations. But for many in the development community, it represented the only credible antidote against crony capitalism.

Over the last few decades, structural adjustment in Latin America and Sub-Saharan Africa, and regime change in the Middle East and North Africa have provided powerful illustrations of the drive toward economic and political liberalization. Depending on the region, the hope was to reduce rent seeking or to undo state capture. The paper by Pranab Bardhan rigorously assesses whether these expected co-benefits of liberalization, beyond the worthy gains in economic efficiency and individual freedom, have actually materialized.

The conclusion is sobering. This conclusion is based on analytical review of two-dozen high-quality papers covering anything from clientelism in West Bengal to the public release of local government audits in Brazil, and from voting behavior in Benin to the embezzlement of resources in politically connected sugar mills in India. Of course, two dozen papers hardly qualifies as a comprehensive review of the literature. A cursory Google Scholar search based on the words 'corruption' and 'liberalization' yields an overwhelming number of articles, books and reports. Even when focusing on the most relevant two hundred entries, there are 76 with more than 100 citations, and 119 with more than 50. But the short list selected by Pranab Bardhan is of high quality, and the findings reported in it are consistent.

Overall, the conclusion is that the reduction in corruption expected as a result of economic or political liberalization often fails to materialize. The multiplicity of counter-examples provided by the selected set of papers shows that corruption takes other forms, or is even amplified, in the context of liberalization. In the words of the author, these regularities "deflate the simplistic view about some exaggerated positive consequences of liberalization for corruption". This candor is certainly refreshing.

However, there are several ways in which the paper leaves the reader waiting for more. Three concerns are worth mentioning:

1. The *definition* of corruption retained by the paper is not linked to the existence of rents, or to the market imperfections and institutional failures that may generate those rents, but rather to the prevailing legal framework. While rent is a universal economic notion, legal frameworks are more idiosyncratic. But this legal plurality makes comparisons across countries, from Benin to India to Brazil, somewhat uneasy. From that perspective, discussing the distinctions between collusive and facilitative corruption, or between outright corruption and well-oiled networks, as the paper does, does not yield insights on the links between the existence of rents and the prevalence of corruption.

   An example may illustrate this point. A colleague who used to work for a private bank in India before joining the World Bank had been sequentially tasked with opening that bank's first branch in Abidjan and in New York. For Abidjan, he was given a briefcase with one million dollars in cash, all of which went into informal payments—some of them extracted at gunpoint by individuals in military fatigues—before a license could be obtained. By contrast, the process in New York was extraordinarily 'clean': a lawyers' cabinet took care of the necessary paperwork ... which it billed at one million dollars. Focusing on the legality of the proceedings in one case and not in the other may somewhat miss the point, as there were rents to be appropriated in both cases.

   The paper itself recognizes this shortcoming. At one point it states that "the boundary between non-corrupt and corrupt lobbying is rather murky". Elsewhere, it notes that "dodgy rentier income in politically-connected firms in 'rent-thick' sectors (like, land, natural resources, defense, finance, construction, telecommunication, etc.) is often legal and not counted as corrupt". This leads to the paradox of Singapore coming up as one the 'cleanest' countries according to international corruption rankings, while at the same time being high in the crony-capitalism index of *The Economist* magazine. The latter is based on the share of billionaire wealth originating in rent-thick sectors.

Overall, a rigorous discussion of the types of corruption (legal or not) which are relevant from the point of view of the paper would have been welcome.

2. The *mechanisms* through which economic or political liberalization affect the scope for corruption are only hinted at, rather than analyzed in detail. With 31 bullet- and sub-bullet points (roughly one every 120 words) the paper seems to offer a typology more than a framework. The coherence provided by such framework would have been especially important in the case of an analytical survey relying on only two dozen papers. Greater depth could have naturally made up for limited thoroughness. Instead, the reader is told that liberalization did not reduce corruption in the way it was expected, but is left to wonder why this was so. This seems a missed opportunity: given his vast knowledge of the issues, Pranab Bardhan was better positioned than many to shed light on the mechanisms at play.

In the case of economic liberalization, the reader is left with the impression that the issue was not a breakout of the link between the existence of rents and the prevalence of corruption, but rather a breakout of the link between liberalization and rent dissipation. The examples provided in the paper suggest a second-best interpretation, in which some markets were liberalized whereas other market imperfections and institutional failures were left intact, resulting in the creation of rents elsewhere, or even in the amplification of the original rents. For example:

* Economic liberalization has so far focused on product markets, much less so on primary *factor markets*, including land and natural resources. With economic growth fueled by the reforms, land and natural resources become more valuable than before, generating new rents and hence more corruption opportunities.
* Economic liberalization has taken place in a context of *asymmetric information*. When it involves the divestiture of state assets, one of

the big unknowns is the price purchasers should pay for those assets. Because of this murkiness, privatization can involve large transfers of wealth to crony oligarchs.

* Progress in liberalizing markets has been faster than progress in building the *legal infrastructure* for a market economy. With faster growth leading to more commercial disputes, courts become more clogged and normal contract enforcement more difficult, leading to greater judicial corruption.

Unfortunately, there is less clarity on the mechanisms at play in the case of political liberalization. The paper refers to common-pool problems in public decision-making, to populism and the race to the bottom, to politically influential networks based on ethnicity in heterogeneous societies, to the growing importance of campaign finance, and to the concentration of private corporate ownership of media. The stories proposed sound plausible, but the reader wonders whether different but equally plausible stories could also have been told. Perhaps the richest discussion concerns the links between decentralization, liberalization and corruption ... but again it is essentially inconclusive.

A few clearly spelled-out hypotheses, to be contrasted with the findings of the literature, could have made for a richer discussion.

3. Not surprisingly, given the previous two points, the *implications* of the paper for development policy are unclear. The sobering conclusion that economic and political liberalization may fail to reduce corruption is clearly not a call to stop or undo reforms. But at the end of a review like the one proposed in the paper, the reader would have expected to find some guidance on how to liberalize differently, or how to identify the features of liberalization that seem more vulnerable to corruption. Perhaps more ambitiously, one could presume that economic and political liberalization are not random occurrences, with their focus and timing also depending on the constellation of rents and their distribution across key stakeholders.

The paper provides a few suggestions about measures that could complement economic and political liberalization in order to reduce the scope for corruption. All of those suggestions seem related to increasing competition in other areas: among service providers, between jurisdictions of courts, and even among bureaucrats. But it is not clear why these approaches would work, especially in light of the inconclusive discussion regarding the impact of decentralization.

Some additional insights could have been gained by looking not only at cases of economic and political liberalization, but also at episodes where the prevalence of corruption clearly diminished. Such episodes include the Progressive Era in the early twentieth century in the US, and the experience of smaller countries such as Georgia and Uruguay more recently. In fact, one of the striking features of corruption indices across countries is their relative stability, even throughout periods of major economic turbulence and policy reforms. The very few countries that defy this regularity could provide more insights than the very many that embraced economic or political liberalization at one point or another.

Despite the absence of a clear framework, a discussion of the implications of the main findings for development policy would have made for a more rounded paper.

References

Ades, Alberto, and Rafael Di Tella. 1999. Rents, Competition and Corruption. *American Economic Review* 89: 982–993.

Banerjee, Abhijit V., and Rohini Pande. 2009. *Parochial Politics: Ethnic Preferences and Politician Corruption.* Working Paper, Kennedy School, Harvard.

Bardhan, Pranab. 1997. Corruption and Development: A Review of Issues. *Journal of Economic Literature* 35: 1320–1346.

Bardhan, Pranab, Sandip Mitra, Dilip Mookherjee, and Abhirup Sarkar. 2009. Local Democracy and Clientelism: Implications for Political Stability in Rural West Bengal. *Economic and Political Weekly* February: 46–58.

Bardhan, Pranab and Dilip Mookherjee. 2012. *Political Clientelism Cum Capture: Theory and Evidence from West Bengal.* Working Paper.

Bobonis, Gustavo J., Luis Cámara R. Fuertes, and Reiner Schwabe. 2015. *Monitoring Corruptible Politicians.* Working Paper.

Drugov, Mikhail. 2010. Competition in Bureaucracy and Corruption. *Journal of Development Economics* 92: 215–231.

Ferraz, Claudio, and Frederico Finan. 2008. Exposing Corrupt Politicians: The Effects of Brazil's Publicly Released Audits on Electoral Outcomes. *Quarterly Journal of Economics* 123: 703–745.

———. 2011. Electoral Accountability and Corruption: Evidence from the Audits of Local Governments. *American Economic Review* 101: 1274–1311.

Fujiwara, Thomas, and Leonard Wantchekon. 2013. Can Informed Public Deliberation Overcome Clientelism? Experimental Evidence from Benin. *American Economic Journal: Applied Economics* 5: 241–255.

Harstad, Bard, and Jakob Svensson. 2011. Bribes, Lobbying and Development. *American Political Science Review* 105: 46–63.

Kang, David C. 2002. *Crony Capitalism: Corruption and Development in South Korea and the Philippines*. Cambridge: Cambridge University Press.

Kapur, Devesh, and Milan Vaishnav. 2015. *Builders, Politicians, and Election Finance*. Discussion Paper, Carnegie Endowment for International Peace.

MacIntyre, Andrew. 2001. Investment, Property Rights, and Corruption in Indonesia. In *Corruption: The Boom and Bust of East Asia*, ed. Jose Edgardo Campos. Manila: Ateneo University Press.

Min, Brian, and Miriam Golden. 2014. Electoral Cycles in Electricity Losses in India. *Energy Policy* 65: 619–625.

Persson, Torsten, and Guido Tabellini. 2009. Democratic Capital: The Nexus of Economic and Political Change. *American Economic Journal: Macroeconomics* 1: 88–126.

Polinsky, A. Mitchell, and Steven Shavell. 2001. Corruption and Optimal Law Enforcement. *Journal of Public Economics* 81: 1–24.

Robinson, James A., and Thierry Verdier. 2013. The Political Economy of Clientelism. *Scandinavian Journal of Economics* 115: 260–291.

Rose-Ackerman, Susan. 1978. *Corruption: A Study in Political Economy*. New York: Academic press.

———. 1994. Reducing Bribery in the Public Sector. In *Corruption and Democracy*, ed. Duc V. Trang. Budapest: Institute for Constitutional and Legislative Policy.

———. 1999. *Corruption and Government: Causes, Consequences, and Reform*. New York: Cambridge University Press.

Shleifer, Andrei, and Robert Vishny. 1993. Corruption. *Quarterly Journal of Economics* 108: 599–617.

Sukhtankar, Sandip. 2012. Sweetening the Deal? Political Connections and Sugar Mills in India. *American Economic Journal: Applied Economics* 4: 43–63.

Svensson, Jakob. 2003. Who Must Pay Bribes and How Much? Evidence from a Cross Section of Firms. *Quarterly Journal of Economics* 118: 207–230.

Treisman, Daniel. 2000. The Causes of Corruption: A Cross-National Study. *Journal of Public Economics* 76: 399–457.

Wantchekon, Leonard. 2003. Clientelism and Voting Behavior: Evidence from a Field Experiment in Benin. *World Politics* 55: 399–422.

6

Why is Italy Disproportionally Corrupt?: A Conjecture

Diego Gambetta

Corruptissima republica, plurimae leges
Tacitus, Annals, III, 27

Italy is an anomaly in terms of corruption: various indicators show that her level of corruption is on a par with or worse than that of much less developed countries while being far above the level of similarly developed countries. Some of the evidence, such as the widely used Transparency International Corruption Perception Index, relies on the opinions of experts and various economic agents, and some scholars question its accuracy. Still, other sources too, including citizens' reports of their corruption experiences and behavioral experiments, corroborate these indexes, and their possible inaccuracies, however plausible, are most

D. Gambetta (✉)
European University Institute, Florence, Italy
e-mail: Diego.Gambetta@EUI.eu

© The Author(s) 2018
K. Basu, T. Cordella (eds.), *Institutions, Governance and the Control of Corruption*, International Economic Association Series,
https://doi.org/10.1007/978-3-319-65684-7_6

unlikely to subvert the ranking in any drastic way. The basic fact of the Italian anomaly seems solid enough to be taken seriously and to make it worth trying to explain it.

However, where the puzzle lies exactly, whether in corruption or in development, is not clear. It could go in both directions: why is as developed a country as Italy so disproportionally corrupt? But also, how can such a corrupt country have reached a high level of socio-economic development? The latter direction of the puzzle is a challenge to the many who argue that corruption is an obstacle to development. But the former direction of the puzzle too defies those who believe that a developed society, relying to some degree on market competition, a free press and the rule of law, should not foster a "culture of corruption", certainly not to the point of making it as widespread as it appears to be in Italy.

It is not easy to disentangle this chicken and egg dilemma. Ceaseless political altercations aim to make Italian corruption seem like the fruit of the greed and moral bankruptcy of the parties in government at any one time. But, while there have been differences in how loud political parties have turned up the volume of corruption, the evidence suggests that corruption cuts long and deep into Italian society,[1] and has coexisted with many different governments, including the Fascist regime, for a very long time (Ricciuti and Petrarca 2013; Bosworth 2006).

An implication of the puzzle is that either the outcomes of corruption "Italian style" or its underlying mechanisms must be compatible with at least *some* development. But I believe that Italy's social quirkiness—often an uncomfortable thorn on the side of unadventurous social science beliefs—allows us to go further. Here I propose a bolder conjecture, namely that the same micro processes that make corruption thrive in Italy have a sunnier side and also help development to hobble forward.

The paper is organized as follows. I first present the data on Italian corruption. I then review how the explanations that have been proffered do not account for the evidence. Third, I present a micro mechanism—sharing compromising information (SCI)—that could sustain corrupt deals, and some evidence thereof. Fourth, I conjecture on the possible reasons why this mechanism could work so well in Italy, better than elsewhere, and why it could sustain not just corrupt deals, which by being a crime cannot by definition rely on legal enforcement, but also *any* deal that cannot count on effective state enforcement.

The Italian Anomaly: The Evidence

Relative to what we should expect, in comparative perspective, Italy shows a much higher level of corruption.[2]

Let us first look at the distribution across the world most developed countries of the *Corruption Perception Index* (CPI), compiled yearly by Transparency International (Fig. 6.1): in 2015 Italy had a CPI of 44 points (a CPI of 0 means maximum corruption and a CPI of 100 zero corruption). Out of 167 countries for which the CPI is produced in 2015, this score corresponds to the 61st rank a rank that Italy shares with Lesotho, Montenegro, Senegal and South Africa. Among EU countries only Bulgaria and Rumania (not shown in the figure) do worse than Italy.

Consider now Fig. 6.2. Out of the 167 countries, I took the subset of developing countries with a CPI that is equal or lower (that is better) than that of Italy. I then plotted the distribution of both the CPI and the

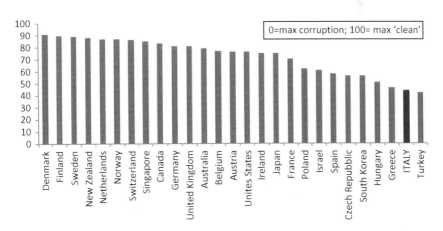

Fig. 6.1 Corruption Perception Index for a selection of developed countries, Transparency International, 2015. Source: http://www.transparency.org/cpi2015

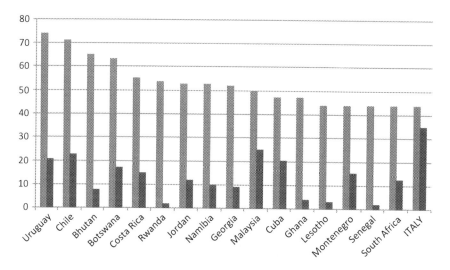

Fig. 6.2 CPI (blue bar) and GDP per capita (red bar, 000 of US $) in a set of developing countries, whose CPI is either equal or worse than that of Italy. Source: CPI: http://www.transparency.org/cpi2015; GDP per capita, World Bank Data (http://data.worldbank.org/indicator/NY.GDP.PCAP.CD) 2011–2015

GDP per capita of these countries. The picture is striking: Italy's GDP is no less than one third *higher* than the GDP of the most developed of these countries (Malaysia), and is much higher than that of all other countries, which however do either as well as or better than Italy in terms of corruption. "Cleaner" cases are found in Asia, Africa, and in Central and Latin America, where Chile and Uruguay distinguish themselves as outliers in the opposite direction to that of Italy.

Finally, let us look at Fig. 6.3. On the vertical axis I plot Italy's *ranking* on the CPI, and compare it with Italy's rankings among world countries on a host of other measures of socio-economic development. This shows that corruption is an outlier, not just compared both with more and with less developed countries, but also compared with Italy's *own* achievements in other spheres. The only other index in this group on which Italy is performing poorly is freedom of the press. I return to this in the last section for this could play a part in explaining Italy's anomaly.

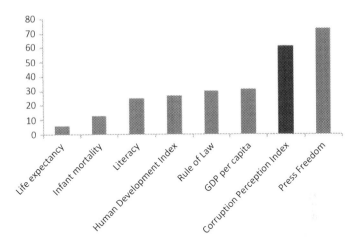

Fig. 6.3 Italy's ranks among world countries on CPI and various development indexes, the higher the rank the worse Italy's position among world countries for which the corresponding measures are available (2015 or nearest year). Sources: Life expectancy, WHO; Infant mortality, CIA; Literacy, UNESCO; Human Development Index, UN; Rule of Law, World Justice Project; GDP per capita, IMF; Corruption Perception Index, TI; Press freedom, Reporters Without Borders

Other corruption indexes show a very similar pattern. The 2010 corruption index produced by the Quality of Government Institute is based on "the combination of national level international expert assessments from the World Bank and the largest QoG survey to date", namely a survey of approximately 34,000 EU citizens. Although the sources are very different from those used by the CPI, the ranking is closely consistent with the CPI distribution (Fig. 6.5a). Also the 2010 Eurobarometer index recording citizens' personal *experience* of corruption in the previous 12 months is highly correlated with the CPI (Vannucci 2012: 85–86) and confirms the Italian anomaly. This is striking since the citizens' experience index is not strongly correlated in general with the CPI (Treisman 2007: 31–32), and is deemed to be a good index, which has been used to identify some errors in the indexes derived from experts' opinions (Razafindrakoto and Roubaud 2010).

Finally, evidence that we are dealing with an anomaly comes from *Progetto Integrità*, carried out by the Scuola Superiore di Amministrazione; they calculated what they dubbed the *Excess Perceived Corruption Index* for EU countries, the US and Japan: this index estimates the deviations of the observed CPI from the CPI that we would expect given various measures of development. Once controlling for the Human Development Index, for instance, Italy shows the second furthermost deviation from the expected value (Vannucci 2012: 89–90).

These indexes rely on the views of various economic agents, or on citizens' reported experience, and one could question their objectivity (Treisman 2007).[3] There is for instance a cultural bias that I have been able to appreciate by living for many years in the UK: when confronted with a case of bribery the British typical interpretation follows "the bad apple" model, while the Italian interpretation follows "the tip of the iceberg" model. The expectation of corruption yet to be discovered is infinitely larger among Italians than among the British—a people who, as Alexis de Tocqueville observed, are peculiarly resistant to generalization. Paradoxically, the more cases of corruption are uncovered by the Italian authorities the more people think not "oh good, we have an effective judiciary catching the scoundrels!", but rather "damn, this country is even more corrupt than I thought!".[4] This bias could influence the replies and inflate the answers for Italy and deflate those for the UK (it could also have a self-fulfilling force and induce further corruption among the Italians, "if they do it why not I?", kind of reasoning).[5]

Despite these doubts, a systematic study by Charron (2016) found that "the consistency between actual reported corruption, as well as citizen and expert perceptions of corruption, is remarkably high and such perceptions are swayed little by 'outside noise'" (p. 147). Furthermore the CPI has been validated *behaviorally* in two experiments. One is a famous natural experiment on UN diplomats' unpaid fines received for parking violations in New York City (Fisman and Miguel 2007). They found that the correlation between unpaid fines and the perception indexes of the diplomats' countries is very high. The other is an experiment carried out by Abigail Barr and Danila Serra (2010) with Oxford undergraduates who played a game in which subjects could choose whether to ask for bribes and, if asked, could choose whether to pay the bribes or refuse.

They found that both paying and asking for bribes in the experiment are highly correlated with the CPI values of the country of origin of the participants. "In 2005, we took a sample of individuals living and studying in Oxford but originating from 34 countries with markedly different levels of corruption, presented them with a corruption decision associated with an exogenously defined set of monetary costs and benefits, and found that, among the undergraduates, we could predict who would and who would not engage in corruption with reference to the level of corruption prevailing in their home country" (Barr and Serra 2010: 869). Both experiments validate the CPI generally, but even looking at their country-level data we find—admittedly relying on only a handful of cases—that Italian diplomats and Italian undergraduates in Oxford conform to the general correlation. The conclusion of these studies is that the disposition to corruption has seeped into the *culture* of the countries of origin and it sticks to its citizens, old and young, wherever they may be.

The Italian Anomaly: Explanations

There is a comprehensive test of the Italian anomaly based on observational data: it does not just show Italy as an anomaly, but that this anomaly is not accounted for by any of the many factors that could plausibly explain corruption. This test can be extracted from Daniel Treisman's (2000) cross-country model of corruption, in which—drawing from a wide range of theories and previous findings—he includes most of the conceivable variables that could affect corruption. Corruption, he argues, should be *lower* in countries in which

* Democracy is stronger
* Economic development is higher
* People are better educated and aware of the public/private distinction
* There is greater freedom of the press, and livelier civic associations
* Public servants wages are higher
* There is more exposure to competition from imports

* There is an efficient legal system—"common law" better than "civil law"
* There is a protestant tradition

By contrast, corruption should be *higher* in countries in which the state is more present in the economy, there are significant natural resources, and there are ethnic divisions. Finally, Treisman included measures of Federalism and Political instability, which, scholars have conjectured, could produce effects *in both directions.*

The outcome of Treisman's model that interests us is reported in Fig. 6.4: Italy comes top in terms of *unexplained corruption* as measured by the residuals obtained by regressing all of the above variables on the CPI index. The Italian puzzle survives the toughest of spins in the statistical mixer, even after all plausible ingredients are thrown in.[6]

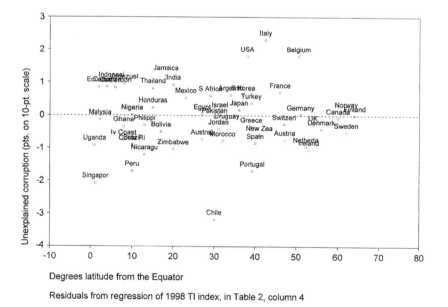

Fig. 6.4 "Residual unexplained corruption, Transparency International 1998 rating." Source: Treisman 2000, p. 438

There is however one ingredient, itself *the* most deep-rooted of Italian peculiarities, which Treisman's model omits: regional disparities. The Quality of Government Index, which has been calculated for 181 European regions (Quality of Government Institute 2010: 39), reveals that regional variations are astonishingly high in Italy, much higher than in *any* other EU country (Fig. 6.5a and b)—Italy contains massive disparities, and virtuous regions coexist with vicious ones, especially in the south. If we treat the two sets of regions, the south and the rest, as if they were separate countries the puzzle would lessen in the south since there both corruption is higher and economic performance is lower, and the two variables thus become more aligned. So partly the Italian corruption puzzle can be explained away as the result of a composition effect.

However, as the map in Fig. 6.6 shows, the QoG corruption index remains high in the rest of the country relative to western and northern EU countries, and is on a par with that of the less developed EU countries in the east. Consider also that socio-economic development is much *higher* in the north, which implies that the tension between corruption and development is not relaxed. The anomaly may lessen somewhat when we take the southern regions out of the picture, but if anything it could become even stronger in the rest of Italy.

Having established with reasonable confidence that Italy is a corruption anomaly, in the next section I will leave the macro picture and delve into the micro mechanisms that preside over corruption.

Sharing Compromising Information

Corrupters and corruptees may be white-collared and meeker than others, but they are criminals nonetheless. Like villains of many stripes they too face two perils. One is of course being caught and to suffer the consequences. The other is being cheated by their partners in crime. The two perils combine when partners inform on one, but each can materialize independently of the other.

The problem with the latter peril is that criminals cannot easily trust one another. This is because they *are* criminals, people who by their very

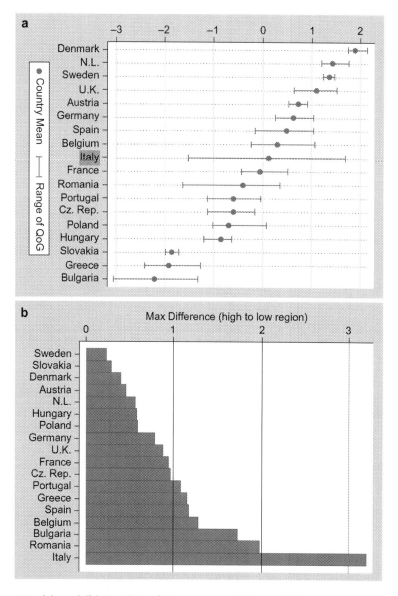

Fig. 6.5 (a) and (b) Quality of Government Index, within country regional variations. Source: Quality of Governance Institute 2010, p. 137

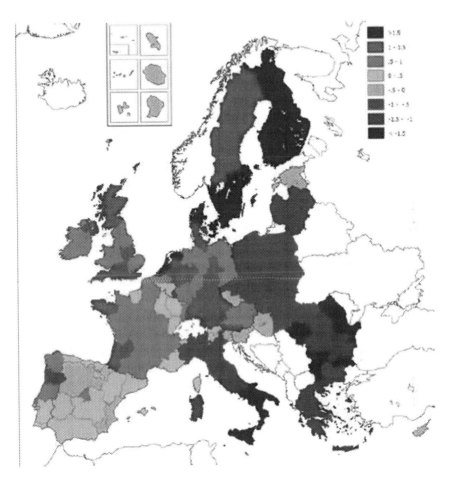

Fig. 6.6 "Combined corruption pillar with regional data." Source: Quality of Governance Institute 2010, p. 147

behavior reveal to have, more than average, the character dispositions—for example, selfish preferences, risk-taking attitudes, lack of morals and lack of respect of social norms—to rip other people off. Unlike law-abiding citizens, criminals cannot trust their partners' good character or socialization into pro-social norms: they are the first to expect little honor among thieves. It stands to reason that in order to thrive in business, the agents of corruption, who renounce by their very nature the option to resort to the law for redress, have to find some strategy to buttress their cooperation (Gambetta 2009: Chap. 2). Trust that their partners will neither cheat them nor turn them in. My general conjecture is that a solution of the puzzle could lie in some comparative advantage that Italians must have in this regard. What could this be?

The criminal quandary of whether or not to trust one's partners is far from having a perfect solution, and this deters many would-be criminals. Those who persist in engaging in crime make do in various ways (not mutually exclusive). Some criminals restrict their dealings to *family* circles, a reassuring choice that however imposes severe limitations on business expansion. Or they arm themselves and rely on the threat of *violence*—but, as I have argued in *Codes of the Underworld*, this solution while good for movies can be bad for business as it deters those potential partners who are too intelligent or too squeamish to get mixed up with a violent lot. Some other villains enjoy indefinitely *repeated interactions* that sustain their honest dealings—as the illegal lotto in Naples or the peculiar travel insurance that pay the fines of commuters caught traveling without a ticket which is found in Mumbai (Gambetta 2011: 153). Repeated interactions, however, sustain self-enforcing cooperation only if the law does not disrupt business continuity—to function it requires ineffective or corrupt law enforcement. The luckiest criminals of all are perhaps those who can count on stable and independent enforcing agencies, entrenched monopolies of violence with an incentive to provide even-handed protection to illegal transactions—aka *mafias* (Gambetta 1993). The lively fauna of mafias that has plagued Italy's southern regions for at least a century and a half provide a pseudo-government of the underworld: they enforce illegal deals, including corrupt deals, thus increasing the incentive to engage in them. They make corrupters and corruptees stick to their promises and refrain from cheating one another, while ensuring *omertà* and decreasing the chances of detection. These institutions give Italy a comparative advantage in terms of corruption.

Are mafias then the solution to our puzzle? There are two reasons to doubt it. First, while helping criminals, mafias impose a "tax" on legal transactions too; they stifle competition in the economy and in politics, worsen the quality of public services and public works, and encourage the exodus of creative and civic individuals. In other words, mafias may well explain the higher corruption levels in the south of Italy, but as their modus operandi is incompatible with economic development they do not explain the other horn of our puzzle. Next, mafia enforcement is not a necessary condition of corruption in Italy. Many cases that have come to the surface, even in recent times, have occurred in Milan and in Venice.[7] These cases involve vast networks of complicity and seem to have functioned well—till they were discovered of course—without third-party enforcement. How did the people involved manage to sustain their cooperation?

In earlier work I have identified another mechanism that solves the problem of criminal cooperation, and which does not require recourse to in-house violence or mafia protection; it benefits from but does not require repeated interactions either. It is the modern version of hostage exchange: instead of exchanging people what is exchanged is *compromising information* (Gambetta 2009: Chap. 3). This idea originates from an intuition of Thomas Schelling: consider the case, he wrote, in which "both the kidnapper who would like to release his prisoner, and the prisoner, may search desperately for a way to commit the latter against informing on his captor once released, without finding one". This is an instance in which two agents would like to agree on an action that leads to an outcome that they both prefer to all other outcomes, but one of them cannot trust the other's promises. The kidnapper in this case fears that once freed the victim will inform on him. Schelling proposed a solution: "If the victim has committed an act whose disclosure could lead to blackmail, he may confess it [to the kidnapper]; if not, he might commit one in the presence of his captor, to create the bond that will ensure his silence" (Schelling 1960: 43–44).

The example of the kidnapper is somewhat extreme and asymmetric for the victim already has compromising information on the kidnapper—that is the inevitable by-product of the kidnapper's crime. Only the victim needs to show evidence of her misdeeds to rebalance the situation thereby gaining the trust of the kidnapper. While inspiring, it is not the form typically taken by the exchange of compromising information. In criminal circles it is rather symmetric: all participants worry about each other's loyalty, and all disclose compromising information about themselves to one another. Just witnessing each other commit a joint crime, for instance, seals their bond. Mark Hiaasen, the thriller writer, summed up the strategy tersely: "The best part about this deal" [Eddie Marsh] said, "is that nobody's in a position to screw anyone else. You've got shit on me, I've got shit on you, and we've both plenty of shit on Snapper. That's why it's going down so clean" (1995: 234).

Schelling's solution identifies a counterintuitive case in which there is an advantage to opening up one's cupboard for others to see our skeletons. Worse still, the agents may have an interest in filling their cupboards with some skeletons, which may come in handy. The same reason that makes incriminating information best kept secret is also that which gives it its persuasive force. Sharing credible evidence of having done bad deeds makes us vulnerable and, because of that, makes our promises credible.

As an example let me quote the spiel that a researcher recruited by a public Italian institution received from the head of his unit: "You are deluding yourself if you think that your brilliant academic achievements in foreign universities matter for your career. You see, in order to be promoted and have career prospects I had to collect a thick dossier full of not so praiseworthy facts which make me blackmailable. This is my real asset, what guarantees to those who appoint me my loyalty, my pass for my career" (Anonymous, personal communication, my translation).

The advantages of SCI are considerable: as a means of enforcement it is cheap, for someone else once informed bears the cost of administering the punishment for you—it grows perversely in the shadow of the law or indeed of any normative system that punishes infractions. Unlike the very few people one cares about who could be sacrificed as hostages, there is plenty of raw material of potential infractions that one can use as compromising information. Evidence is easier to carry, to hide even just in one's head as a potential witness, and does not need to be fed. And it is more effective as the vulnerable person is not a relative as in the case of hostage exchange but the very agent of the transaction.

SCI has drawbacks to be sure. It can be difficult to initiate SCI "cold turkey" in ways that do not leave only one partner vulnerable to the other—"you go first", "no you go first!" kind of impasse. SCI is naturally exposed to sudden shocks that modify payoffs, for example, accidental disclosure, arrest, changes in the law de-penalizing previously prosecuted crimes—homosexuality, for instance, was likely the source of strong bonds of loyalty among politicians, but now in many countries this can no longer be the case. No criminal venture is deprived of risk. But on balance the advantages of this solution outweigh the disadvantages.

Over the years I have gathered diverse pieces of evidence of SCI at work, which I now summarize. A typical case concerns recruitment into illegal or extra-legal organizations that require loyalty: novices are required to commit bonding crimes that give recruiters evidence against them. This is a well-documented case in organized crime and in insurgents groups, but as the quotation above suggests, it may also permeate the dark side of otherwise legal organizations and political circles. A stark digital case can be gauged from the way in which pedophiles were admitted to join online networks of like-minded individuals—they had to supply a certain amount of *new* indecent pictures, which increased the asset of the group but also compromised the new members. Close to the topic of this paper, there is abundant evidence flowing from corruption trials and defendants' confessions that agents in corrupt networks ensure their loyalty through the potential damage they can inflict on one another by revealing their crimes (for details see Gambetta 2009: Chap. 3; many examples of how *kompramat* is used in Russian politics are in Ledeneva 2006: Chap. 3).

In another study Jennifer Flashman and I show that the SCI theory has a reach outside of career criminals' circles. We apply it to explain the patterns of homophily among deviant adolescents. Individuals who engage in deviant behaviors are more likely to be friends with other deviants compared to non-deviants—this pattern has been observed across different types of deviant activities and among different age groups. We test whether SCI theory can explain homophily among deviants. Deviance makes one vulnerable to the risk of being caught and sanctioned. This vulnerability imposes a stringent constraint on deviants, who must pick their friends from among people on whom they can solidly rely. We conjecture that a way to establish trust consists of making oneself "blackmailable" by disclosing compromising information of one's misdeeds. If two individuals share their illicit behaviors with one another, both are made vulnerable and a friendship can be established. Using data from the National Longitudinal Study of Adolescent Health in the US we estimate adolescents' preferences for deviant and non-deviant friends, within and across types of activities, and across different social contexts.

We find that (a) the more secretive an illicit activity, and thus the stronger the need to trust one's friends, the higher is the homophily, and that (b) the tougher the sanctions incurred for a certain infraction, and thus again the stronger the need to trust one's friends, the higher is the homophily. Taken together these tests allow us to distinguish the effect of SCI from that of alternative explanations of homophily (Flashman and Gambetta 2014).

The evidence above relies either on case studies or on observational data, which do not provide causal validity. This is why Wojtek Przepiorka and I tried to recreate the complicity of SCI in the lab to see if even in simplified artificial conditions naïve subjects grasp the strategic potential of it (Gambetta and Przepiorka 2016). Here is a summary of what we did. In a computerized laboratory experiment we ask subjects go through a series of dyadic interactions involving trust, without at first disclosing the details of the whole experiment; then we assign the label "dove" to subjects who prove cooperative in those interactions and the label "hawk" to the uncooperative subjects. In the remainder of the experiment subjects go through the same interactions again, and we vary whether

* subjects' labels are revealed to their interaction partners automatically or by their choosing (within-subject).
* hawks, who are revealed or make themselves known as such, can be inflicted a monetary penalty by their interaction partner (between-subject).

When labels are automatically revealed and without the possibility to inflict a penalty on hawks, we find that doves cooperate with doves but avoid hawks, whereas hawks seek to interact with both doves and hawks but, unlike doves, mostly defect. The cooperation rates among doves and among hawks are 63% and 23%, respectively.[8] Both these rates differ significantly from the cooperation rate in the control condition, in which all subjects interact not knowing the label of their partner.[9] This pattern hardly changes after subjects are given the choice to reveal their label before each interaction.

Once the option to penalize hawks is introduced, subjects' behavior changes dramatically. First, doves become less reluctant to interact and cooperate with hawks, but hawks, fearing the "stick", prefer to avoid doves. Second, if labels are automatically revealed the proportion of hawks, who cooperate with each other increases from 23% to 39%.[10] Finally, among hawks who choose to reveal their label, when revealing is an option, the cooperation rate increases further, from 39% to 67%.[11] The majority of hawks follow a rather blunt strategy: hide their label and defect. But a minority of hawks understand the strategic advantage of SCI and do so to cooperate with each other. These hawks know to use their sticks conditionally, that is only if the other does. Our results corroborate SCI.

Why Do Italians Do It better?

Although SCI seems to be employed far and wide, this says nothing about how it could solve our corruption puzzle. To argue that SCI is part of the solution, we need to argue that Italians somehow "do it better" than people in other countries: what are the conditions that could make it *easier* for Italians to rely on it?

Let us imagine that we want to build a mechanical device mimicking SCI optimal properties. (This amounts to building a homemade equivalent of the *Doomsday Machine*). Each party to a deal should have:

* a sword hanging over each party's head, which follows them around wherever they go;
* unique and private access to a button controlling the sword menacing the other party. By pressing the button each party can cause the sword to drop on the head of the other party;
* neither party can dodge the strike of the sword once released;
* no other force can cause the sword to be released—release is activated only by the buttons controlled by the parties;
* the buttons should have a short delay, short enough for a party not to avoid the strike but long enough to give time to the target party to realize the sword is falling and reach for his own button to retaliate.

There are two equilibria: indefinite truce or mutual destruction. The requirement to sustain the truce is the belief that neither party would refrain from retaliation if attacked. The case is similar, Schelling again, to "mutually assured destruction"—a theory applied to international relations especially after 1945 with the advent of nuclear weapons, and yet arguably so ubiquitous in an unarmed venial form in ordinary life to have remained invisible.

The ensemble of these five properties of our SCI device is not easy to come by in the real world, but my surmise is that the Italian situation approximates them. First of all, Italy is a country of myriad laws (Fig. 6.7). The legal landscape is inordinately large and bewilderingly complex, written in a convoluted obscure jargon that spreads uncertainty and allows manipulation. The surfeit of laws has two important consequences for our purposes. First, it is hard for Italians to go through a day without violating at least one law or even just *fearing* that they violated one unbeknownst to them. This causes an "overproduction" of compromising information, the raw material of SCI. Italians are, as it were, followed everywhere by lots of variedly sized swords that could fall on their head at any moment. As the majority of Hawks in our experiment, most Italians do not go

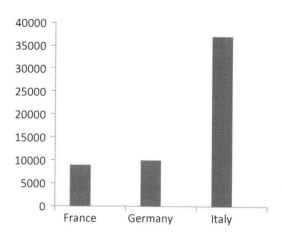

Sources: Servizio Studi Camera Deputati; Luigi Tivelli 2006

Fig. 6.7 Number of laws in three European countries

around advertising their infractions—they are nervous rather, fearful of the legal quagmire that may envelop them. Yet, most people have some "dirt" on some other people without even looking for it—they know of their landlords' tax evasion, of their neighbors' illegal building extensions, of their colleagues' shirking and of friends' cheating in exams, drink-driving, dope-smoking or patronizing prostitutes. The pervasiveness of relatively small infractions fosters a folk culture of *tacit complicity*. No one dares to turn anyone else in. (Two commonly heard injunctions up and down the peninsula are "mind your own business" and "don't cast the first stone"—we are all sinners and a bigger stone could come back and hit you). Most importantly for our puzzle, this broth gives people who can appreciate the strategic advantage of making good use of compromising information for criminal purposes, plenty of opportunities. This state of affairs satisfies condition (a) of our SCI device.

What about the other conditions? The second consequence of this congested legal setting is that law enforcement agencies and the judiciary are overburdened, which implies that they seldom can afford to pursue violations suo motu, with the exception of serious and violent crimes. This raises the probability of impunity, which may go somewhere toward explaining the Italian anomaly. But we should not forget that those who consider embarking on corrupt deals face two perils, being caught by the law is one of them, the other is being cheated by their partners. Impunity directly guards against the former. But to understand how impunity indirectly can guard against the latter we need to take the matter to a greater depth.

One could suppose that if law enforcement is made inefficient by being overburdened and impunity is high, then the potential blackmailing effect attached to violations evaporates. Information about violations would be compromising in theory only. I can shout as much as I like that I can prove that you are a crook, but if nobody takes any notice what is the point of SCI? But this is not so. For the probability of being caught and convicted for any one violation in an overburdened system comes to depend almost entirely on whether someone will inform the authorities and induce them to act rather than on the latter's independently initiated investigations. *The fear of sanctions becomes ancillary to the fear of someone informing on one.*

Even so, one might further suppose, an inefficient law enforcement is itself open to corruption, and this too could make the button malfunction as people could buy their way out of troubles. But this is not the case in Italy. Paradoxically, precisely because Italy has a largely independent and incorruptible law and order system, this system becomes a crucial cog that makes the SCI wheel turn smoothly. Italy has the worst judiciary that money cannot buy. It is the combination of being both overburdened *and* independent that makes the law liable to be exploited by SCI. It means that one can press the button—that is alert the law of a transgression—and get results. By informing on people one can trigger the response of the law and its unpleasant consequences. This satisfies conditions (b) and (c) of our SCI device.

This near-automaticity of the investigative process rests on the fact that the judiciary in Italy has a duty to open an investigation whenever it receives information of a crime (*notitia criminis*). This can occur not only when the police or a hospital personnel alert the prosecuting judges of a crime, but also when citizens report a crime of which they or a third party are the victim, or a media source uncover evidence of criminal activities. Even evidence received anonymously or from an undisclosed police informant, while not admissible in court, can nonetheless trigger an investigation.[12] Whenever one wants to reveal compromising evidence, effective disclosure still requires some ingenuity and care. An entrepreneur who typed an anonymous letter denouncing the members of the cartel to retaliate against his exclusion was identified through his typewriter by the *Carabinieri* and indicted with the rest. But disclosure can be awfully safe and simple too: an anonymous graffiti scribbled on the walls of a nursery in Lastre a Signa near Florence, Italy, sufficed to induce police to launch an investigation, which led to corruption charges against three civil servants.[13] The ease with which one can land someone else in trouble makes the threat derived from SCI credible, and discourages people from taking advantage of each other. So much so that the parties to corrupt deals seldom need to carry the threat out and release the compromising information.

Condition (d) is satisfied first and foremost by the dearth of suo motu investigations, but also by that of investigative journalism and the muffled freedom of the press (see Fig. 6.3): these conditions jointly decrease the chance that a sword will fall on someone's head independently of a SCI deals. Lastly, condition (e) is easily satisfied as at some point, often quite early on, one is informed by prosecutors that one is under investigation, and has ample opportunity to retaliate—he may even be encouraged to do so by the prosecutors eager to secure more convictions and ready to negotiate a sentence discounts for those who turn state witness.

When all these conditions are fulfilled it becomes not so risky for corrupters and corruptees to seek each other out—either of them can propose a deal with little fear the recipient will rush to turn him in lest he too gets turned in. And the consequence of pushing the "mutual destruction" buttons are so severe that by and large corrupt people will stick to their promises, or at least never deviate enough to motivate the other party to trigger the compromising information.

Conclusions

The five conditions that I described could support the lively corruption scene that makes Italy such an anomaly. But what about the other half of the puzzle, namely that the country is far more developed than its level of corruption would predict—why should SCI-driven corruption not be crippling, but just holding the country back, arguably keeping it on a slower growth path than it could otherwise enjoy?

By supporting anti-meritocratic practices antithetical to development—if for example public servants operate as in the case I reported above—I have little doubt that SCI is a major force in keeping institutions in a lamentable state. But here is the twist: by promoting corruption SCI works against economic development, yet SCI in itself is not applicable only to enforce criminal deals: this web of secret-sharing can sustain *any* contract. Why would that matter? Italians who wish to pursue perfectly normal businesses too need to trust their partners, and although unlike their criminal counterparts they can have recourse to the law when disputes arise, they are discouraged from doing so lightly by the slow Italian legal process (starkly illustrated in Fig. 6.8a and b). Ending up in court is not a prospect anyone cherishes, and makes settling business disputes extremely costly for entrepreneurs. The slowness of the legal

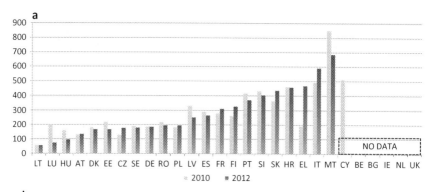

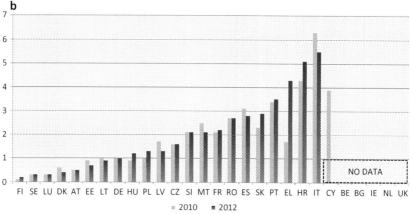

Fig. 6.8 **(a)** and **(b)** Pending cases in civil courts (in millions) and time to reach a verdict (in days). Source: graphs: http://www.eunews.it/2014/03/17/giustizia-italiana-penultima-in-ue-per-la-lentezza-e-ultima-per-il-numero-di-processi-pendenti/13462; the data of the graphs are from CEPEJ 2014

process should discourage people from going into business, and it most certainly does. So it seems something of a miracle that in spite of this institutional bottleneck Italy has had any economic growth at all.

My surmise is that the same web of complicity that sustains corruption might have a sunnier side and be a substitute to the slow justice system. While mafias exact a heavy cost on development, SCI is cheap, non-violent, manageable without third-party interference, and requires minimal organization. Nothing prevents people from exploiting SCI as a mutual insurance to cooperate in legal ventures (or play on both the legal and illegal table at the same time). People who would otherwise stay out of business may still embark on it thanks to SCI. It has often been noticed that Italians prefer to do business with people they know rather than with strangers, even if strangers might provide better quality. This is ascribed to the fact that people one knows are more trustworthy, but they are also people about whom one *knows* about their misdeeds and can ensure that they behave trustworthily. SCI does not need to operate upfront, it is not, except in extreme conditions, vented out crassly by nasty utterances, evoking threats, blackmail, complicity—it is often implicit, a reassuring backdrop of complicity. It is plausible that SCI might paradoxically help cooperation and entrepreneurship, and thus square the puzzling circle of corruption *cum* development.

I do not have an empirical test of this conjecture to propose. Broadly speaking, any law, whether introduced or abolished that affects behavior should have an impact on SCI by respectively increasing or restricting the raw material of it. Suppose for instance that alcohol prohibition was introduced in a country in which people are fond of drinking so that not many would be deterred. Drinkers would be pushed underground, but at the same time would acquire barrels of compromising information on each other that would strengthen their bonds. These bonds may remain within the confines of saloon banter and private friendship, but can also spill over into illegal business life. It is not easy to construct a test that exploits changes in the law, but perhaps not inconceivable either. There is however one question the answer to which may afford us easier progress: are there other countries which fulfill the same five conditions, and if so do they too have the same pattern of both high corruption and economic development? Treisman suggests a list of candidates that may be worth some collective examination: "Some countries have grown extremely rapidly in recent decades despite a perception that their states were highly corrupt. Among the fastest were China, South Korea, Thailand, India, and Indonesia" (2007: 19).

Finally, if SCI were the right explanation of the Italian anomaly would there be any policy implication? Reforming and simplifying the Italian legal system is a daunting task, even if politicians were of unshakeable determination and enjoyed solid majorities in parliament it could take generations. More modestly, with a logic akin to that suggested by "the broken window theory", one could invest more vigorously on combating the myriad smaller and easily observable infractions to dry up the swamps in which every day anti-legal complicity feeds and festers, rather than to persist in thinking that the task of an overburdened law and order system is to focus only on serious crimes. By reducing the expectation of impunity and the belief that suo motu one can be duly punished even for small violations, one would make citizens more wary of bigger violations, and weaken both the direct incentive to corruption offered by impunity and the perverse exploitation of the law on which SCI thrives.[14]

Comments by Juan Dubra, Universidad de Montevideo

Gambetta's interesting and well-written paper documents that Italy is both very corrupt, and very developed. This poses a puzzle "regardless" of our view of the relationship between corruption and development. If one thinks that corruption hinders development the puzzle is "how could such a corrupt country become so developed?" If one thinks that the fight against corruption is a normal good, so that rich countries tend to fight corruption because it does not look good, then the puzzle is "how can such a developed country tolerate so much corruption?" This form of the puzzle is also relevant to the view that a developed country would not foster corruption because of its reliance on the rule of law, competitive markets, a meritocracy in its bureaucracy and a free press.

Gambetta's conjecture is that the Italian environment is particularly good for producing "something" that produces both corruption and development. This something is the SCI. When two people know compromising things about each other it is possible to sustain transactions which on the one hand improve both parties' welfare, and on the other would not be possible in the absence of the mutual knowledge. To illustrate how revealing compromising information about oneself could be beneficial, imagine for example that one person wants to buy a car from another, but has no money now, and there are no good credit markets, and it is hard to recover the car in good condition if the buyer refuses to pay. If the current owner of the vehicle could implicitly or explicitly threaten the buyer with sending him to jail for something he did in the past, if the car is not paid in the future, the transaction could take place. Even though it seems like it would be bad for the buyer to have compromising information about him being known by others, in this case it would help him obtain the car. This example shows that making compromising information about oneself known can help in transactions; it does not illustrate the mutual SCI (more about this below). Still, in Gambetta's theory, SCI can improve welfare, or development and SCI also fosters corruption.

The article's hypothesis is that Italy is "unique" in its capacity for SCI to play an important role in both generating development and corruption. The reason is that a lot of compromising information is generated, and this promotes transactions, both corrupt and development-augmenting. Moreover, this information has no costs. I will focus on three aspects that according to Gambetta explain Italy's uniqueness in this regard.

* Lots of dirt being generated on everybody.
    - Lots of laws (and lawyers), with no enforcement because judiciary is overburdened, so "everybody" breaks laws all the time.
* It is easy to use it in a damaging way.
    - Clean judiciary responds when a bad deed is reported.
* If nobody "pulls the trigger" on you, dirt is harmless.
    - No good press, so bad deeds do not get aired.
    - Overburdened judiciary, so no investigation without finger-pointing.

Gambetta's theory is intriguing, and certainly has a truthiness to it. Still, as the paper's title makes clear, it is only a conjecture, and more empirical analysis is needed in order to establish whether SCI is in fact a cause of both high development and corruption. In order to guide my discussion, and where more empirical research might be needed, I will focus on three main points:

* I will argue that Uruguay has those "same" conditions that promote SCI according to Gambetta, but no corruption or development.
* In Gambetta's theory the link between conditions 1–3 above and corruption is not analysed in the paper. This points to the need of sharpening the conjecture, which might bring in new variables that would "kill" Uruguay as a counterexample to Gambetta's theory.
* As a general point, Gambetta's argument highlights the fact that some variables that might affect the level of corruption in a country have "complementarities": a high level of one variable generates corruption only if another variable is also high. For example, lots of laws are bad, only if the judiciary is overburdened (or there is no free press). In the empirical analysis of corruption such complementarities are often not central. This complementarity is not central in most analysis of the determinants of corruption, and in that sense Gambetta's paper is another illustration that theory should inform empirical exercises in this topic.

One way to stress test Gambetta's theory is to produce a country that has the same values in the explanatory variables ("right hand variables") as Italy, but the opposite outcome. Uruguay is one such case. Fig. 6.2 shows that Uruguay is both poorer and less corrupt than Italy.

In addition, in terms of explanatory variables, Uruguay is similar to Italy. One of the main drivers of SCI (or corruption, according to Tacitus) is the proliferation of laws, and lawyers. However, Uruguay has more lawyers per capita than Italy (see Fig. 6.9), and that is despite the fact that in Uruguay only about a third of kids finish high school, while in Italy that same number is 81%.

Also, while still lower than Italy (see Fig. 6.7), the number of laws in Uruguay is very high, about 20,000, that is even despite its young age. Although counting laws is admittedly a hard problem.

As another example of how laws and regulations make life "complicated", leading to the potential generation of compromising information,

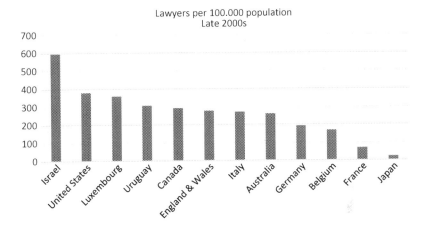

Fig. 6.9 Lawyers per 100,000 population during late 2000s. Source: Author's elaboration with data from Ramseyer and Rasmusen (2010), the Council of Bars and Law Societies of Europe, and Caja de profesionales del Uruguay

Table 6.1 Procedures, time and cost of opening a business

	Procedures	Time (in days)	Cost (% GDP p/c)
Italy	5	5.5	13.8
Uruguay	5	6.5	22

Source: Author's elaboration with data from World Bank's doing Business database

Table 6.1 illustrates the time, number of procedures and cost of opening a business in Italy and Uruguay.

I conclude with three comments that might help sharpen the theory, and validate it empirically.

I mentioned above the need to sharpen the theory in order to exclude a "counterexample" like Uruguay, and that might come from the exploration of how SCI also helps corruption: there may be features which make SCI good for corruption, which are not present in Uruguay. Another point that I would like to see studied further is how can (mutual) SCI foster legal transactions that would not happen otherwise. To be concrete, suppose two parties want to engage in a transaction in which either party can cheat the other and steal a sum of money $x (above what would be the normal profits of the activity). If SCI will support this transaction, parties have to share information which is more damaging to them than $x. In that case, it seems that the threat is "don't cheat on me, or I'll disclose what I know about you, and you will lose more than the $x you will have stolen from me". But if one of the partners cheats the other, he might say, "Now I have cheated on you. Don't reveal what you know about me, or I'll reveal what I know about you." Since for the cheated party there is no benefit ex post of revealing the information, it seems that SCI would not accomplish its ex ante objective.

In terms of validating Gambetta's theory, two avenues might be worth exploring. First, one can estimate again whether Italy is still an outlier in Treisman's 2000 estimates in terms of corruption (Fig. 6.4) if one includes in the analysis the variables that make for a good environment for SCI. Moreover, as pointed out earlier, one would have to include those variables in a way which is consistent with the theory, in terms of the complementarities that Gambetta points out.

Finally, an important aspect of Gambetta's theory is that an individual will not be prosecuted unless a finger is pointed in his or her direction. If Italy is characterized by a lot of SCI, and some contracts are breached, the number of trials started by finger-pointing should be higher than elsewhere. This would be an "observable" consequence of a lot of SCI going on. The general point I am trying to make is that one should look at observable consequences of SCI, and see whether these are more prevalent in Italy than elsewhere.

Concluding Remarks

The paper is very interesting, and the hypothesis put forward is quite intriguing. The data presented to support the conjecture is rich, and seems to point in the right direction. Of course, as the paper admittedly presents "only" a conjecture, some aspects of the theory need to be refined or clarified (what is the connection between SCI and corruption?), and a deeper understanding of the data is necessary.

Acknowledgements I would like to thank Valeria Pizzini Gambetta and Alberto Vannucci—as well as Avinash Dixit, Juan Dubra, Frank Fukuyama, Francesca Recanatini and the other participants in the IEA Roundtable—for their comments and suggestions.

Notes

1. Daniel Treisman points out that: "Italy's corruption rating fell sharply—by more than one and a half points on the Transparency International Index—between the early and mid-1990s, possibly because of the public outrage and judicial campaign against political corruption. But, for its level of economic development, democracy and openness to trade, Italy before these changes *had an abnormally high corruption rating*" (2000: 441–442, my italics). In that short period of time the judiciary came down the hardest on political corruption in an operation known as "Mani Pulite", causing a positive blip in the index; but since then matters have gone back to … abnormal.
2. For a comprehensive account see Vannucci 2012, esp. Chap. 3.
3. A new index, based on corruption cases prosecuted in one country but which occurred in a different country, proposed by Saarni Escresa and Lucio Picci, gives some evidence that the CPI may make Italian corruption seem worse than it is (2017).
4. An interesting bias in corruption beliefs is revealed by Olken (2009: 951): "Villagers in more ethnically heterogeneous villages are less likely to report trusting their fellow villagers, and more likely to attend project monitoring meetings, than those in homogeneous villages, which may explain why there is greater perceived corruption in heterogeneous villages but lower missing expenditures."
5. A different bias is mentioned by Treisman: "It is possible that the ratings we have been analysing measure not corruption itself but guesses about its extent in particular countries that experts or survey respondents have derived by applying conventional theories about corruption's causes, the same conventional theories that inform the hypotheses of researchers, which turn out—surprise!—to fit the data well. Believing democracy reduces corruption, the experts give high grades to democracies; researchers then discover that democracy predicts a low corruption rating" (2007: 32). Paradoxically, if this were the reason why we cannot rely on these indexes,

then the Italian case should be reassuring for these variables that explain corruption levels elsewhere, do not explain the Italian case well.

6. The results also confirm Chile as a positive anomaly, but not Uruguay, which is on the expected line.

7. See, for example, http://espresso.repubblica.it/inchieste/2014/06/09/news/confessate-a-milano-tangenti-per-tre-milioni-1.168631; http://corrieredelveneto.corriere.it/veneto/notizie/cronaca/2016/13-aprile-2016/tangenti-mose-via-processo-gli-imputati-matteoli-orsoni-240299413428.shtml; www.ilfattoquotidiano.it/2015/12/21/mose-a-giudizio-il-sistema-delle-tangenti-processo-per-lex-ministro-fi-matteoli-e-lex-sindaco-orsoni/2324332/.

8. $\chi^2(1) = 29.07$, $p < 0.001$.

9. 39% vs 63%: $\chi^2(1) = 18.75$, $p < 0.001$; 39% vs 23%: $\chi^2(1) = 8.52$, $p = 0.004$.

10. $\chi^2(1) = 4.58$, $p = 0.032$.

11. $\chi^2(1) = 4.13$, $p = 0.042$.

12. www.diritto.it/articoli/penale/chiaia.html.

13. http://firenze.repubblica.it/cronaca/2016/09/22/news/lastra_a_signa_il_pm_azzera_l_ufficio_tecnico_del_comune-148260467/.

14. The value of concentrating on preventing small acts of deviancy rests on different and deeper reasons, illustrated by evidence coming from neuroscience: "Behaviorally, we show that the extent to which participants engage in self-serving dishonesty increases with repetition. Using functional MRI, we show that signal reduction in the amygdala is sensitive to the history of dishonest behavior, consistent with adaptation. Critically, the extent of reduced amygdala sensitivity to dishonesty on a present decision relative to the previous one predicts the magnitude of escalation of self-serving dishonesty on the next decision. The findings uncover a biological mechanism that supports a 'slippery slope': what begins as small acts of dishonesty can escalate into larger transgressions" (Garrett et al. 2016: 1727).

References

Barr, Abigail, and Danila Serra. 2010. Corruption and Culture: An Experimental Analysis. *Journal of Public Economics* 94: 862–869.

Bosworth, Richard J.B. 2006. *Mussolini's Italy: Life Under the Dictatorship.* London: Penguin.

CEPEJ. 2014. Study on the Functioning of Judicial Systems in the EU Member States, Facts and Figures from the CEPEJ 2012–2014 Evaluation Exercise. European Commission for the efficiency of justice. http://ec.europa.eu/justice/effective-justice/files/cepj_study_scoreboard_2014_en.pdf

Charron, Nicholas. 2016. Do Corruption Measures Have a Perception Problem? Assessing the Relationship Between Experiences and Perceptions of Corruption Among Citizens and Experts. *European Political Science Review* 8: 147–117.

Escresa, Laarni, and Lucio Picci. 2017. A New Cross-National Measure of Corruption. *The World Bank Economic Review*: 31(1): 196–219.

Fisman, Raymond, and Edward Miguel. 2007. Corruption, Norms, and Legal Enforcement: Evidence from Diplomatic Parking Tickets. *Journal of Political Economy* 115: 1020–1048.

Flashman, Jennifer, and Diego Gambetta. 2014. Thick as thieves: Homophily and Trust among Deviants. *Rationality and Society* 26: 3–45.

Gambetta, Diego. 1993. *The Sicilian Mafia: An Industry of Private Protection*. Cambridge, MA: Harvard University Press.

———. 2009a. *Codes of the Underworld. How Criminals Communicate*. Princeton, NJ: Princeton University Press.

———. 2011. "Response" to 'Roundtable on Codes of the Underworld. *Global Crime* 12: 150–159.

Gambetta, Diego, and Wojtek Przepiorka. 2016. Sharing Compromising Information: How 'Crime' Begets Cooperation in the Lab. Unpublished manuscript, European University Institute.

Garrett, Neil, Stephanie C. Lazzaro, Dan Ariely, and Tali Sharot. 2016. The Brain Adapts to Dishonesty. *Nature Neuroscience* 19: 1727–1732.

Hiaasen, Carl. 1995. *Stormy Weather*. New York: Alfred A. Knopf.

Ledeneva, Alena. 2006. *How Russia Really Works: The Informal Practices That Shaped Post-Soviets Politics And Business*. Ithaca: Cornell University Press.

Olken, Benjamin A. 2009. Corruption Perceptions vs. Corruption Reality. *Journal of Public Economics* 93: 950–964.

Quality of Government Institute. 2010. *Measuring the Quality of Government and Subnational Variation*. Report for the European Commission Directorate-General Regional Policy Directorate Policy Development, Department of Political Science, University of Gothenburg, Sweden.

Ramseyer, J. Mark, and Eric Rasmusen. 2010. *Comparative Litigation Rates*. Cambridge, MA: Harvard Law School.

Razafindrakoto, Mirelle, and François Roubaud. 2010. Are International Databases on Corruption Reliable? A Comparison of Expert Opinion Surveys and Household Surveys in Sub-Saharan Africa. *World Development* 38: 1057–1069.

Ricciuti, Roberto, and Ilaria Petrarca. 2013. The Historical Economics of Corruption and Development Within Italy. *International Journal of Monetary Economics and Finance* 6: 186–202.

Schelling, Thomas. 1960. *The Strategy of Conflict.* Cambridge, MA: Harvard University Press.

Tivelli, Luigi. 2006. *La fiera delle leggi.* Bologna: Il Mulino.

Treisman, Daniel. 2000. The Causes of Corruption: A Cross-National Study. *Journal of Public Economics* 76: 399–457.

———. 2007. What Have We Learned About the Causes of Corruption from Ten Years of Cross-National Empirical Research? *Annual Review of Political Science* 10: 211–244.

Vannucci, Alberto. 2012. *Atlante della corruzione.* Torino: Edizioni Gruppo Abele.

7

Cohesive Institutions and the Distribution of Political Rents: Theory and Evidence

Timothy Besley and Hannes Mueller

Introduction

The past twenty years have seen a transformation in the way economists think about economic development routinely bringing in insights from political economy. Moreover, the idea that effective institutions lie behind

Paper prepared for the roundtable on Institutions, Governance and Corruption organized by IEA and RIDGE in Montevideo, Uruguay on May 26–27, 2016. We are grateful to the conference participants, especially our discussant Steve Knack, for comments.

T. Besley (✉)
LSE, Houghton Street, London, UK

CIFAR, Toronto, ON, Canada
e-mail: t.besley@lse.ac.uk

H. Mueller
IAE (CSIC), Barcelona, Spain

MOVE, Barcelona, Spain

GSE, Barcelona, Spain
e-mail: hannes.mueller@iae.csic.es

© The Author(s) 2018
K. Basu, T. Cordella (eds.), *Institutions, Governance and the Control of Corruption*, International Economic Association Series,
https://doi.org/10.1007/978-3-319-65684-7_7

the economic development process is now widely accepted by economists and political scientists alike. Yet there is still much debate about the mechanisms at work and the kinds of policy distortions that are important. Knowledge that is widely applicable is most likely to be made by developing models of policy making and assessing their empirical relevance.

This paper discusses the role of institutions in distributing the benefits from government spending. We look at a world where two sets of institutions can affect policy outcomes building from the simple model of Besley and Persson (2011a). First, there are those institutions which affect access to political power. This would include at one extreme rules of hereditary succession and at the other processes for conducting open, free and fair elections. Broadly speaking, the history of political development in the past two hundred years has been to open up access to political office and the introduction of elections where all citizens are eligible to run for office and the franchise encompasses all adult citizen. Second, there are institutions that regulate how power is used once it has been acquired. These include the processes for achieving legislative approval for policy decisions and the framework of law within which policy is made. Particularly important is whether there is a framework of independently enforced rights which the policy process must respect. Besley and Persson (2011a) formalize the idea of cohesive institutions and argue that strong executive constraints are a crucial component. As in the case of openness, the direction of travel over the past two centuries has been toward more constraints on executive power and a stronger role of independent judicial authority.

Whether it is openness or executive constraints at issue, how policy outcomes are affected by political systems is a function of both formal and informal rules. Whether there is electoral intimidation, control of the media or a threat of violence by an incumbent if he loses support is an equilibrium outcome rather than a function purely of the rules. Many closed systems, such as USSR, held elections but under highly restricted conditions and there are many de facto one-party systems in the world. Whether there is real legislative oversight is similarly a function of the way that the game of politics is played. The same goes for judicial oversight which depends on how judges are selected and whether they can be overruled by politicians. As late as the 1930s in the United States, there was still a question of where the limits of supreme court power lie and this has been established over time through the interplay of judicial and executive authority.[1]

A second contribution of the paper is to try to build an explicit link between institutional choices and the distribution of resources across groups with a focus on the welfare properties of different institutional arrangements. There are basically two distinct normative approaches to democratic institutions. The first is an intrinsic value tradition which argues from the nature of human agency.[2] The second argues for democracy more from the instrumental benefits that it brings. For example, democracy can make governments more responsive to the preferences of citizens which lead to better social provision. The latter is more appealing from a traditional welfare-economic approach. Here we develop a normative approach based on a Rawlsian view, specifically we look at how well groups do based on a "worst case scenario" where they are politically powerless. We discuss how this perspective can be used to make a normative case for strong executive constraints.

After developing a simple model of resource allocation, we look at the link between political institutions and between-group inequality. The underlying data for this exercise come from the geographical distribution of luminosity at night which can be used to look at ethnic group inequality by linking this to maps of the homelands of specific groups. We find that having strong executive constraints is associated with less inequality between ethnic groups. We then look at within-country variation in institutions and exploit differences across ethnic groups according to whether they are politically excluded. We find that it is politically excluded groups which benefit particularly from strong executive constraints.

This paper is tied to debates about the use and abuse of political power. The state is frequently used to pursue private interest with some individuals or groups benefitting from having control of some aspects of policy. At one extreme, this can lead to personal enrichment in the form of corruption which is widely condemned. The case of political rents due to office holding is more of a grey area. To the extent that these compensate for historical disadvantage, then allocating these rents toward groups in power could be normatively justified. Indeed, a range of initiatives to increase the representation of traditionally disadvantaged groups are in place such as ethnic, gender or caste quotas. However, there is also a dark side to political favoritism. Favoritism can harm the efficiency of the allocation of state spending and, even worse, can destabilize the state, particularly when a political elite is entrenched. The instrumental benefit of institutional constraints is best seen in this context. Even if the political rents distributed are not illegal, they are a source of long run inequalities which, if not held in check, can fracture otherwise stable polities.

The remainder of the paper is organized as follows. In the next section, we discuss some background literature and issues. Section "Theory" discuss some background theory and Section "Evidence" looks at the data. Section "Concluding Comments" offers some concluding comments.

Background

Who gets benefits from government spending is a classic issue in political economy. This has been studied in the voluminous literature known as the study of "distributive politics" among political scientists. While this originated in studying the U.S., there is now a much wider interest in these issues across a range of countries (see Golden and Min 2013, for a recent review). As conventionally modeled, for example by Dixit and Londregan (1996) and Lindbeck and Weibull (1987), two parties who compete for office make promises of transfers as a means of enhancing their electoral chances. Hence, the main focus is on *pre-election* politics and the promises that are made. A key issue is whether parties tend to target loyal supporters or swing voters. In the basic models, political control does not matter per se as this simply involves fulfilling pre-election pledges.

In the basic models, little attention has been paid to what makes electoral promises credible. Lack of commitment implies a tendency for winners to favor their own group regardless of any pre-election promises as in Besley and Coate (2003). Selection of candidate types then becomes a core issue. This perspective is particularly relevant for studying ethnic politics. Moreover, within-country studies of resource allocation find strong evidence of ethnic favoritism. For example, Franck and Rainer (2012) find, using the spatial variation in the micro data of the Demographic and Health Surveys (DHS) that ethnic leaders in Africa appear to target their own ethnic groups when in power. Hodler and Raschky (2014) use satellite data in a panel of more than 38,000 sub-national regions in 126 countries for the years 1992–2009 to show that luminosity is higher in the birthplace of a country's political leader. They also show that this effect is attenuated in countries with higher polity scores.[3] We will use data from Alesina et al. (2016) which has mapped ethnic inequality within countries with a particular focus on how endowments affect ethnic inequality.

Also relevant to this paper is the large literature on the consequences of institutional reform for patterns of development. In particular, there is an interest in how and why democratization matters where the Polity IV project has provided a way of tracking patterns of institutional change in some detail. It is now well appreciated, see for example Persson and Tabellini (2008), that the relationship linking growth and development is quite heterogeneous with the possibility of two-way causality between growth and institutions. Moving beyond growth, a range of outcome measures have been studied. For example, Burgess et al. (2015) provide a case study for Kenya which also shows that democratization affects the allocation of road spending. Kudamatsu (2012) uses the DHS data to show that democracy has reduced infant mortality in Africa.

A growing theme in the political economy literature is the need to disaggregate institutions beyond a unidimensional democracy index. This has emerged from both theoretical and empirical studies. Besley and Persson (2011a) suggest a simple bivariate classification between institutions which affect access to power (openness) and institutions which regulate use of power (executive constraints). On a world scale, openness and strong executive constraints have both become more widespread over the past two centuries, executive constraints lag behind openness. This can be seen in Fig. 7.1, which comes from the Polity IV data where we measure strong executive constraints as a dummy variable which is equal to one when a country in a given year receives the highest score on this basis (on a seven-point scale) and openness as dummy variable which is equal to one if a country receives the highest score (on a four-point scale). We graph the fraction of countries in the dataset which receive the highest score on each indicator for two groups of countries: the fifty countries that were in that data, i.e. were independent polities, in 1875 and all countries in the data. The latter has countries entering the data over time, e.g. as they become independent entities. The pattern is quite consistent with both types of institutions growing but with openness ahead of executive constraints.

This disaggregation is underpinned by theory as we shall see below. Besley and Persson (2011a) observed that cohesiveness is related to executive constraints and is related to the incentive to build state capacity. However, this is not so true of openness; a more open political system may simply increase political instability. Besley and Persson (2011b) argues that strengthening executive constraints is particularly important in thinking about incentives for political violence. This echoes Collier (2009) who has argued that elections can be problematic in a polarized environment when there is a "winner takes all" structure. More generally, it reinforces the need to think about components of liberal democracy in its widest sense with a more central role for the rule of law and what sustains it as argued, for example, in Fukuyama (2011) and Mukand and Rodrik (2015).[4]

In fact, this argument has a much older provenance. Some of the earliest discussion of democratic institutions were concerned about the "tyranny of the majority" as a consequence of elections whereby the winning group governs in its own interests to the detriment of those excluded from power. Beginning with John Adams in practical debates around the founding of the United States, it was taken up by Alexis de Tocqueville and J.S. Mill. Separation of powers can help by preventing one group capturing all spheres of government. Mill (1859), for example, described a limit to the power of a ruler that can be achieved through "[…] establishment of constitutional checks, by which the consent of the community, or of a body of some sort, supposed to represent its interests,

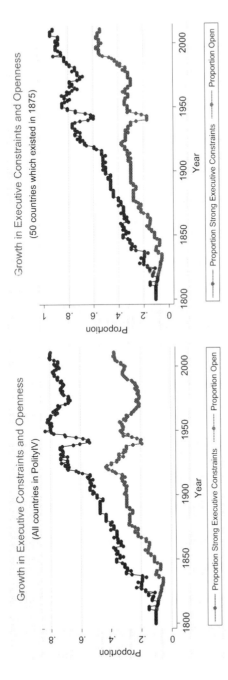

Fig. 7.1 Executive Constraints and Recruitment. **Notes**: Source: Besley and Persson (2017). The data come from the Polity IV website http://www.systemicpeace.org/polityproject.html. For executive constraints, we use xconst which is measured by a dummy variable which is equal to 1 if the value of this variable in a given country-year is equal to 7; for openness, we use xropen which is measured by a dummy variable which is equal to 1 in a given country-year is equal to 4. The left-hand panel is for all countries which are in the Polity IV dataset in 1875 and the right-hand panel for all countries in the data in a given year

was made a necessary condition to some of the more important acts of the governing power." However, strong legal protection of minorities upheld by courts and long-run players such as established political parties which act as broad coalitions of interests can also help to diminish the concern that government is run in the interests of narrow group. Here we show that executive constraints are important in explaining lower ethnic inequality and in raising the incomes of politically excluded groups building on Mueller and Tapsoba (2016) who find that the exclusion from executive power translates into decreases in night-light but only in absence of institutional constraints on the executive.

We make use of data derived from light density at night per capita to measure the distribution of income across groups. This approach follows Henderson et al. (2012) who show that a 100% increase in night light density per capita is associated with around a 30% increase in GDP per capita. A range of studies, such as Alesina et al. (2016) and Michalopoulos and Papaioannou (2014), have used these data to look at spatial development patterns and historical institutions. This is useful since it is difficult otherwise to get at the spatial distribution of income within a country. This is particularly influential in the literature on ethnic conflict where it is possible to exploit locational differences in conflict and relate these to economic outcomes. This has been exploited, for example, in Girardin et al. (2015) and Cederman et al. (2010).

Our welfare criterion will be informed by a maxmin approach in which we worry about the ethnic groups which are politically excluded. In this we follow Rawls (1971) who made the argument that decisions taken behind a veil of ignorance would pay more attention to downside risks in society. Behind the veil of ignorance each member of society might worry about the members of society who are worst off. Second, there could be important externalities arising from politically and economically excluded groups. The maxmin criterion then arises from a desire for robustness.

There is an important issue that we do not cover in this paper, namely the concern that political conflict can arise from ethnic inequality.[5] Besley and Persson (2011b) argue that strong executive constraints might prevent political conflict because the incentives to capture the state are diminished. Goldstone et al. (2011) and Michalopoulos and Papaioannou (2016) show that discrimination of ethnic groups implies a higher likelihood of conflict. The cautiousness implied by a maximin approach would only strengthen our argument in the context if strong constraints were able to limit the risk of descent into violence.

Theory

In this section, we develop a simple conceptual framework to think through the issues. In the model, which is based on Besley and Persson (2011a), an ethnic group is in power and political institutions affect the probability that a group is in power as well as constraining the use of power once acquired.

Set-Up There are M groups each with population share σ_i labeled so that $\sigma_1 > \cdots > \sigma_M$. In each period one group is the incumbent group which controls the government which has access to revenue per capita τ. This tax revenue can be spent on private transfers or public goods. The per capita transfer made to the ruling group is T while that made to other groups is t and spending on the public good whose price is normalized to one is denoted by G. Hence the government budget constraint when group k is in power is:

$$\tau = G + \sigma_k T + (1 - \sigma_k)\, t. \tag{7.1}$$

Preferences in each group are identical and denoted by:

$$\alpha \phi\,(G) + x_i$$

where x_i is private consumption in group i. The income of group i is y_i. We suppose that all groups pay τ per capita in taxes. The focus here is exclusively on between group inequality so we allow the income to be the same in each group.

Institutions There are two aspects of institutions. First, there is an ex post restriction on the use of power which we refer to as cohesiveness as in Besley and Persson (2011a). This says that for every dollar of transfers that the incumbent makes to its group it has to give $\theta \in [0, 1]$ dollars to the other groups. Hence, if $\theta = 1$, there is full equality while if $\theta = 0$, the incumbent "takes" all. From an empirical point of view, we think of θ as reflecting executive constraints. However, as we argue further below, it could also reflect informal constraints on behavior due to social norms.

The way that we model this is somewhere between the two extreme views of how legislative institutions distribute local public goods and transfers that have been developed in the literature.[6] At one extreme, legislative politics is governed by minimum winning coalitions as emphasized, for example, by Buchanan and Tullock (1962), Riker (1962), and Baron and Ferejohn (1989), there will always be a group comprising around 50% of legislators which then chooses policy. This would be wider than a single group deciding policy but would still exclude some groups. The alternative is a more cooperative legislature as modeled by Weingast (1979) and Weingast et al. (1981). On the limit this view gives no advantage to the insider at all with all groups getting an equal share. But it is important to recall that executive constraints is wider than just legislative institutions as it includes judicial or constitutional protection available to excluded groups.

The second aspect of institutions regulates access to power. Thus, let γ_i be the probability that group i holds office. The most closed system is where $\gamma_i = 1$ for a single group. The most open system would arguably be one where $\gamma_i = 1/M$ for all i so that each group has equal access to power regardless of group size.

As in the case of θ, we expect these parameters to reflect a mixture of formal and informal rules. Thus, the case where $\gamma_i = 1$, and there is a monopoly ruling group this is likely to reflect a range of factors possibly including repression. Control of media outlets is a frequent device for controlling electoral processes beyond more crude devices such as intimidating candidates and voters. All of these are likely in practice to affect the allocation of power in a political system. Almost every country in the world holds some form of elections so formal openness and real contests for power are likely to be only loosely correlated.

Policy Choice Suppose that group k is in power and consider its policy choice. Since executive constraints bind then $t = \theta T$. Using this in (7.1), its decision problem boils down to selecting G such that[7]

$$G_k^* (\theta, \alpha, \tau) = \arg\max \left\{ \alpha \phi (G) - \frac{G}{\sigma_k + (1 - \sigma_k) \theta} \right\}.$$

Define

$$\alpha \phi' \left(\hat{G}_k (\theta, \alpha) \right) = \frac{1}{\sigma_k + (1 - \sigma_k) \theta}.$$

Then the level of public goods provided is:

$$G_k^* (\theta, \alpha, \iota) = \min \left\{ \hat{G}_k (\theta, \alpha), \tau \right\}.$$

It is immediate that this is (weakly) increasing in θ. So executive constraints increase spending on public goods and reduce transfer spending. Using this, the level of utility of group j when it is in power is:

$$V_{kk}^I (\theta, \alpha, \tau) = \alpha \phi \left(G_k^* (\theta, \alpha, \tau) \right) + \frac{\tau - G_k^* (\theta, \alpha, \tau)}{\sigma_k + (1 - \sigma_k) \theta} + y_k - \tau$$

for the incumbent and

$$V_{jk}^N (\theta, \alpha, \tau) = \alpha \phi \left(G_k^* (\theta, \alpha, \tau) \right) + \theta \frac{\tau - G_k^* (\theta, \alpha, \tau)}{\sigma_k + (1 - \sigma_k) \theta} + y_j - \tau$$

for others. Thus the value of being in power, i.e. the political rent is:

$$V_{kk}^I (\theta, \tau, \alpha) - V_{jk}^N (\theta, \tau, \alpha) = (1 - \theta) \frac{\tau - G_k^* (\theta, \alpha, \tau)}{\sigma_k + (1 - \sigma_k) \theta} \geq 0.$$

Thus the model makes precise the link between θ and political rents which are lower with strong executive constraints. In the limiting case where it is infeasible for the incumbent group to favor itself, $\theta = 1$, then all tax revenues are spent on public goods and the group receives no rents from holding power.

Dynamic Implications Since we wish to look at data drawn from a number of years, we now add a temporal dimension to the model. Suppose then that we consider a dynamic model with date $s = 1, 2, \ldots$ and that there is an impact of past transfers on future incomes. We do not specify why this is true but there a variety of micro-foundations. One possibility is to think of T_i being partly in the form of an investment in a productivity enhancing local public good. Suppose, specifically, that income in group i at date s is

$$y_{is} = Y_i + \sum_{u=1}^{s-1} \lambda^{s-u} m_{iu}$$

so Y_i is a group-specific source of economic advantage or an endowment and λ is a "persistence" parameter where

$$m_{iu} = \begin{cases} \tau - G_i^* \, (\theta, \alpha, \tau) & \text{if group } i \text{ is in power at date } u \\ \theta \left[\tau - G_j^* \, (\theta, \alpha, \tau) \right] & \text{if group } j \neq i \text{ is in power at date } u. \end{cases}$$

This formulation will imply that there are persistent effects from past political control. This is important as it is likely that data on group-inequality will reflect this amplifying the consequences of long-term political exclusion.

The Distribution of Consumption Total consumption of group i at date s is

$$X_{is} = y_{is} - \tau + m_{is} + G_s$$

where G_s varies exclusively due to switches in political control.[8] The share of total income of group i at date s is

$$\chi_{is} = \frac{X_{is}}{\sum_{j=1}^{M} \sigma_j X_{js}} = \frac{y_{is} - \tau + m_{is} + G_s}{\sum_{j=1}^{M} \sigma_j y_{js}}$$

$$= \frac{y_{is} - \tau + m_{is} + G_s}{\sum_{j=1}^{M} \sigma_j y_{js} + G_s}.$$

This will reflect an immediate advantage due to m_{is} being greater from holding office and a longer term advantage due to past transfers if a group has been in office before. So if $\theta < 1$, then political control which favors one group generates a permanent advantage.

Inter-Group Inequality and the Allocation of Political Power One simple way of thinking about access to power is to distinguish between two groups: the politically powerful where $\gamma_i > 0$ and the politically excluded where $\gamma_i = 0$. Let $\delta_i = 1$ denote being a member of a politically powerful group. The distribution of income will now reflect the distribution of political control.

A simple ex ante measure of between group inequality is

$$\Delta = \left[\sum_i \sigma_i \left[\frac{\delta_i y_{is}}{\sum_j \delta_j \sigma_j} - \frac{(1 - \delta_i) y_{is}}{\sum_j [1 - \delta_j] \sigma_j} \right] \right]$$

$$+ \sum_i \sigma_i \left[\frac{\delta_i \left[\gamma_i [\tau - G_i] + \sum_{\ell \neq i} \gamma_\ell [\tau - G_\ell] \theta \right]}{\sum_j \delta_j \sigma_j [\sigma_i + (1 - \sigma_i) \theta]} \right.$$

$$\left. - \frac{(1 - \delta_i) \theta \sum_\ell \gamma_\ell [\tau - G_\ell]}{\sum_j [1 - \delta_j] \sigma_j [\sigma_i + (1 - \sigma_i) \theta]} \right]$$

The first term is a long-run effect of political power on income and the second a short-term effect reflecting differences in transfers at date s. Both of these terms depend upon the distribution of political control. Note that since group specific control is a sufficient statistic for G the second term does not depend explicitly on time.

If there is a single ruling group, k, the latter term collapses to

$$\frac{[\tau - G_k](1 - \theta)}{\sigma_k + (1 - \sigma_k)\theta}$$

which is decreasing in θ.

More generally, one construct a range of inequality measures on between-group inequality. We will mainly use the between-group Gini coefficient which corresponds to a social welfare function which has rank order weights and for a vector of income per capita by group $x_{1s}, \ldots, x_{2s}$, is:

$$W(x_{1s}, \ldots, x_{2s}) = \frac{1}{M}\left(M + 1 - 2\frac{\sum_i (M + 1 - i) x_{is}}{\sum_i x_{is}}\right).$$

Below we will explore how these are related to executive constraints at the country level (which we think of as capturing variation in θ) and openness (which we think of as telling us something about cross country variation in $\{\gamma_i\}_{i=1}^{M}$).

A Rawlsian Approach to Cohesive Institutions We now explore the case for cohesive institutions, as represented by higher θ using a Rawlsian argument. This would suggest comparing institutions based on a comparison of institutions behind the veil of ignorance where no group is certain of its place in the polity, in particular whether it will enjoy political power.

We will suppose that there is a range of possible polities $\theta_1, \ldots, \theta_P$ ordered so that $\theta_P > \cdots > \theta_1$ so that polity P is the most cohesive society. We also suppose that there is a range of possible patterns of political control $c = 1, \ldots, C$ where $C > M$ in each society $\left\{\{\gamma_{ic}\}_{i=1}^{M}\right\}_{c=1}^{C} \in \Gamma$. We suppose that $C > M$ and make the following key assumption:

Assumption   For all i, there exists c such that $\gamma_{ic} = 0$.

This says that each group has to contemplate political exclusion in each possible society. We will consider what kind of society will be preferred.

Since choice is behind the veil of ignorance, we suppose that the exact pattern of political control is uncertain for each group. Thus it has to form beliefs about expected political control. A conventional decision-making approach would be to allow each group to form a subjective probability distribution over its prospects of being politically powerful. Were this the case, there would be a conflict of interest behind the veil of ignorance with groups which expect to be powerful preferring lower θ while those with low prospects of holding power prefer θ to be high.

To capture the spirit of Rawls, we suppose that there is uncertainty over political control in the Knightean sense and follow the suggestion of Gilboa and Schmeidler (1989) to use the max min expected utility criterion which motivates the criterion used by a Rawlsian paradigm. However, the test here is quite specific based on uncertainty about the allocation of political control.[9]

The procedure that we have described here will yield unanimity in the institutional choice, leading to a preference for the polity where θ_p is highest. This is because the worst case for each group is political exclusion. In this case, the payoff of group i when group $k \neq i$ is in power in society p is

$$y_{is} - \tau + \alpha\phi\left(G_k\right) + \frac{\theta_p\left(\tau - G_k\right)}{\sigma_k + \left(1 - \sigma_k\right)\theta_p}$$

which is increasing in θ_p for all i, k. Thus, each group will prefer to have the highest possible value of θ_p. This argument is summarized in:

Proposition 1. *With uncertainty about the allocation of political control a Rawlsian approach to institutional choice yields a unanimous preference for a polity where θ_p is highest.*

This reasoning underpins a normative approach to cohesive institutions which is directly linked to the distribution of political rents. Once the comparison is made for $\gamma_{ic} = 0$, then there is unanimity since every excluded group will prefer to have the highest value of θ_p no matter whichever other group is in power.

This analysis can be tied into an observation in Rawls (1971) who says that:

> the effects of injustices in the political system are much more grave and long lasting than market imperfections. Political power rapidly accumulates and becomes unequal; and making use of the coercive apparatus of the state and its law, those who gain the advantage can often assure themselves of a favored position. …Universal suffrage is an insufficient counterpoise; for when parties and elections are financed not by public funds but by private contributions, the political forum is so constrained by the wishes of the dominant interests that the basic measures needed to establish just constitutional rule are seldom properly presented. …We are in the way of describing an ideal arrangement, comparison with which defines a standard for judging actual institutions, and indicates what must be maintained to justify departures from it.

It is clear from this that Rawls understood that openness, which he refers to in the form of universal suffrage, is not sufficient for justice to prevail. The notion of cohesiveness here tries to capture this element of Rawlsian justice.

While this is an attractive argument, it is developed for a stylized model. However, the reasoning seems quite general—finding ways of creating greater universalism in the use of political power will be attractive to groups who have little chance of holding agenda setting power in government. This could explain why the kind of norm of universalism in the U.S. congress studied by Weingast (1979) could emerge as a norm to improve the resilience of a political system by creating a stake for politically excluded groups.[10]

This result motivates an empirical exercise developed below which looks at the fate of politically excluded ethnic groups and whether they do better in countries with more cohesive institutions. If they do, then we can use this as the basis of a normative argument for strengthening cohesiveness based on the reasoning that we have developed here.

Evidence

Data We use two sources of data as measures of between-group inequality. The first is from Alesina et al. (2016) who construct the measures of ethnic inequality based on aggregating (via the Gini coefficient formula) luminosity per capita across the homelands of ethnic groups. For this, they use two different approaches for identifying the groups. The first is the Georeferencing of Ethnic Groups (GREG) data which is the digitized version of the Soviet Atlas Narodov Mira (Weidmann et al. 2010). This portrays the homelands of 928 ethnic groups around the world for the early 1960s. The second source is the 15th edition of the Ethnologue (Gordon 2005) that maps 7581 language-country groups worldwide in the mid/late 1990s, using the political boundaries of 2000. The Gini coefficient for a country's population then consists of a set of groups with values of luminosity per capita for the historical homeland of each group. This gives two sets of cross-sectional data, one for each underlying ethnic atlas, on the Gini coefficient across ethnic groups within a country based on night-light per capita for 155 countries in 2010. Alesina et al. show that this inequality reflects differences in geographic attributes across ethnic homelands. We will include their variable on the inequality in geographical endowments as a control below.

The second source of data is the unified platform for geographical research on war (GROW^{up}). This comes from Girardin et al. (2015) who merge and update data on Ethnic Power Relations (EPR) from Cederman et al. (2010) with data on night light emissions (NOAA-NGDC, 2013). The data covers 564 ethnic groups in 130 countries in the period 1992–2010. The dataset covers all countries with the exception of failed states, overseas colonies and countries with fewer than 500,000 people. It includes all politically relevant ethnic groups; with an ethnic group being classified as relevant if at least one political organization claims to represent it in national politics or if its members are subject to political discrimination by the state. It gives us yearly panel data on access to political power and night light emissions as well as interpolated population data. The data also captures access to power documenting participation of members of relevant ethnic groups in the executive. Here there are seven subcategories: discriminated, powerless, self-excluded, junior partner, senior partner, dominant and monopoly. These categories are intended to capture how well the group is represented in the executive of a country. Thus, if a group is coded as having a monopoly, then elite members from this group hold monopoly power in the executive to the exclusion of members of other ethnic groups. A group classified as being a junior partner means that representatives of the group share access to executive power with a more powerful group. We will categorize groups as excluded if they are discriminated, powerless or self-excluded.

As our core measures of institutions, we merge these data with Polity IV measures of strong executive constraints where we create a dummy variable that is equal to one if the variable *xconst* is equal to 7 and high openness which is a dummy variable equal to one if the variable *xropen* is equal to 4. We will interpret these, following Besley and Persson (2011a) as measures of the theoretical parameters θ and γ. However, they are only proxy measures for a variety of reasons, not least because they are largely attempts to capture formal rules. Both are measured at a country-level for each year.

To get a feel for what the variable captures, a good starting point is the Polity IV code book which describes the construction of *xconst* as follows:

> Operationally, this variable refers to the extent of institutionalized constraints on the decision making powers of chief executives, whether individuals or collectivities. Such limitations may be imposed by any "accountability groups." In Western democracies these are usually legislatures. Other kinds of accountability groups are the ruling party in a one-party state; councils of nobles or powerful advisors in monarchies; the military in coup-prone polities; and in many states a strong, independent judiciary. The concern is therefore with the checks and balances between the various parts of the decision-making process.

This makes intuitive sense as a way of measuring constraints on incumbent power and hence a reasonable candidate measure of θ. The case of *xconst* equal to 7 is where "accountability groups have effective authority equal to or greater than the executive in most areas of activity".

We will investigate whether this way of capturing constraints is correlated with the distribution of resources across groups remains to be seen. Even though it has a clearly-defined rationale, a cut-off threshold of 7 for this variable is somewhat arbitrary. Below, we will check what happens if we use a lower threshold to capture "strong" executive constraints.

Measuring the nature of political institutions is inevitably imprecise and judgemental. Hence, it is also fruitful to compare the results using variables in the Polity IV dataset with other measures of political institutions data such as those available from Freedom House or the updated database of political institutions based on Beck et al. (2001) and Keefer and Stasavage (2003). While all dimensions of democratic institutions are positively correlated, there is some institutional variation captured in these variables. For example, Keefer and Stasavage (2003) propose a measure based on the *number* of checks on the executive, *checks_lax*, which while positively correlated with the measure based on *xconst*, is based on a rather different procedure. For example, as we discuss in the Appendix, the *checks_lax* does not seem to include judicial independence as a criterion. For *checks_lax* > 3 around 60 percent of all country/years also have strong executive constraints. Below, we will use this as an alternative measure.

The variable *xropen* is described in the Polity IV user's manual in the following terms:

> Recruitment of the chief executive is "open" to the extent that all the politically active population has an opportunity, in principle, to attain the position through a regularized process.

The notion of a regularized process is quite open to interpretation. A score of 4 denotes a case in which chief executives are chosen by elite designation, competitive election, or transitional arrangements between designation and election. We also use the variable called *eiec* from the World Bank's database of political institutions. We use the threshold *eiec* = 7 which is intended to capture a situation in which the executive is elected in competitive elections, i.e. in which the largest party received less than 75 percent of the votes.

Summary statistics on all three samples we use are in Table 7.5.

Determinants of Inequality We look at purely cross-sectional variation to see whether ethnic inequality is higher with strong executive constraints. The specification that we run is:

$$Gini(light\ per\ capita)_c = \alpha_1 \times constraints_c + \alpha_2 \times openness_c + \theta_r$$
$$+\beta X_c + \epsilon_c \qquad (7.2)$$

where $constraints_c$ and $openness_c$ are the share of years before 2000 in which the country had the respective institutions, θ_r are continent dummies and X_c are other controls, the mean values (for each country) of distance to sea coast, elevation, precipitation, temperature, and land quality for agriculture. We use the Gini constructed by Alesina et al. (2016) as well as constructed from the GROWup data. In the former case, we use Alesina et al. (2016)'s composite index of inequality in geographic endowments which is their main variable of interest. It is measured as the first principal component of five inequality measures (Gini coefficients) measuring inequality across ethnic/linguistic homelands in distance to the coast, elevation, precipitation, temperature, and land quality for agriculture. Controlling for this allows us to show that our interest in institutions has additional explanatory power to their variable.

As a robustness check on our results, we instrument executive constraints using Acemoglu et al. (2001)'s settler mortality variable, i.e. where the first stage is:

$$\widehat{constraints}_c = \zeta \times \log(mortality_c) + \omega_r + \kappa X_c + \eta_c \qquad (7.3)$$

This has certain advantages since it may be that there is some joint determination of institutions and the level of ethnic inequality. However, there is also a cost since it reduces the sample of countries that can be studied and the exclusion restriction is quite demanding, i.e. that effects of settler mortality come entirely through institutions. The reader will note, however, that that is precisely the claim in Acemoglu et al. (2001).

The results for the variables in Alesina et al. (2016) are in Table 7.1. In columns (1) through (3) and (8), we use the GREG data and columns (4) through (6) and (9) use the Ethnologue data. Across the board, the results show that there is a strong and consistent negative correlation between ethnic inequality and experience with strong executive constraints for both measures. When we include openness, it does not affect the core result and is not significant. But this could well be because there is much less variation in openness than in executive constraints across the sample—a much higher proportion of countries have always been open. The results are robust to whether or not controls are included. To get a sense of the size of the effect note that the ethnic Gini has a mean of 0.43 and standard deviation of 0.26. So the effects estimated are quite sizeable.

Column (7) estimates (7.3)—the F-statistic on the instrument is bigger than 10. And in the subsequent columns, we find that there is a larger and strongly significant IV estimate between ethnic inequality and strong executive constraints.

In Table 7.2, we estimate the results using our own estimates of ethnic inequality from the GROWup data. These are time varying since we have data from 1992 to 2010 so all of the variables in (7.2) should now be time subscripted and we include year dummies to capture any macro trends. The results are very similar to those in Table 7.1 with a strongly negative correlation between share of years in strong executive constraints and ethnic inequality. Columns (4) and (5) show that these results are robust to instrumenting and we have a very strong first stage. The results in Table 7.2 are also robust to using alternative measures of cohesive institutions. This level of the analysis does not allow us to distinguish which dimension of democratic institutions is responsible for the strong pattern in the data.

Overall, these results are highly suggestive—strong executive constraints seem to reduce ethnic inequality. Of course, this is only a one-dimensional take on the theory which is not specific about the salient dimension of group inequality which could be religion or some kind of non-ethnic geographical basis. However, the finding is still striking in view of the model and the role that it gives to strong constraints in creating a more even distribution of public expenditures.

Table 7.1 Ethnic inequality in 2000 and history of strong executive constraints

Variables	(1) (OLS)	(2)	(3)	(4)	(5)	(6)	(7) (First stage) Share under strong executive constraints	(8) (IV)	(9)
	Gini (light per capita) across ethnic homelands (GREG data)			Gini (light per capita) across ethnic homelands (Ethnologue data)				Gini (light per capita) across ethnic homelands	
Share of years under strong executive constraints	−0.184*** (0.0622)	−0.202*** (0.0600)	−0.187*** (0.0651)	−0.188*** (0.0594)	−0.162*** (0.0522)	−0.170*** (0.0579)		−0.406*** (0.1480)	−0.267 (0.2200)
Share of years under high openness			−0.0363 (0.0473)			0.0203 (0.0584)			
Inequality in Geography across ethnic homelands (PC)	0.0819*** (0.0100)	0.0797*** (0.0106)	0.0812*** (0.0111)	0.115*** (0.0127)	0.110*** (0.0122)	0.110*** (0.0122)	−0.0216 (0.0277)	0.0745*** (0.0168)	0.0910*** (0.0198)

	(1)	(2)	(3)	(4)	(5)	(6)	(7)	(8)	(9)
Log settler mortality							−0.147*** (0.0492)		
Region fixed effects	Yes	Yes	Yes	Yes	Yes	Yes	Yes	Yes	Yes
Additional controls	No	Yes	Yes	No	Yes	Yes	No	No	No
Observations	155	155	155	155	155	155	60	60	60
R-squared	0.497	0.551	0.553	0.62	0.696	0.696	0.435	0.464	0.571

Robust standard errors in parentheses. ***p <0.01, **p <0.05, *p <0.1. The dependent variable is the ethnic Gini coefficient that reflects inequality in lights per capita across ethnic/linguistic homelands, using the digitized version of Atlas Narodov Mira (GREG) in (1)–(3), (8) and Ethnologue in (4)–(6) and (9). Share of years under strong executive constraints is the share of past years a country had strong executive constraints (xconst=7). Share of years under high openness is the share of past years a country had open recruitment to the executive (xropen=4). All other data is from Alesina et al. (2016). The inequality in geography is the first principal component of five inequality measures (Gini coefficients) measuring inequality across ethnic/linguistic homelands in distance to the coast, elevation, precipitation, temperature, and land quality for agriculture. The mapping of ethnic homelands follows the digitized version of Atlas Narodov Mira (GREG) in columns (1)–(3), (8) and of Ethnologue in columns (4)–(6) and (9). Columns (3) and (6) include as controls the mean values (for each country) of distance to sea coast, elevation, precipitation, temperature, and land quality for agriculture. Region fixed effects are dummies for regions on earth (similar to continents). Log settler mortality is from Acemoglu et al. (2001)

Table 7.2 Ethnic inequality in 2010 and history of strong executive constraints (GROWup data)

Variables	(1) OLS	(2)	(3)	(4)	(5) IV
	Gini (light per capita) across ethnic homelands			Share under strong executive constraints	Gini (light per capita)
Share of years under strong executive constraints	−0.114*** (0.0053)	−0.0459*** (0.0048)	−0.0391*** (0.0076)		−0.390** (0.1760)
Log settler mortality				−0.0459*** (0.0125)	
Year fixed effects	Yes	Yes	Yes	Yes	Yes
Region fixed effects	No	Yes	Yes	Yes	Yes
Country-specific time trends	No	No	Yes	No	No
Observations	2115	2115	2115	913	913
R-squared	0.099	0.306	0.773	0.282	

Robust standard errors in parentheses. ***$p<0.01$, **$p<0.05$, *$p<0.1$. Night light per capita data is from the GROWup database which gives night light and population for each relevant ethnic group in a country. The Gini coefficient is re-calculated every year based on this data. "Strong executive constraints" is defined by xconst=7 in the Polity IV dataset. Log settler mortality is from Acemoglu et al. (2001)

Excluded Groups We now turn to a within-country analysis to examine how excluded groups fare with strong executive constraints. We do so by looking at the light per capita at a group level within country during periods of strong and weak executive constraints comparing groups which are excluded from power to those that are part of the government. For this purpose, we define an excluded group based on the GROWup data as being excluded if they are either classified as being powerless, discriminated or self-excluded.

Our core specification for group i in country c in year t is:

$$log(light\ per\ capita)_{ict} = \alpha_1 \times excluded_{ict} \tag{7.4}$$

$$+\alpha_2 \times excluded_{ict} \times weakconstraints_{ct}$$

$$+C_{ct} + \eta_i + \epsilon_{it}$$

where C_{ct} are country/year fixed effects, η_i are group fixed effects. Specifically, the variable $excluded_{ict}$ is the share of years the group was excluded from political power and $excluded_{ict} \times weakconstraints_{ct}$ is the share of years the group was excluded in a year with weak executive constraints. We look at other measures of institutions as a robustness check.

It bears remarking that this specification is quite demanding as it allows for an arbitrary pattern of within country over time variation and also group fixed effects. If strong executive constraints reduce political rents to incumbents then we expect to find that $\alpha_2 < 0$.

The results are in Table 7.3. Column (1) gives the basic result. It finds that $\alpha_1 < 0$, so that all excluded groups have a lower value of light per capita. It is also shows that this effect is larger under weak executive constraints. Light per capita is about 20 percent lower in weak groups that were not protected by constraints. This corresponds to around a 7% lower GDP per capita. Column (2) reports a weighted regression where the weight is the population share of each ethnic group. We continue to find that $\alpha_2 < 0$. Column (3) controls for time trends in urbanization, population and area and shows that the results remain robust.

In Table 7.4 we consider some alternative ways of capturing political institutions. In column (1) we use the same dimension from the Polity IV dataset, *xconst*, but use a different cut-off to define strong executive

Table 7.3 Political exclusion and night light

Variables	(1) ln(light per capita)	(2) ln(light per capita)	(3) ln(light per capita)
Share of years excluded from power	−0.168*	−0.0504	−0.0503
	(0.0966)	(0.0548)	(0.0553)
Share of years excluded from power in weak executive constraints	−0.210**	−0.139***	−0.152***
	(0.0932)	(0.0538)	(0.0542)
Country/year fixed effects	Yes	Yes	Yes
Group fixed effects	Yes	Yes	Yes
Population, urganization and area trends	No	No	Yes
Observations	9107	9107	9037
R-squared	0.975	0.99	0.974

Robust standard errors in parentheses. ***p <0.01, **p <0.05, *p <0.1. All regressions use GROWup data at the ethnic homeland level. Light per capita is the amount of night light per capita emitted by the ethnic homeland in that year. Columns (2) and (3) use ethnic group size as a regression weight. Column (3) controls for time trends in urbanization, population and area. "Excluded from power" are powerless, discriminated and self-excluded ethnic groups

constraints, namely we include the intermediate scores of 6. If anything, this less demanding way of looking at constraints actually strengthens our main result somewhat. In column (2) we use our measure of openness. Being excluded from power when openness is low does not seem to mean that a group does worse which is what we would expect if openness captures γ_i rather than θ. In column (3) we use the aggregate polity2 score of larger 5, again from Polity IV, to define democracies. This general measure leads to similar results as those in Table 7.3. This is not inconsistent with some dimensions of democracy being more important than others. In columns (4) and (5) we use alternative measures from the World Bank's Database of Political Institutions 2012. The first dimension we look at is a measure of the competitiveness of elections in electing the executive, *eiec* using a cut-off value of 7 as discussed above. The results are similar to when we use openness with no apparent worsening of the consequences of being excluded when there is a stronger electoral constraint. We also find no additional effect of being excluded in a society with few checks and balances as captured by the variable *checks_lax*.

Table 7.4 Political exclusion and night light (robustness)

Variables	(1) ln(light per capita)	(2) ln(light per capita)	(3) ln(light per capita)	(4) ln(light per capita)	(5) ln(light per capita)
Share of years excluded from power	0.000963 (0.0473)	-0.167*** (0.0534)	-0.0636 (0.0564)	-0.143** (0.0717)	-0.194*** (0.0548)
Share of years excluded from power in weak executive constraints	-0.225*** (0.0409)				
Share of years excluded from power with low openness		-0.0292 (0.0731)			
Share of years excluded from power in non-democracy			-0.153*** (0.0482)		
Share of years excluded from power without competitive elections				-0.0506 (0.0811)	
Share of years excluded from power with few checks and balances					0.0191 (0.0414)
Country/year fixed effects	Yes	Yes	Yes	Yes	
Group fixed effects	Yes	Yes	Yes	Yes	
Observations	9232	9232	9219	9219	9216
R-squared	0.99	0.99	0.99	0.99	0.99

Robust standard errors in parentheses. ***$p<0.01$, **$p<0.05$, *$p<0.1$. All regressions use GROWup data at the ethnic homeland level. Light per capita is the amount of night light per capita emitted by the ethnic homeland in that year. Column (1) defines weak executive constraints by an xconst score smaller than 6. Column (2) defines high openness by xropen=4 in the Polity IV dataset. Column (3) uses a polity2 score of >5 to define democracies. Column (4) uses eiec=7 as a criterion for competitive elections. Column (5) uses the cut-off of 4 or more on the variable checks_lax to define many checks and balances. For sources and definitions see the main text and Appendix

This raises the question of what is specific about the way that the Polity IV measures executive constraints in particular in comparison to our measure of checks and balances. In the Appendix we show that the difference is not entirely surprising once the coding of *xconst* and *check_lax* is compared. Executive constraints in Polity IV are defined through constitutional arrangements and judicial independence as opposed to the composition of parliament. For example, South Africa where the ANC dominates both the executive and legislature can be coded as having strong executive constraints due to strong judicial independence and constitutional arrangements which give the national assembly the power to elect the president. Hence this could be telling us that it is consideration of judicial independence as mentioned in the construction of *xconst* that is crucial. However, such a claim is somewhat speculative at this point and merits further investigation.

In summary, the first set of our results is highly robust across a broad set of measures for political institutions although the downside of political exclusion seems specific to using the executive constraints measure from the Polity IV dataset. Overall, the results provide persuasive evidence that the distribution of income between ethnic groups depends on political exclusion and that this effect is particularly strong when executive constraints as measured by Polity IV are weak. Such constraints are "worth" around 5–7% of GDP per capita to politically excluded groups. This speaks directly to the Rawlsian argument for strong executive constraints. Moreover, this gives a precise sense in which these are indeed "inclusive institutions" in the sense of Acemoglu and Robinson (2012).

Concluding Comments

This paper has contributed to debates about how institutions affect economic development. However, the main focus has been on inclusiveness rather than whether growth and development respond to institutional differences. We have argued that having strong executive constraints has a special normative role since it can help to protect those who are politically excluded. We have presented a model where this was true but ultimately, it is an empirical question whether strong executive constraints protect excluded citizens.

The results presented here provide a window on a set of wider debates in political economy. In many respects using *xconst* from Polity IV as a measure of institutional cohesion (as captured by θ in the model) is quite crude so it is interesting that it delivers robust empirical results. The result that other dimensions of polity do not seem to prevent redistribution away from the politically excluded is interesting and confirms findings in Mueller and Tapsoba (2016). What is somewhat puzzling is the fact that measures on checks and balances based on the composition of the parliament do not yield similar results. A closer look at the two measures of institutional constraints suggests that the fact that Polity IV captures constitutional differences and an independent judiciary might be driving this difference.

However, the interpretation is open. Suppose that societies must first develop values that lead to institutional change, then these findings would simply be reflections of these values rather than institutions. This line of argument is developed in Besley and Persson (2016) who propose a model where values and institutions coevolve. This is linked to the idea championed in political science by Putnam (1993) and Fukuyama (2011) that a strong civil society is needed to underpin effective states. Others, such as Weingast (1997), look at this in terms of coordinating on a focal equilibrium where the rule of law and inclusive democracy prevails.

In the end, it does not matter much whether it is values or institutions that matter when interpreting the findings above. However, for policy purposes it is key. Introducing institutions in places where the values are poorly entrenched may just lead to institutions being compromised or even abandoned. The process of foreign intervention in trying to establish political institutions is replete with such examples and countries which were given post-colonial constitutions with nascent executive constraints saw these abandoned (see Acemoglu et al. 2001, for a discussion). Hence, this paper only reinforces the need to understand the dynamic of institutional and value change better.

Comments by Stephen Knack

This chapter contributes to a growing literature on how democratic institutions can influence development outcomes. A second contribution is its emphasis on the multidimensionality of democracy. Some aspects of democracy may matter much more than others, for particular outcomes. Distinctions among these multiple dimensions of democracy also raise questions about the interpretation of popular indicators of democracy and political freedoms.

There is still no consensus on whether democracy is conducive to higher growth: the most obvious pattern in the data is a higher dispersion in growth rates among non-democracies, rather than a lower (or higher) mean. Democracies have much higher per capita incomes on average, but there is still debate on whether causality runs primarily from income to democracy or the other way around.

Nevertheless, the empirical literature has progressed in important respects, by disaggregating democracy, and by looking at other outcomes such as conflict and inequality. Besley and Mueller add to a strand of this literature that focuses on ethnic divisions, and specifically on how the impact of ethnic divisions on outcomes depends on political institutions. Burgess et al. (2015) show that road investments across Kenyan districts are biased in favor of the political leadership's ethnic groups, but this favoritism disappears during periods of greater democracy. Hodler and Raschky (2011) show that political leaders favor their birthplace regions, as measured by luminosity from satellite data, for 126 countries. This effect is smaller, however, in countries with lower scores on the Polity index of democracy.

Several other studies have used luminosity data for analyzing ethnic favoritism, given the absence of reliable data on per capita income at the sub-national level. The most closely-related to the Besley and Mueller chapter is a recent paper by Mueller and Tapsoba (2016). For 564 ethnic groups in 130 countries over the 1992–2010 period, they find luminosity increases for an ethnic group's region if it gains access to executive power, and especially if it gains a monopoly on executive power. However, this effect is largely absent where there are strong constraints on executive power (i.e. for countries scoring 6 or 7 on Polity's 7-point index of "Executive Constraints"). Alesina et al. (2016) use the luminosity data to construct measures of inequality across ethnic groups within countries, and show that disparities across groups can be explained to a surprising degree by differences in geographic endowments.

In their chapter, Besley and Mueller build on these earlier studies, making use of the same datasets and a distinction between political "openness" (institutions which affect access to power) and "executive constraints" (institutions which regulate the use of political power). They operationalize these concepts using two indicators from the Polity dataset (XROPEN and XCONST), and present two major findings. First, inequality across ethnic homelands is significantly lower in countries with a history of strong executive constraints. In contrast, a history of "openness" (open access to executive power) has no significant effect on inequality. Second, using panel data and controlling for country-year fixed effects and ethnic group fixed effects, they find that luminosity is lower for groups excluded from power; moreover, the negative effect of exclusion is significantly larger where executive constraints are weaker.

These findings add to other evidence on the importance of executive constraints for preventing exploitation of ethnic or other minorities protecting rights of citizens more generally. Table 7.8 shows the mean scores on the Freedom House indexes of Political Freedoms and Civil Liberties, for each level of Executive Constraints. These indexes take into account not only the rights of ethnic minorities, but of religious and other minorities, as well as individual rights and freedoms (of speech, assembly, etc,) for all citizens. The data in Table 7.8 are pooled for all countries with available data, for the 2003-onward period for which Freedom House has published these 0–100 indexes (from which their more widely-known 1–7 indexes are derived). Each increment in Executive Constraints is associated with significantly higher mean scores for both Political Freedoms and Civil Liberties. The significant effect of Executive Constraints is robust to controlling for income, population, and country and year effects. Moreover, other aspects of democracy appear to matter less. "Openness" is not significant for either outcome, while age of democracy is significant for Political Freedoms but not for Civil Liberties.

Of course, showing that constraints on the executive is a key aspect of democracy does not tell us much about how to obtain more effective constraints on the executive. As Besley and Mueller acknowledge, interpretation of their findings with respect to institutional reform is problematic. If "societies must first develop values that lead to institutional change" then their findings could "simply be reflections of these values rather than institutions." In the absence of a supportive civic culture, attempts at institutional reform in less-developed countries may be ineffectual or merely create the form (but not the function) of constitutional checks on the executive that characterize political systems in advanced democracies.

Note that although executive constraints are conceptually distinct from openness and competitiveness of executive selection, one can affect the other. For example, weakly-constrained executives might restrict access of some groups to power, potentially creating a one-party state or dictatorship. Where access to power is restricted, for example through hereditary succession, chief executives may attempt to block any constraints on their power, unless they perceive that doing so will provoke active opposition that may result in loss of power.

It is not well understood how effective constraints on executives emerged even in the advanced democracies, although there have been promising if not fully-satisfying attempts at explanations (e.g. Weingast, 1997). One possibility is that constraints emerge and become credible over time with democratic consolidation. Using Polity's Executive Constraints variable and a measure of age of democratic systems from the DPI (Database on Political Institutions), in regressions that control for income, population, and country and year fixed effects, I found a positive and significant relationship between age of democracy and executive constraints. This relationship may partly reflect endogeneity, of course, and the quantitative effect is very small: on average, it takes nearly 100 additional years of democracy to attain a 1-point increment in the 1–7 executive constraints index.

Moreover, finding that executive constraints, as measured by Polity, matters for development outcomes does not tell us specifically which constraints matter. The definition in Polity's codebook[11] mentions legislatures as one constraint, as well as independent judiciaries, ruling parties, and even the military in a coup-prone state. The new "Varieties of Democracy" (V-Dem) measurement project[12] constructs hundreds of more finely-grained indicators, and could be used in conjunction with the Polity indicator to help understand better what are the particular institutions reflected in the Executive Constraints measure. V-Dem's specific constraints indicators could also be used more directly in analyses such as those of Besley and Mueller, as a substitute for the more opaque and multidimensional Polity measure.

Besley and Mueller note long-term positive trends (going back to at least 1875) in both political openness and executive constraints, based on the Polity measures. They argue that progress on executive constraints "lag behind openness," as shown in their Fig. 7.1. Although this pattern accords with intuition, it is potentially an artifact of the measures they use. "Open" countries are those with the maximum value of 4 on Polity's 1–4 XROPEN (openness of executive recruitment) index, and countries with strong constraints are those with the maximum value of 7 on the 7-point XCONST (executive constraints) variable. Other things equal, attaining the maximum value on a 4-point scale should be easier than attaining the maximum on a 7-point scale.

It is instructive, however, to compare the strength of executive constraints at the dawn of political openness in each country (i.e. the year when countries graduate from hereditary to open-recruitment executives), for the group of 22 long-time DAC donors (mostly advanced democracies) and for other countries. Most of the donor countries (17, or 77%) already had strong executive constraints the first year that Polity assigns them the top score on openness. (Polity data begin in 1800, for countries that were already in existence at that time.) Of the other 137 countries in the data, only 34 (25%) had the top executive constraints score the first year they had the maximum openness score. Most of them (73%) had ratings of 5 or below on the 1–7 index. This difference suggests that early- and late-democratizers may be on different paths, with civic culture and constraints on executive power co-evolving and emerging endogenously in the early democratizers. In contrast, late democratizers—whether in imitation of the early democratizers or in response to pressure from them—struggle to adopt the forms of democracy in the hope that function (and a facilitating civic culture) will eventually follow.

Another important distinction among democracies is whether political parties tend to be "programmatic" (offering a platform of policy positions that can be characterized as center, left of center, or right of center) or "clientilistic" (non-ideological parties offering jobs and private or semi-public goods in exchange for votes Keefer (2011). Younger democracies tend to have fewer programmatic parties than mature democracies. With time, a party's promises regarding programmatic policies may become more credible, so that as democracies age there is a gradual shift from clientilistic to programmatic politics. Such a shift can reduce the salience of ethnicity, which often forms the basis of clientilistic parties.

There is some hope, therefore, that as democracies age the problems of ethnic inequality and exclusion analyzed by Besley and Mueller will gradually become less severe, as executive constraints strengthen and parties compete on programmatic platforms rather than patronage. However, these trends are gradual and hold only on average: in some countries weak constraints on the executive and clientilistic politics may be a long-run equilibrium. As Besley, Mueller and other leading scholars in the political economy of development continue their research on these topics, our understanding of reform possibilities should gradually improve.

Appendix: Discussion of Constraints Measure

Summary statistics are in Table 7.5. In this appendix we discuss the difference between executive constraints as measured by the variable *xconst* in the Polity IV dataset and the strength of checks and balances as measured by *checks_lax* in Keefer and Stasavage (2003) (Table 7.5).

In Table 7.6 we plot the share of country-years which are coded *xconst=7* for values of *checks_lax* from 1 to 7+. Two patterns are clear. First, categories with very low values of *checks_lax* also contain very few country/years with strong executive constraints. Second, for larger values of *check_lax* the two measures diverge. There are many country/years which are coded as strong executive constraints but have relatively low values of *checks_lax* and vice versa. Only at values of *checks_lax* = 6 there is a large majority of observations which are also coded as strong executive constraints. Typically, the share is closer to 50 percent.

Table 7.5 Summary statistics

	Obs	Mean	SD	Min	Max
Panel A: Sample from Alesina et al. (2016)					
Gini (light per capita) across ethnic homelands (GREG data)	173	0.4236	0.2597	0	0.9661
Gini (light per capita) across ethnic homelands (Ethnologue data)	173	0.4463	0.333	0	0.982
Inequality in geography across ethnic homelands (PC), GREG	164	0	1.7267	−2.555	5.659
Inequality in geography across ethnic homelands (PC), Ethnologue	164	0	1.7153	−2.67	5.133
Share of years under strong executive constraints	163	0.1972	0.3127	0	1
Share of years under high openness	163	0.6707	0.3352	0	1
Log (settler morgality)	63	4.6776	1.2378	2.1459	7.9862
Panel B: GROWup sample (country level)					
Gini (light per capita) across ethnic homelands	2115	0.127	0.1584	0	0.753
Share of years under strong executive constraints	2115	0.2799	0.4313	0	1
Log (settler morgality)	913	4.8176	1.1546	2.7081	7.9862
Panel C: GROWup sample (ethnic group level)					
ln(light per capita)	9232	−4.3213	2.0291	−19.93	0.97
Share of years excluded from power	9232	0.5424	0.483	0	1
Share of years excluded from power in weak (<7) executive constraints	9232	0.4434	0.4765	0	1
Share of years excluded from power in weak (<6) executive constraints	9232	0.3883	0.4676	0	1
Share of years excluded from power with low openness	9232	0.1124	0.2947	0	1
Share of years excluded from power in non-democracy	9232	0.3457	0.4493	0	1
Share of years excluded from power without competitive elections	9219	0.2683	0.4154	0	1
Share of years excluded from power with few checks and balances	9216	0.2629	0.405	0	1

Table 7.6 Strong executive constraints and checks and balances

Checks_lax	Share of observations with strong executive constraints	Number of observations
0	0.03	464
1	0.01	2387
2	0.29	605
3	0.44	1196
4	0.61	987
5	0.66	436
6	0.84	117
7+	0.58	108

Note: "checks_lax" is a measure of checks and balances based on Keefer and Stasavage (2003). Strong executive constraints is defined by xconst=7 in the Polity IV dataset

In Table 7.7 we show which countries drive this divergence. The most striking feature is that many developed democracies are coded as facing executive constraints but not a high number of checks and balances. Examples are: Sweden, Spain, the UK, Italy, Japan, New Zealand and Norway. Instead, the checks data codes many Latin American countries like Argentina, Brazil, Colombia or Venezuela as having strong checks and balances.

The core of this divergence lies in the way the two variables are coded. The executive constraints variable *xconst* is available on a seven-point scale. As noted in the text above, the Polity IV manual explains the variable's construction as follows:

Operationally, this variable refers to the extent of institutionalized constraints on the decision making powers of chief executives, whether individuals or collectivities. Such limitations may be imposed by any "accountability groups." In Western democracies these are usually legislatures. Other kinds of accountability groups are the ruling party in a one-party state; councils of nobles or powerful advisors in monarchies; the military in coup-prone polities; and in many states a strong, independent judiciary. The concern is therefore with the checks and balances between the various parts of the decision-making process.

Table 7.7 Comparing veto player and executive constraints

Panel A: Weak constraints but 4+ checks		Panel B: Strong constraints but <4 checks	
Country	Number of years	Country	Number of years
Algeria	5	Albania	8
Argentina	15	Belarus	3
Bangladesh	10	Belgium	6
Belarus	1	Bolivia	3
Bosnia and Herzegovina	4	Botswana	15
Botswana	2	Bulgaria	17
Brazil	19	Cape Verde	11
Colombia	14	Chile	8
Congo	4	Colombia	3
Congo (DRC)	6	Comoros	8
Dominican Republic	13	Costa Rica	9
Ecuador	10	Croatia	7
El Salvador	18	Cyprus	13
Ethiopia	5	East Timor	11
Fiji	13	Ecuador	2
France	21	Estonia	12
Guatemala	1	Finland	4
Guyana	1	Greece	20
Haiti	7	Haiti	3
Honduras	8	Hungary	10
Indonesia	5	Israel	6
Iraq	2	Italy	9
Korea	13	Jamaica	9
Liberia	7	Japan	14
Macedonia	3	Kenya	5
Madagascar	3	Kyrgyzstan	2
Malawi	15	Latvia	4
Malaysia	21	Lesotho	12
Mauritania	8	Lithuania	16
Mexico	15	Madagascar	5
Nepal	8	Mauritius	18
Nigeria	13	Moldova, Rep.of	16
Pakistan	5	Mongolia	21
Panama	10	New Zealand	12
Papua New Guinea	21	Nicaragua	8
Paraguay	1	Niger	4

(continued)

Table 7.7 (continued)

Philippines	16	Norway	4
Poland	3	Paraguay	7
Romania	11	Portugal	21
Russian Federation	15	Slovakia	4
Senegal	1	Slovenia	5
Slovakia	5	Solomon Islands	8
Sri Lanka	15	South Africa	19
Suriname	6	Spain	5
Taiwan	4	Sweden	4
Tajikistan	4	Switzerland	17
Tunisia	1	Taiwan	4
Uganda	5	Thailand	1
Ukraine	12	Trinidad and Tobago	12
Venezuela	9	Turkey	14
Zambia	6	United Kingdom	13
Zimbabwe	4	Uruguay	8

Table 7.8 Executive constraints and individual rights

Executive constraints	Political freedoms	Civil liberties	Number of country-year observations
1	2.8	8.1	104
2	7.7	18.1	234
3	10.7	21.6	279
4	15.7	26.4	99
5	22.5	33.9	265
6	27	37.9	295
7	34.4	49.7	757

The table shows, for each level of executive constraints, the mean scores on the Freedom House indexes of political freedoms and civil liberties, pooling all country-year observations from 2003 onward

The rules code $xconst = 1$, for example, when there is unlimited authority in which there are no regular limitations on the executive's actions (as opposed to irregular limitations such as the threat or actuality of coups and assassinations) and category $xconst = 7$ means that accountability groups have effective authority equal to or greater than the executive in most areas of activity (Table 7.8).

This is fairly abstract and not easy to interpret. It is therefore important to check the arguments made for coding in some examples. South Africa, for example, is coded as executive parity or subordination (7) for much of its history. The reasoning given in the coding report is:

> The type of presidential system found in South Africa places significant constraints on the political autonomy of the chief executive. While the president is not directly accountable to the legislature (as is in the case in a traditional parliamentary system), nevertheless, s/he is chosen by the National Assembly. Moreover, under the terms of the 1997 constitution, political power is shared between the president and the Parliament.
>
> While the institutional design of the South African government provides for significant horizontal accountability, the dominance of the ANC in the post-apartheid era has provided the executive branch with significant power to chart the course of the country with little interference from the legislature. In 2003 the ANC, through opposition party defections, achieved a two-thirds majority in parliament. The political dominance of the ANC was reaffirmed with their landslide. The judiciary is largely independent from executive influence. (Centre for Systemic Peace, Polity IV Country Reports 2010)

The United Kingdom is also coded as featuring executive parity or subordination (7). The reasoning given in the report is:

> The parliamentary structure of government found in the United Kingdom places significant constraints on the autonomous actions of the chief executive. The prime minister is elected by, and is directly accountable to, the legislature. Although Britain does not have a written constitution, historical conventions and norms, as well as legal precedents, serve as the foundations of horizontal accountability in this country. The judiciary, while weaker than in many OECD countries, is autonomous from executive interference. (Centre for Systemic Peace, Polity IV Country Reports 2010)

The variable *checks_lax* from Keefer and Stasavage (2003) is coded as follows:

Checks_lax equals one if LIEC OR EIEC is less than 5 – countries where legislatures are not competitively elected are considered countries where only the executive wields a check.

In countries where LIEC and EIEC are greater than or equal to 5:

* *Checks_lax is incremented by one if there is a chief executive (it is blank or NA if not).*
* *Checks_lax is incremented by one if the chief executive is competitively elected (EIEC greater than six).*
* *Checks_lax is incremented by one if the opposition controls the legislature.*

In presidential systems, Checks_lax is incremented by one:

* *for each chamber of the legislature UNLESS the president's party has a majority in the lower house*
* *AND a closed list system is in effect (implying stronger presidential control of his/her party, and therefore of the legislature).*
* *for each party coded as allied with the president's party and which has an ideological (left-right-center) orientation closer to that of the main opposition party than to that of the president's party.*

In parliamentary systems, Checks_lax is incremented by one

* *for every party in the government coalition as long as the parties are needed to maintain a majority*
* *parties in the government coalition, regardless of whether they were needed for a legislative majority).*
* *for every party in the government coalition that has a position on economic issues (right-left-center) closer to the largest opposition party than to the party of the executive.*

From these coding rules it is clear that the composition of parliament receives more weight than the constitutional rules which govern the interplay between legislature and executive. Also, the independence of the judiciary is only mentioned in the description of *xconst* as a factor which certainly explains a part of the divergence. If judicial control is important this is an important difference between the two measures.

Notes

1. See Dahl (1957) for an insightful discussion of the New Deal period. By the time that he was writing, New Deal legislation comprised one third of all legislation that had been declared unconstitutional by the supreme court.
2. See, for example, Sen (1999).
3. Luca et al. (2015) also find proof of ethnic favoritism but do not find political institutions affect this.
4. An alternative argument is that independence of central bankers and other bureaucrats provides efficiency benefits. For a review of this literature see Mueller (2015).
5. See, Alesina and La Ferrara (2005), for a summary.
6. See Besley and Coate (2003) for a discussion and synthesis.
7. To understand this problem note that for every dollar not spend on G the transfer T can go up by $(\sigma_k + (1 - \sigma_k)\theta)^{-1}$ dollars.
8. Note that we are simply adding the per capita cost of providing public goods consumption here, utility is $\alpha\phi(G_s)$. This is common in distributional analyses by statistical agencies which attempt to take public spending into account to create a measure of post-transfer income. Nothing would change qualitatively in our analysis if we would take a different view.
9. The idea that institutions should have this kind of robustness property follows a recent literature in macro economics on policy rules which do not require a unique prior. See Barlevy (2011) for a review of the ideas.
10. Dixit et al. (2000) also develop a model where political compromise arises as the equilibrium of a dynamic game played between political parties. This equilibrium could be interpreted as a social norm which mitigates "winner-takes-all" politics.
11. See http://www3.nd.edu/~mcoppedg/crd/PolityIVUsersManualv2002.pdf.
12. See https://www.v-dem.net/en/fordescriptionsanddatadownloads.

References

Acemoglu, Daron, and James Robinson. 2012. *Why Nations Fail*. New York, NY: Crown Publishers.

Acemoglu, Daron, Simon Johnson, and James A. Robinson. 2001. The Colonial Origins of Comparative Development: An Empirical Investigation. *American Economic Review* 91: 1369–1401.

Alesina, Alberto, and Eliana La Ferrara. 2005. Ethnic Diversity and Economic Performance. *Journal of Economic Literature* 43: 762–800.

Alesina, Alberto, Stelios Michalopoulos, and Elias Papaioannou. 2016. Ethnic Inequality. *Journal of Political Economy* 124 (2): 428–488.

Barlevy, Gardi. 2011. Robustness and Macroeconomic Policy. *Annual Review of Economics* 3: 1–24.

Baron, David, and John Ferejohn. 1989. Bargaining in Legislatures. *American Political Science Review* 83: 1181–1206.

Beck, Thorsten, George Clarke, Alberto Groff, Philip Keefer, and Patrick Walsh. 2001. New Tools in Comparative Political Economy: The Database of Political Institutions. *World Bank Economic Review* 15: 165–176.

Besley, Timothy, and Stephen Coate. 2003. Centralized Versus Decentralized Provision of Local Public Goods: A Political Economy Approach. *Journal of Public Economics* 87: 2611–2637.

Besley, Timothy, and Torsten Persson. 2011a. *Pillars of Prosperity: The Political Economics of Development Clusters*. Princeton, NJ: Princeton University Press.

Besley, Timothy, and Torsten Persson. 2011b. The Logic of Political Violence. *Quarterly Journal of Economics* 126: 1411–1445.

Besley, Timothy, and Torsten Persson. 2016. Democratic Values and Institutions. Unpublished typescript.

Buchanan, James, and Gordon Tullock. 1962. *The Calculus of Consent*. Ann Arbor: University of Michigan Press.

Burgess, Robin, Remi Jedwab, Edward Miguel, Ameet Morjaria, and Gerard Padro i Miquel. 2015. The Value of Democracy: Evidence from Road Building in Kenya. *American Economic Review* 105: 1817–1851.

Cederman, Lars-Erik, Andreas Wimmer, and Brian Min. 2010. Why Do Ethnic Groups Rebel? New Data and Analysis. *World Politics* 62: 87–119.

Collier, Paul. 2009. *Wars, Guns, and Votes: Democracy in Dangerous Places*. New York: Harper.

Dahl, Robert. 1957. Decision-Making in a Democracy: The Supreme Court as a National Policy-Maker. *Journal of Public Law* 6: 279–295.

Dixit, Avinash, and John Londregan. 1996. The Determinants of Success of Special Interests in Redistributive Politics. *Journal of Politics* 58: 1132–1155.

Dixit, Avinash, Gene M. Grossman, and Faruk Gul. 2000. The Dynamics of Political Compromise. *Journal of Political Economy* 108: 531–568.

Franck, Raphael, and Ilia Rainer. 2012. Does the Leader's Ethnicity Matter? Ethnic Favoritism, Education and Health in Sub-Saharan Africa. *American Political Science Review* 106: 294–325.

Fukuyama, Francis. 2011. *The Origins of Political Order: From Prehuman Times to the French Revolution.* New York, NY: Farrar, Straus and Giroux.

Gilboa, Itzhak, and David Schmeidler. 1989. Maxmin Expected Utility with Nonunique Prior. *Journal of Mathematical Economics* 18: 141–53.

Girardin, Luc, Philipp Hunziker, Lars-Erik Cederman, Nils-Christian Bormann, and Manuel Vog. 2015. GROWup - Geographical Research On War, Unified Platform. Zürich: ETHZurich. http://growup.ethz.ch/.

Golden, Miriam, and Brian Min. 2013. Distributive Politics Around the World. *Annual Review of Political Science* 16: 73–99.

Gordon, Raymond G., Jr. (ed.). 2005. *Ethnologue: Languages of the World*, 15th ed. Dallas, TX: SIL International.

Henderson, Vernon J., Adam Storeygard, and David N. Weil. 2012. Measuring Economic Growth from Outer Space. *American Economic Review* 102: 994–1028.

Hodler, Roland, and Paul A. Raschky. 2014. Regional Favoritism. *Quarterly Journal of Economics* 129: 995–1033.

Keefer, Philip. 2011. Collective Action, Political Parties and Pro-development Public Policy. *Asian Development Review* 28(1): 94–118.

Keefer, Philip, and David Stasavage. 2003. The Limits of Delegation: Veto Players, Central Bank Independence and the Credibility of Monetary Policy. *American Political Science Review* 97: 407–423.

Kudamatsu, Masa. 2012. Has Democratization Reduced Infant Mortality in Sub-Saharan Africa? Evidence from Micro Data. *Journal of the European Economic Association* 10: 1294–1317.

Lindbeck, Assar, and Jorgen W. Weibull. 1987. Balanced-Budget Redistribution as the Outcome of Political Competition. *Public Choice* 52: 273–297.

Luca, Giacomo De, Roland Hodler, Paul A. Raschky, and Michele Valsecchi. 2015. Ethnic Favoritism: An Axiom of Politics? Working Paper Series 5209, CESifo.

Michalopoulos, Stelios, and Elias Papaioannou. 2014. National Institutions and Sub-National Development in Africa. *Quarterly Journal of Economics* 129: 151–213.

Michalopoulos, Stelios, and Elias Papaioannou. 2016. The Long-Run Effects of the Scramble for Africa. *American Economic Review* 106 (7): 1802–1848.

Mill, John Stuart. 1859. *On Liberty.* New York: Bartleby.com.

Mueller, Hannes. 2015. Insulation or Patronage: Political Institutions and Bureaucratic Efficiency. *BE Journal of Economic Analysis and Policy* 15: 961–996.

Mueller, Hannes, and Augustin Tapsoba. 2016. Access to Power, Political Institutions and Ethnic Favoritism. Working Paper 901, Barcelona GSE.

Mukand, Sharun, and Dani Rodrik. 2015. The Political Economy of Liberal Democracy. Working Paper No. 21540, NBER.

NOAA-NGDC. 2013. Version 4 DMSP-OLS Nighttime Lights Time Series (Average Visible, Stable Lights, & Cloud Free Coverages). National Oceanic and Atmospheric Administration-National Geophysical Data Center. http://ngdc.noaa.gov/eog/dmsp.html.

Persson, Torsten, and Guido Tabellini. 2008. Political Regimes and Economic Growth. In *Institutions and Economic Performance*, ed. Elhanan Helpman. Cambridge, MA: Harvard University Press.

Putnam, Robert. 1993. *Making Democracy Work: Civic Traditions in Modern Italy*. Princeton NJ: Princeton University Press.

Rawls, John. 1971. *A Theory of Justice*. Cambridge MA: Harvard University Press.

Riker, William. 1962. *The Theory of Political Coalitions*. New Haven: Yale University Press.

Sen, Amartya. 1999. Democracy as a Universal Value. *Journal of Democracy* 10: 3–17.

Weidmann, Nils B., Jan Ketil Rod, and Lars-Erik Cederman. 2010. Representing Ethnic Groups in Space: A New Dataset. *Journal of Peace Research* 47: 491–499.

Weingast, Barry. 1979. A Rational Choice Perspective on Congressional Norms. *American Journal of Political Science* 23: 245–262.

Weingast, Barry. 1997. The Political Foundations of Democracy and the Rule of Law. *American Political Science Review* 91 (2): 245–263.

Weingast, Barry, Kenneth Shepsle, and Christopher Johnson. 1981. The Political Economy of Benefits and Costs: A Neoclassical Approach to Distributive Politics. *Journal of Political Economy* 89: 642–664.

8

If Politics is the Problem, How Can External Actors be Part of the Solution?

Shantayanan Devarajan and Stuti Khemani

Despite a large body of research and evidence on the policies and institutions needed to generate growth and reduce poverty (synthesized, for example, in Commission on Growth and Development [2008]), many governments fail to adopt these policies or establish the institutions. Research advances since the 1990s have explained this syndrome, which we generically call "government failure", in terms of the incentives facing politicians, and the underlying political institutions that lead to those incentives. Meanwhile, development assistance, which is intended to generate growth and reduce poverty, has hardly changed since the 1950s,

We are grateful to our discussant, Santiago Levy, and other participants at the Roundtable on Institutions, Governance and Corruption in Montevideo, Uruguay, May 26–27th, for helpful comments. Authors' views do not necessarily coincide with those of the institution with which they are affiliated.

S. Devarajan (✉) • S. Khemani
World Bank, Washington, DC, USA
e-mail: sdevarajan@worldbank.org; skhemani@worldbank.org

K. Basu, T. Cordella (eds.), *Institutions, Governance and the Control of Corruption*, International Economic Association Series,
https://doi.org/10.1007/978-3-319-65684-7_8

when it was thought that the problem was one of market failure. Most assistance is still delivered to governments, in the form of finance and knowledge that are bundled together as a "project". The canonical example is a dam or bridge, which requires both money and technical assistance for its design and implementation. When the policies to make these projects productive were lacking, development assistance was extended to budget support, "conditional" on policy reforms. This paper asks whether these forms of development assistance can actually achieve what is needed to solve government failures. Drawing on recent research on the politics of government failure, we show how traditional development assistance can contribute to the persistence of perverse political incentives and behavioral norms.

We propose a new model of development assistance that can help societies transition to better institutions. Specifically, we suggest that knowledge be provided to citizens to nourish the transparency that is needed for citizens' engagement, to build their capacity to select better leaders who wield power in government, as well as sanction them if they fail to deliver. Transparency policies that are thus targeted at citizens' political engagement can contribute to building political will and the legitimacy of leaders to pursue policies on the basis of technical merit. As for the financial transfer, which for various reasons has to be delivered to governments, we propose that this be provided in a lump-sum manner (that is, not linked to individual projects), conditional on governments following broadly favorable policies and making information available to citizens.

Section "From Market Failure to Government Failure: A Potted History of Development Economics" of the paper provides a history of development economics, tracing the evolution of both thinking and assistance from an initial concern with market failures to the recognition that government failures were standing in the way of development. We examine various ways that development assistance has attempted to address government failure, and find them falling short in tackling the political incentives that lead to the government failure. In section "A Framework for Government Failure", drawing on recent research, we unpack the politics of government failure as the breakdown in a series of principal-agent relationships. In section "How Can Political Engagement and Transparency Be Harnessed to Overcome Government Failures?", we show how citizen engagement and transparency—two forces that are changing quite rapidly—can help to restore accountability in these relationships, and hence enable politics to play a positive role in overcoming government failure. We then derive, in section "Implications for Development Assistance", the implications of these findings for development assistance. Given the recent and unmistakable increase in citizen engagement in selecting and sanctioning the leaders who wield power in government, this new approach may be the tide "which, taken at the flood, leads on to fortune".

From Market Failure to Government Failure: A Potted History of Development Economics

The field of development economics, which sought to help poor countries grow and reduce poverty, was initially focused on correcting market failures. The analytical foundations were provided by early writers such as Rosenstein-Rodan (1943) and Chenery (1959), who pointed to coordination failures if investment decisions were left to the market. The profitability of a port, say, depends on whether there was a road leading to it. They advocated that governments undertake a "big push" to achieve development results. Others such as Nurkse (1966) noted that low savings could leave poor people (and hence poor countries) in a poverty trap. A transfer of capital from rich countries would enable poor countries to escape the trap and achieve sustained economic growth. This thinking won support from the general field of economics, which was emerging from the Keynesian revolution, which made a strong case for government intervention in the economy, albeit for short-run stabilization purposes. The apparent success of the Soviet Union in industrialization with a planned economy provided compelling empirical evidence.

With this backdrop, governments in developing countries intervened in almost all aspects of the economy. To solve the coordination problem, governments set up enterprises, producing everything from steel to shoes to baked goods (World Bank 1995). To help nascent public and private enterprises grow, governments protected them from import competition with tariffs and quotas, invoking the "infant-industry" argument. As part of the big push, governments built and operated power plants, water systems, roads and other infrastructure. Mimicking the current systems in their former colonial powers (France and Britain), governments provided health and education free of charge.

Development assistance complemented governments' efforts to overcome market failures. Not only would the external resources help countries escape the low-savings poverty trap, but they could finance the building of infrastructure whose costs exceeded domestic resources. They could also finance the health and education systems. Furthermore, since many countries lacked the technical expertise to design and carry out these infrastructure and social-sector programs, donors would provide technical assistance as well. The idea of a development project—where financial and technical assistance was bundled in a package—was born. It soon became—and still is—the dominant mode of delivering development assistance.

In this setting, the interests of donors, governments and the general public were assumed to be aligned. Governments were correcting market failures, which is what governments are supposed to do, so they could take credit for improving social welfare. And donors, since they were supporting governments in this effort, could also be seen as contributing to the betterment of poor people's lives.

Unfortunately, the actual performance of most developing countries that followed this approach was disappointing. India, which embraced central planning for the first three decades after independence, had achieved neither growth nor significant poverty reduction (Lewis 1964). In Africa, South Asia and to some extent Latin America, import-substituting industrialization had promoted neither industrialization nor exports (Bhagwati 1978). For example, the Morogoro shoe factory, financed by the World Bank in Tanzania, never exported a single pair of shoes. Meanwhile, East Asian countries that had followed export-promoting policies were seeing rapid growth in GDP and employment. Significantly, these countries also adjusted more effectively to the oil price shocks of the 1970s. Despite billions of dollars in foreign aid to finance infrastructure, health and education, most of Sub-Saharan Africa through the mid-1990s was mired in poverty (African Strategic Review Group 1981). Much of the public infrastructure was breaking down (Foster 2008). Water was available for only a few hours a day; power cuts were commonplace; roads were impassable. While primary school enrollment rates were rising, student learning outcomes were extremely poor (van Fleet et al. 2012). Less than 40 percent of Ugandan children aged 10–16 have literacy and numeracy skills at the Grade 2 level (Jones 2012).

Why, despite the logic of market failures and the clear role for government to correct them, were the outcomes so disappointing? The proximate reason is that the public interventions, such as import tariffs, state-owned enterprises, infrastructure investment and provision of health and education, created a set of government failures that overshadowed the intended benefits from correcting the original market failures.

The government failures fall into two categories. The first has to do with the incentives in the public sector, which are different from those in a competitive private market. For instance, state-owned enterprises operated under what Kornai (1986) called a "soft budget constraint": the government covered their losses. Unlike their private-sector counterparts, these enterprises had little incentive to minimize costs or maximize profits, much less innovate and upgrade their technology. Industrialization failed to materialize. Public electricity and water utilities, since these services were typically subsidized, were not accountable to the consumer. Utility managers let grid maintenance deteriorate to the point where power and water cutoffs were common, making industrialization even more difficult (Devarajan and Harris 2007). Teachers in public schools and doctors in public clinics were paid whether they were present or not. As a result, they were absent 25–40 percent of the time (Chaudhury et al. 2006), contributing to poor learning outcomes; most people resorted to the private sector for health care (World Bank 2004a).

The second type of government failure was that these interventions were captured by politically powerful groups who then resisted their reform. Import protection resulted in a coalition between the owners and workers of the protected industries, and government bureaucrats who, when the protection was in the form of import quotas, wielded enormous power in being able to hand out scarce import licenses. These groups, who stood to lose enormous "rents" if the protection were removed in favor of greater export promotion, were able to keep the system in place even though it was not delivering (Krueger 1974). Similarly, the subsidized public utilities were an instrument of political patronage: politicians could control who got access to electricity and water and also use them for giving jobs to their constituents—the practice of "featherbedding". Furthermore, defending the status quo was politically easy, since the alternative—removing the subsidy and raising the price—would be seen as discriminating against poor people (even if the reality was the opposite). Finally, in many countries, teachers managed the political campaigns of local politicians (Béteille 2009). If the politician won, he gave the teacher a job from which he could be absent.

Starting in the late 1970s, the donor community realized that development assistance, which was largely delivered as investment projects, was not being productive in the wake of these policy distortions and institutional weaknesses (many of which were created by previous donor-funded projects and advice to correct market failures). The structural adjustment era was born. The World Bank and IMF in particular set out to help countries reform their policies and institutions, so that development projects could generate higher returns (Isham and Kaufmann 1999). Since many countries were also experiencing balance of payments or budgetary difficulties (due to terms of trade shocks such as the oil price spikes), the Bank and the Fund provided financing—budget or balance of payments support—in return for removing some of the major distortions in the economy, such as overvalued exchange rates, prohibitive tariffs and insolvent public enterprises.

While a few of the egregious distortions were removed, the general consensus was that this form of "conditionality" did not work as intended, especially in Africa. By the mid-1990s, after two decades of structural adjustment, Africa was saddled with low growth, high poverty, undiversified economies and a crushing debt burden (that was subsequently alleviated with debt-relief). Moreover, many of the distortions that prevented projects from generating returns and the economy from growing were still in place. For instance, Kenya had implemented no agricultural price reforms—despite three World Bank structural adjustment loans with such reform as conditions (Devarajan et al. 2001).

That conditionality did not lead to significant reforms is not surprising if the reason for the original distortions was politics. A coalition of bureaucrats and owners of protected industries could block import tariff reforms, say, even if much-needed budget support were at stake. In some cases, governments would agree to the reforms, get the money and then reverse the policies. In others, different parts of government were responsible for negotiating the loans and implementing the policies. For instance, the Zambian government signed a structural adjustment loan with maize price reform as a condition—without consulting the Minister of Agriculture. When it came time to implement the reform, the Minister refused (Devarajan et al. 2001). Finally, incentives within donor organizations, such as the desire to show substantial transfers of aid (Svensson 2006) or defensive lending (Basu 1991) played a role. And coordination failures among donors played into the hands of rent-seeking local leaders.

The fundamental problem is that the alignment of interests among donors, government and the general public, which is assumed when everyone is trying to solve market failures, does not hold up when the problem is government failure.[1] As pointed out above, a government failure persists because politically powerful people are earning rents from the distortion. External actors who are trying to remove the distortion to benefit the general public bump up against the same political force that is benefiting from the distortion. Often this force is within government, the same government to whom the aid is given.

The international community has sought to address this problem in at least three ways. The first and most common is to recognize that there are limits to how much the government will reform, but continue to provide the aid on grounds that there are poor people in the country who would benefit from the money. Typical examples include infrastructure projects, where the project document identifies all the price and regulatory distortions in the sector, but concludes that the country nevertheless has a huge infrastructure "deficit" that needs to be filled, and thereby justifies the project. But if the distortions are not removed, the additional aid could be making the problem worse. The welfare loss from the existing distortions is amplified. Furthermore, the financial assistance may give the government breathing room to postpone or even avoid reforms altogether—a syndrome observed in many reviews of aid to Africa (Devarajan et al. 2001). The three structural adjustment loans to Kenya mentioned earlier likely enabled the government to postpone agricultural price reforms. In fact, most of the reforms in Kenya took place in 1992, when the donors cut off aid. In the words of Michael Bruno, the then chief economist of the World Bank, "We did more for Kenya by cutting off aid for one year, than by giving them aid for the previous three decades."

The second approach is to provide knowledge assistance to government officials and leaders on the benefits of policy and institutional reforms, to increase the chances that such reforms will take place. Examples include reports on the benefits of trade reform in India, or fertilizer subsidy reform in Tanzania. While they are of high technical quality and may ultimately be useful, these reports do not necessarily help shift the political equilibrium in favor of reform. Those in favor of the reforms already know this information; those opposed—because they are earning rents from the status quo—are unlikely to change their mind based on technical analysis.[2]

Levy (2015) has proposed a third approach, "Working with the Grain". At the risk of caricature, the approach can be described as follows: assume we already know what the "right" policies are. We then use the available political analysis, such as North et al. (2012), to identify entry points where it will be politically feasible to adopt the right policies or to move in the appropriate direction in incremental or "second-best" ways that satisfy political constraints. However, second-best policies that are feasible in a dysfunctional political setting may not be solutions at all, having little impact on economic outcomes. For instance, politicians who are reluctant to reform the public educational system (because they rely on absentee teachers for their electoral campaigns) may be willing to experiment with an NGO-run school in a particular district. While the students attending this school may benefit, the overall education system will likely remain dysfunctional.

Furthermore, there is an inherent hubris in assuming that external actors will have the capacity to identify the appropriate entry points and engineer reforms in the right direction, simultaneously solving both the technical policy problem and that of adapting it to political constraints. Ex ante, there is little reason to believe that the selected entry points are the right ones; they may make the situation worse. The incentives of donor organizations to show results and count reforms as success are further reasons to search for other approaches that do not depend entirely upon external agencies getting both the economics and the politics right.

More recently, another instrument has come to the fore as a means of improving development outcomes despite government failures: providing financing directly to citizens and non-state actors, who would then demand and deliver public services. Initiatives such as GiveDirectly have emerged on the basis of research evidence of the impact of direct cash assistance in reducing poverty. Grants to local communities, civil society and non-governmental organizations (NGOs) for "community-driven development" have increased. Yet, even if such initiatives result in improved outcomes by making citizens provide public goods for themselves, bypassing the problem of government failure means, logically, that it remains a constraint on development. Unless direct transfers combined with citizen engagement eventually lead to pressure on governments to improve performance in providing public goods, the original market-failure rationale for development assistance—not to mention for government in general—will remain unaddressed.

In sum, the development community still has to confront the problem of delivering aid in the presence of government failure. These failures cannot be side-stepped. Recent research has reinforced the point that prosperity cannot be sustained without sufficient state capacity to maintain law and order and provide the institutions that support competitive markets (Besley and Persson 2009, 2011; Acemoglu et al. 2015). For development to be sustained, government failure to build state capacity has to be solved.

Fortunately, some recent research has increased our understanding of the politics underlying government failure, which in turn points to potentially transformative ways in which external assistance can help developing countries overcome these failures. The research identifies two current forces of change—greater citizen engagement and increased transparency in the political process—and shows how they affect how leaders who wield power within government are selected and sanctioned. In the next section, we describe these findings. In section "Implications for Development Assistance", we draw on these findings to propose a different way of providing development assistance, one that harnesses the power of citizens and transparency to help countries overcome government failures.

A Framework for Government Failure

The report, *Making Politics Work for Development* (World Bank 2016), untangles a vast and complex literature on the political economy of development to pull out a common thread—political engagement—which both explains government failures and holds the key to solving or averting these failures (World Bank 2016).[3] Political engagement is the participation of citizens in selecting and sanctioning the leaders who wield power in government, including by entering themselves as contenders for leadership. Government failures have been examined in economic theory as a series of principal-agent problems: between citizens and political leaders; between political leaders and public officials to whom responsibility is delegated to manage a myriad agencies within government; and between public officials who lead government agencies and the frontline providers they manage (Fig. 8.1). Political engagement influences each of these principal-agent relationships.

Political engagement happens in every institutional context, from democracies to autocracies, albeit in different ways. The main contrast examined in the literature is between when there is scope for greater political engagement by a large number of individual citizens, acting as voters or as contenders for leadership; and when there is not—that is, when power over leaders is instead concentrated among elites or organized groups of citizens such as political parties (Keefer 2011). It may seem that the difference has to do with electoral institutions. But diffused participation by non-elite citizens can happen in informal ways that constrain leaders even in authoritarian contexts, such as through

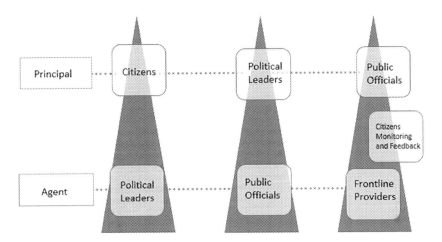

Fig. 8.1 The principal-agent relationships of government. Source: World Bank (2016)

protests, revolutions and the threat thereof (Acemoglu and Robinson 2000). Research examining differences in outcomes across countries with different national political institutions concludes that the key question that applies to both autocracies and democracies is whether leaders are selected and sanctioned on the basis of performance in delivering public goods (Besley and Kudamatsu 2008).

Citizens' political behavior—what issues they consider when selecting and disciplining leaders, and their attitudes toward the public sector—underpins the functioning of all three principal-agent relationships. Political engagement shapes the incentives and characteristics of leaders who in turn select within-government management policies to address the principal-agent problem vis-à-vis public officials and providers. Leaders and public officials also determine whether to provide citizens with powers of monitoring and feedback on frontline providers. Non-political citizen engagement has become a prominent feature of efforts to improve government performance and fits into this framework as how leaders choose to engage citizens to solve their within-government management problems. For example, a middle-tier bureaucrat like a district executive officer who has formal powers over teachers, health workers, agricultural extension workers, road work contractors and so on, can engage civil society organizations and request feedback from beneficiaries as an input into internal management practices.

Unhealthy political engagement, when leaders are selected and sanctioned on the basis of their provision of private benefits rather than public goods, casts a long shadow. It can diminish accountability not only of elected leaders but also within the principal-agent relationships between leaders, public officials and frontline providers. Leaders directly influence incentives and norms within public bureaucracies through the management policies they select. When political leaders provide jobs in the government as political patronage, they prevent the professionalization of bureaucracies. A growing body of research provides evidence on the behavior of officials in the public sector that is consistent with the implications of such patronage politics. For example, doctors with connections to political leaders are more likely to be absent from public health clinics, and the public officials who manage these doctors are more likely to report political interference when trying to apply sanctions (Callen et al. 2014).

Unhealthy political engagement undermines the legitimacy of leaders, weakening their ability to manage complex organizations and effectively implement policies (Akerlof 2015). For example, leaders can use new technologies to monitor frontline providers, reducing opportunities for graft (Banerjee et al. 2008; Muralidharan et al. 2014; World Bank 2016). But when leaders lack legitimacy, they may face resistance from frontline public providers to take up these technologies. Time-stamp machines that were installed to monitor attendance of staff in public health clinics in India were sabotaged by the staff (Banerjee et al. 2008). Widespread electricity theft and non-payment of dues to public electric utilities in the developing world are further examples of the lack of legitimacy of the state in environments of unhealthy political engagement (Min and Golden 2014; Min 2015).

If political norms allowed vote buying and patronage to flourish in elections, those same norms would influence how leaders manage public officials, how public officials manage frontline providers and how citizens engage with the public sector. Leaders who can get away with poor service delivery during their term in office by purchasing votes at election time also tend to provide jobs to public officials and to frontline providers as political patronage and *not* hold them accountable for service delivery. When frontline providers are patronage appointees, citizens do not expect that monitoring them or providing feedback on their performance will have any effect and therefore do not engage to improve the third principal-agent problem. Citizens' expectations of how political power is exercised within government can maintain this vicious cycle, leading to citizens demanding private benefits only and unhealthy political engagement persisting.

Citizens' roles as monitors in the third type of principal-agent problem is also subject to free-riding problems. Monitoring is a public good and so any individual citizen lacks the incentive to provide it. An influential strand of the literature has focused on the free-rider problems that plague collective action and how group organization and cohesion play a role in outcomes (Olson 1965; Lowi 1972; Wilson 1973). Powerful local elites can capture civil society and invert the role of citizens in the third principal-agent problem, again, through their control over local institutions of coercion or economic resources (Acemoglu et al. 2014; Andersen et al. 2015). Rather than being engaged to hold public officials accountable, citizens can be engaged to deliver public services for themselves, letting leaders and public officials off the hook in fulfilling their responsibilities.

Unhealthy political engagement arises out of conflict of interest among citizens. It exacerbates the accountability problem and can lead to "inversions" in each of the principal-agent relationships of government. Powerful elites with control over the coercive institutions of the state can subvert formal democratic and governance institutions. For example, the first principal-agent problem can become one in which leaders hold citizens accountable for providing political support by using violence and clientelist strategies such as vote buying (Stokes 2005; Acemoglu and Robinson 2006).

Even in contexts where power is more dispersed among citizens, rather than controlled by a few elites, there can nevertheless be conflict of interest among citizens with pernicious consequences for accountability for public goods. Citizens are heterogeneous in their beliefs about the role of government and what they demand from public policies and government leaders. Subsets of citizens organized as "special interests" can capture leaders and extract private rents from public policies (Grossman and Helpman 2001). Groups can form to engage in collective action with the objective of obtaining group-specific benefits that may come at the expense of public benefits that are shared with other citizens who are not organized (this is clearly conveyed, for instance, in Grossman and Helpman 1996). Public officials and frontline providers can each organize as special interests (for example, teacher unions) that wield political power over leaders, thus inverting the second two principal-agent relationships within government. Social conflict leads to inefficient outcomes because those in power can choose policies to serve their interest and there is no outside agency with the capacity to control them (Acemoglu 2003).

Alongside explaining how political engagement underpins government failures, this framework lends itself to distilling policy lessons for how transparency can contribute to changes in the nature of political engagement to improve outcomes. The very experience of political engagement, and the outcomes it produces for quality of government and service delivery, can lead to evolution in political behavior to solve government failures. Growing experience with political engagement and the learning that comes from it, sometimes through frustration and indignation with bad outcomes, can contribute to endogenous changes in political behavior, over time (Bidner and Francois 2013).[4]

For example, a rise in demand by the elite for public goods has been linked to historical episodes of institutional reform. Lizzeri and Persico (2004) explain the extension of suffrage by English elites in the mid- to late-1800s as arising from an increase in the value of urban public goods following the industrial revolution (public health infrastructure such as sewerage, waterworks and paved roads). A majority of the franchised elite pushed for reforms to extend the suffrage so that political parties would have stronger incentives to deliver these public goods. Consistent with their explanation, the authors document that following suffrage reforms, spending by municipal corporations on public health infrastructure increased substantially. Demand for common-interest public goods and inclusive political institutions are highlighted by Besley and Persson (2009) as part of the explanation for the origins of state capacity. The building of legal and fiscal institutions of the state, which are needed to support markets, protect property rights and provide public goods, are linked in their model to conditions that enable citizens to come together for a common purpose.

If citizen beliefs and demands are important because they shape political engagement, one avenue to improving outcomes would be to foster interventions that affect those beliefs and demands for common-interest public goods. The literature on transparency offers guidance on how it can interact with institutions for political engagement to bring about the changes in political behavior that are needed to build state capacity and overcome government failures. Empirical evidence on the impact of transparency suggests that citizens, even in the poorest countries, are ready to use information to hold leaders accountable (World Bank 2016). Transparency's impact in one area—voting behavior—is significant across all regions and in a variety of institutional contexts. Whether the responsiveness of voting behavior to transparency will bring about sustained changes in the institutions of governance in poor countries, where these institutions are weak to begin with, is an open question. The historical experience of rich and middle-income countries suggests that transparency works hand in hand with political engagement to enable societies to gradually build better institutions that serve the goals of economic development (Lizzeri and Persico 2004; Glaeser and Goldin 2006; Camp et al. 2014).

Working together, transparency and political engagement could not only hold elected leaders more accountable, but they could improve the incentives, political beliefs, and behavioral norms of appointed officials and of citizens. These forces together influence institutional change not only by affecting the "political will" or incentives of leaders to take up formal reforms, but also by changing informal behavioral norms in the public sector to act upon them.

Political engagement is a blunt instrument for accountability. Other strong institutions beyond the ballot box, such as supreme audit institutions and independent judiciaries, are needed. The problem is how to build such institutions from a weak base. Change in formal institutions alone is not sufficient to change actual behavior. Research has found that healthy and unhealthy political behaviors can coexist and vary within the same formal institutional context (Acemoglu et al. 2014; Andersen et al. 2015; Banerjee et al. 2005). The importance of informal behavior is further highlighted in research that examines persistent effects of historical institutions, even when those institutions (such as slavery) have long disappeared and been formally replaced by others (Nunn 2014, provides a review). A wealth of experience with efforts to strengthen institutions has shown that programs that replicate successful rich-country institutions in developing countries (often by providing equipment and training to bureaucrats) often fail (Pritchett et al. 2013; Andrews et al. 2013; IDS 2010). Effective institutions are more likely to be homegrown, using local knowledge and tailored to local contexts (Dal Bó et al. 2010; Rodrik 2000).

Political engagement and transparency, and the leaders selected through it, can foster these homegrown institutions by shifting political beliefs and promoting cooperative behavioral norms among citizens. Leaders can play this role as "prominent agents" who signal a shift in beliefs among society at large (Acemoglu and Jackson 2015).[5] Multiple levels for political engagement, such as through local electoral institutions within countries, can enable transitions to healthy political behavior by increasing the supply of leaders who have built a reputation for responsible management of public resources (Myerson 2006, 2012). Both the spread of local political competition and instruments for transparency, such as new communication technologies, can lower barriers to entry for new political contenders (Campante et al. 2013). Changes in political engagement at the local level could potentially translate into larger changes at the national level, with local levels serving as the training ground for citizens to develop their political beliefs and behavioral norms (Giuliano and Nunn 2013).

How Can Political Engagement and Transparency Be Harnessed to Overcome Government Failures?

Conditions in today's poor countries resemble those described in historical accounts of institutional transition in rich countries. These conditions include: widespread political engagement by citizens, even the poor and less educated; broad-based demands for improvements in public services; dissatisfaction with the politics of patronage and vote buying; and availability of cheap and accessible mass media such as television and radio. But good outcomes are far from guaranteed, with many risks of unhealthy political engagement by citizens and perverse responses by leaders. This section draws lessons on ways to manage the risks and channel these forces toward the goals of economic development.

Transparency can be targeted to nourish the growing political engagement and thereby complement other capacity building efforts to establish effective public sector institutions. Research on the attributes of transparency that bring about positive change suggests that external actors may have two advantages: the technical capacity for generating new data and credibility of information through politically independent expert analysis.

A global shift in political institutions is providing space for greater political engagement. The dramatic spread of elections at national and at local levels, even within countries with authoritarian national political institutions, has created unprecedented opportunities for citizens to influence governance. Citizens are engaging as never before in the political process, as individual voters and as contenders for political office. Figure 8.2 plots the distribution of countries ranked by the Polity IV measure of democracy, with higher values corresponding to greater space for political engagement by citizens. During the past three and a half decades, the distribution of political institutions across countries has steadily shifted toward greater political engagement. Although some individual countries have experienced reversals to more autocratic institutions or seen little change, the overall trend has been toward greater opportunities for political engagement.

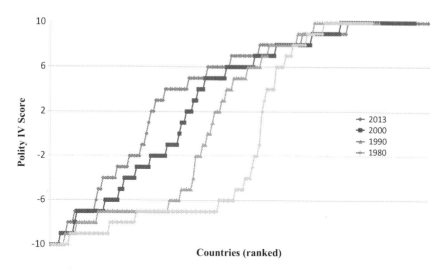

Fig. 8.2 Global Shift toward democratic institutions for political engagement, 1980–2013. Source: World Bank (2016) using data from the Polity IV project. *Notes:* The Polity IV Score is a measure of state authority that is widely used in research, varying on a 21-point scale ranging from −10 (which corresponds to hereditary monarchy) to +10 (which corresponds to the Polity IV view of consolidated democracy). Higher values are associated with more democratic institutions

Political engagement within countries is also growing through elections at the local level, even under different national political institutions. National leaders across the political spectrum are concerned about monitoring and managing public officials at the local level, who are often on the front lines of service delivery. National leaders even in authoritarian regimes are considering how best to use citizen engagement and transparency to solve this "last-mile" problem, including through local elections. For example, local elections at the village level in China have been found to support local accountability and to improve local government performance in delivering public goods, compared with bureaucratic monitoring through upper-level governments (Martínez-Bravo et al. 2011; Martínez-Bravo et al. 2014). Three country cases—India, Indonesia and Uganda—offer a picture of how political engagement is growing at the local level across very different national institutional contexts (World

Bank 2016). In Indonesia and Uganda, space for political engagement has grown as the result of proliferation of new subnational political units. India has seen a marked increase in contending political parties in state elections.

At the same time, the conduct of elections in many poor countries is marred by violence, fraud, vote buying and ethnic favoritism, leading researchers and observers to discount the role of elections in bringing about accountability (Collier 2009; Kaplan 2000; Chua 2002; Zakaria 2003). Furthermore, some observers doubt the capacity of poor and less educated citizens to exercise their vote responsibly. Robert D. Kaplan (2000 p. 62) states that "if a society is not in reasonable health, democracy can be not only risky but disastrous". In the regions where most of the poorest people live, Africa and South Asia, more than 70 percent of respondents report voting. Citizens with less than a primary education, and therefore likely to be relatively poor, are *more* likely to report voting. Citizens in Africa with less than a primary education report voting 7 percentage points more than others; in South Asia the gap is 10 percentage points (World Bank 2016). Pande (2011) finds that in many developing countries less educated and income-poor citizens tend to be more politically active than those with greater education and income.

Electoral malpractice does *not* imply that authoritarian institutions that bypass or suppress political engagement would necessarily improve outcomes. One study finds that ethnic favoritism led to distortions in public resource allocation even under authoritarian regimes in Kenya, but that periods of transition to multiparty electoral competition were in fact associated with *reductions* in these ethnicity-based policy distortions (Burgess et al. 2015). The same factors that explain unhealthy political engagement, such as the ability of political elites to punish voters through economic sanctions, violence and coercion, can also prevent autocratic arrangements from being successful (Acemoglu and Robinson 2006; Besley and Kudamatsu 2008).

The diversity of successful institutions around the globe might tempt reform leaders to find ways of bypassing the messiness of electoral politics rather than improving it. It may even be interpreted as evidence in favor of restricting political engagement and establishing institutions run by benevolent dictators and organized elites. For example, some have attributed the East Asian growth "miracle" to institutions that restricted citizen engagement, allowing leaders to select and implement policies on technical merit.[6] This view, however, begs the question of where benevolent dictators come from, and whether the "miracle" can be replicated in other countries. Societies in which elites do not sanction poor leaders, or where elites benefit from poorly-performing leaders' remaining in office, are unlikely to be successful autocracies (Besley and Kudamatsu 2008). Why are some autocratic settings successful in selecting and sanctioning leaders on the basis of competence and performance, and others disastrous at it? There is little research available to guide us on this question, and even less on whether messy democracies can eschew elections, however flawed they may be, and become well-functioning autocracies.

In contrast to researchers and external observers, citizens who experience electoral malpractice tend to believe that elections do matter, that through their votes they can improve their lives. The two panels of Fig. 8.3 show the share of individuals by region who described elections as being very or rather important on a personal and national level, respectively.

Similar patterns were obtained from two Afrobarometer surveys undertaken in Uganda and Nigeria on the eve of their elections in 2011 and 2007, respectively. In these surveys, about 80 percent of respondents in Uganda and 70 percent in Nigeria said that they believed the way they voted could make things better (Fig. 8.4). Those respondents, many of whom are likely to be poor, with low education and reporting food insecurity, are just as likely as others to express the belief that the way they vote could make things better.

Not only do Ugandan and Nigerian citizens believe in the importance of voting, and vote at high rates, but they also express interest in receiving information about elections. More than 80 percent of respondents said they wanted a little more or a lot more information ahead of the 2007 elections in Nigeria and the 2011 elections in Uganda (Fig. 8.5). Again, those with less education and food security are just as interested in receiving more information as others.

There is substantial evidence that political engagement responds to transparency within and across a variety of institutional contexts.

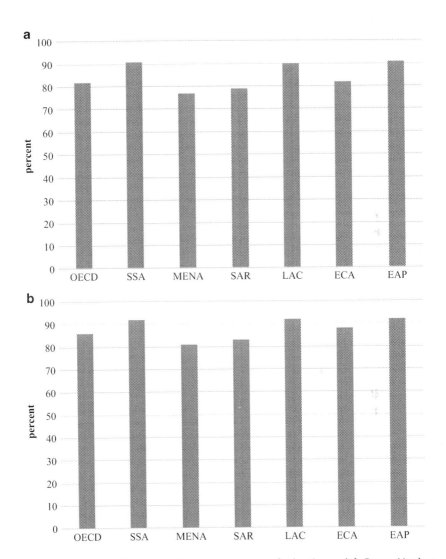

Fig. 8.3 Citizens' Views of the Importance of Elections. (**a**) Does Having Honest Elections Make a Lot of Difference in Your and Your Family's Lives? Percentage of respondents answering "Very" or "Rather" Important. (**b**) How Important Is Having Honest Elections for Whether the Country Develops Economically? Source: World Bank (2016) using World Values Survey (Wave 6 undertaken over 2010–2014)

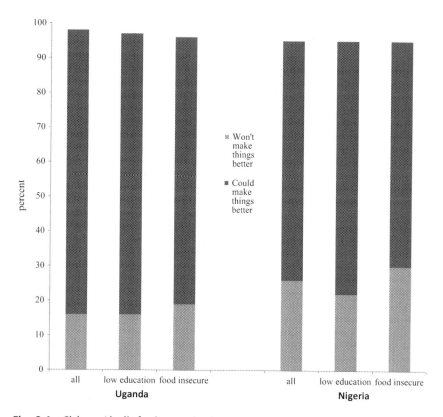

Fig. 8.4 Citizens' beliefs about whether the way they vote could make things better, Uganda and Nigeria. Source: World Bank (2016) using data from Afrobarometer Round 4.5.2 (Uganda 2011), Round 3.5 (Nigeria 2007). *Notes:* The survey question is the following: "Which of the following statements is closest to your view? Choose Statement 1 or Statement 2. Statement 1: No matter how you vote, it won't make things any better in the future. Statement 2: The way you vote could make things better in the future"

Transparency can increase voter turnout or shift the distribution of vote shares in countries as diverse as India, China, Malaysia, Mozambique, and Pakistan (Giné and Mansuri 2011; Banerjee et al. 2011; Guan and Green 2006; Aker et al. 2013; Miner 2015). Even where corruption is rampant, concrete information on the extent of corruption, as revealed by public audits of government spending, can increase the likelihood

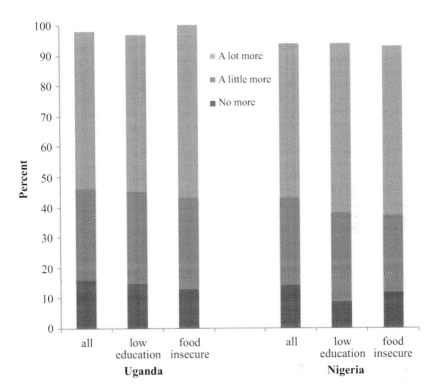

Fig. 8.5 How much more information do citizens want in order to decide how to vote, Uganda and Nigeria. Source: Afrobarometer Round 4.5.1 (Uganda 2011), Round 3.5 (Nigeria 2007). Notes: The survey question is the following: "In order to decide how to vote in the upcoming elections, how much more information would you like to have?"

that corrupt leaders are removed from office (Ferraz and Finan 2008). Where ethnic favoritism and vote buying are widespread, the use of these clientelist practices to win office can be reduced by providing greater information about the quality of leaders and their performance in delivering public services (Casey 2015; Fujiwara and Wantchekon 2013; Keefer and Khemani 2014, Banerjee et al. 2011).

Mass media, such as radio, television, newspapers and the Internet, are important in bringing about changes in voting behavior. Leaders respond to mass media because it amplifies the role of political engagement to hold them accountable (Besley and Burgess 2002; Snyder and Stromberg 2010). World Bank (2016) discusses the evidence on how citizens around the world can obtain news from plural sources. For example, in a region like Sub-Saharan Africa where poverty is widespread and effective literacy may be low, a Gallup World poll shows that citizens rely on radio as the most important source for becoming well-informed about events in their countries. Research on the impact of radio in Africa has found that it provides information which helps relax ethnic and partisan loyalties, and promotes demand for broad public services in health and education (Casey 2015; Keefer and Khemani 2014).

Yet, the type of information, its source, and its "fit" with the institutional context are important. Information has sometimes had the opposite effect of discouraging voter turnout or increasing vote buying. The direction of impact depends upon the timing of information provision, the nature of the media market and the extent to which the information is credible or reflects political biases and polarization. The same type of information can have different effects depending on the credibility of the source. The pattern of evidence does not suggest that lack of impact or detrimental impact of transparency is limited to weak institutional settings or that successful impacts occur only in strong institutional settings. Yet, despite overwhelming evidence of the responsiveness of political engagement to transparency, there is no clear evidence on whether transparency's impact is sufficient to get leaders to respond with sustainable or long-term improvements in outcomes, using the powers of their office to strengthen institutions. The extent to which incumbent politicians and party elites can undo any positive effects of information on voting behavior is not clear.

Implications for Development Assistance

To summarize the argument so far: government failures are constraining development. These failures, defined here as a series of principal-agent relationships between citizens, politicians, policy makers and service providers, are the result of politics. The political failures in turn can be understood as unhealthy citizen engagement to select and sanction leaders on the basis of receiving private benefits, which comes at the expense of broad public goods. Transparency can help strengthen and improve political engagement so that citizens can hold leaders accountable for public goods.

In this setting, how can development assistance help promote growth and poverty alleviation? As we mentioned earlier, the traditional mode of development assistance—the investment project—was based on overcoming market failures. That mode has not proved to be effective when the problem was government failure. Investment projects do not by themselves reform policies or institutions. Budget support based on conditions for policy reform has its limitations when the distortions that the reforms are meant to correct is the result of a political equilibrium. Knowledge assistance, provided only to the government, is unlikely to dislodge the political equilibrium. And looking for politically-feasible entry points or giving cash directly to citizens do not directly address the flawed principal-agent relationships that created the government failure in the first place.

For development assistance to be effective, the tradition of "bundling" knowledge and financial assistance—in a project, for instance—has to be abandoned. Knowledge assistance should be provided to citizens to help them in holding the government accountable. External actors should target transparency to nourish the growing forces of political engagement. External agents have technical capacity for generating new data and credible information through politically independent expert analysis. This technical advantage stands in sharp contrast to their lack of such advantage when it comes to building capacity and organizations for collective action from the outside (Mansuri and Rao 2013; Pritchett et al. 2013; Andrews et al. 2013; IDS 2010). Even though there is less established evidence from the poorest countries (in contrast to rich and middle-income countries) about the eventual impact of transparency on governance and institutions, what is available shows that political engagement is highly responsive to transparency. The theory on how changes in political engagement bring about larger institutional changes, going beyond the ballot box, and the supporting evidence on specific channels of the selection and sanctioning of leaders, are consistent with the potential of targeted transparency to work together with political engagement to gradually build better institutions in developing countries.

Research also indicates which attributes of transparency are important to cultivate healthy political engagement to overcome government failures. These attributes, discussed below, also imply that the aid architecture should be transformed to de-link financing from the knowledge transfer, to enable the latter to be more effective in helping countries build homegrown institutions and deliver results using the aid they receive.

Transparency is most effective when it supports specific, reliable and impartial evidence on the performance of leaders. The information provided through transparency must be specific about both policy actions and the resulting outcomes, so that citizens can use this information to select and sanction leaders. Information that is not specific in this way will erode the benefits of transparency. For example, information only on budget allocations is of limited use without information on how these allocations were spent and what the spending accomplished. Naturally, the information provided must also be reliable, and must be accepted as impartial and untainted by partisan political considerations.

Media markets are crucial to foster healthy political engagement. Policies can promote healthy competition in media markets, and can be complemented by interventions to support public-interest programming that provides impartial information to cultivate citizens' political engagement. Even when media are independent from state control and markets are competitive, citizens can choose to access primarily entertaining programs that do not sufficiently inform them about public-interest issues. Sponsorship of appealing programs, or "infotainment", to communicate evidence on the actions of leaders and the effects of public policies, has the potential to persuade citizens to shift political beliefs in favor of good leaders and good policies.

The information and access to media has to be relevant and timely to the political process. A key dimension of relevance is jurisdictional: information on the performance of public policies needs to be targeted to the jurisdictions in which citizens select leaders. Information on public goods provision at the local level is more relevant to voters' decisions in local elections than is information at the national level. Timeliness matters as well: performance assessments of both current incumbents and of challengers, delivered regularly during a term in office but also at the time of elections, can make it easier for citizens to use information to decide on how to vote. Information that enables citizens to assess the potential of political contenders, not just incumbents, can be useful to avoid incumbency bias. Relevant information broadcast through media that citizens actually access and pay attention to can make it easier for candidates to compete on platforms of improving public policies and government performance.

Transparency can improve the functioning of local electoral institutions. Not only are local governments at the last mile of service delivery, but they are also at the "first mile" at which citizens determine the platforms on which leaders are selected and sanctioned. These platforms, whether they are the healthy ones of good public performance or the unhealthy ones of vote buying and ethnic favoritism, not only determine the incentives and quality of selected local leaders but can also shape the behavioral norms in the public sector as a whole. This first mile can matter for building legitimacy and capacity of state institutions in fragile contexts; for building capable and accountable local governments in rapidly urbanizing environments; that plan well for urban development and mobilize the domestic resources needed for sustainable development. The local level can matter for improving political attitudes and behavior of citizens in rich-country contexts as well, where the national stage appears to be hopelessly mired by political polarization among citizens. Targeting transparency to improve the functioning of local institutions of political engagement along the lines described above can therefore address some of the growing areas of economic concern throughout the world.

What is different about the recommendation here is the importance of communicating to citizens, in ways that effectively shift citizens' political beliefs and behavior on the basis of technical evidence. The traditional policy approach has treated leaders as the sole audience of expert analysis, and has treated communication to citizens as a matter not requiring scientific investigation. Communicating information to influence beliefs and political behavioral norms requires an understanding of the institutions within which and through which citizens form these beliefs. Research has offered a better understanding of how political engagement, and the leaders selected through it, shape beliefs and behavior in the public sector. Transparency can be targeted at these political institutions to try to improve beliefs and behavior toward solving shared problems of public goods for economic development.

Applying these policy lessons for transparency depends upon the characteristics of existing government jurisdictions: which tasks are assigned to which leaders, and who are the citizens who select and sanction them? If government jurisdictions have clearly assigned responsibilities for public goods, then it is easier to generate data on performance that can be attributed to the leaders of those jurisdictions, and to communicate that information to enable citizens to hold those leaders accountable for public goods. Most places will have a complex set of political and bureaucratic institutions that share responsibilities for the provision of public goods. In these cases, higher-order transparency, such as civic education about the roles of different government jurisdictions and officials, can play a role in strengthening political engagement.

What about the financial transfer? If it is in the form of a sovereign loan, the transfer has to go to the government. But it should be transferred in such a way that maximizes citizens' ability to hold the state to account, to complement the efforts by the knowledge transfer of improving the quality of political engagement through transparency. This can be achieved if the financing is transferred in a lump-sum fashion to the government budget. Note that this is the polar opposite of a traditional project, where the money is transferred only if it will be spent on a particular project (and disbursed only when expenses against that project are incurred). But aid where the donor specifies how the money should be spent weakens citizens' ability to verify—not to mention have a say in—whether the government is spending according to their preferences. The proposed method of transfer is also different from policy-based lending, which is usually conditioned on certain policies being enacted. This type of conditionality, imposed by the donor, again goes against citizens' efforts at demanding policy changes from their governments.

While this proposal may at first glance appear radical, it is in fact not very different from how aid is transferred now. For example, the World Bank (and other multilateral development banks [MDBs]) allocate aid to low-income countries according to a formula, based on the Country Policy and Institutional Assessment and other factors. The formula indicates the total amount of aid to a particular country that will be productive. Typically, the actual aid provided to a country is equal to this formula-based amount. The only difference is that the total is usually broken up into specific projects on health, transport, water and the like. But as pointed out above, these projects do not address the government failures plaguing low-income countries. Since the Bank has already determined that the formula-based total amount of aid will be productive, they should transfer that amount directly. If the country wants to build a road or school or hospital, it is welcome to use the aid resources to finance these investments. However, the decision should be the government's—so that the government can be held accountable—rather than the donor's. We should add that there is considerable evidence that project-specific aid is fungible (Feyzioglu et al. 1998). That is, when the donor is financing a project that the government would have undertaken anyway, then the aid is replacing government resources, which are now spent on other items in the budget. In other words, even project-specific aid is effectively budget support. Finally, this lump-sum aid could still be conditional, but it should be conditional on those measures that promote citizen engagement and transparency, so that the financial transfers contribute to overcoming the government failure.

To be sure, this transition in the aid architecture will not take place overnight. The development community is accustomed to a traditional way of doing business, where knowledge and finance are bundled, and the two are primarily delivered to the government. However, the same development community has for a long time recognized that government failures are the main obstacle to faster growth and poverty reduction and, more recently, that these failures are political. Now that we have a better understanding of how politics contributes to government failures, and the role of citizen engagement and transparency in turning a vicious cycle to a virtuous one, the development community must re-think its mode of delivering aid, so that external actors can contribute to, rather than detract from, citizens' ability to select leaders who have the political will and the legitimacy to deliver the public goods needed for development.

Comments by Santiago Levy[7]

This is an interesting and very relevant paper that discusses a central issue for MDBs and, more broadly, international agencies involved in promoting development. The paper argues that the current mechanism used by MDBs to help developing countries—financial assistance and technical knowledge bundled in the form of the project loan—is targeting the wrong problem, namely, market failures of various varieties. The paper suggests that, instead, the central constraint that needs to be tackled is government failure, in particular, the capture of political leaders by various interest groups that, on one hand, impede the adoption of technically sound policies; and, on the other, weaken State capacity to deliver quality public goods in a context of absence of transparency and accountability. The paper then argues that MDBs should explicitly aim to correct government failure changing the nature of their engagement with developing countries. In particular, it makes a rather bold proposal to unbundle knowledge from financial assistance; deliver knowledge directly to citizens and not governments with the explicit aim of increasing transparency and political engagement; and deliver financial assistance to governments as a lump-sum transfer delinked from individual projects, conditional only on governments adopting broadly favorable policies. The claim is that increasing citizens' access to specific, reliable and impartial evidence on the performance of political leaders will allow citizens to select and sanction them, improve the functioning of electoral institutions, and facilitate the adoption of development friendly policies.

There is indeed much to be in agreement with Devarajan and Khemanis' paper (henceforth D&K). There is by now substantial evidence that governments captured by special interests, and characterized by rent-seeking, corruption, opacity and lack of accountability are exactly the opposite of what is needed for equity and growth. Further, it is clear that State capacity is a critical determinant of performance, arguably much more important than access to concessional finance. Key inputs for the proper functioning of markets and social welfare depend on State capacity: protection of property rights, setting appropriate macro policies, providing citizen security and delivering quality public services for health, education and so on.

D&K argue, and I would agree with them, that State capacity cannot be replaced by "community-driven" development, or by NGOs. This of course does not mean that communities and NGOs cannot make a positive contribution to development; they certainly can. But it should be clear that their contribution is a complement and not a substitute for a well-functioning State. Neither communities nor NGOs can set trade or exchange rate policy, defend citizens from crime with the use of force, adjudicate justice or collect taxes. A well-functioning State is a *sine qua non* for development.

I have three broad reactions to D&K. First, although as a general proposition more transparency and better access to information is always welcome, one needs to ponder whether there is an automatic association between more transparency and information and more political engagement. Clearly, if citizens know that a medicine costs 100 dollars and a government official paid 200 dollars for it, this will likely trigger an investigation and eventual punishment for presumably corrupt behavior. This is simple and straightforward. But there are cases when things are not so clear. Assume a government official in the Finance Ministry colludes with a private international bank and places government bonds at a higher cost (commission, interest rate, maturity) than warranted by the country's risk profile (no explicit bribe involved, but eventually that government official will be hired by that international bank). The damage to the country might be much higher than the extra 100 dollars paid for medicines. But the information to detect this behavior is not so easy for the majority of citizens to interpret and act upon, even if the terms and conditions of the financial operation are open and transparent to all. Should the maturity have been ten years instead of eight? Should the interest rate have been 6.75 rather than 7.15 percent? Should the currency be euros rather than dollars? Citizens might have all the information, but there is no substitute for an authority within the government (or the Central Bank) that has the technical ability and the right incentives to offer a qualified opinion. Information in the hands of citizens is good, but by itself at times insufficient.

Further, citizens' reactions to more information need not always be *constructive*. If cumulatively the information about corruption by government officials is available to all citizens, but does not lead to punishment, citizens might feel frustrated. Further, they may feel that since nobody is playing by the rules of the game, then they should not either, making them more willing to pay bribes or break the rules themselves. Citizens can became disillusioned, even cynical, when they know that government officials (and other citizens) are breaking the rules but nothing happens. More information may be a necessary but not sufficient condition for more constructive political engagement by citizens. There must be consequences for bad behavior; otherwise there may be two equilibriums from more information.

My second reaction to D&K is associated with the connection between more political engagement and better public policies. Broadly, I agree with D&K that more political engagement should translate into reduced corruption, less vote buying and patronage politics and limits to rent-seeking behavior. In a context of active political engagement by citizens and mechanisms to enforce accountability, more information about teacher absenteeism will most likely lead to teachers showing up for work more often. This is better but not enough to achieve quality education, which is the ultimate aim. Even without corruption or rent-seeking, there can be genuine disagreements about the public policies needed to improve the quality of education. Should teachers be promoted based on their own evaluations or on evaluations of their students? Should they be paid monetary incentives on the basis of performance?

In my view, the connection between more political engagement and better public policies is there, but perhaps not as strong, or at least as direct, as D&K would have us believe. Certainly more political engagement can reduce the more egregious types of dysfunctional behavior, and remove obstacles for adopting better policies that emanate from corruption or rent-seeking. Still, more political engagement may not immediately result in better public policies. What it may lead to is a *process* of trial and error by which better policies can eventually be found. Perhaps this is all that can reasonably be aimed for. That said, it is much better than the status quo in many developing countries, and in that sense D&K are quite right in that greater political engagement is a critical input into (eventually, I would add) better policies.

My third comment centers on the proposal made by D&K for MDB action, which is in two parts: deliver information and knowledge only to citizens, and deliver financial aid to governments through a lump-sum transfer conditional only on broadly favorable policies. I consider first the suggestion that MDBs deliver information and knowledge directly to citizens. To discuss this, it is useful to distinguish between two types of government failure (a distinction made by D&K at the beginning of their paper but then abandoned in the discussion and policy proposal). Type I government failure, so-to-speak, associated with political capture, corruption, vote buying and lack of accountability, which weakens State capacity and leads to insufficient or low quality public goods. But there is a, so-to-speak, type II government failure, associated with governments pursuing the wrong policies, even if they are honest, transparent, accountable, un-captured and well-intentioned. Perhaps the government is fixing the exchange rate to combat inflation, even though the resulting appreciation is taxing the export sector with broadly negative consequences. Perhaps the government is subsidizing energy to all households as a way of helping the poor, even though this is regressive and fiscally very costly. Perhaps the government has set up a pay-as-you-go pension system that under current demographics is not viable, but not as a result of rent-seeking by anybody, but because it thinks it is the best way to deal with longevity risks. The list of type II failures can be very long.

D&K are concerned about type I failures, but type II might be equally relevant. And MDBs may have useful knowledge and policy advice to convey to governments regarding type II failures. Indeed, much of the day-to-day work of MDBs is associated with precisely this. So a policy prescription that says that MDBs should only provide information to citizens about type I failures might be unnecessarily strict and limiting. Of course, MDBs policy advice as to how to deal with type II government failures should be available to all, but there is no reason to exclude governments, who in the end are the counterparts to the MDBs for any policy change. This suggests that D&K recommendation should perhaps be more nuanced. MDBs should provide information and knowledge to all, governments and citizens, about both type I and type II; they are not mutually exclusive. The nature of the information will be different in each case. And the key important difference vis-à-vis what MDBs are doing today is that MDBs would be producing and disseminating much more information about type I failures than at present.

There are some issues associated with this part of the D&K proposal that merit more discussion. How would MDBs identify the citizens to whom information of type I failures is to be delivered? Would these be political parties in opposition? Would they be NGOs, local think-tanks and academia? Would MDBs establish direct relationship with the local media and brief them on a regular basis? Or would they establish web-based portals? The devil here is in the details, as usual. But the point here is that these are not minor operational considerations, but substantive issues that would have large implications for the modus operandi of MDBs.

In parallel, one has to also consider what the reactions of governments would be to a systemic effort by MDBs to provide information about type I government failures to their citizens. Perhaps some governments would argue that they are being wrongly accused of corruption, or of rigging elections. Some would argue that under the pretext of development, MDBs are unduly interfering in their country's political life (and may eventually decide not to engage with MDBs). This aspect of the D&K proposal also merits further discussion.

A related set of issues that also needs more discussion is associated with the quality and veracity of the information that MDBs would provide to citizens, and the set of issues covered. D&K rightly point out that information is more effective in promoting political engagement when it is specific, reliable and impartial. This would pose new challenges to MDBs, as they would have to judge whether accusations of corruption are indeed true or not (is it the case that during the construction of the road from A to B officials at the Transport Ministry manipulated the bidding process to help some contractors over others?); whether depictions of behavior are accurate (is the absentee rate of doctors at the public clinics x and not z percent); or whether electoral processes were fair or characterized by vote-rigging (did all political parties have fair access to the media?). It would be important for MDBs to be judged impartial by all, and to have credibility, a situation that in my view at present is not always the case.

I turn quickly to make two observations on the second component of the D&K proposal, namely, delivering financial aid through a lump-sum transfer rather than through project finance. First, I think that this component of the proposal is secondary and not essential to the main issue raised by D&K: fostering political participation by citizens by giving them more information. Indeed, MDBs could add to their current tasks some mechanism to achieve the above, and still continue with standard project finance focusing on infrastructure, say, or standard policy-based loans focused on addressing type II government failures. It is not indispensable that financial aid be given through a lump-sum transfer to achieve D&K's aims. The second observation follows from the first: the proposal to deliver financial aid through a lump-sum transfer rather than individual project finance should be justified on different grounds. This brings us to a different and long-standing debate on the merits of various type of lending. D&K do mention that the lump-sum transfer would be conditional on the country following broadly favorable policies, but do not dwell on what these policies would be. Thus, one can interpret this second component of the D&K as really not that different from policy-based lending, or potentially very different. There are, for instance, substantive implications for how the work of MDBs would be coordinated with the work of the IMF in cases of macroeconomic stress, or even without that coordination, about the proper mix of lending by MDBs on their own. This debate takes us far from the core point raised by D&K and, again, needlessly so.

The issues raised above are not meant to disqualify the proposal made by D&K, but rather to identify some implications that need more careful consideration and research. Nor should raising these issues deter attention from the broader, and in my view correct, point made by D&K: type I government failures are systemic and a real hindrance to development, and cannot be ignored by MDBs.

While the various implications of the D&K proposal are more carefully considered, MDBs can deepen their involvement in an agenda of work in which they are already involved, which is complementary to the transparency and better governance agenda raised by D&K. As with most issues of development, this on-going agenda needs to be applied on a case-by-case basis, but broadly should pursue a multipronged approach of lending, policy advice, knowledge dissemination and capacity building to, inter alia: (a) spread the use of internet and/or improve its regulation to reduce costs and raise quality; (b) create or strengthen anti-trust agencies to increase efficiency but also reduce the power of private trusts that engage in costly rent-seeking activities; (c) strengthen laws regarding transparency and accountability in tax and spending operations, extending them to all levels of government; (d) create or strengthen capabilities in independent national audit agencies; and, (e) together with other agencies or institutions like the OECD and the IMF, extend protocols on global transparency and the exchange of information for tax purposes or for combatting money laundering. Even if these measures are by themselves insufficient to improve the political process in developing countries, implementing them more widely and systematically can make a direct contribution to having more informed citizens, to combat corruption and rent-seeking, and to facilitate more political participation.

In parallel, research needs to deepen our understanding of the multiple factors that determine the extent and nature of political participation, and the mechanisms by which this participation translates into better policies and stronger State capacity. We need better metrics of corruption, more evidence of what information is more relevant to promote political participation, and a better understanding of the circumstances under which political participation induces constructive changes in the relation between those governing and those being governed.

Notes

1. There is also the possibility of government failure in donor countries, which leads to aid not in fact being targeted at fixing market failures in recipient countries (World Bank 2004b).
2. As we will discuss in the following sections, providing the knowledge to citizens more broadly, going beyond government officials and leaders, is a strategy that may help shift the political equilibrium.
3. This section draws upon World Bank (2016), *Making Politics Work for Development: Harnessing transparency and citizen engagement*, Policy Research Report, Washington DC: World Bank.
4. A body of research examining regional differences in governance within Italy has attributed the presence of greater social capital and of public interest or "civic" voting to earlier experience with participatory democracy (Putnam et al. 1993; Guiso, Sapienza, and Zingales 2006; Nannicini et al. 2013; Alesina and Giuliano 2015).

5. Beamen et al. (2009) and Beaman et al. (2012) provide evidence on how female leaders shift social norms related to gender.
6. Isham, Kaufmann and Pritchett (1997) suggest that this is the argument in a World Bank report on the growth performance of East Asian countries.
7. Inter-American Development Bank. Author's views do not necessarily coincide with those of the institution he is affiliated with. If, on one hand, development will not occur (or at least will occur very slowly and imperfectly), without a proper functioning State; and, on the other hand, there is abundant evidence that in many developing countries constructing such a State is being undermined by corruption, patronage politics and rent-seeking, then D&K argue that doing something about malfunctioning governments should be *the* central mission for MDBs. And that that something should be to nurture the main mechanism that can improve the functioning of governments and strengthen State capacity, namely, more active political participation by better informed citizens.

References

Acemoglu, Daron. 2003. Why Not a Political Coase Theorem? Social Conflict, Commitment, and Politics. *Journal of Comparative Economics* 31: 620–652.
Acemoglu, Daron, Camilo García-Jimeno, and James A. Robinson. 2015. State Capacity and Economic Development: A Network Approach. *American Economic Review* 105: 2364–2409.
Acemoglu, Daron, and Matthew O. Jackson. 2015. History, Expectations, and Leadership in the Evolution of Social Norms. *Review of Economic Studies* 82: 1–34.
Acemoglu, Daron, Tristan Reed, and James A. Robinson. 2014. Chiefs: Economic Development and Elite Control of Civil Society in Sierra Leone. *Journal of Political Economy* 122: 319–368.
Acemoglu, Daron, and James A. Robinson. 2000. Why Did the West Extend the Franchise? Growth, Inequality and Democracy in Historical Perspective. *Quarterly Journal of Economics* 115: 1167–1199.
———. 2006. De Facto Political Power and Institutional Persistence. *American Economic Association Papers and Proceedings* 96: 325–330.
African Strategic Review Group. 1981. *Accelerated Development in Sub-Saharan Africa: An Agenda for Action. World Bank Regional and Sectoral Studies.* Washington, DC: World Bank.

Aker, Jenny C., Paul Collier, and Pedro C. Vicente. 2013. *Is Information Power? Using Mobile Phones and Free Newspapers During an Election in Mozambique.* Working Paper 328, Center for Global Development, Washington.

Akerlof, George. 2015. A Theory of Authority. Unpublished.

Alesina, Alberto, and Paola Giuliano. 2015. Culture and Institutions. *Journal of Economic Literature* 53 (4): 898–944.

Anderson, Siwan, Patrick Francois, and Ashok Kotwal. 2015. Clientelism in Indian Villages. *American Economic Review* 105: 1780–1816.

Andrews, Matt, Lant Pritchett, and Michael Woolcock. 2013. Escaping Capability Traps Through Problem Driven Iterative Adaptation (PDIA). *World Development* 51: 234–244.

Banerjee, Abhijit, Esther Duflo, and Rachel Glennerster. 2008. Putting a Band-Aid on a Corpse: Incentives for Nurses in the Indian Public Health Care System. *Journal of the European Economic Association* 6: 487–500.

Banerjee, Abhijit, Lakshmi Iyer, and Rohini Somanathan. 2005. History, Social Divisions, and Public Goods in Rural India. *Journal of the European Economic Association* 3: 639–647.

Banerjee, Abhijit V., Selvan Kumar, Rohini Pande, and Felix Su. 2011. *Do Informed Voters Make Better Choices? Experimental Evidence from Urban India.* Working Paper.

Basu, Kaushik. 1991. *The International Debt Problem, Credit Rationing and Loan Pushing: Theory and Experience.* Princeton Studies in International Finance. Princeton, NJ: Princeton University.

Beaman, L., R. Chattopadhyay, E. Duflo, R. Pande, and P. Topalova. 2009. Powerful Women: Does Exposure Reduce Bias? *The Quarterly Journal of Economics* 124 (4): 1497–1540.

Beaman, L., E. Duflo, R. Pande, and P. Topalova. 2012. Female Leadership Raises Aspirations and Educational Attainment for Girls: A Policy Experiment in India. *Science* 335 (6068): 582–586.

Besley, Timothy, and Robin Burgess. 2002. The Political Economy of Government Responsiveness: Theory and Evidence from India. *Quarterly Journal of Economics* 117: 1415–1451.

Besley, Timothy, and Masayuki Kudamatsu. 2008. *Making Autocracy Work.* Research Paper DEDPS48. London School of Economics.

Besley, Timothy, and Torsten Persson. 2009. The Origins of State Capacity: Property Rights, Taxation, and Politics. *American Economic Review* 99: 1218–1244.

————. 2011. *Pillars of Prosperity: The Political Economics of Development Clusters*. Princeton, NJ: Princeton University Press.

Béteille, Tara. 2009. Absenteeism, Transfers and Patronage: The Political Economy of Teacher Labor Markets in India. Unpublished Doctoral Dissertation, Stanford University.

Bhagwati, Jagdish N. 1978. Foreign Trade Regimes: Overall Conclusions. In *Anatomy and Consequences of Exchange Control Regimes*, 205–218. Cambridge, MA: NBER.

Bidner, Chris, and Patrick Francois. 2013. The Emergence of Political Accountability. *Quarterly Journal of Economics* 128: 1397–1448.

Burgess, Robin, Remi Jedwab, Edward Miguel, Ameet Morjaria, and Gerard Padró i Miquel. 2015. The Value of Democracy: Evidence from Road Building in Kenya. *American Economic Review* 105: 1817–1851.

Callen, Michael, Saad Gulzar, Ali Hasanain, and Yasir Khan. 2014. The Political Economy of Public Employee Absence: Experimental Evidence from Pakistan. Unpublished, Harvard Kennedy School, Cambridge.

Camp, Edwin, Avinash Dixit, and Susan Stokes. 2014. Catalyst or Cause? Legislation and the Demise of Machine Politics in Britain and the United States. *Legislative Studies Quarterly* 39: 559–592.

Campante, Filipe, Ruben Durante, and Francesco Sobbrio. 2013. *Politics 2.0: The Multifaceted Effect of Broadband Internet on Political Participation*. NBER Working Paper 19029, National Bureau of Economic Research, Cambridge.

Casey, Katherine. 2015. Crossing Party Lines: The Effects of Information on Redistributive Politics. *American Economic Review* 105: 2410–2448.

Chaudhury, Nazmul, Jeffrey Hammer, Michael Kremer, Karthik Muralidharan, and F. Halsey Rogers. 2006. Missing in Action: Teacher and Health Worker Absence in Development Countries. *Journal of Economic Perspectives* 20: 91–116.

Chenery, H.B. 1959. The Interdependence of Investment Decisions. In *The Allocation of Economic Resources*, ed. Abramovitz et al. Stanford, CA: Stanford University Press.

Chua, Amy. 2002. *World on Fire: How Exporting Free Market Democracy Breeds Ethnic Hatred and Global Instability*. New York: Doubleday.

Collier, Paul. 2009. *Wars, Guns, and Votes: Democracy in Dangerous Places*. New York, NY: Harper Collins.

Commission on Growth and Development. 2008. *The Growth Report: Strategies for Sustained Growth and Inclusive Development.* Washington, DC: World Bank.

Dal Bó, P., A. Foster, and L. Putterman. 2010. Institutions and Behavior: Experimental Evidence on the Effects of Democracy. *American Economic Review* 100: 2205–2229.

Devarajan, Shantayanan, David R. Dollar, and Torgny Holmgren. 2001. *Aid and Reform in Africa: Lessons from Ten Case Studies.* Washington, DC: World Bank.

Devarajan, Shantayanan, and Clive Harris. 2007. Does India Have an Infrastructure Deficit? *India Economy Review* 2007: 24–27.

Ferraz, Claudio, and Frederico Finan. 2008. Exposing Corrupt Politicians: The Effect of Brazil's Publicly Released Audits on Electoral Outcomes. *Quarterly Journal of Economics* 123: 703–745.

Feyzioglu, Tarhan, Vinaya Swaroop, and Min Zhu. 1998. A Panel Data Analysis of the Fungibility of Foreign Aid. *World Bank Economic Review* 12: 29–58.

Foster, Vivien. 2008. Africa Infrastructure Country Diagnostic: Overhauling the Engine of Growth: Infrastructure in Africa. Unpublished draft report, World Bank.

Fujiwara, Thomas, and Leonard Wantchekon. 2013. Can Informed Public Deliberation Overcome Clientelism? Experimental Evidence from Benin. *American Economic Journal: Applied Economics* 5: 241–255.

Giné, Xavier, and Ghazala Mansuri. 2011. *Together We Will: Evidence from a Field Experiment on Female Voter Turnout in Pakistan.* Working Paper 5692, World Bank Policy Research.

Giuliano, Paola, and Nathan Nunn. 2013. The Transmission of Democracy: From the Village to the Nation-State. *American Economic Review* 103: 86–92.

Glaeser, Edward, and Claudia Goldin. 2006. *Corruption and Reform: Lessons from America's Economic History.* Chicago, IL: University of Chicago Press.

Grossman, Gene M., and Elhanan Helpman. 1996. Electoral Competition and Special Interest Politics. *Review of Economic Studies* 63: 265–286.

———. 2001. *Special Interest Politics.* Cambridge: MIT Press.

Guan, Mei, and Donald P. Green. 2006. Noncoercive Mobilization in State-Controlled Elections: An Experimental Study in Beijing. *Comparative Political Studies* 39: 1175–1193.

Guiso, L., P. Sapienza, and L. Zingales. 2006. Does Culture Affect Economic Outcomes? *Journal of Economic Perspectives* 20 (2): 23–48.

Institute of Development Studies. 2010. *An Upside Down View of Governance.* Brighton: Institute of Development Studies, University of Sussex.

Isham, Jonathan, Daniel Kaufmann, and Lant H. Pritchett. 1997. Civil Liberties, Democracy, and the Performance of Government Projects. *World Bank Economic Review* 11 (2): 219–242.

Isham, Jonathan, and Daniel Kaufmann. 1999. The Forgotten Rationale for Policy Reform: The Productivity of Investment Projects. *Quarterly Journal of Economics* 114: 149–184.

Jones, Sam. 2012. Are Our Children Learning? Literacy and Numeracy Across East Africa. Uwezo and Hivos/Twaweza, Nairobi, Kenya, August. http://www.educationinnovations.org. Improving the status and quality of teachers in developing countries 231: 4–52.

Kaplan, Robert D. 2000. *The Coming Anarchy: Shattering the Dreams of the Post Cold War.* New York: Random House.

Keefer, Philip. 2011. Collective Action, Political Parties, and Pro-development Public Policy. *Asian Development Review* 28: 94–118.

Keefer, Philip, and Stuti Khemani. 2014. *Radio's Impact on Preferences for Patronage Benefits.* Working Paper 6932, World Bank Policy Research.

Kornai, János. 1986. The Soft Budget Constraint. *Kyklos* 39: 3–30.

Krueger, Anne O. 1974. The Political Economy of the Rent-Seeking Society. *American Economic Review* 64: 291–303.

Levy, Brian. 2015. *Working with the Grain: Integrating Governance and Growth.* Oxford: Oxford University Press.

Lewis, John P. 1964. *Quiet Crisis in India.* New York: Doubleday.

Lizzeri, A., and N. Persico. 2004. Why Did the Elites Extend the Suffrage? Democracy and the Scope of Government, With an Application to Britain's 'Age of Reform'. *Quarterly Journal of Economics* 119: 707–765.

Lowi, Theodore J. 1972. Four Systems of Policy, Politics and Choice. *Public Administration Review* 32: 298–310.

Mansuri, Ghazala, and Vijayendra Rao. 2013. *Localizing Development: Does Participation Work? World Bank Policy Research Report.* Washington, DC: World Bank.

Martínez-Bravo, Monica, Gerard Padró-i-Miquel, Nancy Qian, and Yang Yao. 2011. *Do Local Elections Increase Accountability in Non-democracies? Evidence from Rural China.* Working Paper 16948, National Bureau of Economic Research.

———. 2014. *The Effects of Democratization on Public Goods and Redistribution.* Working Paper 18101, National Bureau of Economic Research.

Min, Brian. 2015. *Power and the Vote: Elections and Electricity in the Developing World*. New York: Cambridge University Press.

Min, Brian, and Miriam Golden. 2014. Electoral Cycles in Electricity Losses in India. *Energy Policy* 65: 619–625.

Miner, Luke. 2015. The Unintended Consequences of Internet Diffusion: Evidence from Malaysia. *Journal of Public Economics* 132: 66–78.

Muralidharan, Karthik, Paul Niehaus, and Sandip Sukhtankar. 2014. *Building State Capacity: Evidence from Biometric Smartcards in India*. Working Paper 19999. National Bureau of Economic Research.

Myerson, Roger. 2006. Federalism and Incentives for Success of Democracy. *Quarterly Journal of Political Science* 1: 3–23.

———. 2012. *Standards for State Building Interventions*. Working Paper, University of Chicago.

Nannicini, Tommaso, Andrea Stella, Guido Tabellini, and Ugo Troiano. 2013. Social Capital and Political Accountability. *American Economic Journal: Economic Policy* 5: 222–250.

North, Douglass C., John Joseph Wallis, and Barry R. Weingast. 2012. *Violence and Social Orders: A Conceptual Framework for Interpreting Recorded Human History*. Cambridge: Cambridge University Press.

Nunn, Nathan. 2014. Historical Development. In Handbook of Economic Growth, ed. Philippe Aghion and Steven Durlauf, Vol. 2, 347–402. Amsterdam: Elsevier.

Nurkse, Ragnar. 1966. *Problems of Capital Formation in Underdeveloped Countries*. Oxford: Oxford University Press.

Olson, Mancur. 1965. *The Logic of Collective Action*. Cambridge: Harvard University Press.

Pande, Rohini. 2011. Can Informed Voters Enforce Better Governance? Experiments in Low-Income Democracies. *Annual Review of Economics* 3: 215–237.

Pritchett, Lant, Michael Woolcock, and Matt Andrews. 2013. Looking Like a State: Techniques for Persistent Failure in State Capability for Implementation. *Journal of Development Studies* 49: 1–18.

Putnam, Robert, Robert Leonardi, and Raffaella Y. Nanetti. 1993. *Making Democracy Work*. Princeton, NJ: Princeton University Press.

Rodrik, Dani. 2000. Institutions for High-Quality Growth: What They Are and How to Acquire Them. *Studies in Comparative International Development* 35: 3–31.

Rosenstein-Rodan, Paul. 1943. Problems of Industrialisation of Eastern and South-Eastern Europe. *The Economic Journal* 53: 202–211.

Stokes, Susan C. 2005. Perverse Accountability: A Formal Model of Machine Politics with Evidence from Argentina. *American Political Science Review* 99 (3): 315–325.

Snyder, James M., and David Strömberg. 2010. Press Coverage and Political Accountability. *Journal of Political Economy* 118: 355–408.

Svensson, Jakob. 2006. The Institutional Economics of Foreign Aid. *Swedish Economic Policy Review* 13: 115–137.

van Fleet, Justin W., Kevin Watkins, and Lauren Greubel. 2012. *Africa Learning Barometer*. Washington, DC: Brookings Institution.

Wilson, James Q. 1973. *Political Organizations*. New York: Basic Books.

World Bank. 1995. *Bureaucrats in Business: The Economics and Politics of government Ownership*. A World Bank Policy Research Report. Washington, DC: World Bank.

———. 2004a. *World Development Report 2004: Making Services Work for Poor People*. Washington, DC: World Bank.

——— 2004b. Donors and Service Reform. In *World Development Report 2004*, Chap. 11, 203–217. Washington, DC: World Bank.

———. 2016. *Making Politics Work for Development: Harnessing Transparency and Citizen Engagement*. World Bank Policy Research Report. Washington, DC: World Bank.

Zakaria, Fareed. 2003. *The Future of Freedom: Illiberal Democracy at Home and Abroad*. New York: Norton.

9

Fighting Political Corruption: Evidence from Brazil

Claudio Ferraz and Frederico Finan

JEL: D72, D78, H41, K42, O17

Introduction

Corruption is considered by many a major impediment to economic development, and yet it remains pervasive throughout the world. Developing countries, in particular, provide seemingly endless examples of politicians diverting funds intended for basic public services and

C. Ferraz (✉)
Department of Economics, Pontifícia Universidade Católica do Rio de Janeiro (PUC-Rio), Rua Marquês de São Vicente, 225- Gávea, Rio de Janeiro, Brazil

BREAD, Cambridge, MA, USA
e-mail: cferraz@econ.puc-rio.br

K. Basu, T. Cordella (eds.), *Institutions, Governance and the Control of Corruption*, International Economic Association Series,
https://doi.org/10.1007/978-3-319-65684-7_9

obtaining bribes to favor particular firms.[1] While there has been growing research on corruption in the past decade, most work has focused on diagnosing corruption and explaining its causes. Glaeser and Goldin (2006) argue that reduction in corruption over time in the U.S. was due to a combination of increasing political competition, an active media uncovering corruption scandals, and an independent judiciary that successfully prosecuted corrupt officials. What policies are effective to fight corruption in developing countries remain poorly understood.[2]

This chapter examines the effects of anti-corruption policies with a focus on political corruption—corrupt practices by political leaders. We focus on anti-corruption policies that have been adopted in Brazil since early 2000s. We use the case of Brazil for two important reasons. First, the Federal Comptrollers Office (CGU) adopted a randomized audits policy in 2003 that allow us to use audit reports to objectively measure corruption. Thus, we are able to overcome one of the biggest barriers to study corruption which is the difficulty in measuring it. Second, this policy and its variations allows us to answer some important questions regarding anti-corruption policies by overcoming empirical identification challenges.

We start by describing the "web" of institutions that foster horizontal accountability in the Brazilian context and how the Comptrollers Office (CGU), responsible for the Randomized Audit Policy, interact with other institutions responsible for monitoring government activities, investigating suspected corruption, and punishing corrupt practices.[3] We then describe the institutional details of the Randomized Audit Program that started in Brazil in 2003 and has audited more than 2000 municipalities. Following this institutional background, we describe how numerous

F. Finan
Department of Economics, UC Berkeley, 508-1 Evans Hall, Berkeley, CA 94720-3880, USA

BREAD, Cambridge, MA, USA

IZA, Bonn, Germany

NBER, Cambridge, MA, USA
e-mail: ffinan@berkeley.edu

number of studies have used audit reports to build measures of corruption. We then use the existing literature based on these audits reports to answer three questions: (1) whether information from audit reports affect electoral outcomes, (2) whether the threat of being exposed affects politicians' behavior, and (3) whether audits are effective to ultimately reduce corruption.

Horizontal Accountability and Anti-Corruption Institutions in Brazil

Brazil has a number of accountability institutions that were put in place after the 1988 constitution to constrain corrupt practices under a largely decentralized government structure. These institutions form a "web" of horizontal accountability that occupy the middle ground between electoral and judicial systems at the federal level. They are responsible for three types of activities: (1) monitoring government activities to identify potential corruption, (2) investigation of suspected corruption, and (3) punishment of corrupt practices.[4]

Until the early 2000s most of the monitoring of government activities was done by the Tribunal de Contas da União or Federal Audit Court (TCU). The TCU is the primary agent responsible for oversight of all federal public spending for the legislative and executive branches, with responsibilities ranging from overseeing expenditures, correcting irregular spending patterns, auditing and authorizing public accounts, to applying punitive fines and other sanctions against irregular acts. But the effectiveness of the TCU to monitor and detect corruption was limited by the fact that TCU ministers are politically appointed and the focus on routine tasks and analysis of financial accounts took most of their time. This was specially true after the adoption of the Fiscal Responsibility Law in 2000 that sets rigid limits on spending and requires the provision of transparent fiscal information that had to be checked by the TCU for all levels of governments.[5]

While the TCU act as an oversight agency, the investigation of corruption cases is undertaken by the Federal Police who is in charge of investigating infractions that occur when the Federal Government delivers goods and services. While they are in charge of investigations of criminal activity, they cannot prosecute cases. This is done by the Federal Public Ministry or Ministerio Public Federal (MPF)—an independent body of the executive and judicial branches with prosecution power. Many view the Federal Public Ministry as the most important institution of accountability at the federal level in Brazil due to its autonomy and highly qualified and motivated personnel.[6]

From the 1990s until early 2000s several corruption scandals emerged in Brazil and the success of these institutions in preventing corruption was limited as anti-corruption laws were weakly enforced (Taylor and Buranelli 2007). At the municipal level, corruption was widespread, fueled by the large amount of resources transferred to municipalities after the 1988 constitution and the lack of control for their use.[7] But since the mid-2000s these patterns have started to change considerably and many authors consider the anti-corruption policies and implementation since the mid-2000s a success (Praca and Taylor 2014). One of the most important innovations in the fight against corruption was the creation of the Controladoria Geral da União or General Comptrollers Office (CGU) in 2001 and its upgrade to a Ministry status in 2003. The CGU centralized all the internal control activities across the Federal government and had an explicit mandate to prevent corruption in the public administration.

While the creation of the CGU improved significantly the monitoring and oversight of public resources, the process of horizontal accountability was strengthened in the past decade by the interaction between the CGU, the Federal Public Ministry (MPF) and the Federal Police. When the CGU uncovers irregularities, they generally pass along their findings to the federal police and the Ministrio Público for analysis and investigation. If credible evidence of wrongdoing were found, the Ministrio Público would proceed to trial in the judiciary. There has been a significant increase in the number of investigations undertaken since the mid-2000s due to an increase in resources available for the Federal Police and an increase in the cooperation between the Federal Police, MPF and other investigative bodies, such as state MPs, Revenue Service Inspectors and ministries (Prado and Carson 2016).

Anti-corruption crackdowns and prosecutions have become more common as task-forces and collaborative efforts between the CGU, the

Public Ministry and the Federal Police have emerged. To measure this institutional change Avis et al. (2016) build a dataset on the joint CGU-Federal Police crackdowns using the information available on the CGU homepage, as well as internet searches.[8] For each year starting in 2003, the CGU lists the name of the Special Operations and a description of the target. For each crackdown, we searched for the name of each operation together with the names of the targeted municipalities and keywords such as "mayor" or "corruption". The dataset is comprised of the name of each municipality targeted by the special operation, a description of the findings, and whether the mayor or public servants of the targeted municipalities were involved in and/or arrested during the crackdown.

In Fig. 9.1 we plot the number of joint operations between the CGU and the Federal Police that took place in Brazil's municipalities between 2007 and 2015. The number of crackdowns have increased considerably,

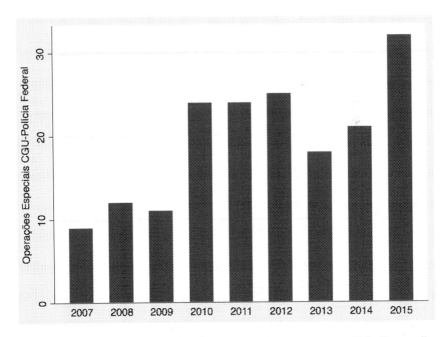

Fig. 9.1 Number of CGU-Federal Police Operations. Notes: This figure displays the number of CGU-Federal Police operations

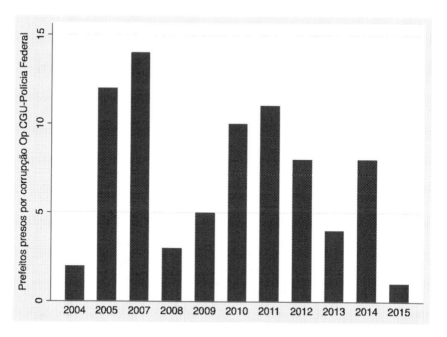

Fig. 9.2 Number of mayors arrested in CGU-Federal Police Operations. Notes: This figure displays the number of mayors arrested in CGU-Federal Police operations

specially after 2010. A significant number of crackdowns resulted from irregularities uncovered initially from audit reports of the CGU and led into the arrest of mayors, secretaries, and other local bureaucrats responsible for malfeasance of public funds as shown in Fig. 9.2.

The Public Ministry have also significantly increased the number of prosecutions and many mayors have been convicted of wrongdoings since the early 2000s. Avis et al. (2016) put together data on the convictions of mayors for misconduct in public office obtained from the *Cadastro Nacional de Condenaes Cíveis por ato de Improbidade Administrativa e Inelegibilidade.* This database, administered by the National Council for Justice (CNJ), includes the names of all individuals charged of misconduct in public office. We downloaded the data in 2013 so the dataset includes all agents convicted up to that point. For each individual we observe the type of irregularity (e.g. violation of administrative principles

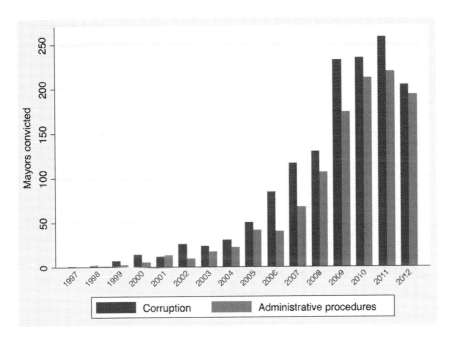

Fig. 9.3 Convictions of mayors. Notes: This figure displays the number of mayors convicted for corruption and administrative procedures by Brazil's civil courts

or diversion of resources), the court where the conviction took place, and the date. In Fig. 9.2 we plot the number of mayors convicted by civil courts. In Fig. 9.3 we observe a sharp increase for mayors that ruled municipalities in the mid-2000s given that it takes, on average, approximately 6 years for a case to be judged by the courts.

Monitoring Corruption Through Randomized Audits

In 2003 the CGU launched a new anti-corruption program based on the random auditing of municipal governments expenditures. The program, named *Programa de Fiscalizao por Sorteios Públicos* or Monitoring

Program through Public Lotteries, consists of random audits of municipalities for their use of federal funds. The first audit drew 26 randomly selected municipalities, one in each state of Brazil. The program was then expanded to auditing 50 and later 60 municipalities per lottery, from a sample of all Brazilian municipalities with less than 450,000 inhabitants. The program has since expanded to incorporate audits for state governments as well.[9] The random selection of municipalities was initially held every two to three months and drawn in conjunction with the national lotteries in Brasilia. Representatives of the press, political parties, and members of the civil society are all invited to witness the lottery to ensure transparency and fairness. All municipalities with a population of up to 500,000 inhabitants are eligible for selection. As of February 2015, there have been 2241 audits across 40 lotteries in 1949 municipalities and over R$22 billion dollars worth of federal funds audited. In Fig. 9.4 we plot the number of municipalities chosen every year since 2003.

Lotteries are done by state so the probability of being audited is constant for municipalities within the same state. For smaller states such as Alagoas, only 1 or 2 municipalities are typically drawn in a single lottery, whereas for a large state like Minas Gerais, with over 853 municipalities, as many as 8 municipalities have been drawn in a single lottery. Once a municipality is audited, it can only be audited again after several lotteries have elapsed.[10] Overall, the audit probabilities in any given lottery are between 1 and 2 percent. But given the frequency of the lotteries, the probability of being audited in a political term (four years in office) can be quite high, ranging from 8.6 percent for the state of Minas Gerais to 26.4 percent in the case of Rio de Janeiro.[11]

Once a municipality is chosen, the CGU gathers information on all federal funds transferred to the municipal government during the previous three to four years and issues a random selection of inspection orders. Each one of these orders stipulates an audit task for a specific government project (e.g. school construction, purchase of medicine, etc.) within a specific sector (see endnote 6). Once these inspection orders are determined, 10–15 auditors are sent to the municipality for one to two weeks to examine accounts and documents, to inspect for the existence

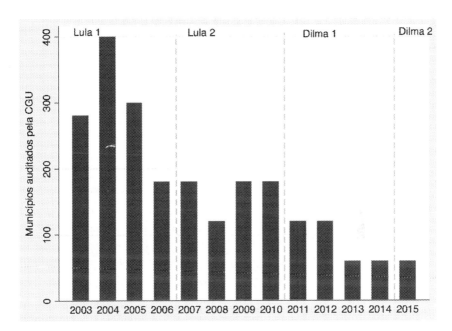

Fig. 9.4 Municipalities audited under the anti-corruption program of randomized monitoring

and quality of public work construction, and to verify the delivery of public services. These auditors are hired based on a competitive public examination and earn highly competitive salaries, thus their incentives for corruption are lower than those of other bureaucrats in the federal level administration. Moreover, the inspections are done by a team which reduces the opportunity for corruption among individual auditors.[12] After the inspections are completed, a detailed report describing all the irregularities found is submitted to the central CGU office in Brasilia. The central unit unifies the information and publishes a report on the internet. These reports are also sent to the Federal Courts of Accounts (TCU), the Federal Prosecutors' Office (MPF), the local judiciary, the Federal Police, and to the municipal legislative branch.

Measuring Corruption Using Audit Reports

One of the main challenges for studying the causes and consequences of corruption and evaluating anti-corruption policies is measuring it. Because corruption is illegal, it is difficult to uncover and measure.[13] The Audit reports available from the CGU under the Monitoring through Lotteries Program provided a unique opportunity to understand and quantify corrupt practices using objective measures.

Ferraz and Finan (2008) use the summary of audit reports posted in the internet by the CGU to measure corrupt practices in Brazil's local governments. Each audit report contains the total amount of federal funds transferred to the municipality and the amount audited, as well as an itemized list describing each irregularity. They read the reports and codified the irregularities listed into those associated with corruption and those that simply represent mismanagement. Most corruption schemes used by local politicians to appropriate resources in Brazil are based on a combination of frauds in procurements, the use of fake receipts or "phantom" firms, and over-invoicing the value of products or services. In addition, the audit reports also suggest that some politicians simply embezzle resources for personal purposes. Ferraz and Finan (2008) define political corruption as any irregularity associated with fraud in procurements, diversion of public funds, or over-invoicing. For each municipality, they sum up the number of times each one of these three irregularities appears.[14]

The information released by the CGU to citizens only provided a partial picture of corrupt practices as it does not contain information on the amount of resources embezzled. Ferraz and Finan (2011) built a measure of corruption by quantifying the value associated with each irregularity uncovered in the audits. To illustrate the approach, it is useful to use an example. In the municipality of Capelinha, for example, the Ministry of Health transferred to the municipality R$321,700 for the Programa de Atenção Básica. The municipal government used fake receipts valued at R$166,000 to provide proof of purchase. Furthermore, there is no proof that the goods were purchased since there were no registered entries of the merchandise in the stock. Also, in 2003 the municipality bought medicine valued at R$253,300 without procurement. In 2004, the value was R$113,700, also without procurement. They classified this violation as an incidence of irregular procurement and diversion of public funds in the area of health and coded this as a diversion of R$166,000. For each municipality, Ferraz and Finan (2011) sum the amount estimated as diversion and express it as a share of the total amount of resources audited.

The coding of audit reports require judgement over what is considered corrupt practices. An alternative approach is to use the classification used by the auditors themselves. Starting with the 20th lottery in March 2006, the CGU began to code the information contained in the reports for internal use. For each inspection order, the dataset contains information on the sector and government program, the amount transferred to the municipality, and a list of findings. For each finding, the auditors describe the irregularity found and assign a code that classifies irregularities into one of three categories of wrongdoing: (1) irregularities associated with mismanagement (e.g. documents were not properly filled out, or improper storage of food supplies and medical equipment), (2) moderate acts of corruption, (3) severe acts of corruption. Based on this information, Avis et al. (2016) construct measures of corruption and mismanagement at the municipality-lottery level. They measure corruption as the number of irregularities classified as either moderate or severe while mismanagement is measured as the number of irregularities associated with administrative and procedural issues.[15]

Does Exposing Corrupt Politicians Affect Elections?

When the program was launched in 2003 it produced information about local corrupt practices that have never been disclosed before. Ferraz and Finan (2008) describe several newspaper articles suggesting that information from the audit reports were widely used in the political campaigns. An article from the newspaper Diario de Para, in the North of Brazil, illustrates the use of the audit reports in the political campaign and how this information came as a complete surprise to the public:

The conclusions from the CGU were used extensively in the political campaigns, by not only the opposition parties but those that received positive reports as well...The reports were decisive in several cities. In the small city of Vicosa, in Alagoas, where a lot of corruption was found, the mayor, Flavis Flaubert (PL), was not reelected. He lost by 200 votes to Pericles Vasconcelos (PSB), who during his campaign used pamphlets and large-screen television in the city's downtown to divulge the report. Flaubert blames the CGU for his loss (Diario do Para (PA), 10/18/2004).

The information that was made publicly available through audits of local governments was used by candidates, political parties, and citizens in elections. Using data from the first batch of audit reports released before the 2004 municipal elections in Brazil, Ferraz and Finan (2008) examine the effects of exposing corrupt practices of mayors on electoral outcomes. Prior to the October 2004 municipal elections, the CGU had audited and released information on the corruption practices of 376 municipalities randomly selected across eight lotteries. Because municipalities were selected at random, the set of municipalities whose audit reports were only made available after the elections represent a valid control group. Ferraz and Finan (2008) use audit reports for 300 municipalities that were released after the municipal elections as a comparison group. The timing allows them to have information on corruption levels for two groups of municipalities: those whose corruption levels were released prior to the elections—potentially affecting voters perceptions of the mayor's corruptness—and those that were audited and had their results released only after the elections.

We estimated a model that includes an interaction of whether the municipality was audited prior to the elections with the level of corruption discovered in the audit to capture voters' prior beliefs about the incumbent's corruption activities. Our findings suggest that municipalities that were audited and had their findings disseminated prior to the municipal elections exhibit a striking downward-sloping relationship between reelection rates and corruption. Among the municipalities where not a single violation of corruption was discovered, approximately 53% of the incumbents eligible for reelection were reelected. Reelection rates decrease sharply as the number of corrupt irregularities increase. The estimated relationship suggests that voters care about corruption and hold corrupt politicians accountable when provided with the appropriate information. Ferraz and Finan (2008) use variation in the presence of local radio stations across Brazil and provide evidence that local radio played a crucial role in providing information to voters that allowed them to punish corrupt politicians. They find that audits had a differential effect by both the level of corruption reported and the presence of local radio measured by the number of AM radio stations. The effects of audits were much more pronounced in municipalities that had both higher levels of reported corruption and more radio stations to diffuse that information. While radios are not randomly allocated across the territory, the findings are not driven by schooling levels as we do not find any significant differences on the impact of the audits by literacy rates. In sum, the information disclosed by the anti-corruption policy based on municipal audits provided new information to voters about corrupt practices of their mayors. Voters used this information to update their priors and punish politicians that were found to be more corrupt than on average. The audit effects were in turn more pronounced in areas where the local media could disseminate these findings more widely.

These results are not unique for the Brazilian context. Similar results were found by Larreguy et al. (2014) using data from Mexico's Auditoria Superior de la Federacion (ASF). The ASF is an auxiliary entity to the Lower House of Congress that audits funds transferred to municipalities on a yearly basis. The ASF selects municipalities in each state to be audited according to unknown fixed criteria, which prioritize municipalities with higher variation in federal transfer amounts across years and those not audited in previous years. They examine the release of these audit reports and the extent to which voters reward or punish incumbent parties for irregularities in mayoral distribution of FISM funds. They use the timing of the release of municipal audit reports around elections and compare incumbent parties whose mayor was revealed to have engaged in malfeasant behavior before an election to similarly malfeasant mayors whose audit reports were not published until after the election. They also use spatial location of media outlets to exploit within-neighboring precinct variation in access to local and non-local commercial quality radio and television signals. They find that each additional local radio or television station reduces the vote share of incumbent political parties whose mayor was revealed to be corrupt or to have misallocated funds earmarked for projects benefiting the poor by up to one percentage point.

Bobonis et al. (2016) study the effects of the audits conducted by the Office of the Comptroller of Puerto Rico (OCPR), an independent body that systematically conducts municipal government audits and makes the findings publicly available to media sources. They exploit variation in the pre-determined timing of the audits to examine how audits that are disclosed before elections affect corrupt practices and electoral outcomes. They find that foreseeable audits that will have results released before elections induce a large short-term reduction in municipal corruption, as well as a reduction in the probability of a successful reelection for incumbent mayors in municipalities with negative audit outcomes, conditional on running for reelection. They also find that in municipalities that had an audit before the election, voters are more likely to reelect the mayor in the following election—specially in more competitive municipalities—a result that is consistent with audits acting as a mechanism to positively select politicians.

While audits can play an important role in allowing citizens to select better politicians, there are instances in which the information provided can trigger responses that can undo the potential informational effects. Brollo et al. (2013) use data from the CGU audit reports in Brazil and combine the identification strategy used by Ferraz and Finan (2008) with discontinuous thresholds on the amount of resources that municipalities receive as transfers from the federal government in Brazil. They compare the electoral punishment of disclosed corruption just above and below the population thresholds and find evidence that the electoral punishment for corruption is weaker when mayors have access to larger transfers to buy more support.

Does the Threat of Exposure Affect Politicians' Behavior?

While political selection is one of the mechanisms through which audits might affect corruption, the threat of an audit can also discipline politicians that have career concerns.[16] When politicians believe that information from audits can hurt their prospective careers, they might refrain from corruption. This is likely to change the behavior of politicians if they think that information from audits can be used in elections. Bobonis et al. (2016) use variation from municipalities in Puerto Rico where the order that municipalities are audited is pre-determined. They find that the number of corrupt violations drops significantly during the last two years of a mayor's term when he knows, ex-ante, that he would very likely be audited before the next election. This result is consistent with Ferraz and Finan (2011) who show that indeed the motivation to get reelected can discipline politicians and reduce corrupt practices. They examine the case of mayors in Brazil that face a two-term limit and compare corruption and mismanagement practices of mayors that are elected for office and can get reelected with those that have been reelected for office and face a term-limit. Using a large number of specifications that control for other differences between these two types of mayors, they find that mayors that face reelection concerns divert less public resources compared to those mayors that face a term-limit. Their results are also consistent with Ferraz and Finan (2009) who compare the performance of city-level legislators across Brazilian cities to examine their performance as salaries increase and the opportunity cost of losing office rises. They find that legislators in cities that pay higher wages perform better and have higher reelection rates consistent with how motivation to remain in office affects politicians' behavior.

In a different context, Zamboni and Litschig (2015) examine the effects of a randomized policy experiment that was designed together with Brazil's Comptroller's Office (CGU) to test whether higher audit risk deters corruption and irregularities in Brazil's municipalities. They randomly chose 120 municipalities and informed that 30 of them would be selected to be audited in the following year. This increased the annual probability of auditing from close to 5–20 percent. The randomization was carried out by the CGU through a lottery and publicly announced in May 2009. Mayors of these 120 municipalities received a letter from the CGU stating that they were part of a group of 120 municipalities and 30 of them would be audited in the following year. They find that a temporary increase in the annual audit risk by 20 percentage points reduced the share of audited resources involved in corruption by 10 percentage points and the proportion of local procurement processes with evidence of corruption by 15 percentage points. The corruption reduction is entirely driven by procurement modalities that restrict competition and afford discretion to procurement officials in their choice of suppliers.

Does Information from Audits Increase Investigations and Convictions of Politicians?

The monitoring of corruption through audits can affect not only political selection, but also the investigation and prosecution of corruption cases as the Federal Police and the Federal Public Ministry (MPF) have access to information from corrupt practices. Avis et al. (2016) examine the relationship between audits and subsequent investigations of the Federal Police and Convictions for mismanagement and corruption.

They build a dataset on the convictions of mayors for misconduct in public office using data obtained from the Cadastro Nacional de Condenações Cíveis por ato de Improbidade Administrativa e Inelegibilidade. They scrapped the dataset administered by the National Council for Justice (CNJ) that contains the names of all individuals charged of misconduct in public office. They downloaded the data in 2013 so the dataset includes all agents convicted up to that point. For each individual the dataset contains the type of irregularity (e.g. violation of administrative principles or diversion of resources), the court where the conviction took place, and the date. Individuals on this list are banned from running for any public office for at least five years.

They also built a dataset on the joint CGU-Federal Police crackdowns using the information available on the CGU homepage, as well as internet searches. For each year starting in 2003, the CGU lists the name of the Special Operations and a description of the target. For each crackdown, we searched for the name of each operation together with the names of the targeted municipalities and keywords such as "mayor" or "corruption". They created a dataset comprised of the name of each municipality targeted by the special operation, a description of the findings, and whether the mayor or public servants of the targeted municipalities were involved in and/or arrested during the crackdown. Using this information they created an indicator that equals to one if a municipality was subject to a crackdown in a given year and the mayor was involved in the irregularities and/or arrested.

Avis et al. (2016) test whether municipalities that are audited have a higher likelihood of a federal conviction or investigation by the Federal Police. They use the randomized choice of municipalities audited and compare audited to non-audited municipalities using a panel dataset where they follow convictions and Federal Police crackdowns over time. They find that municipalities that have been audited in the past are 0.5 percentage points more likely to face a legal action compared to those that have not been audited. This effect implies that the audits led to an increase of approximately 30 legal actions from a base of 140 among control municipalities. These effects are largely concentrated in places with the presence of a court. And among these municipalities, the treatment increased the likelihood of a legal action by 35.4 percent. Avis et al. (2016) also examine the relationship between the findings of the audits and future legal actions. They regress the measures of legal action on measures of mismanagement and corruption uncovered in the audits. They find that past corruption is strongly associated with the likelihood of a legal action, but acts of mismanagement are associated with any legal costs. Overall these findings suggest that the legal costs of engaging in corruption are substantial.

Do Audits and Judicial Checks Reduce Corruption?

Most of the existing literature on how audits affect corruption has focused on political mechanisms. Audits allow for the monitoring of politicians by releasing information that allow voters to select better politicians or make politicians accountable through reelection. But in countries where institutions can take corrupt politicians to courts, judicial checks and balances on the executive can play an important role in disciplining politicians (La Porta et al. 2004). In this context, policies that increase the monitoring of politicians can supply important information for investigations and prosecutions of corrupt politicians. Thus the threat of legal consequences of rent extraction should also discipline politicians (Becker 1968; Becker and Stigler 1974).

Litschig and Zamboni (2015) use variation in the location of courts in Brazil to examine whether corruption is affected by the presence of courts. State-level prosecutors and judges provide the checks on local officials within their entire jurisdictions but are not physically present in every municipality. Less than half of all municipalities in Brazil have a local judicial presence and the location depends on characteristics such as population, government revenues, and judicial caseload. They use an Instrumental Variable approach that exploits the fact that population is one of the main determinants of court location. Intuitively, they compare corrupt practices in municipalities that are the largest in their district to municipalities with identical population from other districts in the same state, where they are not the most populous. Their findings suggest that the local presence of courts reduces the share of inspections with irregularities related to corruption by 10 percent. The results are concentrated in corrupt practices as they find no effects for procedural irregularities, consistent with the intuition that less serious infractions are less likely to be prosecuted by the judiciary.

Avis et al. (2016) complement the evidence on the location of courts by asking whether audits can reduce corruption by increasing judicial checks to politicians. They examine the role of audits in reducing political corruption among Brazil's local governments by providing information for investigation and prosecution of corruption cases. They exploit the randomized choice of municipalities to be audited and the fact that since 2003 almost 2000 have been chosen at random, many of which multiple times. Using information from audit reports, Avis et al. (2016) compare the corruption levels discovered among the municipalities that are being audited for the first time to the corruption levels of municipalities that had been previously audited. Because municipalities are selected at random, this simple comparison estimates the causal effects of a past audit on future corruption levels, in a setting in which both groups face the same ex-ante probability of being audited. They find that municipalities that had been audited in the past have significantly fewer irregularities than those that had not been previously audited. They estimate a reduction of 7.9 percent in acts of corruption compared to those that had not been audited in the past. Differently from corruption, mayors that have been audited in the past do not change mismanagement practices. If we consider that the average municipality in their sample received R$15,000,000 in federal transfers per year, their estimates suggest that audits reduced corruption by R$355,000 per year per municipality.

Because under the Randomized Audits Program mayors might learn from other municipalities being audited, Avis et al. (2016) also estimate a model where they test for spillover effects of audits. They regress corruption on whether the municipality has been audited in the past or whether neighboring municipalities were audited in the past. They find that for each additional neighbor that was audited, a municipality reduces its corruption when the local media is present to diffuse information across municipalities. An additional audited neighbor decreases corruption by 7.5 percent when AM radio is present. These results are consistent with Lichand et al. (2016) who also examine the effects of Brazil's audit program with a focus on corruption in health. Using a difference-in-differences strategy, the study tests whether corruption is lower in municipalities that neighbor municipalities that were audited in the past. Consistent with our spillover effects on corruption across all sectors, they find that corruption in health reduced by 5.4 percent in places that neighbor an audited municipality.

There are several reasons why the audits might have reduced local corruption in Brazil. First, as documented in Ferraz and Finan (2008), the audits may have induced a political selection effect. In places that were audited before the election, voters were able to reward good and punish bad incumbents who were up for re-election. Second, the audits may have led to a stronger electoral disciplining effect, specially for mayors with political career concerns as suggested by Ferraz and Finan (2011). Third, the audits may have affected the political environment more generally by inducing a better selection of candidates. This might have been important in localities where the mayor faced a term-limit. Finally, as previously discussed, the audits might have triggered investigations and prosecutions that increased the judicial checks on the local executive. Avis et al. (2016) estimate a structural model to interpret the main findings and examine these different mechanisms that lead into reductions of corruption. Their results suggest that the disciplining effects from legal costs can explain 72 percent of the reduction in local corruption, while 28 percent is due to electoral discipline and less than 1 percent is due to selection.

Concluding Remarks

This chapter reviews the evidence on the effects of Anti-Corruption Policies in Brazil, with a special focus on the use of audits. We summarize the evidence from a number of papers that use audit reports of municipal governments to quantify corruption. Our summary suggests that, during the early phase of the program, the release of information about corrupt practices had a significant effect on electoral outcomes. But this selection effect cannot account for the long-term reduction in corruption. The evidence suggests that disciplining politicians through elections and legal actions play a crucial role in fighting corruption.

Our results suggest that, despite the excitement with the use of information obtained through audits to promote electoral accountability, this channel alone might not be sufficient to reduce corruption in the long run if public officials adjust their electoral strategies (e.g. Bobonis et al. 2016; Brollo et al. 2013). The fight against corruption might require, not only information and transparency, but also policies aimed at improving the capacity to detect and prosecute corrupt politicians. Strengthening anti-corruption agencies who can implement well-executed random audits may be an important step toward this direction. Also, institutions that can investigate and prosecute corrupt politicians, as well as a judiciary system that convicts politicians, are needed to increase the judicial checks on corrupt politicians (Alt and Lassen 2008; Besley and Persson 2011; Glaeser and Shleifer 2002; La Porta et al. 2004).

Finally, other policies that ban corrupt politicians from running for office and policies that reduce the incentives for politicians to give contracts in exchange for bribes can also play an important role in the fight against corruption. In the case of Brazil, the *Lei da Ficha Limpa* or "Clean Politician Law" that forbids politicians convicted in the judiciary to run for political offices has helped in the process of political selection. Also the recent reform that bans campaign contributions from firms, while too recent to be evaluated, might reduce the incentives that politicians have to exchange campaign resources with corrupt contracts, a practice that has been widespread in Brazil for many decades.

Comments by Laura Chioda

Anti-corruption policies are often designed either to affect the certainty (the probability of getting caught) or the severity of sanctions (punishment), which ultimately determine the expected punishment. The evidence reviewed by Ferraz and Finan (2017) in this volume provides further evidence that public officials respond to monitoring and punishment, as predicted by basic incentive theory, and complements the conclusions of Olken and Pande (2012). Borrowing from Becker's (1968) framework, let Y denote the gain from the act of corruption (normalizing income to zero in the absence of gains from corruption, for simplicity); let P represent the punishment (or monetary equivalent) conditional on being detected and found guilty; let $U_i(\cdot)$ be utility over income and $p(p_{audit})$ be the probability of detection which is a function of the probability of getting audited (p_{audit}), both increasing in their arguments.

The expected utility from engaging in corruption is then:

$$E(U_i) = pU_i(Y - P) + (1 - p)U_i(Y)$$

Punishment for corrupt practices can operate along four distinct channels. A discipline channel, which is a pure general deterrence mechanism related to an increase in the subjective probability of being detected and experiencing disciplinary action; a reputation effect that is linked to diminished reputational stock should the politician be found guilty of corruption, which in turn lowers future occupational and earnings prospects (due to the reputation of being corrupt or even being prosecuted); an electoral feedback channel, whereby the electorate may punish politicians whose illegal behavior has been exposed (by audits, in the current context); and an entry effect, which can be thought of as an anticipatory response to the electoral feedback and to the discipline channels and leads to positive selection of politicians entering electoral races based on their (lower) propensity for corruption.

As noted by Ferraz and Finan, the mechanisms through which an increase in the probability of detection leads to a reduction in acts of corruption are a combination of the discipline and electoral feedback effects. First, there are electoral consequences (i.e. an electoral feedback): in Brazil (Ferraz and Finan, 2008), Mexico (Larreguy et al. 2015), and Puerto Rico (Bobonis et al., 2016), voters punish politicians who are exposed as having committed acts of corruption by voting them out of office at much higher rates than in municipalities in which there is (as yet) no evidence of misconduct. The media appear to play an important role in these conclusions, as they are the vehicle by which news of the malfeasance is disseminated to the electorate. Indeed, the decline in the likelihood of reelection of corrupt candidates is steeper in municipalities with greater numbers of radio outlets.

It is important to highlight two central implicit assumptions needed for audits, which represent an increase in the probability of detection, to serve as effective deterrence mechanisms. Political competition and independent media reporting on corruption scandals are condicios sine qua non for the electoral feedback channel. Similarly, an independent judicial system, which holds corrupt politicians accountable, is likewise central to the efficacy of the discipline channel (and reputation effect). Indeed, political competition, active media coverage, and an independent judiciary were the three factors highlighted by Glaeser and Goldin (2006) as leading to a reduction in corruption over time in the US and that can be identified as pre-conditions for audits to be effective.

Adapting Becker (1968)'s model to the current context, the following expression for expected utility reflects the electoral feedback and discipline channels:

$$E(U_i) = pE(U|guilt) + (1-p)U_i(Y)$$

where

$$p * E(U|guilt) = p_{audit} * p_{judicial}(1 - p_{media}) * U_i(Y - P_{legal})$$
$$+p_{audit} * (1 - p_{judicial})p_{media}U_i(Y - P_{electoral})$$
$$+p_{audit} * p_{judicial} * p_{media} * U_i(Y - P_{legal} - P_{electoral})$$
$$+p_{audit} * (1 - p_{judicial})(1 - p_{media})U_i(Y)$$

where p_{audit}, p_{media}, $p_{judicial}$, denote the probabilities of an audit, of media reporting, and of the judicial system holding guilty politicians accountable, respectively, while P_{legal} denotes the punishments by the judiciary (e.g. in the form of legal costs or jail time) and $P_{electoral}$ represents the punishment by the electorate should audits uncover irregularities.

Given the substantial costs associated with corrupt practices in the event of an audit, a natural question is whether these induce a behavioral response from politicians to avoid them. That is, does the risk of punishment generate deterrence, thereby disciplining politicians (discipline channel)? Bobonis et al. (2016), Ferraz and Finan (2011), and Zamboni and Litschig (2015) document that, in the short run, local officials who face reelection (and positive probability of audit) reduce corrupt practices and divert fewer resources, consistent with monitoring having a deterrent/disciplining effect.

Lastly, the ultimate goal of monitoring is not simply to identify corrupt practices but to reduce overall corruption. Avis et al. (2016) document that the incidence of corruption is substantially lower among municipalities that have, by chance, previously been audited relative to municipalities on their first audit: audits exhibit positive temporal spillovers. Furthermore, the spillovers have a geographical component: municipalities adjacent to previously audited municipalities also register fewer instances of malfeasance than observationally similar municipalities whose neighbors were never audited.

The Behavioral Response to Audits

This section discusses some of the possible behavioral responses associated to random audits that may be relevant for policy design. This discussion does not have implications for the validity of identification strategies nor the evidence reviewed by Ferraz and Finan, but highlights some additional avenues for future research.

Changes in Subjective Probability The behavior of politicians is of course dependent not only on the objective probability of detection but on subjective perceptions of the probability. Avis et al. (2016) study how a municipality's experience of an audit affects future corruption and find that a prior audit increases the perceived likelihood of getting audited. In our notation, the expected utility is now given by

$$E(U_i) = p(\hat{p}_{audit}) * E(U|guilt) + (1 - p(\hat{p}_{audit}t)) * U_i(Y)$$

where the subjective probability of being audited, $\hat{p}_{audit}$, is a nonlinear function of time elapsed since a previous audit, the history of audits in neighboring municipalities, and of the objective probability of audit:

$$\hat{p}_{audit} = f(p_{audit}, t, history_{neigh})$$

The determinants of the wedge between objective and subjective probabilities of being audited is not only of academic interest, but could inform policy design to increase the efficiency of audits and their optimal temporal spacing. It is conceivable that the impact of experienced audits on behavior exhibits nonlinearities in their temporal distance through changes in the subjective probability of detection over time. For instance, the saliency of audits may be declining in the time since the previous audit, such that more recent audits are more salient and have greater impact on current behavior.

Optimal Combination of Severity vs. Efficiency For any given amount of expected punishment (given by the product of the probability and severity of the punishment), different combinations of severity and certainty will give rise to different levels of efficiency with respect to deterrence. Empirical evidence can inform the discussion regarding the optimal combination of policy parameters governing the certainty of detection and severity of sentences to maximize the overall deterrence effect of monitoring. To illustrate the trade-off between certainty and severity parameters, holding constant the level of expected punishment, consider two regimes with the same expected punishment of 0.1 years of prison. Regime A is characterized by 1% probability of detection and a sentence for corruption of 10 years; regime B instead has a 10% probability of detection and a 1 year sentence. If the elasticities of corruption with respect to certainty and severity are identical, the same level of corruption will be observed in both regimes. However, the crime literature has documented that property and violent crimes are more sensitive to certainty parameters, while deterrence exhibits rapidly diminishing returns with respect to severity of punishment (Nagin 2003; Chalfin and McCrary 2017; Chioda 2017). It remains an open question whether the same conclusion applies in the context of corruption. Because of the multidimensional nature of the punishment and the likelihood that career politicians exhibit higher than average degrees of patience, there may be ranges of severity and certainty over which this conclusion is reversed.

Compensating Behavior Existing evidence on monitoring interventions intended to reduce corruption documents the short-run effects of these policies. However, it is difficult to establish whether the short term effects reflect a net reduction in rent extraction or merely substitution over time—with high audit risk municipalities making up at least some lost rents in subsequent periods. It could take corrupt officials time to learn how to manipulate a new system, resulting in smaller long-run effects of anti-corruption policies than in the short run. Similarly, officials may substitute from one form of corruption to another. In the Brazilian context, while Ferraz and Finan document declines in corruption related to the allocation of federal funds, corrupt officials may compensate by concentrating their efforts on other sources, e.g. in the allocation of local funds.

Olken (2007), for instance, reports a decline in missing expenditures resulting from audits of road projects, but documents an increase in the number of project officials family members hired to build the roads. In the context of India's largest rural welfare program, Niehaus and Sukhtankar (2013) document a reduction in government officials theft of piece-rate jobs following an increase in the wages of daily wage jobs (and hence in the ability of officials to steal from those workers): most of the increase in the daily wage owed to beneficiaries was syphoned away by officials. Burgess et al. (2012) find that illegal logging falls in Indonesian districts following increases in their oil and gas revenue, which provide an alternate source of rent extraction for local district officials.

Previous research suggests that the short- and long-run impacts of monitoring could differ materially (Olken and Pande, 2012). Bobonis et al. (2016) provide the first evidence on the diverging long- and short-run impacts of monitoring on political corruption. They find that audits lead to a significant short-term decline in municipal corruption, as well as an increase in incumbent mayors' electoral accountability. However, the level of municipal corruption in the subsequent round of audits is on average the same in municipalities audited preceding the previous election as those whose audits became publicly available afterward.

Because the Brazilian anti-corruption program targets municipal governments, but municipalities are audited only for their use of federal government funds, politicians might react by shifting their focus to state and/or municipal sources of funding. Even if the allocation of local funds is not audited, data on the procurement/disbursement of these funds may be informative. For instance, identifying whether funds are more likely to be awarded to members of the mayors family network may be possible by exploiting conventions in the structure of Brazilian last names; alternatively, discrepancies might be detected between the allocation of grants and actual expenditures via estimation by subtraction (Reinikka and Svensson 2005).

The Size of the Gamble A second behavioral response to the increased likelihood of monitoring may result in changes in the size distribution of corrupt acts, conditional on graft. That is, the conditional distribution of acts of corruption in an environment with audits may lie to the right of the conditional distribution of Y in an environment without audits. That is, the higher probability of detection may be compensated by raising the payoff to corruption, in terms of expected utility. An indirect test of this hypothesis could be derived by evaluating whether the distribution of resources across sectors systematically favored larger sectors following the introduction of the audits or in municipalities that face a higher likelihood of monitoring.

Long Run Effects and the Role of the Media A third channel that may mediate the long run effect of audits involves the relationship between the electoral feedback channel and the media. Bobonis et al. (2016) and Ferraz and Finan (2008) documented the complementary role of the media in disseminating audit results in support of electoral accountability, which may both benefit clean and harm malfeasant incumbent parties. Larreguy et al. (2015) not only confirm these findings but further document that the local media market structure can explain substantial variation in electoral accountability.

Two possible mechanisms may lead to attenuations of the media-electoral accountability relationship: habituation and discouragement effects. The timing of audits and news matters, but their frequency may be equally important. That is, the salience and appeal of reports of corruption to voters may decline over time such that they are reported less frequently or simply carry less new information than when audits started (i.e. news fatigue/habituation). Even in the absence of news fatigue, reports of corruption may have demoralizing effects on voters and depress voter turnout. That is, voters may become jaded and simply stop paying attention to local politics. Even if audits are timely and sustained Bobonis et al. (2016), the timing and spacing of media reports may contribute to a divergence between short- and long-run impacts of monitoring on political corruption.

Acknowledgements We thank Laura Chioda and seminar participants at the World Bank/RIDGE/IEA Roundtable on Institutions, Governance, and Corruption for helpful discussions and comments.

Notes

1. See, for example, Di Tella and Schargrodsky (2003), Ferraz et al. (2012), Fisman et al. (2014), Olken (2007).
2. See Olken and Pande (2012) for a review of the literature.
3. See Power and Taylor (2011).
4. See Mainwaring (2003), Taylor and Buranelli (2007), Power and Taylor (2011), Praca and Taylor (2014), Prado and Carson (2016).
5. See Taylor and Buranelli (2007), Speck (2011), Praca and Taylor (2014), Prado and Carson (2016).
6. See Taylor and Buranelli (2007) and Arantes (2011).
7. See Ferraz and Finan (2011) for an overview of corruption practices in Brazil's local governments.
8. See http://www.cgu.gov.br/assuntos/auditoria-e-fiscalizacao/acoes-investgativas/operacoes-especiais.
9. See Ferraz and Finan (2008) and Loureiro et al. (2012) for details.
10. This rule has changed over time going from 3 to 12 lotteries.
11. See Avis et al. (2016).
12. Ferraz and Finan (2008) find no evidence that auditors manipulate the audit reports according to municipal and mayor characteristics such as political competition or specific parties. In a recent study of Brazil's federal government, Bersch et al. (2016) found the CGU to be one of the government's most autonomous and least politicized agencies.
13. Olken and Pande (2012) summarize different approaches taken by researchers to uncover and measure corruption.
14. A similar measure was used by Brollo et al. (2013).
15. These data are similar to those used by Zamboni and Litschig (2015), except that our dataset spans a longer period of time. The classification used by the CGU to distinguish between moderate and severe irregularities does not map directly onto the categories used either by Ferraz and Finan (2008) or Brollo et al. (2013). See Zamboni and Litschig (2015) for a discussion of this point.
16. See Besley (2007) for a theoretical framework that describes discipline and selection effects.

References

Alt, James E., and David D. Lassen. 2008.   Political and Judicial Checks on Corruption: Evidence from American State Governments. *Economics and Politics* 20 (1): 33–61, March.   https://ideas.repec.org/a/bla/ecopol/v20y2008i1p33-61.html.

Arantes, Rogerio B. 2011.   The Federal Police and Ministerio Publico.   In *Corruption and Democracy in Brazil: The Struggle for Accountability*, Chap. 8, ed. T.J. Power and M.M. Taylor. Notre Dame: Notre Dame Press.

Avis, E., Ferraz, C., and Finan, F. 2016. Do Government Audits Reduce Corruption? Estimating the Impacts of Exposing Corrupt Politicians. Working Paper 22443, National Bureau of Economic Research.

Becker, Gary S. 1968. Crime and Punishment: An Economic Approach. *Journal of Political Economy* 76 (2): 169–217.

Becker, Gary, and George Stigler. 1974.   Law Enforcement, Malfeasance, and Compensation of Enforcers. *The Journal of Legal Studies* 3 (1): 1–18. http://EconPapers.repec.org/RePEc:ucp:jlstud:v:3:y:1974:i:1:p:1-18.

Bersch, Katherine, Srgio Praa, and Matthew M. Taylor. 2016.   State Capacity, Bureaucratic Politicization, and Corruption in the Brazilian State. *Governance* 30: 105–124. ISSN 1468-0491. doi:10.1111/gove.12196. http://dx.doi.org/10.1111/gove.12196.

Besley, Timothy. 2007.   *Principled Agents?: The Political Economy of Good Government*. Number 9780199283910 in OUP Catalogue. Oxford: Oxford University Press. https://ideas.repec.org/b/oxp/obooks/9780199283910.html.

Besley, Timothy, and Torsten Persson. 2011.   *Pillars of Prosperity: The Political Economics of Development Clusters*. Princeton: Princeton University Press.

Bobonis, Gustavo J., Fuertes, Luis Cámara R., and Schwabe, Rainer. 2016. Monitoring corrupt politicians. *The American Economic Review* 106 (8): 2371–2405.

Brollo, Fernanda, Tommaso Nannicini, Roberto Perotti, and Guido Tabellini. 2013. The Political Resource Curse. *American Economic Review* 103 (5): 1759–1796. doi:10.1257/aer.103.5.1759. http://www.aeaweb.org/articles.php?doi=10.1257/aer.103.5.1759.

Burgess, Robin, Benjamin A. Olken, and Stefanie Sieber. 2012. The Political Economy of Deforestation in the Tropics. *Quarterly Journal of Economics* 127 (4): 1707–1754.

Chalfin, Aaron, and Justin McCrary. 2017. Criminal Deterrence: A Review of the Literature. *Journal of Economic Literature*, 55 (1).

Chioda, Laura. 2017. *Stop the Violence in Latin America: A Look at Prevention from Cradle to Adulthood.* Washington, DC: World Bank. https://openknowledge.worldbank.org/handle/10986/25920.

Di Tella, Rafael, and Ernesto Schargrodsky. 2003. The Role of Wages and Auditing During a Crackdown on Corruption in the City of Buenos Aires. *Journal of Law and Economics* 46 (1): 269–292. http://EconPapers.repec.org/RePEc:ucp:jlawec:y:2003:v:46:i:1:p:269-92.

Ferraz, C., and Finan, F. 2008. Exposing Corrupt Politicians: The Effects of Brazil's Publicly Released Audits on Electoral Outcomes. *The Quarterly Journal of Economics* 123 (2): 703–745.

Ferraz, Claudio, and Frederico Finan. 2009. Motivating Politicians: The Impacts of Monetary Incentives on Quality and Performance. Working Paper 14906, National Bureau of Economic Research, April. http://www.nber.org/papers/w14906.

Ferraz, C., and Finan, F. 2011. Electoral accountability and corruption: Evidence from the audits of local governments. *American Economic Review* 101 (4): 1274–1311.

Ferraz, Claudio, Frederico Finan, and Diana B. Moreira. 2012. Corrupting Learning: Evidence from Missing Federal Education Funds in Brazil. *Journal of Public Economics*, 96 (9–10): 712–726. https://ideas.repec.org/a/eee/pubeco/v96y2012i9p712-726.html.

Fisman, Raymond, Florian Schulz, and Vikrant Vig. 2014. The Private Returns to Public Office. *Journal of Political Economy* 122 (4): 806–862. https://ideas.repec.org/a/ucp/jpolec/doi10.1086-676334.html.

Glaeser, Edward L., and Claudia Goldin. 2006. Corruption and Reform: Introduction. NBER Chapters in *Corruption and Reform: Lessons from America's Economic History*, 2–22. Cambridge: National Bureau of Economic Research, Inc, February. https://ideas.repec.org/h/nbr/nberch/9976.html.

Glaeser, Edward L., and Andrei Shleifer. 2002. Legal Origins. *The Quarterly Journal of Economics*, 117 (4): 1193–1229. https://ideas.repec.org/a/oup/qjecon/v117y2002i4p1193-1229..html.

La Porta, Rafael, Florencio Lopez-de-Silanes, Cristian Pop-Eleches, and Andrei Shleifer. 2004. Judicial Checks and Balances. *Journal of Political Economy* 112 (2): 445–470, April. https://ideas.repec.org/a/ucp/jpolec/v112y2004i2p445-470.html.

Larreguy, Horacio A., John Marshall, and Jr. James M. Snyder. 2014. Revealing Malfeasance: How Local Media Facilitates Electoral Sanctioning of Mayors in Mexico. Working Paper 20697, National Bureau of Economic Research, November. http://www.nber.org/papers/w20697.

Larreguy, H. A., Marshall, J., and James M. Snyder, J. 2015. Publicizing Malfeasance: When Media Facilitates Electoral Accountability in Mexico, Working Paper.

Lichand, Guilherme, Marcos Lopes, and Marcelo Medeiros. 2016. Is Corruption Good for Your Health? Working Paper.

Litschig, Stephan, and Yves Zamboni. 2015. Judicial Presence and Rent Extraction. Working Papers 796, Barcelona Graduate School of Economics, August. https://ideas.repec.org/p/bge/wpaper/796.html.

Loureiro, Maria Rita, Fernando L. Abrucio, Cecilia Olivieri, and Marco A. C. Teixeira. 2012. Do controle interno ao controle social: A mltipla atuao da CGU na democracia brasileira. *Cadernos Gesto Pblica e Cidadania* 17 (60): 54–67.

Mainwaring, Scott. 2003. Introduction: Democratic Accountability in Latin America. In *Democratic Accountability in Latin America*, ed. Scott Mainwaring and Christopher Welna, 3–34. Oxford: Oxford University Press.

Nagin, Daniel S. 2013. Deterrence: A Review of the Evidence by a Criminologist for Economists. *Annual Review of Economics*.

Niehaus, Paul., and Sandip Sukhtankar. 2013. The Marginal Rate of Corruption in Public Programs. *Journal of Public Economics* 104: 52–64.

Olken, B. 2007. Monitoring Corruption: Evidence from a Field Experiment in Indonesia. *Journal of Political Economy* 115: 200–249.

Olken, Benjamin A., and Rohini Pande. 2012. Corruption in Developing Countries. *Annual Review of Economics* 4: 479–509.

Power, T.J., and M.M. Taylor. 2011. Introduction: Accountability Institutions and Political Corruption in Brazil. In *Corruption and Democracy in Brazil: The Struggle for Accountability*, Chap. 1, ed. T.J. Power and M.M. Taylor, 1–28. Notre Dame: Notre Dame Press

Praca, S., and M. Taylor. 2014. Inching Toward Accountability: The Evolution of Brazil's Anticorruption Institutions, 1985–2010. *Latin American Politics and Society* 56 (2): 27–48.

Prado, M. M., and L. D. Carson. 2016. Brazilian Anti-Corruption Legislation and Its Enforcement: Potential Lessons for Institutional Design. *Journal of Self-Governance and Management Economics* 4 (1): 34–71.

Reinikka, R., and Svensson, J. 2005. Fighting Corruption to Improve Schooling: Evidence from a Newspaper Campaign in Uganda. *Journal of the European Economic Association* 3 (2–3): 259–267.

Speck, B.W. 2011. Auditing Institutions. In *Corruption and Democracy in Brazil: The Struggle for Accountability*, Chap. 6, ed. T.J. Power and M.M. Taylor. Notre Dame: Notre Dame Press.

Taylor, Matthew M., and Vincius C. Buranelli. 2007.   Ending Up in Pizza: Accountability as a Problem of Institutional Arrangement in Brazil. *Latin American Politics and Society* 49 (1): 59–87.   ISSN 1548-2456. doi:10.1111/j.1548-2456.2007.tb00374.x.   http://dx.doi.org/10.1111/j.1548-2456.2007.tb00374.x.

Zamboni, Y., and Litschig, S. 2015. Audit Risk and Rent Extraction: Evidence from a Randomized Evaluation in Brazil. Working Papers 554, Barcelona Graduate School of Economics.

10

What Drives Citizen Perceptions of Government Corruption? National Income, Petty Bribe Payments and the Unknown

Nancy Birdsall, Charles Kenny, and Anna Diofasi

Introduction

Low trust in government appears to be a global phenomenon, and a challenge to effective governance.[1] A related (potentially causal) phenomenon is the widespread sense that governments are corrupt.[2] This has important implications for a government's ability to raise revenues and to implement effective policies. Where there is a perception of corruption in tax offices, for example, there is lower willingness to pay tax.[3] Perceptions of corruption also feed into assessments about a country's long-term development prospects. Short of any measure of actual corruption, the

We are grateful for assistance from Ben Crisman.

N. Birdsall • C. Kenny (✉) • A. Diofasi
Center for Global Development, Washington, DC, USA
e-mail: nbirdsall@cgdev.org; ckenny@cgdev.org; adiofasi@cgdev.org

K. Basu, T. Cordella (eds.), *Institutions, Governance and the Control of Corruption*, International Economic Association Series,
https://doi.org/10.1007/978-3-319-65684-7_10

perception of corruption by people and/or by "experts" is used as an input to "governance"; and governance is then (often) treated as a determinant of growth and other outcomes within and across countries. In the aid system, the resulting measure of governance is sometimes used as an indicator of whether and how much aid a country "deserves" and can effectively absorb.

How useful is the recourse to perceptions of corruption as an input to measuring governance (and to allocating aid)? What leads to a perception of corruption among citizens? Is the perception of corruption related in any systematic way to actual (unmeasurable) corruption? Or is it the result of a generalized (and also unmeasurable) sense that corruption is the norm so that government officials cannot be trustworthy, perhaps especially in relatively poor, "particularistic" as opposed to rules-based societies.[4] Are citizens' perceptions of corruption influenced by progress under a certain government in growth or schooling or other measurable outcomes in their country; or affected by such conventionally conceived aspects of "governance" as the right to engage and participate in the political process?

Compared to the literature on expert perceptions of corruption, empirical work on citizens' perceptions is still relatively small.[5] We know very little about the association between citizens' perceptions of corruption and, for example, actual conditions in their communities and countries or other factors beyond average income or GDP per capita in their country, such as levels of inequality, reliance on natural resources, and political and civil rights. This paper is an attempt to begin filling that gap.

In this paper we examine the correlates of citizen perceptions of corruption and citizens' self-reported bribe-paying using data (the Transparency International Global Corruption Barometer [GCB]) from nationally representative surveys of individuals across 117 countries in the years 2004 to 2011. In these surveys—along with their demographic characteristics—individuals were asked about their perception of corruption across various government institutions or services, including medical and health services, police, and political parties, as well as their contact and experience of paying bribes in those services. We explore perceptions of corruption at the individual level using information on individuals' education, age, sex, employment status and their self-reported income (in three categories only). We then look at perceptions of corruption at the country level, using country averages of individual perceptions, and adding data on such service outcome measures as infant mortality, Programme for International Student Assessment (PISA) scores, power outages and homicides (meant to reflect the effectiveness of the various government services), and on national-level indicators of democracy, inequality, civil rights and GDP per capita. In analyzing perceptions of corruption, we include bribe-paying in the individual and country-level regressions as a right-hand side, explanatory variable.

We then turn to a comparable exploration at the individual and country levels of bribe-paying[6] as the left-hand side, "dependent" variable.

Our results suggest that citizen perceptions of corruption are at best a very noisy measure of an underlying reality of corruption. They are consistent with an interpretation that suggests higher GDP per capita lowers perceptions of corruption because of its association with lower reported bribe payments, an interpretation further suggested by the fact that in the case of political parties (where direct bribe payments by citizens are likely to be very rare), higher GDP per capita is not strongly associated with lower perceptions of corruption.

A plausible conclusion would be that the one reliable tool we have to reduce popular perceptions of corruption in developing countries in particular is development evidenced by sustained economic growth: at the county level, higher GDP per capita is consistently associated with lower perceived corruption. That raises the question whether better "governance" (at least using the measures we have) is at best a tool to achieve development, but not a direct tool to change perceptions of corruption.

Data

Dependent variables. Our dependent variable data on perception of corruption and bribe payments come from the most recent wave of the Transparency International GCB. Survey respondents are asked to rate their perception of corruption of various services from 1 (not at all corrupt) to 5 (extremely corrupt). They are asked if they have had contact with the same services over the past year, and, if so, they are asked if they paid a bribe to a service provider. We use the most recent survey year available for each service by country[7]; for the country-level overall corruption perception variable, we use the most recent survey year for the country as a whole,[8] for which Appendix 1 lists all data used and their sources.

Independent variables. Our data on individual characteristics—used as independent variables in the individual-level regressions—comes directly from the GCB surveys. For our analysis of the country-level aggregates of corruption and bribe payments, we added data service performance indicators as a proxy for outcomes and overall quality of services, and thus for a lower association with perception of corruption and bribe payment in that service.

* For education we use the average country score of the three PISA components covering mathematics, science and reading. The PISA is designed as an internationally comparable measure of learning outcomes of students. It is overseen by the OECD. Learning outcomes are connected with factors outside the education service including parental education, health and income. Controlling for GDP per capita should reduce this concern.

* For judiciary we use the quality of judicial processes index from the World Bank's Doing Business report. This is designed to reflect whether each economy has adopted a series of good practices that promote quality and efficiency in the commercial court system. Note that as a doing business indicator, it reflects de jure rather than de facto performance and is limited to commercial courts.

* For the health service we use the under-five mortality rate as a (comparatively) well-measured health outcome, although this is clearly connected with factors outside the health service including sanitation and income. Controlling for GDP per capita should reduce this concern.

* For police we use intentional homicides per 100,000 people as an outcome indicator. This is a limited measure of policing outcomes, and related to a range of other factors including culture, education, income and human rights.[9] We control for some of these factors.

* For registry and permit services we use an Index of three standardized indicators linked to registering property (no. of procedures, no. of days and costs) from Doing Business. Again, as a doing business indicator, this reflects de jure rather than de facto performance.
* For utilities we use Enterprise Survey data on the probability that businesses experienced a power outage in the last (fiscal) year. Note that this measure only covers one utility service, although it is the service that ranks as the highest concern in enterprise surveys.
* For tax collection we use taxes as a share of total government revenue. Note that this is an arguable outcome measure that may still be connected with a capricious and inefficient tax regime.

We also added three measures of civil and political rights and freedoms: Freedom House's measure of civil liberties; Freedom House's (sub-)measure of individual rights; and the Polity 2 indicator of democracy developed at the University of Maryland. The Freedom House measure of civil liberties provides a top score to countries and territories which "enjoy a wide range of civil liberties, including freedoms of expression, assembly, association, education, and religion". The individual rights measure is a component of a country's civil liberties score and considers rights and freedoms such as citizen freedom of travel, choice of residence, employment and education as well as personal social freedoms, including gender equality, choice of marriage partners and the absence of economic exploitation. The polity 2 measure was designed to reflect differences between democratic and authoritarian political systems, with the highest score awarded to consolidated democracies.[10] The two Freedom House measures are obviously correlated with each other. All three measures are based on expert assessments; as with all such expert perception measures, there are significant concerns with the gap between what they purport to measure and what they actually measure.[11]

Appendix Table 10.8 provides information on the construction, units and sources for the variables used. Appendix Tables 10.9–10.16 present descriptive statistics for the data.

Potential data issues. Within countries there are large swings in year-on-year reporting of perceptions, contact with services and bribing, which suggest care in detailed interpretation of various correlates for any one country in any one year on the basis of the GCB data. While perceptions might plausibly shift from one year to the next thanks to a reported scandal (as it might be), this seems less likely with contact and bribes. Yet there are 37 countries where there was a 20 percentage point change in contact with at least one service between two survey years.[12] For example, the population reporting contact with the medical service in the Philippines jumped from 23% in 2006 to 53% in 2007 (Fig. 10.1). In nine countries, there was a 20 percentage point change in reported contact in three or more services. The data show similarly large year-on-year shifts in the incidence of bribe-paying: there are 27 countries where there was a 15 percentage point or greater difference in reported bribe-paying in at least one service between two survey years. Take Cameroon: the population reporting a bribe payment in the education sector fell from 53% in 2007

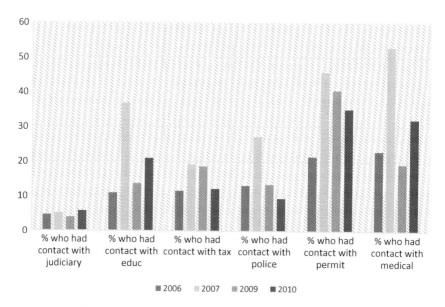

Fig. 10.1 Philippines: reported contact by sector over time

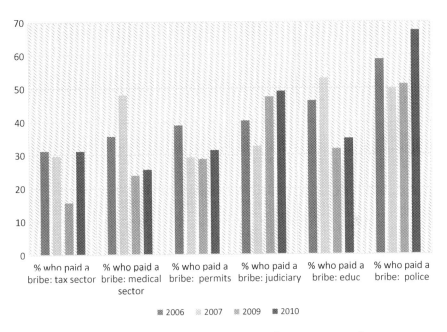

Fig. 10.2   Cameroon: reported bribe payments by sector over time

to 32% in 2009 (Fig. 10.2); in the same period reported bribe payments to the judiciary rose from 33% to 49%.

Some of these differences may reflect genuine changes in contact or bribe payments due to changes in regulations or policy, but given the magnitude and cross-service nature of many of the jumps, at least some are likely to reflect disparities in data collection in different years. This suggests some concern with data quality regarding contact at least. While we raise this concern, excluding some of the countries with the greatest discrepancies across years from the analysis below did not significantly affect our results.

Some respondents may also be reticent about reporting that they paid bribes.[13] And what counts as a bribe payment is considerably socially constructed (is my tip to a postal worker at the end of the year a bribe? Is my payment for private tutoring to my child's public school teacher a bribe?), in which case the causality between perceiving corruption and reporting a bribe payment may run in both directions.

Analysis

We estimate for each service (political parties, education, judiciary, medical, permit and registry services, police, tax and utilities) for the latest survey year where responses to that particular service are available:

$$P_{ics} = \alpha \times [I] + \beta \times [S_c] + \gamma \times [C] + \varepsilon \qquad (10.1)$$

where P_{ics} is perception of corruption for individual i in country c for service s; [I] is a matrix of individual-level characteristics including education, self-reported income bracket, employment and age; S is a dummy variable indicating "contact" with service S and/or bribe payment in service S; and C is a set of dummy variables for countries.

Then, we estimate using aggregate perceptions on a country level as our dependent variable, by service:

$$P_{cs} = \beta \times [S_c] + \gamma \times [C] + \varepsilon$$

where $[S_c]$ includes measures of service performance in country C calculated from the data sources below (as well as probability of contact and bribe payment in the given service), $[C]$ is a matrix of country characteristics including GDP per capita, a measure of inequality, and measures of civil liberties and individual rights enjoyed by citizens.

We perform the same analysis with bribe payments as the left-hand side variable.

We run each of the regressions above separately for high-income country[14] (HIC) respondents and non-high income country (non-HIC) respondents to explore whether the drivers behind perceptions of corruption and bribe payments differ between high-income and lower-income settings.[15]

Results

A few points are worth making before turning to regression results. First, across all countries there is a negative relationship between GDP per capita and both perceptions of corruption (Fig. 10.3) and, more obviously, between GDP per capita and incidence of bribe payments (Fig. 10.4). Some countries are outliers (Georgia, Ethiopia) given their GDP per capita, with both low perceived corruption and low incidence of bribe-paying. Some that are outliers on perceived corruption are not outliers on bribe-paying (Ukraine, Panama, Mexico). Even among high-income countries, on the simple 1 to 5 scale, almost no country reported an average perception of corruption across services below 2.

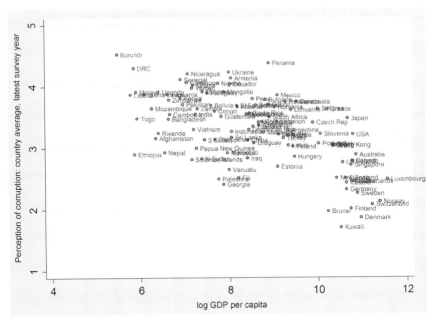

Fig. 10.3 Corruption perceptions and GDP per capita

Table 10.1 Perceptions of corruption[a] and probability of bribe payment (country averages) for HICs and non-HICs, by service

Services	Perception of corruption		Bribe payment (in %) (After contact)	
	HICs	Non-HICs	HICs	Non-HICs
Political parties	3.71	3.76	–	–
Education services	2.66	3.12	3.28	19.91
The judiciary	2.97	3.58	6.67	29.81
Medical services	2.92	3.36	6.56	20.15
The police	3.08	3.86	6.42	40.48
Permit and registry services	2.62	3.41	5.26	27.45
Utilities	2.68	3.11	2.67	16.41
Tax service	2.83	3.49	3.08	20.36

[a]Note that the scale of corruption perceptions goes from 1(best) to 5(worst)

Table 10.1 shows the simple averages, by sector, across countries grouped into high-income (HIC) and non-high income (non-HIC) countries using the World Bank classifications. The differences between the two groups in the perception of corruption by sector appear relatively small (on the 1 to 5 scale) but are statistically different,[16] with perception of corruption higher in the non-HICs. The sole exception is perception of corruption of political parties where corruption is seen as just about as high in the HICs as non-HICs. (In 2010, over 81% of the US public thought that political parties were corrupt—about the same proportion as in Bulgaria, Ghana, Mexico or Mongolia.) In contrast, the differences in reported bribe-paying are substantial, with a much lower likelihood of bribe-paying in the HICs.

Second, perceptions of corruption across services at the national level are correlated, but not in any consistent way. Figure 10.5 presents the relationship between perceptions of corruption in education and in political parties and Fig. 10.6 between perceptions in political parties and in the police. Almost universally the average respondent at the country level

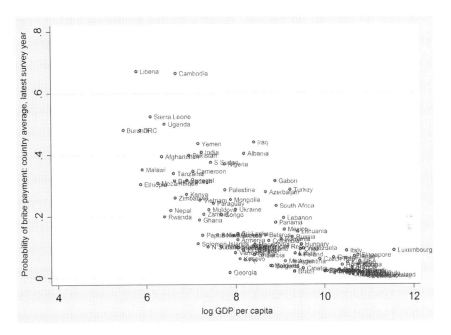

Fig. 10.4 Bribe payments and GDP per capita

perceives politics as a considerably more corrupt sector than education. The relationship for police services compared to political parties varies among countries.

Third, and again at the national level, the relationship between democracy (polity 2 score) and perceptions of corruption is weak (Fig. 10.7)—a brave analyst might suggest an inverse u-shaped relationship,[17] but it would certainly not be a strong one.

Finally, average perceptions of corruption across services and the probability of paying a bribe are (unsurprisingly) related, but clearly measure different things (Fig. 10.8). Perception of corruption ranges widely in countries where reported bribe-paying is relatively low. There is considerably more to views of corruption than a record of reported bribe payments.

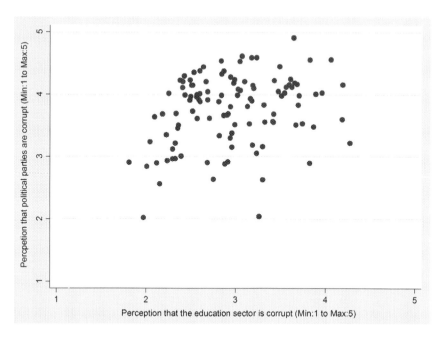

Fig. 10.5 Relationship between perceptions of corruption in political parties and in the education service

Perceptions of Corruption as Dependent Variable

We begin by testing the strength of the relationship between individual perceptions of corruption in a particular service of a country at a particular time. If all of those surveyed in every given country about a particular service reported the same level of perceived corruption in that service, we would expect an R-squared of one. Across services, the R-squared in fact varies between 0.15 and 0.28 for the full sample of countries (and similarly at somewhat lower overall levels for all HICs and all non-HICs), which implies that the country where respondents live explains less than one-quarter of the variation in their perceptions of corruption (though note again the ordinal nature of our data) (Table 10.2).

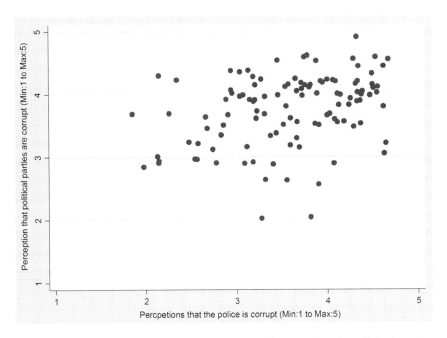

Fig. 10.6 Relationship between perceptions of corruption in political parties and in the police

This suggests that there is at least somewhat of a common sense across individuals of how corrupt a particular service is in their country but also that the bulk of any *individual* response may reflect other factors—including different interpretations of what a 2 means on a 1–5 ordinal scale and different views of the actual scale of corruption in a given service based on individual biases and experiences. There is "signal" in individual perceptions, but also a considerable amount of "noise".

Table 10.3 provides individual results by service for all countries, adding observable individual characteristics. For individual-level results, we report ordinary least squares (OLS) coefficients for ease of interpretation (we also ran ordered logit for perceptions and logit for bribe payments; the results are substantially the same—results available on request). Note the large sample size (N mostly above 40,000) implies that coefficients can be statistically significant while quantitatively irrelevant. While perceptions of corruption reflect individual characteristics, the *observable* individual characteristics that we include in our regression

Table 10.2 Individual-level regressions about corruption perceptions with country dummies only

VARIABLES	Political parties	Education	Judiciary	Medical	Permits	Police	Tax	Utilities
	Perception of corruption (scale: 1–5) about [...] service, individual level (OLS)							
Constant	2.918***	2.910***	3.370***	2.820***	2.934***	3.184***	2.961***	3.015***
	(0.0410)	(0.0407)	(0.0416)	(0.0338)	(0.0350)	(0.0403)	(0.0380)	(0.0369)
Observations	106,389	106,189	106,095	72,461	69,121	107,616	67,812	70,038
R-squared	0.195	0.169	0.239	0.2	0.219	0.28	0.191	0.152
Country dummies	Yes	Yes	Yes	Yes	Yes	Yes	Yes	Yes
VARIABLES	Political parties	Education	Judiciary	Medical	Permits	Police	Tax	Utilities
	HICs only: Perception of corruption (scale: 1–5) about [...] service, individual level (OLS)							
Constant	4.107***	2.405***	3.647***	3.125***	3.928***	3.806***	3.560***	3.544***
	(0.0361)	(0.0386)	(0.0367)	(0.0464)	(0.0395)	(0.0366)	(0.0449)	(0.0444)
Observations	40,077	38,221	39,594	31,191	30,307	38,942	30,183	30,714
R-squared	0.22	0.15	0.253	0.244	0.238	0.243	0.179	0.115
Country dummies	Yes	Yes	Yes	Yes	Yes	Yes	Yes	Yes
VARIABLES	Political parties	Education	Judiciary	Medical	Permits	Police	Tax	Utilities
	non-HICs only: Perception of corruption (scale: 1–5) about [...] service, individual level (OLS)							
Constant	2.918***	2.910***	3.370***	2.820***	2.934***	3.184***	2.961***	3.015***
	(0.0410)	(0.0407)	(0.0416)	(0.0338)	(0.0350)	(0.0403)	(0.0380)	(0.0369)
Observations	66,312	67,968	66,501	41,270	38,814	68,674	37,629	39,324
R-squared	0.183	0.145	0.178	0.145	0.084	0.197	0.118	0.126
Country dummies	Yes	Yes	Yes	Yes	Yes	Yes	Yes	Yes

'*' indicates a p-value $\leq$ 0.1, '**' indicates a p-value $\leq$ 0.05, and '***' indicates p-value $\leq$ 0.01.

Table 10.3 OLS regression results: perceptions of corruption on the individual level across services (all countries), latest year

VARIABLES	Perception that [...] service is corrupt (range 1–5), latest survey year (OLS)							
	Pol. parties	Education	Judiciary	Medical	Permits	Police	Tax	Utilities
Age: 30–50	0.0195**	0.00313	0.0537***	0.0678***	−0.0291**	−0.00749	−0.0518***	0.0263
	(0.0094)	(0.0105)	(0.0101)	(0.0138)	(0.0143)	(0.0093)	(0.0148)	(0.0459)
Age: 51–65	0.0192	0.0161	0.0349***	0.0576***	−0.0831***	−0.0328***	−0.113***	−0.0139
	(0.0120)	(0.0133)	(0.0128)	(0.0175)	(0.0185)	(0.0119)	(0.0191)	(0.0704)
Age: 65 +	−0.02	−0.0288	−0.0164	−0.0114	−0.115***	−0.0940***	−0.220***	−0.326**
	(0.0185)	(0.0203)	(0.0195)	(0.0276)	(0.0296)	(0.0183)	(0.0307)	(0.1490)
Male (dummy)	−0.0122	−0.0189**	−0.0419***	−0.0527***	0.00436	−0.0181**	−0.0777***	−0.0825**
	(0.0077)	(0.0086)	(0.0082)	(0.0111)	(0.0116)	(0.0077)	(0.0120)	(0.0411)
Educ: secondary school	0.0816***	0.0864***	0.0355***	0.00196	−0.0113	0.0522***	−0.01	0.0104
	(0.0115)	(0.0127)	(0.0120)	(0.0161)	(0.0172)	(0.0112)	(0.0178)	(0.0788)
Educ: higher/uni	0.124***	0.102***	0.0315**	0.0172	−0.00224	0.0579***	−0.0226	0.0746
	(0.0124)	(0.0138)	(0.0131)	(0.0181)	(0.0190)	(0.0122)	(0.0197)	(0.0833)
Income: med/med high	0.0058	−0.00572	−0.0257***	−0.0227*	0.0264**	−0.00823	0.0119	−0.0166
	(0.0086)	(0.0094)	(0.0091)	(0.0123)	(0.0129)	(0.0085)	(0.0133)	(0.0448)
Income: high	−0.00998	−0.0007	−0.0842***	−0.0466***	0.0193	−0.00771	−0.0366*	−0.09
	(0.0119)	(0.0133)	(0.0130)	(0.0176)	(0.0186)	(0.0118)	(0.0193)	(0.0710)
Unemployed	−0.0105	0.0228	0.000422	0.0239	0.0223	0.0225*	0.0276	−0.0884
	(0.0140)	(0.0151)	(0.0146)	(0.0226)	(0.0248)	(0.0134)	(0.0251)	(0.0811)

Not working (student, housewife)	−0.0552***	0.0128	−0.0380***	−0.0530***	−0.021	−0.0196*	−0.00908	0.0332
	(0.0106)	(0.0119)	(0.0114)	(0.0155)	(0.0159)	(0.0105)	(0.0166)	(0.0514)
Retired	−0.0424***	0.0224	−0.00728	0.0201	−0.0238	−0.0383**	0.0279	0.000673
	(0.0155)	(0.0168)	(0.0161)	(0.0221)	(0.0238)	(0.0152)	(0.0248)	(0.1000)
Contact dummy		−0.0572***	−0.00145	−0.014	0.0126	0.0128	0.0446***	−0.0026
		(0.0093)	(0.0132)	(0.0118)	(0.0133)	(0.0103)	(0.0135)	(0.0419)
Bribe dummy	0.505***	0.445***	0.580***	0.566***	0.357***	0.649***	0.463***	
	(0.0179)	(0.0233)	(0.0255)	(0.0365)	(0.0149)	(0.0563)	(0.0970)	
Constant	2.909***	2.850***	3.263***	3.929***	3.635***	3.100***	3.600***	2.861***
	(0.0428)	(0.0432)	(0.0438)	(0.0336)	(0.0399)	(0.0424)	(0.0426)	(0.1150)
Observations	93,240	89,156	88,874	48,008	45,693	89,849	44,773	4567
R-squared	0.203	0.178	0.242	0.248	0.243	0.289	0.216	0.067
Country dummies	Yes	Yes	Yes	Yes	Yes	Yes	Yes	Yes

'*' indicates a p-value ≤ 0.1, '**' indicates a p-value ≤ 0.05, and '***' indicates p-value ≤ 0.01.

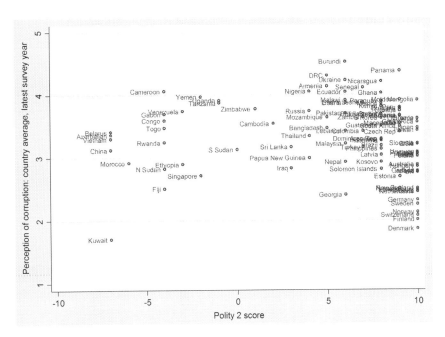

Fig. 10.7   Polity 2 score and corruption perceptions

play a small role. Adding age, gender, education, (self-reported) income group and employment status (along with country dummies) adds only marginally to the explanatory power of the regression (comparing R^2s in Table 10.2 for all countries to R^2s in Table 10.3). The most significant explanatory variable at the individual level is bribe payment, though including bribe payment does not increase much the R^2s of the regressions.

Table 10.3 suggests that women tend to perceive higher levels of corruption in one or another service than men and so do the better-educated. Other variables including employment status and age show inconsistent or negligible relationships across services. These results are similar in regressions (not shown) for HICs and non-HICs, with one exception: in HICs, the more educated and higher-income respondents are consistently less likely to perceive corruption than their non-HIC counterparts (except in the case of political parties—perceived corruption

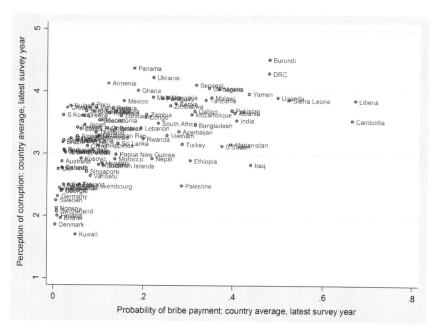

Fig. 10.8 Bribe payments and corruption perceptions

of political parties seems to be universal). We will return to this difference between HICs and non-HICs in looking at bribe-paying below.

Turning to country-level analysis on perceptions of corruption, (Table 10.4), GDP per capita is negatively associated with perception of corruption across many of the services. (GDP per capita alone[18] produces an R-squared of 0.36 in a regression of average perceptions across services; the relationship between median income and perception of corruption is even stronger in every case—these regressions not shown).[19]

Table 10.5 duplicates Table 10.4 with the exception that it adds reported bribe-paying and controls for the share of population that came into contact with the given service and thus had the opportunity to pay a bribe. In this table, GDP per capita is no longer statistically significant, presumably because it is so highly correlated with bribe payments, which are consistently significant across all sectors.

Table 10.4 OLS regression results: perceptions of corruption on the country level across services (all countries), latest survey year

VARIABLES	Perception of corruption (scale: 1–5) about [...] service, country level (OLS)								
	Avg. across services	Political parties	Education	Judiciary	Medical	Permits	Police	Tax	Utilities
log GDP per capita (current $)	-0.154**	0.0581	-0.251**	-0.159*	-0.0855	-0.155*	-0.223***	0.0151	0.00024
	(0.0596)	(0.0622)	(0.1140)	(0.0950)	(0.0920)	(0.0806)	(0.0651)	(0.0700)	(0.0825)
Avg. ten-year annual GDP growth (%)	0.0217	-0.023	0.0305	0.00698	0.0199	-0.000537	0.0251	0.00312	-0.0552
	(0.0231)	(0.0254)	(0.0586)	(0.0304)	(0.0380)	(0.0394)	(0.0265)	(0.0389)	(0.0432)
Gini coefficient, latest available	0.00687	0.0124**	-0.0079	0.00953	-0.0252***	0.00726	0.0118*	0.0031	0.0138
	(0.0056)	(0.0054)	(0.0080)	(0.0075)	(0.0094)	(0.0070)	(0.0059)	(0.0087)	(0.0083)
Share of pop. w/secondary educ or higher (0–1)	0.299	0.152	0.0501	-0.124	-0.19	-0.328	0.313	-0.680*	
	(0.3290)	(0.2890)	(0.4090)	(0.4280)	(0.4660)	(0.5150)	(0.4370)	(0.3790)	
Polity2 score	0.0182	0.0603***	0.0496	0.0134	0.00906	0.00472	0.00444	0.0236	0.0143
	(0.0137)	(0.0174)	(0.0382)	(0.0176)	(0.0195)	(0.0222)	(0.0205)	(0.0182)	(0.0125)

(continued)

Table 10.4 (continued)

VARIABLES	Perception of corruption (scale: 1–5) about [...] service, country level (OLS)								
	Avg. across services	Political parties	Education	Judiciary	Medical	Permits	Police	Tax	Utilities
Freedom House: civil liberties (−7 to −1)	0.197*	0.213**	−0.0841	0.240*	0.300**	0.191	0.207	0.201	
	(0.1020)	(0.0890)	(0.1660)	(0.1260)	(0.1430)	(0.1310)	(0.1340)	(0.1490)	
Freedom House: individual rights (0–16)	−0.117**	−0.141***	−0.0635	−0.127*	−0.256***	−0.163**	−0.117*	−0.235***	
	(0.0485)	(0.0500)	(0.0856)	(0.0650)	(0.0689)	(0.0643)	(0.0615)	(0.0697)	
Service performance/outcome variable			0.00440*	0.0293	−0.00645**	0.00844	0.0156***	−0.00641*	0.785*
			(0.0022)	(0.0232)	(0.0031)	(0.0930)	(0.0050)	(0.0033)	(0.4050)
Resource dependence dummy	−0.0162	0.0901	0.126	0.03	−0.1	−0.216*	−0.13	−0.217*	
	(0.1010)	(0.1150)	(0.1870)	(0.1710)	(0.1700)	(0.1220)	(0.1350)	(0.1150)	
Constant	5.745***	4.459***	3.521*	6.132***	8.772***	6.809***	6.453***	6.967***	2.163**
	(0.7560)	(0.7380)	(1.8300)	(0.9740)	(1.3480)	(1.0830)	(1.1070)	(1.1650)	(0.9280)
Observations	97	97	50	97	62	61	85	57	51
R-squared	0.453	0.383	0.404	0.302	0.397	0.604	0.617	0.587	0.191

'*' indicates a p-value ≤ 0.1, '**' indicates a p-value ≤ 0.05, and '***' indicates p-value ≤ 0.01.

Table 10.5 OLS regression results: perceptions of corruption on the country level across services (all countries) including bribe payments, latest survey year

VARIABLES	Perception of corruption (scale: 1–5) about [...] service, country level (OLS)								
	Avg. across services	Political parties	Education	Judiciary	Medical	Permits	Police	Tax	Utilities
log GDP per capita (current $)	−0.0734	0.0581	−0.225*	−0.0363	−0.0602	−0.0615	−0.126	0.0731	0.000242
	(0.0697)	(0.0622)	(0.1230)	(0.0986)	(0.1020)	(0.0806)	(0.1000)	(0.0759)	(0.0825)
Avg. ten-year annual GDP growth (%)	0.0238	−0.023	0.0213	0.0193	0.0146	0.0404	0.00972	0.0259	−0.0552
	(0.0206)	(0.0254)	(0.0621)	(0.0280)	(0.0435)	(0.0296)	(0.0242)	(0.0416)	(0.0432)
Gini coefficient, latest available	0.0109*	0.0124**	−0.00388	0.0124	−0.0126	0.0180**	0.0159**	0.0111	0.0138
	(0.0061)	(0.0054)	(0.0084)	(0.0083)	(0.0111)	(0.0087)	(0.0066)	(0.0114)	(0.0083)
Share of pop. w/secondary educ or higher (0–1)	0.356	0.152	0.248	−0.0915	−0.597	−0.709	0.546	−0.771*	
	(0.3120)	(0.2890)	(0.3700)	(0.4300)	(0.4950)	(0.4910)	(0.4170)	(0.4140)	
Polity2 score	0.0171	0.0603***	0.0517	0.0151	0.0157	−0.00513	0.0133	0.0197	0.0143
	(0.0128)	(0.0174)	(0.0364)	(0.0177)	(0.0182)	(0.0174)	(0.0198)	(0.0327)	(0.0125)

(continued)

Table 10.5 (continued)

VARIABLES	Perception of corruption (scale: 1–5) about [...] service, country level (OLS)								
	Avg. across services	Political parties	Education	Judiciary	Medical	Permits	Police	Tax	Utilities
	(0.0963)	(0.0890)	(0.1680)	(0.1220)	(0.1560)	(0.1440)	(0.1230)	(0.2130)	
Freedom House: civil liberties (−7 to −1)	−0.106**	−0.141***	−0.0376	−0.121**	−0.11	−0.0471	−0.0979*	−0.148	
	(0.0963)	(0.0890)	(0.1680)	(0.1220)	(0.1560)	(0.1440)	(0.1230)	(0.2130)	
Freedom House: individual rights (0–16)									
	(0.0421)	(0.0500)	(0.0805)	(0.0561)	(0.0772)	(0.0749)	(0.0531)	(0.0960)	
Service performance/outcome variable			0.00366	0.0419*	−0.0042	−0.0711	0.0143***	−0.00807*	0.785*
			(0.0022)	(0.0238)	(0.0027)	(0.0935)	(0.0049)	(0.0044)	(0.4050)
Resource dependence dummy	−0.0267	0.0901	0.1	−0.0056	−0.0712	−0.175	−0.151	−0.26	
	(0.0988)	(0.1150)	(0.1710)	(0.1700)	(0.2050)	(0.1580)	(0.1100)	(0.1790)	

	(1)	(2)	(3)	(4)	(5)	(6)	(7)	(8)	(9)
Share of population with contact (%)		−0.00461	0.00667	0.00279	−0.00278	−0.00595	−0.00365		
		(0.0051)	(0.0096)	(0.0044)	(0.0055)	(0.0051)	(0.0052)		
Probability of bribe payment (%)	0.0117**	0.0162*	0.0136***	0.0158***	0.0144***	0.0116**	0.00978		
	(0.0050)	(0.0049)	(0.0042)	(0.0030)	(0.0046)	(0.0047)	(0.0103)		
Constant	4.523***	4.459***	3.068	4.324***	5.650***	3.750***	4.812***	4.882**	2.163**
	(0.9050)	(0.7380)	(1.9610)	(1.1930)	(1.5670)	(1.3330)	(1.0910)	(1.8190)	(0.9280)
Observations	96	97	50	96	54	53	84	48	51
R-squared	0.491	0.383	0.458	0.378	0.499	0.701	0.667	0.599	0.191

'*' indicates a p-value ≤ 0.1, '**' indicates a p-value ≤ 0.05, and '***' indicates p-value ≤ 0.01.

Apart from GDP per capita and the probability of bribe payments, very few other explanatory variables display a statistically significant relationship with perceptions of corruption. The Gini coefficient is positively associated with higher perceived corruption in political parties, permits and the police.[20] Among the service outcome (service performance) variables, only homicides show a statistically significant correlation with corruption perceptions in its associated sector, police services. (We do not observe this association among non-HICs). We see little statistically significant associations with the perception of corruption of our other outcome indicators. Where the polity measure of democracy enters significantly, it does so with the unexpected sign (more democratic countries associated with higher perceived corruption) and so does the civil liberties measure by Freedom House.[21] Perhaps freer people have a higher standard of intolerance of corruption; perhaps less free people are more likely to be reticent about reporting their sense that corruption prevails.

Bribe Payments as Dependent Variable

In Table 10.6 we return to results at the individual level, now with bribe payments as the dependent variable for all countries. (In this table, which shows odds ratios, any coefficient above one implies a positive relationship and below one a negative relationship.) The results are all conditional on contact with the given service: only those who had contact with the service were asked about bribe payment. Answers from those with no contact and thus no bribe are considered missing observations.

In contrast to their lower perceptions about corruption, men are more likely to report (someone in the household) paying a bribe than are women. The difference is particularly striking when it comes to paying bribes to the police: men are over 30% more likely to report bribe-paying (controlling for country differences and other individual characteristics). That the incidence of reported bribe payments is higher for men and perception of corruption is higher for women speaks (again) to perceptions being about more than bribe payments.

The patterns for having a higher level of education show a similar positive association with bribe payments to that seen with corruption

Table 10.6 Logistic regression results with odds ratios displayed: probability of bribe payment on the individual level across services (all countries), latest year

VARIABLES	Probability of bribe payment in [...] service, latest survey year (logit; odds ratios displayed)						
	Education	Judiciary	Medical	Permits	Police	Tax	Utilities
Age: 30–50	0.983	1.074	1.064**	0.939*	1.003	0.913*	0.932*
	(0.0329)	(0.0553)	(0.0327)	(C.0353)	(0.0378)	(0.0502)	(0.0355)
Age: 51–65	0.835***	0.977	1.011	0.913*	0.835***	0.807***	0.898**
	(0.0432)	(0.0721)	(0.0419)	(C.0498)	(0.0475)	(0.0634)	(0.0490)
Age: 65 +	0.755***	0.813	0.953	0.875	0.599***	0.741**	0.957
	(0.0740)	(0.1100)	(0.0626)	(C.0893)	(0.0649)	(0.1120)	(0.0958)
Male (dummy)	1.110***	1.04	1.021	1.137***	1.309***	1.094*	1.136***
	(0.0336)	(0.0472)	(0.0267)	(C.0386)	(0.0447)	(0.0529)	(0.0395)
Educ: secondary school	1.083*	1.197***	1.116***	1.056	1.188***	0.952	0.956
	(0.0463)	(0.0767)	(0.0404)	(C.0501)	(0.0581)	(0.0663)	(0.0455)
Educ: higher/uni	1.053	1.016	1.076*	1.08	1.263***	0.946	0.924
	(0.0488)	(0.0710)	(0.0433)	(C.0558)	(0.0674)	(0.0706)	(0.0479)
Income: med/med high	1.011	1.137**	1.058**	1.048	1.167***	0.968	0.901***
	(0.0341)	(0.0577)	(0.0303)	(C.0399)	(0.0443)	(0.0527)	(0.0344)
Income: high	1.049	1.205***	1.042	1.251***	1.181***	1.06	0.991
	(0.0505)	(0.0870)	(0.0424)	(0.0655)	(0.0649)	(0.0808)	(0.0522)
Unemployed	1.002	0.962	0.974	0.964	0.853***	1.053	0.968
	(0.0477)	(0.0667)	(0.0419)	(0.0518)	(0.0451)	(0.0839)	(0.0531)
Not working (student, housewife)	0.920**	0.915	0.920**	0.892**	0.849***	0.863**	0.857***
	(0.0356)	(0.0563)	(0.0330)	(0.0405)	(0.0390)	(0.0569)	(0.0385)
Retired	1.081	1.057	0.92	0.829**	0.848**	0.694***	0.699***
	(0.0817)	(0.1120)	(0.0484)	(0.0686)	(0.0707)	(0.0811)	(0.0584)
Constant	0.262***	2.212***	0.268***	0.686***	0.968	1.544***	0.353***
	(0.0302)	(0.2810)	(0.0281)	(0.0882)	(0.1010)	(0.2500)	(0.0505)
Observations	43,662	13,782	58,238	29,215	23,991	26,087	50,051
Country dummies	Yes	Yes	Yes	Yes	Yes	Yes	Yes

'*' indicates a p-value ≤ 0.1, '**' indicates a p-value ≤ 0.05, and '***' indicates p-value ≤ 0.01.

perceptions. Education and self-reported income level are both positively correlated with bribe-paying when looking at all countries together; separate regressions (not shown) for the HICs and non-HICs indicate that those relationships are largely driven by the non-HICs. In the HICs, having a higher level of income and education is negatively correlated with reported bribes. It may be that in non-HICs, public officials target wealthier (and generally better-educated) individuals to maximize the size of bribes, and that the wealthy are more likely to be able to afford bribes and thus do so more often—also implying that wealthier individuals get ahead by circumventing official rules and procedures.

On the country level (Table 10.7), there is the same consistent and strong negative association between GDP per capita and bribe payments as was the case with perception of corruption. A 10% increase in GDP per capita is associated with an 0.7 percentage point decrease in the average (across multiple services) probability of bribe payment. The Gini coefficient shows an interesting—and somewhat puzzling—pattern: controlling for GDP per capita, democracy and personal freedoms, the Gini is negatively associated with bribe payments in medical- and tax services (higher Gini, fewer bribes). However, looking at HICs alone (not shown) we see a positive association between inequality and more frequent reported bribe-paying. Finally, as in the perceptions analysis, the police service outcome variable—homicides—is positively and statistically significantly correlated with the probability of paying a bribe.

In rough summary, we have three major results. First, individual perceptions of corruption of a given service in a country vary widely within populations, largely due to individual unobserved factors—beyond education and reported income for example. The same personal characteristics can be positively related to perceptions of corruption in one service or sector and negatively related to perceptions of corruption in another: being between the ages of 30 and 50, for example, is positively associated with seeing the judiciary and medical services as more corrupt, but negatively associated with views of corruption in permit- and tax services. This underlines the complexity of possible interpretations and biases that may be in play when individuals are asked to judge levels of corruption. The fact that perceptions of corruption by different individuals judging

Table 10.7 OLS regression results: probability of bribe payment (%) on the country level across services (all countries), latest year

VARIABLES	Probability of bribe payment (%) in [....] service; latest survey year available (OLS)							
	Avg. across services	Education	Judiciary	Medical	Permits	Police	Tax	Utilities
log GDP per capita (current $)	-6.826***	-1.984	-6.789***	-3.899**	-7.548***	-9.277***	-5.073***	-5.506**
	(1.695)	(2.216)	(2.275)	(1.859)	(1.774)	(2.771)	(1.902)	(2.424)
Avg. ten-year annual GDP growth (%)	-0.182	1.152	0.121	0.853	-0.196	1.281	-1.701**	-0.314
	(0.669)	(0.989)	(0.876)	(0.752)	(0.823)	(1.014)	(0.770)	(0.839)
Share of pop. w/secondary educ or higher (0-1)	-5.057	-10.21	-7.651	-9.888	-2.553	-17.09	-11.05	-1.655
	(7.988)	(7.341)	(10.640)	(9.424)	(10.460)	(14.080)	(9.203)	(12.990)
Gini coefficient, latest available	-0.316**	0.00257	-0.289	-0.587***	-0.318	-0.31	-0.438**	-0.158
	(0.141)	(0.173)	(0.178)	(0.162)	(0.217)	(0.218)	(0.169)	(0.184)
Polity2 score	0.139	-0.606	0.245	0.0532	-0.244	-0.632	-0.446	0.578
	(0.345)	(0.792)	(0.462)	(0.434)	(0.658)	(0.904)	(0.672)	(0.428)
Freedom House: civil liberties (-7 to -1)	0.467	0.248	-1.289	1.065	-0.147	2.769	-0.629	-1.764
	(2.196)	(3.018)	(2.938)	(2.890)	(2.974)	(4.595)	(2.778)	(3.182)
Freedom House: individual rights (0-16)	-0.949	-0.476	-0.471	-0.623	-0.343	-1.643	-0.923	-0.217
	(1.128)	(1.405)	(1.592)	(1.446)	(1.357)	(2.038)	(1.309)	(1.513)

(continued)

Table 10.7 (continued)

| VARIABLES | Probability of bribe payment (%) in [...] service; latest survey year available (OLS) | | | | | | | |
	Avg. across services	Education	Judiciary	Medical	Permits	Police	Tax	Utilities
Service performance/outcome variable		0.0305	−0.71	0.0821	3.496*	0.311**	−0.014	12.39
		(0.041)	(0.501)	(0.061)	(1.983)	(0.144)	(0.108)	(7.759)
Resource dependence dummy	0.577	1.455	−0.0344	−0.967	−2.048	0.877	−1.686	1.469
	(2.546)	(2.786)	(3.744)	(3.205)	(3.765)	(4.283)	(3.465)	(3.772)
Share of population with contact (%)		−0.0537	0.0879	0.0229	0.0934	0.328**	−0.150*	−0.170***
		(0.068)	(0.210)	(0.082)	(0.145)	(0.135)	(0.084)	(0.062)
Constant	102.6***	29.11	101.5***	81.36***	101.6***	148.8***	106.9***	62.11***
	(18.08)	(34.74)	(25.44)	(25.80)	(25.13)	(36.57)	(22.29)	(21.99)
Observations	96	50	96	95	96	84	84	69
R-squared	0.617	0.52	0.574	0.462	0.567	0.704	0.561	0.486

'*' indicates a p-value ≤ 0.1, '**' indicates a p-value ≤ 0.05, and '***' indicates p-value ≤ 0.01.

the same sector are so wildly dissimilar suggests the danger of small-N, non-random survey measures of fuzzy concepts like corruption or governance of the type behind "expert perceptions" indicators including the World Bank's Country Policy and Institutional Assessment (CPIA).

Second, at the national level, the level of a country's GDP per capita is negatively associated with perception of corruption and with bribe payments, across all countries (and within HICs and non-HICs); and, not surprisingly, GDP per capita and bribe-paying are highly and negatively correlated with each other. The difference between poor (non-HICs) and rich (HICs) countries is greater for bribe-paying than for perception of corruption; perception of corruption appears to be an inherently noisier variable than paying or not paying a bribe.

Third, the relation between better scores on measures of service outcomes and lower perception of corruption is weak. Similarly, "governance" measures including indicators of democracy and civil rights are only weakly related to perceived corruption—and sometimes in an unexpected direction—perhaps because standards are higher in more democratic countries.

A Concluding Note

In the end, our analysis above is based on data and methods that are not sufficient to determine to what extent citizens' perceptions of corruption are a reliable proxy for unmeasurable "actual corruption". However, citizen perceptions' strong association with a reported behavior—paying a bribe—suggests bribe-paying is at least a partial measure of actual "petty" if not "grand" corruption—and possibly a proxy for weak and/or corrupt government in terms of capacity to finance and deliver key services in response to citizens' demands. We use the diagram below to illustrate that basic conclusion, and to speculate about future research.

Figure 10.9 provides a simple visual representation of how citizen perceptions of corruption might relate to "actual" (unmeasurable) corruption and to bribe payments—and how those might be related to

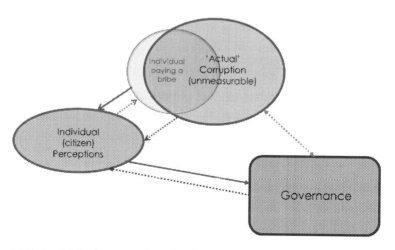

Fig. 10.9 Individual perceptions in the context of bribe payments, actual corruption and governance

(unmeasurable) governance. Because there is more to corruption than bribe payments, we show bribe payments as constituting a good portion but not all of actual corruption.[22] We show a solid arrow from individual bribe payments to "actual" corruption to represent the relationship that our analysis suggests, namely that paying a bribe increases individuals' perception of corruption about a given service. The dotted arrows to and from perceptions and actual corruption represent the possibility that each affects the other, or that a third factor influence both; our analysis does not address causation or effects of unmeasured third factors.

What about the relationship between perceptions of corruption and governance? The solid arrow from citizens' perception of corruption to governance represents the likelihood (supported by other work in this field) that widespread perception of corruption is likely to signal lack of trust in government and thus for example resistance to paying taxes. The dotted arrows from and to governance represent the possibility that governance affects perceptions and is affected by actual corruption (including actual bribe-paying).

Put another way, because of probable reinforcing effects—a potential vicious circle—it seems likely that in the end it is economic growth and development (measured by GDP per capita, median income and so on) that we can be most confident matters. Our analysis suggests that GDP per capita lowers perceptions of corruption, including because it is closely (and negatively) associated with bribe payments; that intuition is reinforced by the fact that in the case of political parties (where direct bribe payments by the average citizen are likely to be very rare), higher GDP per capita is not as strongly associated with lower perceptions of corruption.

We return to where we started in this paper: a plausible conclusion is that the one reliable tool we appear to have to reduce citizens' perceptions of corruption is development. "Governance" is at best a tool to achieve development itself. Better governance in one form or another, independent of more development in one form or another, may have little direct effect on actual probity or perceptions of probity—except perhaps to the extent that better governance reduces the incidence of bribe payments.

An agenda which targets corruption and weak governance through tools from biometric identification and service quality surveys of government employees to open budgeting and contracting alongside registries of beneficial ownership and stolen asset recovery is still very much worthwhile. But the development community might want to be cautious in assuming such measures will significantly reduce popular perceptions of corruption. The better approach to reduce perceptions—and perhaps the reality—of corruption would be to focus on broad-based growth-driven development.

Comments by Francesca Recanatini

> *"There are things known and there are things unknown,*
> *and in between are the doors of perception."*
> — Aldous Huxley

Low confidence and trust in government institutions can significantly undermine the governance in a country. The factors responsible for low levels of trust among citizens are still unclear. Nancy Birdsall, Charles

Kenny and Anna Diofasi offer a novel approach to the issue of trust in government, focusing on the link between perceptions of corruption, actual corruption and quality of governance. The authors move from the consideration that perceptions of corruption are often an input to measuring governance and allocate aid and explores the factors driving perceptions of corruption (and in turn trust in government) at different levels: at the individual level and at the country level. Rather than focusing on experts' perceptions, the authors focus on citizens' perceptions of corruption. A few key messages emerge: at the individual level, citizens' perceptions can provide some information about the problem of corruption in a country but they reflect largely unobserved factors. At the country level, the level of perceptions of corruption is negatively correlated with the GDP of the country and positively correlated with reported bribe payments. Building on these findings, the authors suggest that growth and development could be an effective tool to reduce perceptions of corruption.

The approach proposed by the authors help look at the problem of low trust and corruption from a new angle but the main results of the paper—individual perceptions are mostly driven by unobservable factors and may be reduced by development—open the doors to more questions about the relationship among corruption, governance and trust. These comments focus on some of the additional questions that should be explored for future research building on these initial results:

1. what additional factors may affect and drive citizens' perceptions;
2. how we should think about corruption;
3. how the relationship among perceptions, development and corruption may be changed when we use a broader definition of corruption.

Drivers of Perceptions

The authors use a new approach to the analysis of the challenges to effective governance. Corruption undermines the ability of government to effectively manage public resources. But the perceptions by citizens of corruption can also have a negative impact by promoting distrust and creating incentives for citizens to participate less in government activities (ex. paying taxes). Thus, by changing citizens' perceptions—suggest the authors—government can improve governance too. The question is then what are the factors driving perceptions.

The paper explores the role of individual characteristics (such as education, sex, employment, income) and bribe payment on perceptions but the results suggest that the perceptions are affected by other factors. What could be the other factors driving perceptions?

Perceptions by citizens can provide information on the state of governance of a country as they clearly signal the existence of a governance problem. The paper however does not provide enough evidence to link perceptions to actual corruption. Perceptions of corruption can be influenced by recent scandals and their media coverage with limited connection to the actual extent of corruption in a country. Perceptions can also be affected by changes in freedom and access to information. They can be manipulated by a captured media with the intention of undermining policy reforms.[23]

By their nature perceptions are volatile and noisy and can be affected by the way in which the individual forms his or her views and by the environment in which the individual lives and operates. The three levels of analysis presented in the paper use a mix of both types of factors, as described in detail in the paper. There one additional factor that should be taken into consideration as it can affect both the dependent and the independent variables used in the empirical analysis: the level of impunity occurring in the country.

While news and scandals are likely to affect the perceptions by citizens, it is also the case that observed inaction by the government on allegations and documented cases of corruption (i.e. impunity) will increase the perception of corruption in the country by citizens. This particular factor can impact greatly perceptions even if citizens observed just a few high profile cases of impunity and despite the degree of bribe payment experience first-hand. Moreover, the perceived degree of impunity present in the country can affect the willingness of citizens to report bribe payment and may help explain the observed changes in bribe payment in a few countries of the sample used. If for example during the past 12 months the government acted swiftly following a corruption scandal, citizens may perceive a lower level of corruption and at the same time be less willing to report bribe payment as this may have some direct consequences on them.[24] Thus, perceived impunity can both affect perceptions of corruption and attitude of citizens to report bribe payment. This introduces an omitted variable problem especially relevant when analyzing individual perceptions of corruption.

Perceptions by citizens may also be affected by the type of corruption that citizens observe. The authors propose to use bribe payment for a public service as an additional explanatory variable. While the use of this variable may introduce some issues at the estimation stage, as highlighted above, focusing only on bribe payment as "corruption" poses a more significant challenge at the theoretical level as explained below.

What is Corruption?

The more commonly used definition of corruption is the abuse of public office for private gain (Rose-Ackerman, 1999). Such simple definition captures a phenomenon that however can take many forms and shapes within the same country and across different countries. Box 10.1 offers an example of different forms of corruption that World Bank practitioners have observed in their work. Bribe payment, one of the key variables in this analysis, captures only one form of corruption, the one that has been however more frequently measured by practitioners.

More importantly, corruption is about power and incentives— allocation and misuse of power by public officials and politicians and incentives present. Researchers are increasingly realizing the role of incentives rather than that of laws and regulations when it comes to improve governance and reduce the risk of corruption. Laws and regulations are necessary to establish and define exchanges among citizens and between citizens and government institutions. But, they are not sufficient to guarantee that those transactions will happen in the way specified by the law. In practice, laws and regulations will be implemented differently and to a different degree depending on the system of incentives present in the country.[25]

Moreover, corruption is not only heterogeneous phenomena that require a focus on behavior and incentives. It also requires a reallocation of roles and responsibility within a country, that is a reallocation of powers. These issues may be even more severe for certain types of corruption, particularly where rents are large and interest in maintaining the status quo is strong.[26] As a result, measures to reduce the incidence of petty corruption may receive wider and stronger political support than measures that address other types of corruption (such as public funds' diversion or corruption in public procurement), since the control of petty payoffs will have only a limited impact on the distribution of the most significant rents and power in a country.

Box 10.1 Typologies of Corruption

Corruption in public procurement: use of bribes, gifts and/or favors to alter the public procurement process;

Corruption in budget management: use of bribes, gifts and/or favors to influence budget management decisions and divert funds;

Corruption in personnel management: use of bribes, gifts and/or favors to affect personnel management decisions;

Legal and regulatory corruption: use of bribes, gifts and/or favors to alter regulatory and legal decisions;

Administrative corruption: use of bribes, gifts and/or favors to obtain or hasten the provision of public services.

Source: Author

Acknowledging the complexity of the phenomenon of corruption and the role of power and incentives has some implications for the framework used in the paper and the subsequent empirical analysis. The starting point for the paper's analysis is the hypothesis that individual perceptions of corruption are driven by actual corruption in the form of bribe payment and that in turn perceptions can affect and are affected by quality of governance, as illustrated in Fig. 10.9 in the paper.

An aspect overlooked in the proposed framework in Fig. 10.9 is the heterogeneity of the phenomenon of corruption. Bribe payment is one of the many aspects that "corruption" can take, as the "revised" Fig. 10.10 presented below illustrates. Corruption includes also phenom-

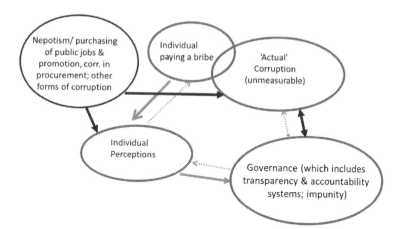

Fig. 10.10 Individual perceptions in the context of bribe payments, actual corruption and governance –Revised. Source: Author

ena like nepotism, embezzlement and state capture. These other forms of corruption can affect citizens' perceptions of corruption. In addition, forms of corruption like nepotism or state capture can have a direct and more significant impact on the quality of institutions of a country and its governance, undermining reform efforts and further exacerbating corruption.

Consider for a moment corruption in the management of human resources of a country. A civil service selected based on favors and bribe payments affect the way in which the public administration operates and manages public resources, leading to a lower quality of public services, misuse and misallocation of public resources (with possible exclusion of some group of citizens to certain services), abuses and support for the status quo. Citizens may not pay bribes to access services but the level of perceived corruption (and distrust) is likely to be high.

Finally, to acknowledge the complexity of corruption and the role of power and incentives is also critical for the interpretation of the conclusion of the paper—that is development as a possible tool to reduce perceptions of corruption. If we focus on bribe payment, there is increasing evidence that bribe payment declines as the level of development in the country increases. A World Bank report published in 2011 uses firm-level data to analyze the experience of a selected group of Eastern European countries between 2005 and 2008. The evidence collected shows how country-specific and targeted policy measures have helped significantly to reduce the incidence of bribes paid by businesses in the majority of the countries analyzed. Although progress has been made in reducing bribe payment by promoting development, practitioners observed no variation or an increase in the level of other forms of corruption, such as diversion of public funds. The observed inability of governments to reduce some forms of corruption points to the role of power and incentives. As countries grow, it is easier for policymakers to address forms of corruption that require a small reallocation of power (like bribe payments), while other forms remain untouched and flourish. Thus, individual perceptions of corruption may be reduced by development since citizens are more likely to observe bribe payment rather than other forms of corruption, but that does not necessarily mean that actual corruption is declining in the country.

In the end, perceptions of corruption can provide some information about the actual extent of corruption. Because of the nature of corruption, perceptions can only get to the tip of the problem, leaving researchers and policymakers with more unanswered questions than answers.

Appendix

Table 10.8 Variables—data and sources

Variable	Details/units	Sources	Year/construction
DV: perception that [….] service is corrupt (individual-level regressions)	Variable that takes on values from 1 to 5, with 1=Not at all corrupt and 5= Extremely corrupt	Transparency International (TI) Corruption Barometer survey	Same as TI survey year
DV: probability of bribe payment in [….] service	Dummy variable; =1 if respondent or household member or respondent reportedly paid a bribe for/to a given service; =0 if no bribe paid. Observations for those with no contact are treated as missing.	TI Corruption Barometer survey	Same as TI survey year
(individual-level regressions)			
Age	Four groups: under 30; 30 to 50; 51 to 65 and 65+	TI Corruption Barometer survey	Same as TI survey year
Male	=1 if respondent is male; =0 if female	TI Corruption Barometer survey	Same as TI survey year
Education	Three groups: no education/only basic education; secondary school; high-level education	TI Corruption Barometer survey	Same as TI survey year
Income	Self-reported, three groups: low/medium low; medium/ medium high and high	TI Corruption Barometer survey	Same as TI survey year

Employment status	Four groups: working full time (incl. self-employed); unemployed; not working (student, housewife); retired	Same as TI survey year
Contact dummy (IV in individual-level regressions)	=1 if respondent had contact with a given institution;	Same as TI survey year
Bribe dummy	=0 if no contact =1 is respondent or household member of respondent reportedly paid a bribe to a given institution (conditional on contact);	Same as TI survey year
(IV in individual-level regressions)	=0 if no bribe was paid, incl. in case of no contact	
DV: perception that [...] service is corrupt (country-level regressions)	Country-level average of corruption perceptions for [...] service. 1=Not at all corrupt and 5= Extremely corrupt	TI Corruption Barometer survey
DV: probability of bribe payment in [...] service	Country-level average of bribe payments (by respondent or household member) for [...] service, expressed as %. Lowest possible value=0%, highest possible=100%	TI Corruption Barometer survey
(country-level regressions)		
GDP per capita	GDP per capita, current US$	World Bank PovcalNet/
Median income/	Median country income or consumption at 2011 Purchasing Power Parity (PPP)	Latest year available
consumption	Diofasi and Birdsall	

(continued)

Table 10.8 (Continued)

Avg. ten-year annual GDP growth	Avg. ten-year annual GDP growth; measured as %	World Bank	Average of ten preceding years' annual GDP growth rates for each TI survey year
Gini coefficient	Range: 0–100	World Bank	Latest year available after 2000
Share of pop. with secondary educ. or higher	Share of surveyed population that reported to have secondary school or higher-level education	TI Corruption Barometer survey	Same as TI survey year
Polity2 score	From −10 (autocracy) to 10 (democracy)	Center for Systemic Peace/ Polity IV project	Same as TI survey year
Freedom House: civil liberties	From 7 (worst) to 1 (best)	Freedom House	Same as TI survey year
Freedom House: individual rights	From 0 (worst) to 16 (best)	Freedom House	Same as TI survey year
Resource dependence (dummy)	=1 if the export share of fuels and ores, metals, minerals and gold is >50%	United Nations Conference on Trade and Development	2013
Share of population with contact	Country-level average of total population that had contact with [. . .] service, expressed as %. Lowest possible value = 0%, highest possible = 100%	TI Corruption Barometer survey	Same as TI survey year

Probability of bribe payment (IV in country-level regressions)	Country-level average of total population (not limited to those with contact) that paid a bribe in [...] service, expressed as %. Lowest possible value = 0%, highest possible = 100%	TI Corruption Barometer survey	Same as TI survey year
Service outcome indicator for education:	Average country score of the three PISA components (mathematics, science and reading)	PISA	Same as TI survey year where available; extrapolated for missing years if data available for more than two years; latest score where only one data point available
Average PISA score			
Service outcome indicator for the judiciary:	Quality of judicial processes index;	Doing Business (World Bank)	Latest available
DB judicial index	from 0 (worst) to 18 (best)		
Service outcome indicator for the medical sector:	Mortality rate per 1000 for children under 5	World Bank	Same as TI survey year
Under 5 mortality			
Service outcome indicator for permit and registry services: ease of property registration index	Index of three standardized indicators linked to registering property (no. of procedures, no. of days and costs); higher values indicate a higher average of the three components	Dcing Business	Same as TI survey year
		(World Bank)	

(continued)

Table 10.8 (continued)

Service outcome indicator for the police: homicide rates	Intentional homicides per 100,000 people	World Bank	Same as TI survey year
Service outcome indicator for tax services: Taxes as a share of total govt. revenue	Taxes as a share of total govt. revenue, measured as %	IMF	Same as TI survey year
Service outcome indicator for utilities: likelihood of power outage	Share of businesses that experienced a power outage in the last (fiscal) year, measured as %	Enterprise Surveys (World Bank)	Same as TI survey year where available; extrapolated for missing years if data available for more than two years; latest year where only one data point available

Summary statistics

Table 10.9 Country-level summary statistics (all countries)

VARIABLES	(1) N	(2) mean	(3) sd	(4) min	(5) max
Perception of corruption	117	3.28	0.59	1.7	4.52
Avg. probability of bribe payment	109	16.38	15.28	0.34	67.12
GDP per capita	117	14,365	19,897	240.6	103,267
Median income/consumption	100	15.25	15.47	1.1	59.5
Avg. ten-year GDP growth	117	4.24	2.5	−3.29	15.29
Gini coefficient	110	38.05	8.26	16.64	63.01
Polity 2 score	110	5.68	5.2	−7	10
Freedom House: civil liberties	115	−2.97	1.62	−7	−1
Freedom House: individual rights	107	10.24	3.64	0	16
Resource dependence dummy	118	0.24	0.43	0	1
PISA avg score (education service var.)	56	470.4	51.79	369	548.3
Quality of judicial processes index (judiciary service var.)	117	8.94	3.01	4	15.5
Under 5 mortality (medical service var.)	115	32.23	34.2	2.4	160.2
Homicide rates (police service var.)	102	6.29	10.07	0.4	64.1
Property registration index (permit service var.)	117	0.024	0.72	−1.39	2.43
Power outage probability (utilities service var.)	85	0.62	0.23	0.16	0.96

Table 10.10 Country-level summary statistics: Average corruption perceptions by service

VARIABLES	(1) N	(2) mean	(3) sd	(4) min	(5) max
Perceptions about political parties	117	3.73	0.59	2.02	4.91
Perceptions about the education service	115	2.95	0.56	1.81	4.27
Perceptions about the judiciary	117	3.36	0.67	1.59	4.63
Perceptions about the medical service	81	3.16	0.6	1.99	4.52
Perceptions about the police	115	3.58	0.7	1.85	4.67
Perceptions about permit and registry services	80	3.04	0.65	1.76	4.41
Perceptions about utilities	81	2.91	0.51	1.91	4.2
Perceptions about the tax service	80	3.18	0.6	1.9	4.39

Table 10.11 Country-level summary statistics: probability of contact by service

VARIABLES	(1) N	(2) mean	(3) sd	(4) min	(5) max
Probability of contact: education	109	49.15	17.8	9.63	100
Probability of contact: judiciary	109	15.93	11.44	0.87	86.28
Probability of contact: medical service	109	63.03	15.47	21.3	94.85
Probability of contact: police	109	26.89	15.14	5.84	88.87
Probability of contact: permits + registry	109	32.37	13.51	7.11	85.36
Probability of contact: utilities	109	55.57	21.89	6.4	98.69
Probability of contact: tax service	109	30.31	17.54	3.61	82.64

Table 10.12 Country-level summary statistics: probability of bribe payment by service (conditional on contact)

VARIABLES	(1) N	(2) mean	(3) sd	(4) min	(5) max
Probability of bribe payment: education	109	13.81	15.27	0	75.69
Probability of bribe payment: judiciary	109	21.31	19.45	0	78.31
Probability of bribe payment: medical service	109	15.16	14.61	0.35	66.45
Probability of bribe payment: police	109	27.98	24.67	0	86.07
Probability of bribe payment: permits + registry	109	19.33	18.55	0.32	75.71
Probability of bribe payment: utilities	109	11.37	14.62	0.29	82.78
Probability of bribe payment: tax service	109	14.02	17.79	0	67.31

Table 10.13 Individual-level summary statistics: respondent characteristics

	(1)	(2)	(3)	(4)	(5)
VARIABLES	N	mean	sd	min	max
Age	115,077	2.057	0.92	1	4
Level of education	114,023	2.149	0.72	1	3
Employment type	114,393	1.917	1.12	1	4
Male dummy	115,357	0.495	0.5	0	1
Income level	101,428	1.711	0.7	1	3

Table 10.14 Individual-level summary statistics: contact dummies by service

	(1)	(2)	(3)	(4)	(5)
VARIABLES	N	mean	sd	min	max
Contact dummy: education	102,001	0.488	0.5	0	1
Contact dummy: judiciary	101,458	0.158	0.37	0	1
Contact dummy: medical service	61,959	0.604	0.49	0	1
Contact dummy: police	102,791	0.269	0.44	0	1
Contact dummy: permits + registry	58,789	0.301	0.46	0	1
Contact dummy: utilities	6960	0.524	0.5	0	1
Contact dummy: tax service	56,943	0.318	0.47	0	1

Table 10.15 Individual-level summary statistics: bribe payment dummies by service

	(1)	(2)	(3)	(4)	(5)
VARIABLES	N	mean	sd	min	max
Bribe dummy: education	48,583	0.158	0.37	0	1
Bribe dummy: judiciary	15,439	0.276	0.45	0	1
Bribe dummy: medical service	28,850	0.097	0.3	0	1
Bribe dummy: police	26,635	0.348	0.48	0	1
Bribe dummy: permits + registry	13,724	0.107	0.31	0	1
Bribe dummy: utilities	3527	0.085	0.28	0	1
Bribe dummy: tax service	14,380	0.04	0.2	0	1

Table 10.16 Individual-level summary statistics: bribe payment as a dependent variable[a] by service

VARIABLES	(1) N	(2) mean	(3) sd	(4) min	(5) max
Bribe dummy as DV: education	51,326	0.155	0.36	0	1
Bribe dummy as DV: judiciary	15,971	0.274	0.45	0	1
Bribe dummy as DV: medical service	66,761	0.152	0.36	0	1
Bribe dummy as DV: police	27,550	0.341	0.47	0	1
Bribe dummy as DV: permits + registry	32,855	0.214	0.41	0	1
Bribe dummy as DV: utilities	58,090	0.1	0.3	0	1
Bribe dummy as DV: tax service	31,038	0.099	0.3	0	1

[a]The values and the number of observations differ between the bribe payment dummy as a dependent variable and bribe payment dummy as an explanatory variable. This is due to the different survey years that apply. For the bribe payment dummy as a dependent variable (Table 10.16), the values represent the latest survey year for each service when the bribe payment question was asked for a given country in the GCB survey. For the bribe payment dummy as an explanatory variable (Table 10.15), the values represent the latest survey year for each service when corruption perception question was asked for a given country in the GCB survey.

Notes

1. See for example: Diamond (2007), Gallup (2015) or Whiteley et al. (2015).
2. Solé-Ollé and Sorribas-Navarro (2014).
3. Anderson (2015); Daude et al. (2012).
4. Mungiu-Pippidi (2015) distinguishes between particularistic and personalistic societies where corruption is the norm, and those where norm-based "ethical universalism" is the default.
5. Individual perceptions of corruption have been found to be consistently affected by factors including age, ethnicity, education, political affiliation (Olken 2009).
6. Note that reported bribe-paying covers both a bribe payment by the survey respondent herself/himself or anyone living in their household. The question posed to respondents with regards to bribes is: "In the past 12 months, have you or anyone living in your household paid a bribe in any form to each of the following institutions/organizations?"

7. Mostly 2010 for perceptions of corruption about political parties, education, the judiciary and the police and mostly 2007 for perceptions of corruption about medical services, permits, utilities and tax services.

8. Mostly 2010 for most countries the country-level overall corruption perception variable is the average of perceptions about the education services, the judiciary and the police—weighted by the number of respondents. For some countries—depending on the data available in the most recent survey year—the overall corruption perception variable also includes medical-, permit-, utilities- and tax services. Perceptions about political parties are not included for any country.

9. See: Cole and Gramajo (2009), Fajnzylber et al. (2002), Neumayer (2003).

10. For a detailed description of these measures, see: https://www.freedomhouse. org/report/freedom-world-2015/methodology#.UuEq87Qo7lI (Freedom House) and http://www.systemicpeace.org/polityproject.html (Polity 2 scores).

11. Given that experts are specifically asked to consider bribes and corruption in their assessment of Freedom House's individual rights measure, any causal argument regarding this measure and our corruption indicators would have to be made with considerable care.

12. Between two consecutive survey years or between 2007 and 2009 (we have no 2008 observations in our data).

13. Azfar and Murrell (2009); Kraay and Murrell (2013).

14. As categorized by the World Bank in FY 2016.

15. Only regression tables with results for all countries (HICs and non-HICs combined) are included in the Appendix. Separate regression results tables for HICs and non-HICs are available from the authors on request.

16. The average across all services is 2.9 for HICs and 3.5 for non-HICs. The differences for all sectors are statistically significant using a two-sample t test with unequal variance.

17. For example, as countries get richer and more educated, citizens become more sensitive to corruption possibilities; as countries get even more rich and educated, perception of corruption decline, presumably as government services improve overall. We find a hint of this possibility in the regression results below, where the education effect is positive on perceptions in developing countries and negative in the high-income countries.

18. In a bivariate regression with perceptions of corruption across sectors as the dependent variable and log GDP per capita as the right-hand side variable.

19. In the case of political parties, the average perception of corruption about political parties is a noteworthy exception to this trend: GDP per capita is not statistically significantly associated with perceptions but—unlike in other services—the average ten-year GDP growth is. Perhaps growth is a good "outcome variable" for political parties. Using three-year growth, the result was not significant for low- and middle-income countries—results available from authors.

20. Using top 10% income share as a measure of inequality produces similar results—available from the authors on request.

21. We also examine the relationship between our country-level perceptions measure and other measures of corruption—the CPIA, expert responses to Bertelsmann Transformation Index's (BTI) questions on impunity and corruption control, and expert responses to three questions regarding corruption in awarding jobs, business licenses and procurement contracts from the Quality of Government Institute's (QoG) 2012 Expert Survey. We see no statistically significant correlation between the CPIA or the corruption-related BTI questions, but the three QoG assessments of corruption do show a significant association with our (GCB) country-level citizen perception aggregates. One potential explanation could be that the QoG questions we tested focus on specific instances of corruption (getting a job, getting a business license, procurement contract), which may be more aligned with citizens' own experiences than indicators that assess government corruption overall (CPIA, BTI). Results available on request.

22. At the same time, some bribe payments may not represent corruption but a misunderstanding on the part of citizens, for example if citizens report a payment to a head teacher that is voluntary for extra school supplies as mandatory and thus a bribe. This is what not all of the bribe-paying is included in the "actual corruption" circle.

23. Dal Bo and Di Tella (2003).

24. The authors could construct a simple dummy variable to capture whether the previous year there was a significant corruption scandal and whether this led to any action by the government.

25. The difference in implementation of laws within a country will also lead to a difference in perceptions of corruption by citizens.

26. This is in line with the "resistance to reforms" argument first highlighted by Fernandez and Rodrik (1991).

References

Anderson, John E. 2015 Trust in Government and the Willingness to Pay Taxes In Transition Countries. Paper Prepared for Presentation at the 71st Annual Congress of the International Institute of Public Finance (IIPF), August 20–23, 2015, Dublin, Ireland. http://papers.ssrn.com/sol3/papers.cfm?abstract_id=2652268

Azfar, Omar, and Peter Murrell. 2009. Identifying Reticent Respondents: Assessing the Quality of Survey Data On Corruption and Values. *Economic Development and Cultural Change* 57: 387–411.

Cole, Julio H., and Andres Marroquin Gramajo. 2009. Homicide Rates in a Cross-Section of Countries: Evidence and Interpretations. *Population and Development Review* 35: 749–776.

Bo, Dal, Ernesto, and Rafael Di Tella. 2003. Capture by Threat. *Journal of Political Economy* 111: 1123–1154.

Daude, Christian, Gutiérrez, Hamlet and Ángel Melguizo. 2012. *What Drives Tax Morale?* Working Papers, No. 315, OECD Development Centre.

Diamond, Larry. 2007. Building Trust in Government by Improving Governance. Paper Presented to the 7th Global Forum on Reinventing Government: "Building Trust in Government". http://stanford.edu/~ldiamond/paperssd/BuildingTrustinGovernmentUNGLobalForum.pdf

Fajnzylber, Pablo, Daniel Lederman, and Norman Loayza. 2002. Inequality and Violent Crime. *Journal of Law and Economics* 45: 1–40.

Fernandez, Rachel, and Dani Rodrik. 1991. Resistance to Reform: Status Quo Bias in Presence of Individual Specific Uncertainty. *American Economic Review* 81: 1146–1155.

Gallup. 2015. Trust in Government. Gallup website. http://www.gallup.com/poll/5392/trust-government.aspx

Kraay, Aart and Peter Murrell. 2013. Misunderstanding Corruption. Research Working Paper 6488, World Bank Policy.

Mungiu-Pippidi, Alina. 2015. *The Quest for Good Governance.* Cambridge, UK: Cambridge University Press.

Neumayer, Eric. 2003. Good Policy Can Lower Violent Crime: Evidence from a Cross-National Panel of Homicide Rates, 1980–97. *Journal of Peace Research* 40: 619–640.

Olken, Benjamin A. 2009. Corruption Perceptions vs. Corruption Reality. *Journal of Public Economics* 93: 950–964.

Rose-Ackerman, Susan. 1999. *Corruption and Government: Causes, Consequences and Reform.* Cambridge: Cambridge University Press.

Solé-Ollé, Albert, and Pilar Sorribas-Navarro. 2014. Do Corruption Scandals Erode Trust in Government? Evidence from a Matched Sample of Local Governments. Unpublished Paper Prepared for the CESifo Area Conference on Public Sector Economics, Munich. Vol. 2426.

Whiteley, Paul, Harold D. Clarke, David Sanders, and Marianne Stewart. 2015. Why do Voters Lose Trust in Governments? Public Perceptions of Government Honesty and Trustworthiness in Britain 2000–2013. *The British Journal of Politics and International Relations.* https://doi.org/10.1111/1467-856X.12073.

11

Doing the Survey Two-Step: The Effects of Reticence on Estimates of Corruption in Two-Stage Survey Questions

Nona Karalashvili, Aart Kraay, and Peter Murrell

> *Economics studies facts, and seeks to arrange the facts in such ways as make it possible to draw conclusions from them. As always, it is the arrangement which is the delicate operation. Facts, arranged in the right way, speak for themselves; unarranged they are as dead as mutton.*
>
> John Hicks, The Social Framework, 1950

Introduction

Cross-country estimates of the extent of corruption rely largely on the self-reports of households, business managers, and government officials. But a long-recognized problem in survey research is that individuals are

The authors can be contacted at nkaralashvili@worldbank.org, akraay@worldbank.org, or murrell@econ.umd.edu We thank discussants of a first version of this paper, presented at the Conference on "Ethics and Corporate Malfeasance: Interdisciplinary Perspectives", organized by the Center

N. Karalashvili (✉) • A. Kraay
The World Bank, Washington, DC, USA
e-mail: nkaralashvili@worldbank.org; akraay@worldbank.org

P. Murrell
University of Maryland, College Park, MD, USA
e-mail: murrell@econ.umd.edu

© The Author(s) 2018
K. Basu, T. Cordella (eds.), *Institutions, Governance and the Control of Corruption*, International Economic Association Series,
https://doi.org/10.1007/978-3-319-65684-7_11

335

reticent to tell the truth about sensitive topics, which extend from illegal activities to behaviors in which a person is simply morally invested. An old example was exaggeration in reports of possession of a library card (Locander et al. 1976), but recent examples abound. Pregnant women, especially those in higher social classes, under-report smoking, even when access to free smoking cessation services depends on such reports (Shipton et al. 2009). A significant number of girls, and even more boys, profess knowledge of the mathematical concepts of declarative fractions and subjunctive scaling, which are fictions (OECD 2015). Either conservatives exaggerate how happy they are or liberals downplay how happy they are, or both (Wojcik et al. 2015).

Notice that this is not simply a problem confined to the estimation of population means of important variables, such as smoking rates or educational attainment. Reticence can also lead to incorrect causal conclusions about matters vital to public policy. A recent example is the attribution of the rise of obesity rates in England to the lessening physical burdens of jobs and housework. This conclusion was driven by survey data that indicated that calorie consumption went down over the time period that obesity was rising. However, later checking of the survey data against other sources led to the conclusion that survey respondents were increasingly under-reporting their calorie consumption.[1]

In attempting to counter the problem of reticence on sensitive topics, the traditional approach in survey research has been to find ways to make respondents more comfortable when answering questions, in order to elicit more candor. For example, researchers have experimented with self-administered questions, telephone interviewing, and variations in the wording of questions (Tourangeau and Yan 2007). One important

for the Study of Business Ethics, Regulation, and Crime (C-BERC), University of Maryland, September 12, 2014. We are grateful to our discussant, Joao de Mello, and to participants in the IEA Roundtable in Montevideo, for helpful comments, and to the Enterprise Survey Team at the World Bank for their collaboration. We are grateful to Patricia Funk for providing data on Swiss referenda. Financial support from the Knowledge for Change Program of the World Bank is gratefully acknowledged. The views expressed here are the authors', and do not reflect those of the World Bank, its Executive Directors, or the countries they represent.

approach in trying to increase respondent comfort level has been the use of unconventional questions that elicit answers that do not reveal precise facts about individuals but yield relevant sample statistics. Such techniques range from the venerable random-response question (RRQ) of Warner (1965) to the new item sum technique of Trappmann et al. (2014). These different approaches have made varying contributions to alleviating the problem of reticence, but as Tourangeau and Yan (2007, p. 878) state, "The need for methods of data collection that elicit accurate information is more urgent than ever".

This urgency appears no more so than in the area on which this paper focuses, measures of corruption that are comparable across countries. These measures perform a vital function. Policy makers and politicians use corruption indicators to monitor governance quality, with consequences for implementation of reforms and for the provision of aid by such entities as the Millennium Challenge Corporation, The United States Agency for International Development (USAID), and the World Bank. Cross-country measures of corruption are often prominent in political debate, as for example in attitudes toward Greece within Europe.[2]

Innovative attempts have been made to obtain evidence on corruption that do not rely on self-reports (Reinikka and Svensson 2004; Olken 2009). However, the effort required to gather such evidence is large and there is great reliance on peculiar country-specific institutional features that create specific opportunities for measurement. Hence, self-reports from surveys will continue to provide the basis for most research on and assessment of corruption in the future. This is especially the case when the focus is on comparisons across countries.

Existing survey evidence indicates that acts of corruption are amazingly common across the globe. Rose and Peiffer (2015) estimate that over a quarter of the world's population regularly pays bribes for public services. Such acts are by definition illegal. Moreover, for obvious reasons, corruption is much more common in countries where the reach of the rule of law is tenuous. But these are exactly the countries where respondents have the most reason to fear that government officials can force survey firms to violate confidentiality agreements. They are the countries where the evidence necessary to support criminal prosecution—or simply political or administrative persecution—is the weakest. They are the places where legal defense against such prosecution or persecution is least likely to be effective. Hence, in the highest corruption environments, there is very good reason to believe that the traditional approach of survey research—increasing respondent comfort—will not eliminate respondent reticence on corruption questions.

Therefore, in aiming to develop valid, self-report-based, cross-country-comparable measures of corruption, we adopt an approach diametrically opposite to the traditional one. We accept that there will always be large numbers of respondents who have a propensity to give false answers to questions on sensitive issues, and we embrace that fact. Instead, we rely on a methodology that allows us to estimate the rate of false answers and therefore the rate of commission of the corrupt act.

The intuition behind our approach is as follows. We formulate a structural model of the behavior of reticent respondents in answering sensitive survey questions. We then apply the model to data that simultaneously reflects the answers to two different types of questions. First, there is a conventional question (CQ) that asks explicitly whether a particular act of corruption has taken place. Naturally, if respondents are reticent, the distribution of yes/no responses on this question will depend on both the level of corruption and the level of reticence. Using this question alone one cannot disentangle the two. We therefore employ the CQ in tandem with a second type of question, a forced-response RRQ (Warner 1965, Boruch, 1971). Importantly, we assume that responses to both the RRQ and the CQ are affected by the same degree of respondent reticence.[3] Then, the distribution of responses on the RRQ will depend on the same corruption and reticence parameters as the distribution for the CQ, but in a different way. Hence, by applying our model to the combination of the responses to the two types of questions, we obtain estimates of structural parameters that separately reflect levels of corruption and degree of respondent reticence. Our analytical approach is fully described in the sections "Modeling Survey Responses" and "Estimation and Definitions of Composite Parameters", where we set up the model of respondent behavior, apply the model to the two types of questions, and show how the key parameters of the model can be estimated.

The analysis follows and expands on that of Kraay and Murrell (2016a). Their initial implementation of the above methodology focused on a CQ that asks all respondents (e.g. company officials acting on behalf of firms) whether a bribe is required when government officials provide some sort of service.[4] This is a very general question that does not generate information on any specific government agency, and as such is not a good guide to specific anti-corruption measures aimed at particular government agencies. To be more useful to policymakers, the CQ must be more specific, asking, for example, about levels of corruption in a named government agency. But then a problem of analysis immediately arises. Whereas most firms are likely to have had interactions with at least one government official and therefore can answer a non-specific question, not every firm will interact with any given agency's officials. This necessitates a subtle change in the nature of the survey question asked, which in turn has significant implications for modeling how respondents answer survey questions.

Consider the subject matter of this paper. The World Bank Enterprise Surveys project (World Bank, 2015; henceforth WBES), from which our data come, asks a two-step question about each of a series of government officials. First, it asks whether the firm has been visited by a specific type of official in the past 12 months. Then, the survey goes on to inquire about whether a gift or payment was required only if the respondent acknowledged that a visit occurred. For such two-step questions, modeling respondent behavior is more complex because respondents might be reticent in answering the question about a visit in order to forestall being asked the follow-up question about the bribe. Additionally, this reticence in acknowledging the visit might depend on whether a request for a bribe had occurred. This adds more complexity to the modeling process, because evaluating the answers to one question (the bribe) cannot be done independently of evaluating the answers to another (the visit). In this paper, we extend the Kraay and Murrell (2016a) analytics to cover the case of two-step questions. We use the example of a two-step question asking about interactions with tax officials, but as we note below analogous two-step questions are very common across a whole range of well-known surveys, and so our methodology is broadly applicable in these other settings as well.

In section "The Data", we provide the background to the current exercise, describing the data sets and survey questions used. We use data from seven countries included in the WBES project—Bangladesh, India, Nigeria, Peru, Sri Lanka, Turkey, and the Ukraine—where we have fielded the RRQs essential to the implementation of our methodology. Thus one contribution of this paper is to compare rates of reticence across countries, then examining the degree to which the underestimation of corruption varies across nations. This has important implications for the production of valid cross-national comparisons of corruption.

Section "Modeling Survey Responses" details how we model a respondent formulating a response to the two-step question. We consider two alternative models with different assumptions on how reticence affects the respondent's approach to the first part of the question on whether a visit occurred. Our first model assumes respondents are reticent only on direct questions on corruption and are candid on questions about the visit of a government official. Our second model assumes that a question about a visit is innocuous to all respondents who have not subsequently experienced a bribe request, but a reticent respondent who has experienced a bribe request will be reticent about reporting visits. We show that estimates of corruption and reticence depend upon which model of respondent behavior is used. Section "Modeling Survey Responses" also describes how we model the responses to RRQs, showing that such responses are a function of the same parameters as responses to the two-part CQ.

Section "Estimation and Definitions of Composite Parameters" describes the maximum-likelihood (ML) estimation procedure. Section "Results: Standard Estimates and Alternative Models of Reticence" presents estimates of the two different models for each of the countries, comparing these to standard estimates of corruption that assume all answers were candid. Section "Results: Preferred Estimates and Analysis" presents summary cross-country results based on estimates for the preferred model for each country. We estimate that the rate at which questions on bribes are answered reticently runs from a low of 27% in Bangladesh to a high of 64% in India. Not surprisingly these rates of reticence cause corruption to be significantly underestimated in all countries.

We introduce the concept of effective corruption, a derived parameter. Effective corruption is the unconditional probability of a randomly selected firm being directly involved in a corrupt interaction with a government official from a specific agency. It is equal to the probability of a visit by an official times the probability of a bribe being solicited on a given visit. The latter probability—that is, the conditional and not the unconditional one—is the one reported in standard sources in the literature, for example by the WBES. Effective corruption adds insights by taking into account the frequency of visits by officials, which is especially important because our estimates show that respondents can be reticent in answering questions about whether visits have occurred. This implies that simple reported rates of visits by government officials cannot be taken at face value, but must be corrected for reticence in a manner similar to that used for reported rates of bribe frequency.

We obtain ML estimates of the degree of downward bias of effective corruption in standard (non-reticence-adjusted) measures of corruption. These estimates range from a low of 12% in Nigeria to a high of 90% in Turkey. That is, only 10% of corruption by tax officials is reported in standard estimates for Turkey! Thus our methods produce startling changes in perceptions of relative corruption: Peru is perceived as more than twice as corrupt as Turkey in standard estimates, while Turkey appears more than twice as corrupt as Peru in our estimates. Estimates of the propensity of officials to make visits to firms are also affected. In India, for example, tax officials visit 50% more firms than standard estimates suggest.

Since effective corruption is the probability of a bribe being solicited by a visiting official times the probability of a visit, we can use our methods to decompose any bias in the perception of effective corruption between bias on estimates of bribes and bias on estimates of visits. In India, our estimates of corruption are 157% higher than standard estimates. This is due to the combination of a rise in the perception of visits by 50% and a rise in the perception of corruption on a visit of 72% (2.57 approximately equals 1.49 times 1.72). In other countries, Turkey, for example, there is no change in the perception of visits and all the rise in effective corruption is due to an increase in the perception of levels of corruption on an official's visit.

The Data

We implement our methodology using data from surveys conducted by the WBES unit (WBES 2015) in Bangladesh, India, Nigeria, Peru, Sri Lanka, Turkey, and the Ukraine. Over the past several years, with the generous cooperation of the WBES team, we have placed forced-response RRQs in these surveys. Each survey polled business owners or top managers in a sample of officially registered firms that is representative of the economy's formal private manufacturing and services sectors.[5] Interviews were conducted face-to-face and covered a wide range of topics, including corruption. The data from the seven surveys were collected in different waves of the WBES between 2007 and 2014. Information on the timing of interviews, the type of interview, and the number of observations included in our analysis for each country is given in Table 11.1. Full details of the subsample of firms used in the analysis are given in Appendix A.

We use responses to two types of questions. The first is a two-step CQ regarding whether an interaction with a government official occurred and if it did whether a bribe interaction took place. Two-step questions with this structure are very common in survey work, appearing for example in the surveys conducted by Transparency International, the World Justice Project, the US Federal Reserve, the US Agency for International Development, and the World Health Organization, as well as the Gallup World Poll and the National Crime Victimization Survey.[6] In the World Bank's Enterprise Surveys, there are a number of such questions with identical structure, varying only in the type of official who is the subject of enquiry. The example used in this paper concerns interactions with tax

Table 11.1 Description of the surveys

Country	Timing of interviews	Method of interviews	Number of observations used in the analysis
Bangladesh	From April 2013 through September 2013	Face-to-face/PAPI	915
India	From June 2013 through December 2014	Face-to-face/PAPI	4623
Nigeria	From January 2007 through December of 2007, and from June 2010 through December 2010	Face-to-face/PAPI	5537
Peru	From April 2010 through April 2011	Face-to-face/PAPI	590
Sri Lanka	From June 2011 through November 2011	Face-to-face/PAPI	443
Turkey	From January 2013 through June 2014	Face-to-face/mix of CAPI and PAPI	964
Ukraine	From January 2013 through November 2013	Face-to-face/PAPI	467

Note: In Nigeria, firms located in different and non-overlapping regions were interviewed in 2007 and 2010 which is why the data from these different time-periods are combined.
CAPI: Computer-assisted personal interview
PAPI: Pen and paper interview.

officials, a question that is in the core questionnaire for the World Bank's Enterprise Surveys and has been asked in a large number of countries. This two-step CQ asks whether firms had an interaction with tax officials over the last year and if so, whether the firms were expected or requested to give gifts to the officials. Responses to this question are the basis of one of WBES's prominent corruption indicators—"Percent of firms expected to give gifts in meetings with tax officials".[7] Appendix A contains the precise wording of all survey questions used in this paper and further details on the samples used in the analysis, including information for each country on how many observations were dropped because questions were not answered.

For simplicity in presentation, and following previous papers, we will rather inaccurately refer to a firm as "guilty" when it was expected or requested to give gifts in the meeting with tax officials. This is the measure of corruption. The standard approach in the literature is simply to assume that all answers to the CQs are honest and to report statistics based on such answers.[8] We call these "standard" estimates of corruption or guilt in what follows.

The second type of question is a forced-response RRQ. For reasons made clear below, our methodology requires responses to more than one RRQ. The ones we use are intended to be on issues that are similarly sensitive to the subject matter on the CQ. This identifying assumption is important because we will assume that the probability of reticent behavior is the same for the CQ and the RRQs. The questions are listed in Table 11.2, together with summaries of the responses to each question in each of the countries.[9] Following Azfar and Murrell (2009), Clausen et al. (2011), and Kraay and Murrell (2016a), survey respondents were presented with a series of ten sensitive questions. They privately toss a coin before answering each question, having previously been instructed to answer "Yes" if the coin comes up heads and otherwise answer the sensitive question. The series of ten questions includes three that ask about less sensitive acts. We do not use the data from these three questions: their inclusion is to give sophisticated reticent respondents the chance to answer "Yes" occasionally without affecting the data that we use. The seven more sensitive questions used in the analysis are identified in bold in Table 11.2, but were not so highlighted in the questionnaire itself.

The data in Table 11.2 provide immediate justification for our assumption that the RRQs do little to encourage respondent candor. Absent reticent behavior, the rate of "Yes" responses on each of the RRQs should be at least 50% given that half of the responses would reflect the outcome of obtaining a heads on the coin toss, which should force a "Yes" response. Yet "Yes" response rates are below 50% in 47 of the 49 relevant cases in Table 11.2 (seven RRQs for each of seven countries). Moreover, if a positive fraction of respondents had in fact done the sensitive acts in

Table 11.2 Summary results from random-response questions

	Percentage of respondents answering "Yes"						
	Bangladesh	India	Nigeria	Peru	Sri Lanka	Turkey	Ukraine
Have you ever paid less in personal taxes than you should have under the law?	52	53.5	49.5	39.2	42.2	15.9	40.5
Have you ever paid less in business taxes than you should have under the law?	48.6	49.5	42.3	41.2	42.4	15	45
Have you ever made a misstatement on a job application?	34.3	13.4	41.4	36.1	39.3	14.5	37.9
Have you ever used the office telephone for personal businesses?	65.6	36.6	49.7	73.7	52.8	48.3	79
Have you ever inappropriately promoted an employee for personal reasons?	37.6	13.8	39.5	39	37.9	25.1	48.2
Have you ever deliberately not given your suppliers or clients what was due?	35.3	10.1	36	36.6	39.7	16.9	41.1
Have you ever lied in your self-interest?	58.4	28.4	50.9	53.2	49	27.2	70.5
Have you ever inappropriately hired a staff member for personal reasons?	47.2	16	39.9	39.5	39.5	25.2	48.6
Have you ever been purposely late for work?	47.5	21.7	47.2	54.7	47.6	30.4	43.9
Have you ever unfairly dismissed an employee for personal reasons?	43.2	9.7	35.1	32	33	17.1	39.2
Number of responses to questions in bold	915	4623	5537	590	443	964	467

question, we should expect even higher rates of "Yes" responses. This provides a first clear indication that a significant proportion of responses reflect reticent behavior.

The data underlying Table 11.2 also provide justification for another assumption that we use in our model, that reticent respondents do not always behave reticently, but sometimes answer questions candidly. In Sri Lanka for example, the existence of reticence itself is clear from the 8.6% of respondents with zero "Yes" responses on all the seven sensitive questions, since if there were no reticence less than 1% would answer the RRQs in this way.[10] Importantly, another 33.6% of respondents answer "Yes" one or two times, while if there were no reticence, only 22% of respondents should do so.[11] This is evidence of significant reticence but also of reticent respondents who answer some questions candidly and others reticently. These points are further amplified if we assume that some respondents have done some of the sensitive acts in question, because candor would then require more "Yes" answers.

Modeling Survey Responses

Our goal in this section is to provide some structure in describing the interaction between an interviewer, who would like to elicit accurate information, and the respondent, who may prefer not to disclose this information. Our particular approach in addressing the problem of respondent reticence means that providing such structure is intrinsic in our methodology. But as we proceed below, it will become obvious that *every* attempt to construct a measure of corruption from similar questions involves making assumptions, either implicitly or explicitly, on the way in which reticent behavior influences respondents' answers. The virtue of an explicit structure is that our assumptions become clear.

We follow the Azfar and Murrell (2009) definition of reticence—a reticent respondent is one who knowingly gives false answers with a non-zero probability when honest answers to a specific set of survey questions could generate the inference that the respondent might have committed a sensitive act. We assume that the probability that respondents answer

"Yes" to a given question depends on (a) whether they are reticent individuals, in the sense that they are sometimes unwilling to truthfully answer a sensitive question, (b) whether those who are reticent individuals choose to behave reticently on a specific question, and (c) whether they have in fact done the sensitive act in question, that is whether they are guilty, allowing for guilt rates to be different for reticent and candid respondents. These are natural assumptions. The first is implied by all of the literature on the under-reporting of sensitive acts. The second—that reticent respondents are not always reticent—is strongly suggested by patterns in the data analyzed in previous research and noted above (Azfar and Murrell 2009; Clausen et al. 2011; Kraay and Murrell 2016a). The third is completely intuitive: the guilty may very well have more incentive to behave reticently.

There are five parameters in our model: the probabilities of (a) receiving a visit, (b) being reticent, (c) behaving reticently on a given question, (d) being guilty if reticent, and (e) being guilty if candid. We make the identifying assumption that the answers to all questions—CQs and RRQs—can be modeled using the same parameter values. This is a strong assumption, but all approaches to using survey data in the face of reticence would need to make some such assumptions. In Appendix B, we review some literature relevant to this assumption and present results that show that our general conclusions are robust to violations of this assumption.

Reticence is an individual-specific trait, with respondents being reticent or candid with probabilities r and $1 - r$. Candid respondents are always honest. However, with probability q, reticent respondents choose to behave reticently on any given sensitive question—that is, they answer in a way that obscures any possible inference of guilt. Sometimes, however, reticent respondents behave candidly, and provide honest answers with probability $1 - q < 1$. We assume that the decision to behave reticently on the two-step CQ is made once, and is independent of the similar decisions on the RRQs. Notice that this set-up makes a distinction between reticence and behaving reticently: reticence is a fixed trait for a single individual, but any reticent individual sometimes behaves reticently and sometimes candidly across different questions.

Tax officials visit or inspect businesses with probability w.[12] We differentiate between two classes of businesses in order to allow for the possibility that guilt and reticence are correlated across respondents. First, in those businesses asked for a bribe with probability $0 \leq g \leq 1$, respondents are reticent. Second, in those asked for a bribe with probability kg ($0 \leq k \leq 1$), respondents are candid. A k less than one induces the correlation between reticent behavior and guilt. However, our estimation procedure does not preclude $k = 1$ as a special case. We can therefore test whether, in fact, the guilty are more likely to give dishonest responses.

Modeling Responses to the Conventional Question

In this subsection we develop two alternative models of how reticent behavior affects the interview process for the two-step CQ, a boiled-down version of which is "(1) was your firm visited by tax officials and (2) if yes, did they expect an informal payment?". Importantly, if no visit is acknowledged in the first step, no bribe question is asked in the second step. This means that reticent respondents can avoid the bribe question, if they so choose, by denying that a visit occurred. Thus, in contrast with Kraay and Murrell (2016a), we must not only decide how to model reticent behavior, but also specify which parts of the two-step CQ are affected by reticent behavior.

We consider two distinct possibilities. In the first, which we refer to as Model A, reticent respondents are always candid in responding to the first part of the CQ, that is the question about the visit. However, they may behave reticently when responding to the sensitive second part of the CQ, that is the question about the bribe. The second possibility, which we refer to as Model B, allows reticent respondents to avoid answering the sensitive second part of the CQ by responding "No" to the first part of the CQ even if a visit did occur. Although the first part of the CQ is not per se sensitive, a "No" answer can put the respondent in the position of avoiding an inquiry on a sensitive act.[13] Specifically, we assume that reticent respondents who received a visit but not a request for a bribe respond candidly to both parts of the CQ. In contrast, reticent respondents receiving a visit and a bribe request and choosing to behave reticently deny that the visit occurred and thereby avoid the sensitive second question.[14]

For notational convenience, we now define a random variable D that fully summarizes the possible responses to the two-part CQ. Specifically, $D = 1$ if no visit is acknowledged, $D = 2$ if a visit is acknowledged but no bribe is reported, and $D = 3$ if a visit and a bribe are both acknowledged. Note that D is defined in such a way that it is non-missing for all respondents that answered either part of the CQ. This is in contrast with the bribe question itself, which is non-missing only for those respondents who acknowledge a visit in the first part of the CQ. The use of a structural model integrating responses on both parts of the CQ therefore will allow us to use the data on all respondents in estimating rates of corruption. This is in contrast to standard estimates that focus only on the subset of the sample corresponding to respondents who acknowledge a visit.

Table 11.3 spells out our assumptions on the likelihood of observing these three possible responses to the CQ. The panels of the table reflect combinations of the models (A and B) and the types of respondents (candid and reticent), with only three panels needed since candid respondents behave the same in both models. Within panels, the rows reflect the three possibilities for the respondents' actual experiences on visits and bribery, that is (a) a visit actually did not occur, (b) a visit did occur without a bribe request, or (c) a visit did occur and a bribe was requested. Of course, these actual experiences are unobserved for the researcher, who only sees survey responses. The columns of the table correspond to the three possible responses to the CQ, which are observed by the researcher. The cell entries spell out the probability of the (observed) response corresponding to the column, given the model, the type of respondent, and the (unobserved) actual experience indicated in the row of the table. Of course, even though the probability of two different values of D can both be positive, the value of D is unique in any given observation in the survey.

Consider the behavior of candid respondents, summarized in Panel 1 of Table 11.3. Candid respondents always answer truthfully, so there are ones on the diagonal and zeros otherwise, indicating that candid respondents always answer truthfully. For example, if there was no visit, they say there was no visit with probability 1. At the bottom of this panel we

Table 11.3 Modeling how reticence affects responses to the conventional question

Actual behavior (unobserved)	Probability of observed responses on two-stage corruption question		
	No visit ($D = 1$)	Visit, no bribe ($D = 2$)	Visit, bribe ($D = 3$)
Panel 1: Candid respondents (both models)			
No visit: $(1 - w)$	1	0	0
Visit, no bribe: $w(1 - kg)$	0	1	0
Visit, bribe: wkg	0	0	1
Probability of observing response	$P[D = 1 \mid C] = (1 - w)$	$P[D = 2 \mid C] = w(1 - kg)$	$P[D = 3 \mid C] = wkg$
Panel 2: Reticent respondents, model A			
No visit: $(1 - w)$	1	0	0
Visit, no bribe: $w(1 - g)$	1	0	0
Visit, bribe: wg	0	q	$1 - q$
Probability of observing response	$P_A[D = 1 \mid R] = (1 - w)$	$P_A[D = 2 \mid R] = w(1 - g + qg)$	$P_A[D = 3 \mid R] = wg(1 - q)$
Panel 3: Reticent respondents, model B			
No visit: $(1 - w)$	1	0	0
Visit, no bribe: $w(1 - g)$	1	0	0
Visit, bribe: wg	q	0	$1 - q$
Probability of observing response	$P_B[D = 1 \mid R] = 1 - w + wgq$	$P_B[D = 2 \mid R] = w(1 - g)$	$P_B[D = 3 \mid R] = wg(1 - q)$

Notes: This table summarizes the probability of observing the three different response possibilities to the two-step corruption question, for candid and reticent respondents, and for the two different models of reticent behavior that we consider. The first column reports the possible unobserved outcomes, that is whether a visit occurred, and if a visit occurred whether a bribe was requested, together with the corresponding probabilities of the three events. The remaining three columns report the observed responses for candid and reticent respondents, for the two different models discussed in the text. Note that q is the probability of reticent behavior on the two-step corruption question report the corresponding population probabilities of observing the three possible responses on the two-part CQ, conditional on respondents being candid, that is $P[D = j | C]$ for the three outcomes $j = 1, 2, 3$, with the conditional C indicating a candid respondent. Since candid respondents respond truthfully, the probability of observing a "Yes" response to the visit question is simply $P[D = 1 | C] = w$, that is the true probability of a visit. Similarly, the probability of reporting a visit but not a bribe is $P[D = 2 | C] = w(1 - kg)$, that is a visit occurs with probability w and a bribe does not occur with probability $1 - kg$. Naturally, the probability of reporting a visit and a bribe is simply the product of the probability of these two events, that is $P[D = 3 | C] = wkg$.

The second and third panels of Table 11.3 present the same analyses for reticent respondents, whose behavior differs between the two models. Under the assumptions of both Model A and Model B, reticent respondents truthfully respond that there was no visit if indeed no visit occurred, as summarized by the 1 in the top-left cell of each the second and third panels. Similarly, if there was a visit and no bribe request occurred, they truthfully acknowledge the visit in the first part of the CQ, and truthfully state that there was no bribe in response to the second part of the CQ. This is represented by a 1 in the center cell of both panels. If a visit and a bribe occurred, under the assumptions of Model A reticent respondents admit the visit but behave reticently with probability q on the second part of the CQ. Specifically, with probability q the reticent respondent denies the bribe, or otherwise the bribe is acknowledged (hence with probability $1 - q$). On the other hand, under the assumptions of Model B, reticent respondents who are guilty might manifest reticent behavior in the first part of the CQ: they deny that the visit occurred with probability q, or otherwise admit to the visit and the bribe (hence with probability $1 - q$).

The different assumptions of Model A and Model B imply different probabilities of observing the three possible responses to the CQ among reticent respondents. In Model A, reticent respondents are always candid about the visit question, and so the probability of denying a visit is just one minus the true probability of a visit, that is $P_A[D = 1 | R] = 1 - w$, the A subscript referencing the model and the conditional R indicating a reticent respondent. In contrast, in Model B reticent respondents who (a) received a visit (with probability w), *and* (b) received a bribe request (with probability g), *and* (c) choose to behave reticently (with probability q) will deny that the visit occurred. These responses are in addition to those of respondents who in fact did not receive a visit (a proportion $1-w$ of respondents), so the overall probability of a response that a visit did not occur is $P_B[D=1|R]=1-w+wgq \geq P_A[D=1|R]$.

In Model B, reticent respondents always acknowledge a visit when a bribe does not occur, so the probability of a response that a visit occurred without a bribe is simply the product of the probability of a visit and the probability of a bribe not occurring, that is $P_B[D=2|R]=w(1-g)$. However, in Model A, there are also some reticent respondents who experienced a visit and a bribe request, but decided to behave reticently on the second part of the CQ and deny that the bribe occurred. This implies a greater likelihood of observing a "No" response to the second part of the CQ in Model B, that is $P_A[D=2|R]=w(1-g+qg) \geq P_B[D=2|R]$. Finally, in both models, reticent behavior reduces the likelihood of respondents admitting both the visit and the bribe by the same amount, that is $P_A[D=3|R]=P_B[D=3|R]=wg(1-q)$. In both cases, a visit *and* a bribe occur with probability wg, and reticent respondents acknowledge this with probability $1-q$. In Model A, the remaining proportion q of respondents admit to the visit but deny the bribe, while in Model B these respondents manifest their reticence by denying the visit, thereby avoiding the question about the bribe.

Combining these observations, we can now summarize how the presence of reticent respondents affects the interpretation of responses to both parts of the CQ. Note first that the probability that a visit is reported in the first part of the CQ is:

$$1-P[D=1] = \begin{cases} w, & \textit{Model A} \\ w(1-rgq), & \textit{Model B} \end{cases} \tag{11.1}$$

In Model A, both candid and reticent respondents are candid in their responses to the question about visits, and so the observed rate of "Yes" responses is a valid estimate of the frequency of visits, w. However, in Model B, a fraction r of respondents are reticent, experience a bribe with probability g, and with probability q choose to behave reticently by denying that the visit occurred. As a result, the observed frequency of visits in the data is an underestimate of the true frequency of visits, and the extent of the downward bias depends on the prevalence of reticent respondents, the likelihood of reticent behavior on the part of reticent respondents, and the frequency of bribery itself.

The interpretation of responses on the second part of the CQ is similarly clouded by reticent behavior. Consider the rate of admission of bribery among those respondents who acknowledge a visit, which is exactly the standard estimate of corruption. Using our notation, this is:

$$
\frac{P[D = 3]}{1 - P[D = 1]} =
\begin{cases}
(1 - r)\, kg + rg\,(1 - q), & \text{Model A} \\[2mm]
\dfrac{(1 - r)\, kg + rg\,(1 - q)}{1 - rgq}, & \text{Model B}
\end{cases}
\tag{11.2}
$$

In Model A, all respondents who were visited by an inspector admit to the visit. Among these, a proportion $1 - r$ are candid and truthfully admit that a bribe occurred with probability kg. In contrast, a proportion r of respondents are reticent. For these, a bribe occurs with probability g but only a proportion $1 - q$ of reticent respondents chooses to behave candidly and answer the question truthfully. The only difference in Model B is that reticent respondents who are guilty and choose to behave reticently deny that the visit occurred rather than admitting the visit but denying the bribe. The probability of this occurring is rgq. In Model A these respondents would have admitted the visit in the first part of the question, but would have responded "No" to the bribe question in the second stage. In Model B these respondents do not advance to the second stage and so the rate of "Yes" responses in the second stage is higher by a factor of $1/(1 - rgq) \geq 1$.

Modeling Responses to the Random-Response Questions

For both models, the interview process for RRQs is modeled as in Kraay and Murrell (2016a). The key assumption here is that reticent behavior is equally prevalent in responses to the RRQ as it is in the CQ. Recall that on each of the questions in the RRQ, the respondent is instructed to answer the sensitive question if the coin comes up tails, and to answer "Yes" if the coin comes up heads. Our definition of a reticent respondent is one who gives knowingly false answers with a non-zero probability when honest answers to a question could generate the inference that the respondent might have committed a sensitive act. Given the assumptions above and this definition, there is therefore a probability q that a reticent respondent will respond "No" even when the coin comes up heads. Similarly, when the coin comes up tails, there is a probability q that the reticent respondent will answer "No" even if the respondent has done the sensitive act in question. The data in Table 11.2 provide reassurance on this assumption. If the outcome of a head on the coin toss actually encourages candor, then all entries in that table would lie above 50%. However, as discussed in the previous section, for the truly sensitive questions the responses are greater than 50% only in 2 out of 49 cases (seven sensitive questions in seven countries).[15]

As discussed in more detail in Kraay and Murrell (2016a), these assumptions imply that the probability of a "Yes" response on any single RRQ is $0.5(1 + g)(1 - q)$. To see this, note that respondents are supposed to answer "Yes" either if they are guilty (with probability g) or if they are not guilty and the coin comes up heads (with probability $0.5(1 - g)$). These two probabilities sum to $0.5(1 + g)$ but must be scaled down by $(1 - q)$, the probability that a reticent respondent provides an honest "Yes" response. For candid respondents, the probability of a "Yes" response on a given RRQ is $0.5(1 + kg)$. Candid respondents can have a lower guilt probability than reticent respondents (i.e. $kg \leq g$), but always answer honestly (i.e. q is not relevant to them).

Define the random variable X as the number of "Yes" responses on the seven sensitive RRQs that are given in bold in Table 11.2. Since both the coin toss and the decision to behave reticently on a given question are independent across questions in the battery of RRQs, X is binomially distributed, with different success probabilities for reticent and candid respondents as noted above, that is a success probability of $0.5(1 + kg)$ for candid respondents and $0.5(1 + g)(1 - q)$ for reticent respondents.

It is also useful to briefly note why we use several RRQs and not just a single RRQ. As discussed in section "The Data", in modeling the data generating process it is important to allow for the possibility that the reticent do not always behave reticently, that is to include in the model a parameter $q < 1$. But then if $k = 1$ or $k = 1 - q$, which are possibilities that we do not want to rule out a priori, the effects of q and r on data gathered on any single CQ or single RRQ are identical.[16] Hence, these parameters would not be separately identified in an estimation that relied on one CQ and a single RRQ. Where these two parameters do have different effects is on the variation in the number of "Yes" responses to a set of RRQs, that is X. Hence, we use a battery of seven RRQ's chosen to approximate the prevalence of guilt and the degree of sensitivity of the CQ.

The intuition for the separate identification of r and q follows from our assumptions that reticence is an individual-specific trait that is fixed across questions for a given respondent, while the event of reticent behavior, that is failure to answer "Yes" when supposed to, is independent across questions. This has the implication that the presence of reticence will be reflected in a covariance across a respondent's answers to the individual questions in an RRQ battery. For example, reticent respondents are less likely to answer "Yes" to all RRQs precisely because they are reticent. This in turn will be reflected in the sample distribution of the number of "Yes" responses to a battery of individual RRQs (X). That is, for any given r, the sample distribution of X will vary with q, giving the information for identification.[17]

Estimation and Definitions of Composite Parameters

We estimate the parameters of our model using ML. With the notation and structure of the previous section in hand, it is straightforward to write down the likelihood function of the observed responses to the CQ and the RRQ, which is:

$$L_i (D, X; w, g, r, q, k)$$

$$= (1 - r) \left(\sum_{j=1}^{3} P[D = j|C] I_{(D=j)} \right) B \left(X; 7, \frac{1 + kg}{2} \right)$$

$$+ r \left(\sum_{j=1}^{3} P_i \left[D = j|R\right] I_{(D=j)} \right) B \left(X; 7, \frac{(1-q)(1+g)}{2} \right) \quad (11.3)$$

for models $i \in \{A, B\}$. $I_{(D=j)}$ is an indicator variable taking the value 1 if $D = j$ and zero otherwise. B(.) is a binomial density function for X successes in seven trials (the number of RRQs) that have the success probability stated in the last argument.

To understand this likelihood function, note that the two lines correspond to the contribution of candid respondents (a proportion $1-r$ of the sample) and the contribution of reticent respondents (a proportion r of the sample). For both groups, their contribution to the likelihood function is the product of the trinomial probability distribution for the three response possibilities for the CQ, and the binomial distribution summarizing the observed responses to the RRQs. Since the responses to the CQ and the RRQ are independent conditional on being candid, the product of these two distributions forms the joint distribution of responses for candid respondents. Finally note that while the response probabilities for the CQ are the same for both models for the candid respondents and are given by $P[D = j| C]$, they are different for models A and B for the reticent respondents, that is $P_A[D = j| R]$ and $P_B[D = j| R]$. By substituting the appropriate functions of (w, g, r, q, k) given in Table 11.3 for these response probabilities and then multiplying across individuals, one obtains the likelihood function for the observed data. In the next section we report the estimates of the parameters obtained by maximizing this likelihood function.

We also define three composite parameters, which provide a more intuitive interpretation of the implications of the two models. The first we call *effective reticence*, which is the probability that a randomly selected respondent will choose to answer a sensitive question reticently, that is rq. The second composite parameter is motivated by the fact that the model assumes that the reticent have a higher rate of guilt than the candid and that the rate of guilt of a randomly selected respondent is therefore a weighted average of the rates of the two types of respondents: $g(r + (1-r)k)$. We call this *average guilt*, which is the probability that a randomly selected respondent will be asked for a bribe given that this respondent is being visited by a tax official. Third, we estimate the unconditional probability that a randomly selected respondent will be both visited by a tax official and asked for a bribe, which is average guilt times the probability of a visit, that is $wg(r + (1 - r)k)$. We call this *effective corruption*, reflecting the fact that in countries where corruption is widespread part of the underlying motive for visits by tax officials is to extract a bribe.

Results: Standard Estimates and Alternative Models of Reticence

Tables 11.4, 11.5, 11.6, 11.7, 11.8, 11.9, 11.10 report estimates of Model A and Model B for the seven countries in our dataset. In each table we report estimates for the five model parameters, g, k, r, q, and w, and for the three composite parameters, *effective reticence*, *average guilt*, and *effective corruption*.[18] Our discussion focuses mainly on the three composite parameters since these are most informative about overall levels of corruption and reticence.

Effective reticence (rq) reflects the proportion of sensitive questions that are not answered candidly in the whole sample. This proportion varies from 28% for Model A in Sri Lanka to 67% for Model A in India. Variation is much greater between countries than between models within a country, the two models telling a quite consistent story about rates of effective reticence. One element of this story is that the countries seem to fall naturally into two groups. Turkey and India have rates of effective reticence approximately twice as high as the rates in all other countries. The estimates for these two countries imply that approximately 64% of the time a respondent would answer the second part of the CQ misleadingly if the respondent had in fact been asked for a gift or informal payment. The analogous percentage for the other countries varies between around 30% and 40%. In all countries, these are high rates of misleading answers. The obvious implication is that overall rates of corruption in standard measures are downward biased, with the degree of underestimation varying markedly between countries.

Examining average guilt, which is the probability that a request for a bribe is made on any visit, our estimates average approximately twice those that would be reported using standard methods. But as expected there also is large variation between countries. For Turkey, the estimate of average guilt is increased either tenfold (Model A) or fourfold (Model B) relative to standard estimates. In Peru, on the other hand, effective guilt is "only" 50% higher than conventional estimates. The significance of allowing for reticence is perhaps best shown by the results for Sri Lanka,

Table 11.4 Estimates of reticence and guilt from the enterprise survey in Bangladesh

	Standard	Model A	Model B
Prob. of interaction with tax official (w) = Pr (inspected)	0.619*** (21.49)	See note below	0.843*** (20.04)
Reticence (r)	0		0.952*** (21.42)
Probability reticent person answers question reticently (q)	0		0.476*** (21.25)
Effective reticence (rq)	0		0.453*** (25.41)
Guilt rate of the reticent (g)	0.420*** (17.26)		0.587*** (20.02)
Reduction in guilt for the candid (k)	1		0.468** (3.20)
Average guilt = Pr(request | inspected)	0.420*** (17.26)		0.572*** (19.65)
Effective corruption = Pr(inspected & request)	0.260*** (13.91)		0.482*** (11.83)
Log likelihood			−2625.048
Number of observations	915	915	915
Number of clusters	100	100	100

Notes: z-statistics based on heteroskedasticity-consistent standard errors clustered at the strata level are reported in parentheses
Note that z-statistics for estimates of k are for the null hypothesis of k = 1
The ML procedure failed to converge for model A
**p < 0.01; ***p < 0.001

Table 11.5 Estimates of reticence and guilt from the enterprise survey in India

	Standard	Model A	Model B
Prob. of interaction with tax official (w) = Pr(inspected)	0.429*** (23.01)	0.429*** (23.01)	0.642*** (19.50)
Reticence (r)	0	0.803*** (46.79)	0.815*** (51.50)
Probability reticent person answers question reticently (q)	0	0.835*** (81.91)	0.784*** (65.29)
Effective reticence (rq)	0	0.671*** (58.92)	0.639*** (54.80)
Guilt rate of the reticent (g)	0.279*** (13.71)	1.000	0.545*** (20.15)
Reduction in guilt for the candid (k)	1	0.182*** (38.03)	0.361*** (18.14)
Average guilt = Pr(request | inspected)	0.279*** (13.71)	0.839*** (49.74)	0.481*** (18.53)
Effective corruption = Pr (inspected & request)	0.119*** (10.69)	0.360*** (21.23)	0.309*** (10.63)
Log likelihood		−12,675.054	−12,668.046
Number of observations	4623	4623	4623
Number of clusters	634	634	634

Notes: z-statistics based on heteroskedasticity-consistent standard errors clustered at the strata level are reported in parentheses
Note that z-statistics for estimates of k are for the null hypothesis of $k = 1$
***$p < 0.001$

because that country generally scores reasonably well in cross-country rankings of corruption, and has relatively low rates of reticent behavior. Even then, average guilt is 69% above standard estimates in Model A and 35% above in Model B.

Effective corruption reflects the unconditional probability of being personally involved in a corrupt exchange with tax officials, that is, it is the probability of having been visited by tax officials and having been expected to give a gift on such a visit.[19] This proportion varies from 6.7% for Model A in Peru to 48% in Model B for Bangladesh. In contrast, standard estimates in these instances give 4.2% for Peru and 26% for Bangladesh. Estimates for Model A increase the perception of overall corruption by approximately 100% on average whereas the corresponding

Table 11.6 Estimates of reticence and guilt from the enterprise survey in Nigeria

	Standard	Model A	Model B
Prob. of interaction with tax official	0.811***	0.811***	0.905***
(w) = Pr(inspected)	(154.37)	(154.37)	(164.04)
Reticence (r)	0	0.429***	0.402***
		(32.37)	(31.37)
Probability reticent person answers	0	0.805***	0.738***
question reticently (q)		(125.72)	(75.41)
Effective reticence (rq)	0	0.345***	0.297***
		(39.19)	(41.72)
Guilt rate of the reticent (g)	0.283***	1.000	0.420***
	(42.15)		(30.57)
Reduction in guilt for the candid (k)	1	0.205***	0.474***
		(134.33)	(23.92)
Average	0.283***	0.546***	0.288***
guilt = Pr(request | inspected)	(42.15)	(43.78)	(40.20)
Effective corruption =	0.230***	0.443***	0.261***
Pr(inspected & request)	(40.66)	(42.12)	(35.82)
Log likelihood		−16,271.138	−16,241.511
Number of observations	5537	5537	5537

Notes: The z-statistics that are reported in parentheses are based on the usual ML standard errors and not on heteroskedasticity-consistent standard errors clustered at the strata level because the sampling information included in the data is incomplete

Note that z-statistics for estimates of k are for the null hypothesis of $k = 1$

***$p < 0.001$

figure for Model B is 75%. Thus the risk of being personally involved in corruption is usually greatly underestimated. But it is not uniformly underestimated. In Turkey, which has low rates of corruption and high rates of reticence based on any yardstick, estimates of effective corruption are tenfold the standard estimates in Model A and fourfold in B. In contrast, Ukraine's estimate of effective corruption in Model B is marginally less than that in standard estimates.

We now turn to brief comments on the estimates of the individual parameters. For w, the probability of a visit by tax officials, estimates vary much more between countries than between models. As discussed in section "Modeling Survey Responses", Model A's estimates are by construction identical to standard estimates, whereas Model B's estimates

Table 11.7 Estimates of reticence and guilt from the enterprise survey in Peru

	Standard	Model A	Model B
Prob. of interaction with tax official (w) = Pr(inspected)	0.551*** (20.18)	0.551*** (20.18)	0.590*** (17.81)
Reticence (r)	0	0.381*** (7.67)	0.367*** (7.91)
Probability reticent person answers question reticently (q)	0	0.754*** (13.74)	0.770*** (17.53)
Effective reticence (rq)	0	0.287*** (9.80)	0.282*** (9.97)
Guilt rate of the reticent (g)	0.0769*** (4.67)	0.212 (1.53)	0.231** (2.65)
Reduction in guilt for the candid (k)	1	0.308** (2.74)	0.266*** (5.58)
Average guilt = Pr(request | inspected)	0.0769*** (4.67)	0.121* (2.49)	0.124*** (3.73)
Effective corruption = Pr(inspected & request)	0.0424*** (4.40)	0.0669* (2.49)	0.0729*** (3.34)
Log likelihood		−1619.5222	−1616.9835
Number of observations	590	590	590
Number of clusters	73	73	73

Notes: z-statistics based on heteroskedasticity-consistent standard errors clustered at the strata level are reported in parentheses

Note that z-statistics for estimates of k are for the null hypothesis of $k = 1$

*$p < 0.05$;**$p < 0.01$; ***$p < 0.001$

are usually in the range of 5–10% higher than standard ones. One exception to this is India, a high corruption, high reticence country, where our estimate of visits by tax officials is more than 50% greater than conventional ones. Such an observation changes perceptions about the mechanisms of corruption in a country, suggesting that the decision of a tax official to visit a business might be an element of that mechanism.

For k, the parameter capturing (inversely) the correlation between reticence and guilt, results vary more between models than for any other of the parameters. For three countries, Model A tells a different story than Model B. For example, in Ukraine Model B finds no significant correlation (k not significantly different from 1) while Model A suggests that the reticent are four times as likely to be guilty as the candid.

Table 11.8 Estimates of reticence and guilt from the enterprise survey in Sri Lanka

	Standard	Model A	Model B
Prob. of interaction with tax official (w) = Pr(inspected)	0.537*** (14.33)	0.537*** (14.33)	0.562*** (12.29)
Reticence (r)	0	0.480** (3.02)	0.519*** (3.69)
Probability reticent person answers question reticently (q)	0	0.574*** (3.49)	0.523*** (4.66)
Effective reticence (rq)	0	0.276*** (10.21)	0.271*** (10.04)
Guilt rate of the reticent (g)	0.0840*** (5.02)	0.244 (1.24)	0.168* (2.19)
Reduction in guilt for the candid (k)	1	0.193*** (3.39)	0.324** (2.60)
Average guilt = Pr(request | inspected)	0.0840*** (5.02)	0.142* (2.33)	0.113*** (4.00)
Effective corruption = Pr(inspected & request)	0.0451*** (4.34)	0.0760* (2.12)	0.0637*** (3.31)
Log likelihood		−1175.5814	−1176.4097
Number of observations	443	443	443
Number of clusters	69	69	69

Notes: z-statistics based on heteroskedasticity-consistent standard errors clustered at the strata level are reported in parentheses
Note that z-statistics for estimates of k are for the null hypothesis of $k = 1$
*$p < 0.05$; **$p < 0.01$; ***$p < 0.001$

However, in general, estimates of k are quite low, implying a strong correlation between reticence and guilt, which is hardly surprising.[20]

Results: Preferred Estimates and Analysis

In this section we draw together the preferred estimates for each country. We choose either Model A or Model B as the preferred model, based on which has the largest value of the maximized log likelihood.[21] Table 11.11 first indicates our preferred model and then the following five rows summarize the preferred estimates of the five parameters of the model, that is w, r, q, g, and k, and the corresponding estimate of effective reticence, rq. In the remaining rows we focus on accounting for the

Table 11.9 Estimates of reticence and guilt from the enterprise survey in Turkey

	Standard	Model A	Model B
Prob. of interaction with tax official (w) = Pr(inspected)	0.609*** (26.27)	0.609*** (26.27)	0.662*** (21.77)
Reticence (r)	0	0.680*** (28.85)	0.684*** (29.04)
Probability reticent person answers question reticently (q)	0	0.933*** (68.31)	0.914*** (84.26)
Effective reticence (rq)	0	0.635*** (27.24)	0.625*** (27.46)
Guilt rate of the reticent (g)	0.0273*** (4.00)	0.387* (2.11)	0.134*** (3.86)
Reduction in guilt for the candid (k)	1	0.0480*** (29.82)	0.153*** (10.77)
Average guilt = Pr(request | inspected)	0.0273*** (4.00)	0.269* (2.17)	0.0983*** (4.06)
Effective corruption = Pr(inspected & request)	0.0166*** (1.00)	0.164* (2.18)	0.0650*** (3.65)
Log likelihood		−2198.3828	−2202.2151
Number of observations	964	964	964
Number of clusters	174	174	174

Notes: z-statistics based on heteroskedasticity-consistent standard errors clustered at the strata level are reported in parentheses
$*p < 0.05$; $***p < 0.001$
Note that z-statistics for estimates of k are for the null hypothesis of $k = 1$

primary question of interest in this paper, which concerns the size and source of downward biases present in measures of corruption that do not take reticent behavior into account. We focus here on estimates of effective corruption, that is the likelihood that a firm is visited by a tax inspector and a bribe request takes place. The standard way to estimate effective corruption without taking reticence into account would be to simply calculate the proportion of all respondents who admit to both a visit and a bribe request. The population frequency of this is $P[D = 3]$ in the notation of section "Modeling Survey Responses". Note that the standard estimate of effective corruption differs from the standard estimate of corruption conditional on a visit occurring, which is described in Eq. (11.2) above and is commonly reported in analysis of the Enterprise Survey data.

Table 11.10 Estimates of reticence and guilt from the enterprise survey in Ukraine

	Standard	Model A	Model B
Prob. of interaction with tax official (w) = Pr(inspected)	0.570*** (22.88)	0.570*** (22.88)	0.605*** (18.36)
Reticence (r)	0	0.409*** (6.48)	0.408*** (5.32)
Probability reticent person answers question reticently (q)	0	0.813*** (25.08)	0.689*** (13.17)
Effective reticence (rq)	0	0.332*** (8.23)	0.281*** (7.79)
Guilt rate of the reticent (g)	0.263*** (9.26)	1.000*** (2726.63)	0.250*** (3.54)
Reduction in guilt for the candid (k)	1	0.230*** (28.47)	0.944 (0.26)
Average guilt = Pr(request | inspected)	0.263*** (9.26)	0.544*** (8.94)	0.241*** (5.60)
Effective corruption = Pr(inspected & request)	0.150*** (9.02)	0.310*** (7.69)	0.146*** (4.65)
Log likelihood		−1411.875	−1420.0272
Number of observations	467	467	467
Number of clusters	94	94	94

Notes: z-statistics based on heteroskedasticity-consistent standard errors clustered at the strata level are reported in parentheses
Note that z-statistics for estimates of k are for the null hypothesis of $k = 1$
***$p < 0.001$

Our goal in this paper is to contrast the standard estimate with the "true" rate of effective corruption, which is the product of the true probability of a visit, w, and the true probability that a bribe encounter occurs, $g(r + (1 - r)k)$. In addition, we would like to decompose the downward bias into the parts due to the under-reporting of visits and the under-reporting of bribe experiences. This decomposition is as follows:

$$\frac{P[D = 3]}{wg(r + (1 - r)k)} = \frac{1 - P[D = 1]}{w} \cdot \frac{\dfrac{P[D = 3]}{1 - P[D = 1]}}{g(r + (1 - r)k)} \quad (11.4)$$

The left-hand side of this expression is the ratio of measured corruption to true effective corruption, which is less than one if there is reticent

Table 11.11 Summary of estimates from preferred model for each country

	Bangladesh Model B	India Model B	Nigeria Model E	Peru Model B	Sri Lanka Model A	Turkey Model A	Ukraine Model A
Panel A: Estimated parameters							
Probability of visit (w)	0.843	0.642	0.905	0.590	0.537	0.609	0.570
Reticence (r)	0.952	0.815	0.402	0.367	0.480	0.680	0.409
Probability of reticent behavior (q)	0.476	0.784	0.738	0.770	0.574	0.933	0.813
Effective reticence (rq)	0.453	0.639	0.297	0.283	0.276	0.634	0.333
Guilt rate of the reticent (g)	0.587	0.545	0.420	0.231	0.244	0.387	1.000
Reduction in guilt for the candid (k)	0.468	0.361	0.474	0.266	0.193	0.048	0.230
Panel B: Conventional versus reticence-adjusted estimates of							
(1) Probability of a visit							
Conventional	0.619	0.429	0.811	0.551	0.537	0.609	0.570
Reticence-Adjusted	0.843	0.642	0.905	0.590	0.537	0.609	0.570
Ratio	0.734	0.668	0.896	0.934	1.000	1.000	1.000
(2) Probability of bribery conditional on visit							
Conventional	0.420	0.279	0.283	0.077	0.084	0.027	0.263
Reticence-Adjusted	0.572	0.481	0.288	0.124	0.142	0.269	0.545
Ratio	0.734	0.581	0.983	0.623	0.593	0.100	0.483
(3) Effective corruption							
Conventional	0.260	0.120	0.230	0.042	0.045	0.016	0.150
Reticence-Adjusted	0.482	0.309	0.261	0.073	0.076	0.164	0.311
Ratio	0.539	0.388	0.881	0.581	0.593	0.100	0.483
z-statistic for test of null hypothesis that right-hand side of Eq. (11.7) equals 1	(25.11)	(56.07)	(42.33)	(5.51)	(2.57)	(37.31)	(30.48)

Notes: z-statistics based on heteroskedasticity-consistent standard errors clustered at the strata level are reported in the last row of the table behavior. The first term on the right-hand side is the ratio of the population value of the standard estimate of the probability of a visit to the true probability, and so measures the downward bias in reported visits due to reticence. The second term on the right-hand side is the ratio of the population value of the standard estimate of bribery conditional on a visit to the corresponding true probability, and so measures the downward bias in reported bribe interactions conditional on a visit being reported.

These two sources of bias are different in the two models we have considered. In particular from Eq. (11.1) we see that the bias in reported visits is:

$$\frac{1 - P[D = 1]}{w} = \begin{cases} 1, & \textit{Model A} \\ 1 - rqg, & \textit{Model B} \end{cases} \tag{11.5}$$

In Model A we assumed there is no reticence in responding to the visit question so there is no bias relative to the true incidence of visits. However in Model B reticent respondents who experienced a bribe behave reticently with probability q, and so there is a downward bias, that is $1 - rqg < 1$. We report standard and reticence-adjusted estimates of the probability of a visit, and the ratio of the two, in the first part of Panel B of Table 11.11. This ratio is equal to 1 for Sri Lanka, Turkey, and Ukraine where Model A is the preferred model. However, for the remaining four countries this ratio is less than one, and substantially so in India (67%) and Bangladesh (73%). On average, for the four countries where Model B is the preferred model, reticent behavior implies that only 81% of visits that actually occur are acknowledged by respondents.

We next turn to the bias in reported bribes which is:

$$\frac{P[D = 3]}{\frac{1 - P[D = 1]}{g(r + (1 - r)k)}} = \begin{cases} \dfrac{r(1 - q) + (1 - r)k}{r + (1 - r)k}, & \textit{Model A} \\ \dfrac{\frac{(r(1 - q) + (1 - r)k)}{1 - rqg}}{r + (1 - r)k}, & \textit{Model B} \end{cases} \tag{11.6}$$

In both Model A and Model B, the frequency of reported bribes among those who report a visit is biased downward relative to the true probability of a bribe occurring, that is this ratio is less than one when there is reticent behavior. Comparing Model A and B, the downward bias is greater in Model A. As discussed in section "Modeling Survey Responses", this is because some reticent respondents simply denied the visit altogether in Model B rather than admit the visit and then deny the bribe. We summarize the estimated downward biases in the second part of Panel B in Table 11.11, reporting standard and reticence-adjusted estimates of rates of bribery among those who admit to a visit, as well as the ratio of the two. This ratio naturally is less than one, but varies widely across countries. At the one extreme, in Turkey we estimate that only 10% of the bribes that actually occur are reported in responses to the second part of the question. At the other extreme, in Nigeria virtually all bribe interactions are acknowledged in the second part of the question. On average across the seven countries, we estimate that 58% of bribes that actually occur are acknowledged.

Inserting Eqs. (11.5) and (11.6) into (11.4), we find that the overall bias in standard estimates of effective corruption relative to actual effective corruption is the same function of the parameters in both Models A and B, that is:

$$\frac{P[D=3]}{wg\,(r+(1-r)\,k)} = \frac{r\,(1-q)+(1-r)\,k}{r+(1-r)\,k} \qquad (11.7)$$

for both models. Standard estimates of effective corruption are biased downward as long as $rq > 0$, that is as long as there is reticent behavior. We report the standard estimates, estimated true effective corruption, and the ratio of the two in the last part of Table 11.11. The downward bias is substantial, with the ratio of standard estimates to actual effective corruption averaging 50% across the seven countries. Naturally, this ratio also varies considerably across countries, from a low of 10% in Turkey to a high of 88% in Nigeria. To assess the significance of these overall downward biases, we also report the z-statistic for the test of the null hypothesis that the ratio on the right-hand side of Eq. (11.7) is equal to one. This null hypothesis is overwhelming rejected in all seven countries.

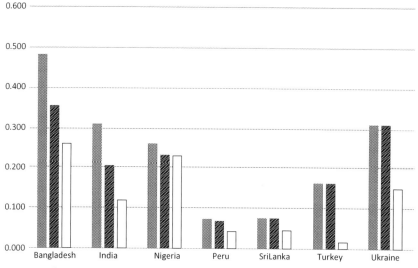

Fig. 11.1 Estimates of effective corruption, adjusted for sources of bias due to reticence

Figure 11.1 depicts the extent to which standard estimates of corruption are biased in the seven countries, how much the degree of bias varies, and the source of the bias, in terms of reticence on visits and reticence on bribes given visits. The solid, blue bar shows our preferred estimates of effective corruption while the white bar shows standard estimates. The varying heights of the first bar show how much corruption levels vary between countries, the contrast between Bangladesh and Peru, for example, being very striking. The ratios of the last to the first bars show how much the underestimation of corruption due to reticence varies between countries, with the contrast between Nigeria and Turkey standing out. Finally, the decomposition of bias is depicted in two steps, when moving from the white bar to the red bar to the solid blue bar, with under-reporting due to reticence on the bribe question first corrected and then under-reporting due to reticence on visits corrected. While Bangladesh, India, and Nigeria evidence a significant portion of their bias from under-reporting on visits, Peru and the three countries with the preferred Model A do not.

Conclusions

We conclude with five points not emphasized above. First, when aiming to produce valid cross-country comparisons of corruption, we highlight how important it is to model responses in terms of structural parameters. Second, we underscore how much cross-country perceptions of corruption can change when such perceptions are cast in terms of structural parameters estimated using models that acknowledge the effect of reticence. Third, we note that similar changes may occur over time, to the extent that reticent behavior changes over time. Fourth, we emphasize the broader applicability of these techniques to other survey settings where reticent behavior is a concern. Finally, we comment on the plausibility of the identifying assumptions that drive our approach.

Our summary in section "Results: Preferred Estimates and Analysis" reflects the results from the single preferred model for each country, basing the choice on which model maximizes the likelihood. As it happens, the preferred model differs between countries. In three of the seven cases the preferred model has no reticence on visits and in the remainder there is reticence on visits when a bribe occurred in the subsequent interaction.[22] This fact speaks to the virtue of our approach of estimating structural parameters that have identical meanings across countries but enter different models in different ways. Because respondent behavior on reticence differs across countries, standard statistics, which reflect varying combinations of those structural parameters, have different meanings across countries. By focusing on the estimates of structural parameters themselves, we are able to generate valid comparisons between countries. Since the design of any anti-corruption program would need access to those structural parameters, such programs would be much better informed by the estimates we present here than by simple summary statistics from two-step questions. Indeed, as we have shown above, the

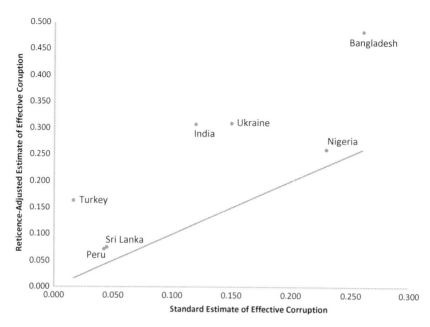

Fig. 11.2 Standard and reticence-adjusted rates of effective corruption

intuitively appealing standard summary statistics might contain little useful information given the biases induced by reticent behavior.

Figure 11.2 depicts how much perceptions of differences in effective corruption across countries can change when using comparisons of rigorously estimated structural parameters rather than comparisons of the intuitively appealing, but informationally obscure, standard estimates. On the horizontal axis we graph the standard estimates of effective corruption and on the vertical axis we report our preferred reticence-adjusted estimates, those appearing in Table 11.11. The upward-sloping line traces out the points where reticence-adjusted estimates equal standard estimates of guilt. The large differences between model-based estimates of effective corruption and standard estimates are readily apparent in the large vertical distance between any data point and the upward-sloping line. More notably, there are very significant reversals of orderings. In standard estimates, Nigeria appears much more corrupt than both India and Ukraine, whereas in our estimates Nigeria is less corrupt than those two countries. Whereas standard estimates place Turkey as the least corrupt of our seven countries, we place the levels of corruption of Sri Lanka and Peru below those of Turkey, with Fig. 11.2 exhibiting a dramatic change in the relative perception of corruption in Turkey. Given that aid allocations are partially based on such rankings, it would seem prudent to use rankings based on models using structural parameters when the data are from sensitive questions asked on surveys.

Our results clearly show that the extent of reticence, and the channels through which it is manifested in survey responses, vary considerably across countries. An open question that we cannot address with our data is the extent to which reticence varies within countries over time. Just as cross-country differences in reticence cloud the interpretation of cross-country differences in survey responses to sensitive questions, it is possible that changes over time in survey responses are affected by changes in reticent behavior. This concern may be particularly acute when comparing survey responses from before and after major political or institutional transitions. For example, it is plausible that a large shift from a repressive regime to a more open regime might simultaneously influence the incentives and opportunities for corruption, and also survey respondents' willingness to acknowledge corrupt acts. Depending on whether these effects complement or offset each other, average survey responses to questions about corruption may exaggerate or understate the effect of the institutional change on actual corruption. In principle, it is possible to address this issue empirically, by applying the methodology in this paper at different points in time in the same country, ideally before and after large institutional reforms. However, at this point we can do little more than speculate about the likely direction of these changes in reticent behavior over time, while emphasizing that our paper suggests they could be considerable.

It should be noted that our methodology is a general one, not restricted to study of corruption, but also applicable in other survey settings where responses to sensitive questions may be influenced by reticent behavior. As noted earlier, two-stage questions regarding sensitive acts are common in many other settings, and our methodology provides a framework for handling reticence in either stage of the question. When considering applications of this methodology in other contexts, we can offer at least some hints of the wider external validity of this approach. For three of the countries included here, Bangladesh, India, and Sri Lanka, we have also applied our methodology in household surveys conducted by the Gallup World Poll. Despite the very different context of household (as opposed to firm) surveys, we find a rank ordering of countries by effective reticence that is remarkably consistent with this paper, with Sri Lanka the lowest, Bangladesh next, and India having much higher rates than the other two.

To be sure, our method does rely on a strong identifying assumption—that we are able to find a set of questions (used for the RRQ's) that are approximately comparable to the CQ in terms of degrees of guilt and reticence. As with most identifying assumptions, this cannot be tested directly. However, we can provide some indirect evidence on the plausibility of our identification strategy by noting that our estimates of reticence are consistent with those in the literature where scholars have been fortunate enough to be able to compare survey responses to direct evidence of the phenomenon under investigation.[23] For example, Wolter and Preisendörfer (2013) present estimates corresponding to our rq and they find a value of 0.40 for self-reports of criminal activity, whereas our country estimates for corruption range from 0.28 to 0.64. Gong (2015) reports on a number of studies of self-reported sexual activity that contain estimates analogous to our rq ranging from 0.22 to 0.48. Funk (2016) compares polls on voting behavior to official data on Swiss referenda, finding reticence varying widely between referenda. For example, her estimates imply an rq as high as 0.45 for a measure on reducing the voting age and one of 0.26 for a measure on easing immigration restrictions. For some studies, the focus is on the proportion of wrong answers, which is comparable to our grq, which ranges from 0.07 to 0.35. The comparable estimate in the meta-analysis of six studies by Lensvelt-Mulders et al. (2005) is 0.38. Therefore, our strong identifying assumption leads to estimates that are consistent with those obtained in contexts where the availability of direct data obviates the need to make such an assumption. But these are exactly the situations where survey methods are not needed—the sought-after information is available directly. For corruption, direct evidence is near-impossible to obtain, necessitating a method such as the one we have developed above and the need for the identifying assumption that we make.

Comments by Joao Manoel Pinho de Mello

Karalashvili, Kraay, and Murrell have a very nice chapter on how to account for respondents' (lack of) honesty in answering survey questions when the question is sensitive. Their application is corruption but the scope of the question is broader. One could easily imagine applications in unsafe sexual behavior, racial biases, tax evasion, and drug consumption, among others.

The paper is important but the reason is a little subtler than the one articulated in the paper. Most corruption measurements are based on experts' perceptions (the most prominent being the Corruption Perception Index from the Transparency International and the Corruption Index of the World Governance Indicators). Evidently, perception surveys may have all sorts of problems. Among them is the fact that perception is affected by *observed* corruption, which is a function of *actual* corruption and enforcement effort; and the fact that experts may detect more higher-level corruption than more pedestrian small corruption; experts' perception may be affected by general rule of law in the country, or ease of doing business, which biases measures of corruption.

The World Enterprise Survey (WES) directly asks managers about corruption. Example: "When establishments like this one do business with the government, what percent of the contract value would be typically paid in informal payments or gifts to secure the contract?" This is a more direct measure of corruption. Clearly, if the questions in the WES are honestly answered, the problem raised by *observed* versus *actual* corruption is mitigated. If respondents answer honestly, of course. Thus the importance of the paper: respondents may respond untruthfully and thus there is a lot a value in correcting for the reluctance in responding honestly.

But its importance of the topic depends on what the user wants. Correcting for (dis)honesty in the WES is important insofar as the WES itself is a better measure of corruption than perception-based indices. If the user wants to make comparisons across countries (even ordinal ones such as country A is more corrupt than country B), then perception-based indices are useless. Experts' biases may drive absolute differences. The WES, properly corrected, is very useful. If the user wants to compare corruption for the same country over time, then perception indices are still problematic unless the user is willing to assume that enforcement effort remains constant. Again, the WES is more useful, unless the relevance of the question changes overtime (getting telephone licenses may become less relevant overtime).

If the user wants to compare how corruption changed differently in different countries, then the value of the WES is diminished. One reason is practical: one has only a few sparse observations per country (not all the same years). Perception indices are panel, short-ones admittedly, but one has some 20 observations for a reasonably large amount of countries. Another is more conceptual. In a panel setting with time and country fixed effects, perception indices are fine insofar as experts' biases and enforcement efforts do not change overtime differently across countries. This is a weak assumption.

It would be nice to have this articulation in the paper. In fact, the method for correcting for dishonesty may be more generally applicable. And in other settings one may be particularly interested in absolute comparisons or in having a standalone measure. For example, one may be interested in the level of unsafe sex in a country. In this case, honest direct answers are extremely valuable. My view is that corruption is an application of a smart method, not an end in and of itself for this paper (not to diminish the importance of corruption). The paper is more interesting than the stated goal of having a cross-country comparable measure of corruption.

A second general comment refers to the reason why some countries are more corrupt than others and, more importantly, why respondents in Peru and Sri Lanka are more forward with surveyors than in Turkey. This is interesting per se, but also as a check to the method. It would be reassuring to have some independent corroboration, even if only qualitative.

On the method itself, the identification assumption seems to be that "answers to all questions—CQs and RRQs—can be modeled using the same parameter values". This assumption, although reasonable in general, could be better defended. In fact, assuming that the answers to questions CQs and RRQs can be modeled with the same parameter values seems to imply that admitting to corruption (the CQs as well as some RRQs) is the same as admitting to discrimination (unfairly dismissing an employee).

The parameter k allows reticence in responding and guilt (being corrupt) are correlated. But it seems that one makes another independence assumptions. For example, being asked a bribe is independent of receiving a visit for an official. This seems far from a trivial assumption. It would be great to have an idea on how results could change if this assumption is violated.

Appendix A: The Survey Questions and the Data

The Two-Step Conventional Question

1. A professional surveyor read the following to the respondent: *"Over the last year, was this establishment visited or inspected by tax officials?"* Respondents could either answer "Yes", or "No", or "Don't know" (DK) or refuse (R) to answer. Respondents answering DK or R were dropped from the sample. The incidence of DK and R responses to these questions is given in Table 11.12.
2. We set $D = 1$ if the respondent did not acknowledge that the visit occurred, that is if the respondent answered "No".
3. If the above question was answered with a "Yes", then the interviewer read the following to the respondent[24]: *"In any of these inspections or meetings was a gift or informal payment expected or requested?"* Respondents could either answer "Yes", or "No", or DK or R.[25] Respondents who answered DK or R were dropped from the sample. The incidence of DK and R responses to these questions is given in Table 11.12.

Table 11.12 Sample attrition due to do not knows, refusals, and interviewer effects

	Total Number of Firms Surveyed[a]	DK or R to the preliminary part of CQ	DK or R to the follow-up part of the CQ	DK or R to the set of RRQs	Answers to both CQ and RRQ available	Observations deleted due to interviewer effects	Sample size used in the estimates	Percentage of firms surveyed that is used in the estimates
Bangladesh	1442	14	74	399	982	67	915	63.5%
India	9281	64	411	1752	7206	2583	4623	49.8%
Peru	1000	2	6	215	778	188	590	59.0%
Sri Lanka	588	7	9	127	448	5	443	75.3%
Nigeria	5544	0	2	5	5537	0	5537	99.9%
Turkey	1344	25	7	361	964	0	964	71.7%
Ukraine	1002	12	140	458	473	6	467	46.6%

Note: Some respondents answer Don't Know or refuse to answer (DK/R) to more than one of the questions and therefore the sum of columns 3, 4, 5, and 6 can be greater than the number in column 2
[a]Includes only the firms that were asked both sets of questions—CQs and RRQs—used in the analysis

4. We set $D = 2$ if the respondent said "No" to the inquiry about the bribe request, and we set $D = 3$ if the bribe request is acknowledged.

The Random-Response Questions

1. A professional surveyor read the following to the respondent: *"We have designed an alternative experiment which provides the opportunity to answer questions based on the outcome of a coin toss. Before you answer each question, please toss this coin and do not show me the result. If the coin comes up heads, please answer 'yes' to the question regardless of the question asked. If the coin comes up tails, please answer in accordance with your experience. Since I do not know the result of the coin toss, I cannot know whether your response is based on your experience or by chance."*
2. The ten sensitive questions used in this battery of questions are given in Table 11.2. Respondents who refused to respond or responded "Don't know" were dropped from the sample.
3. The variable X used in the analysis is equal to the number of the seven bolded questions in Table 11.2 for which the respondent answers "Yes".

The incidence of DK and R responses to these questions is given in Table 11.12.

Cleaning the Data for Interviewer Effects

The RRQ battery is a key ingredient in our methodology, and therefore it is important to ensure that this unusual and cumbersome-to-administer procedure was implemented as designed. Enumerators received specific training on the RRQ methodology. As part of this training, they learned how the RRQ methodology is supposed to provide greater anonymity for respondents. However, they were not briefed on our intention to use the RRQ battery to make inferences about reticence.

Despite these precautions we do find some evidence of interviewer effects in the data that might indicate variation across interviewers in the implementation of the RRQs. In all countries we have information on the identity of the interviewer for each respondent.[26] For each interviewer, we calculated the proportion of respondents with seven "No" responses on the RRQs. For most interviewers in most countries, we found rates of seven "No" responses that were not too different from the corresponding country averages. However, we did find some interviewers with implausibly high rates of seven "No" responses. We speculate that this may reflect differences across interviewers in how the RRQ was implemented. One possibility is that the interviewer incorrectly had the respondent toss the coin only once and let a single outcome govern the responses to all questions in the RRQ battery. This could lead to an upward bias in our estimates of the prevalence of reticent behavior. To avoid such a possibility, we drop all interviews performed by interviewers whose interviewer-specific rate of seven "No" responses on the sensitive RRQ questions was more than five standard deviations above the corresponding country average.[27] Combining all surveys except India, we drop 2% of interviewers who accounted for just under one tenth of all respondents who answered "No" seven times on the RRQ battery. Including India, we drop a total of 4% of interviewers, together accounting for over third of all of the respondents who answered "No" seven times.

This process is necessary in order to pursue the objective of focusing solely on the effects of respondent reticence. Our goal is not to evaluate the properties of survey data as a whole, but rather to investigate the effect of reticent behavior on the CQ as a possible source of bias in estimates of corruption. The goal is furthered by focusing on a subset of the data where one can be most sure that interview procedures were followed faithfully. We also note that while dropping these interviewers naturally increases the rate of "Yes" responses on the RRQ, it only has small effects on the rate of "Yes" responses on the CQ. This treatment of interviewers did not result in any changes in the data from Turkey and Nigeria. It had the biggest effect on the rate of "Yes" responses on the second part of the CQ in the data from India where the rate increased from 9.1% to 11.9%. In Peru, Bangladesh 2011, and Bangladesh 2013, this rate increased by less than one percentage point, and in Ukraine it decreased by less than 0.1 percentage point. This suggests that our concerns about the dropped interviewers applies only to their administration of the RRQs, except in India, perhaps.

Appendix B: The Assumption That Reticence on the CQ and the RRQs Is the Same

Our methodology assumes that rates of reticence on the CQ are the same as on the RRQs. This appears to be a strong assumption because the RRQ was developed with the exact purpose of reducing respondent reticence relative to that on CQs. In this Appendix we justify our assumption in two ways. First, we show that the assumption is reasonable given current evidence in the survey-research literature. Second, we show that one of our major conclusions—the underestimation of corruption—is robust when this assumption is relaxed, that is, assuming the RRQ does reduce respondent reticence.

In a meta-analysis, Lensvelt-Mulders et al. (2005) examined the few studies where RRQs and CQs were used and external validation of survey responses was possible. They found that on average RRQs had 90% of the reticence of conventional face-to-face interview questions (CQs). Holbrook and Krosnick (2010) and Wolter and Preisendörfer (2013) cite a large number of studies of the effects of RRQs versus CQs and both conclude that there are reasons to doubt the efficacy of RRQs. After conducting their own study showing that the use of RRQs actually increased estimates of voter turnout to impossible levels, Holbrook and Krosnick (2010, p. 336) conclude that " . . . among the few studies that have compared RRT and direct self-report estimates of socially admirable attributes, none yielded consistent evidence that the RRT significantly reduced reported rates . . . This calls into question interpretations of all past RRT studies and raises serious questions about whether the RRT has practical value for increasing survey reporting accuracy."[28]

Coutts and Jann (2011) used exactly the technique that we used in our study—forced-response, manual-coin toss RRQ—to examine six sensitive topics. They find that admission rates for RRQs are much lower than for CQs for not buying a ticket on public transport, shoplifting, marijuana use, driving under the influence (DUI), and infidelity, while higher only for keeping extra change when too much was given in a transaction. They attribute their results on RRQs as reflecting the fact that a forced-yes response can feel like an admission of guilt. (Indeed, a yes response should mean that the Bayesian posterior probability of guilt is higher than the prior for anybody but the respondent, such as a judgmental interviewer.) Wolter and Preisendörfer (2013) also compared a CQ to a forced-response RRQ, questioning a sample of known convicted criminals on whether they had committed an offense. Whereas 100% of the sample were guilty, 57.5% acknowledged this in a CQ and 59.6% in an RRQ, a trivial increase in candor. As the qualitative study of Lensvelt-Mulders and Boeije (2007) shows, the forced-response of yes after a coin toss is highly unpopular among respondents, thus suggesting the reason why RRQs might not produce their desired effect.

One can also address the issue analytically. Suppose that the world is such that reticence on the RRQ is less than on the CQ, that is the RRQ has some of the effect that its proponents hoped for. In terms of the parameters of our models, there are now two values of q, one for the CQ and one for the RRQs, and $q^{CQ} > q^{RRQ}$. One can then ask what the biases in our estimation procedure would be given that our procedure embodies the assumption that reticence is the same on the two types of questions. This is easy to answer analytically in one case, when there is a one-step CQ and $k = 1$. (This is equivalent to Model A with $k = 1$, since in that model respondents are always candid about visits). Suppose that our ML estimate of average guilt is denoted g^e and the true value of average guilt is g^a. Then, it is straightforward to show that $\frac{g^e}{(1+g^e)}$ consistently estimates $\frac{g^a}{(1+g^a)} \cdot \frac{(1-rq^{CQ})}{(1-rq^{RRQ})}$.[29] Thus our procedures underestimate the actual rate of guilt in this special case.

When we turn to model B or instances where $k < 1$, or both, the analytics is not as straightforward. Thus, we use simulations for the analysis. A single simulation is as follows. We generate a data set of 10,000 observations using one of our models, for example model B, and parameter values that appear in Table 11.11 for a particular country for

Table **11.13** Simulation results

Model used in estimation	Country whose parameter values are taken from Table 11.11	True value of effective corruption in model simulation (from Table 11.11)	Maximum-likelihood estimate of effective corruption
B	Bangladesh	0.482	0.409 (0.009)
B	India	0.309	0.199 (0.008)
B	Nigeria	0.261	0.234 (0.006)
B	Peru	0.073	0.061 (0.004)
A	Sri Lanka	0.076	0.055 (0.004)
A	Turkey	0.164	0.03 (0.004)
A	Ukraine	0.31	0.095 (0.005)

Note: standard errors of estimates in parentheses

which that model is preferred, for example India. However, when we generate the observations we make one variation on the model: we assume reticence on the RRQ is less than on the CQ. That is, q^{CQ} is set at the value of q in Table 11.11, but $q^{RRQ} = 0.8 \times q^{CQ}$. Then when we estimate the model we incorrectly assume that the simulated world is one where $q^{CQ} = q^{RRQ}$, that is, estimation is as described in section "Estimation and Definitions of Composite Parameters".

The results of the simulations appear in the table immediately above. Because the results are so consistent, and consistent with the analytics for the simple case above, six simulations are sufficient, each one matching our preferred model for a country. In all cases, our procedures severely underestimate the true rates of effective corruption when the world is one in which $q^{CQ} = 0.8 \times q^{RRQ}$ and estimation incorrectly imposes the assumption that $q^{CQ} = q^{RRQ}$. The degree of underestimation varies between 3 standard deviations (Peru) and 43 (Ukraine). Thus, our conclusion that standard estimates of corruption are significantly under-estimated is robust to the criticism that we have incorrectly assumed that the RRQ has no affect in diminishing respondent reticence (Table 11.13).

Notes

1. See "Counting Calories", *The Economist* Aug 13, 2016.
2. "Corruption still alive and well in post-bailout Greece" *The Guardian* December 3, 2014 http://www.theguardian.com/world/2014/dec/03/greece-corruption-alive-and-well.
3. In Appendix B, we argue that this is a reasonable assumption and also summarize some simulation results that show that our estimates of the degree of downward bias in standard measures of corruption are lower than those that would be obtained should the RRQ work as designed.
4. Kraay and Murrell (2016a) used two different data sets in their implementation. For brevity, we focus on their implementation that uses data from the World Bank's Enterprise Surveys project (World Bank 2015), since this project also provides the data for the set of countries on which this paper focuses.
5. Full details of the methodology can be found at http://www.enterprisesurveys.org/methodology. Stratified random sampling was used, with strata based on firm size, geographical location, and economic sector. Given the small sample size and the oversampling of some industries, the pattern of sampling weights is highly skewed. To prevent a small number of firms with very high weights from dominating our results, we report unweighted results throughout the paper. As a result, our results should be interpreted as representative only of the sample of firms in the data.
6. See, for example, Transparency International's survey for the Global Corruption Barometer http://files.transparency.org/content/download/604/2549/file/2013_GlobalCorruptionBarometer_EN.pdf, the questions on gambling in the Fed's Survey of Household Economics and Decision making http://www.federalreserve.gov/econresdata/2014-economic-well-being-of-us-households-in-2013-appendix-2.htm, the questions on health behavior in the World Health Survey of the WHO http://www.who.int/healthinfo/survey/en/, the World Justice Project's questions on corruption http://worldjusticeproject.org/sites/default/files/gpp_2013_final.pdf, the questions on unwanted sexual acts in the National Crime Victimization Survey http://www.bjs.gov/index.cfm?ty=dcdetail&iid=245, and the questions on sexual behavior in the Demographic and Health Surveys of USAID http://dhsprogram.com/What-We-Do/Survey-Types/DHS-Questionnaires.cfm.

7. Several measures of corruption produced and used by the World Bank are available at: http://www.enterprisesurveys.org/data/exploretopics/corruption.

8. With one caveat: refusals to answer are sometimes treated as admissions of guilt, as for example in analysis conducted by the World Bank's Enterprise Surveys unit.

9. Because these RRQs are not part of the core questionnaire for the World Bank's Enterprise Surveys, we placed these questions in selected Enterprise Surveys over the past several years, in collaboration with the Enterprise Survey team at the World Bank. We are particularly grateful to Giuseppe Iarossi, Jorge Rodríguez Meza, Veselin Kuntchev, and Arvind Jain for their cooperation in placing these questions.

10. Specifically, under the assumption that the respondent has done none of the sensitive acts, the probability of observing seven "No" responses is $0.5^7 < 0.01$.

11. Specifically, under the assumption that the respondent has done none of the sensitive acts, the probability of observing one or two "Yes" responses can readily be calculated from the binomial distribution with seven trials and a success probability of 0.5.

12. It is of course plausible that businesses of different characteristics (size, activity, etc.) have different probabilities of getting a visit or inspection by tax officials. However, we do not model tax officials' choices here.

13. On the WBES questionnaires, this tax question appears in the middle (or in Nigeria, at the end) of a series of two-part questions each of which is identical in structure to the question on taxes, but referring to other government agencies. Thus by the time the respondents reach the tax question they should know that acknowledgement of a visit will be followed by a question about a bribe request.

14. We also considered a third model, similar to model B except that all reticence respondents who chose to behave reticently did so on the visit question whether or not a visit had resulted in a bribe request. When evaluating the performance of each model—see section "Results: Preferred Estimates and Analysis" —this third model was the least preferred for all countries and therefore we have not reported any results for this model.

15. Since the assumption that rates of reticence on the CQ and the RRQ are the same is so critical to our procedures, and is non-standard in the context of the existing literature on RRQs, we elaborate on this point in Appendix B. Importantly, in that appendix we report the results of some simulations

showing that if our assumption is not correct in the sense that reticent behavior is less prevalent in the RRQ, then we *underestimate* the degree of downward bias in standard estimates of corruption.

16. This point is trivial to show using equations (1) and (2) and the information appearing in the paragraphs immediately above.

17. See Kraay and Murrell (2016a) for more details.

18. Our test statistics for the parameters are based on heteroskedasticity-consistent standard errors clustered at the strata level. Following Cameron-Miller (Cameron and Miller 2010, pp. 19–20), our coefficient estimates would be consistent even in the presence of significant intra-cluster correlation of observations although they would no longer be the ML estimates. If instead we used the test statistics that were based on standard errors that were not clustered, there would be no substantive differences in our main conclusions.

19. This composite parameter is different from the measure of corruption in dealing with tax officials that is usually publicized (e.g. by the WBES) in that it takes into account the fact that not every business is necessarily involved in the contexts that potentially involve corruption. Average guilt, estimates of which are provided in Tables 11.4, 11.5, 11.6, 11.7, 11.8, 11.9, 11.10, is the concept that is usually reported.

20. This general point is strongly reinforced when we examine the set of preferred estimates in the ensuing section. It is also a strong conclusion in Kraay and Murrell (2016a).

21. Formally, we perform the Vuong (1989) model selection test for non-nested models estimated by ML. The test is very simple and involves forming the difference between the maximized value of the likelihood function between the two models for each observation, and then performing a standard t-test of the null hypothesis that the mean difference is zero. The difference in the maximized values of the log likelihoods for the two models is statistically significant at the 5% level in Ukraine.

22. As noted above, the data for all countries reject a model that reticent respondents treat the visit as a sensitive issue in exactly the same way that they would confront a question on bribes.

23. In producing the information in the following, we made a number of assumptions on how to treat non-responses, whether voters accurately reported whether they voted, and so on. While precise numbers would change if we varied these assumptions, the overall conclusion of this paragraph would be unaltered.

24. The questionnaire contains one other question that is asked between these two questions if the respondent answers yes to the first question: "If visited or inspected by tax officials, over the last year, how many times was this establishment either inspected by tax officials or required to meet with them?" Information from this subquestion is not used here.

25. The World Bank constructs the numerator of the following variable: "Percent of firms expected to give gifts in meetings with tax officials" by including both those who answer "yes" and those who refuse to answer, effectively assuming that a refusal means "yes". In contrast, we drop from the sample those who refuse to answer.

26. With the exception of India where this information is available only for half of the sample and Nigeria where the interviewer code is missing for 2387 out of 5544 interviews. Therefore the procedure described below is not applicable to these observations in India and Nigeria.

27. Specifically, if i in country c carried out n_{ic} interviews, for which a proportion p_{ic} answered "No" to all seven sensitive questions, we dropped all the interviews of this interviewer if $p_{ic} - 5\sqrt{\frac{p_{ic}(1-p_{ic})}{n_{ic}}} > \frac{\sum_i n_{ic} p_{ic}}{\sum_i n_{ic}}$.

28. One very recent study seems to fly in the face of these judgments. Rosenfeld et al. (2016, henceforth RIS) surveyed Mississippi citizens on how they had voted in a controversial ballot initiative and found that the use of a RRQ "recovers the truth well" (RIS p. 794), a judgment made possible because the outcome of the initiative was known. However, Kraay and Murrell (2016b) show that RIS rely on a very unorthodox RRQ, one that has none of the properties that are usually deemed necessary to encourage candid behavior in respondents. Using a model of individual behavior similar to the one employed in this paper, Kraay and Murrell (2016b) also show that the survey results obtained by RIS are internally inconsistent. While there is no doubt that RIS recovered the truth well in this instance, why this was the case is something of a mystery, causing one to doubt the external validity of their methodology.

29. The version of our model with a one-step question and $k = 1$ is analyzed in Kraay and Murrell (2016a). This result follows transparently from the formulae for population moments in that paper.

References

Azfar, Omar, and Peter Murrell. 2009. Identifying Reticent Respondents: Assessing the Quality of Survey Data on Corruption and Values. *Economic Development and Cultural Change* 57: 387–412.

Boruch, Robert.F. 1971. Assuring Confidentiality of Responses in Social Research: A Note on Strategies. *The American Sociologist* 6 (4): 308–311.

Cameron, A. Colin and Douglas L. Miller. 2010. Robust Inference with Clustered Data. In Handbook of Empirical Economics and Finance, ed. Aman Ullah and David E. A. Giles. Boca Raton: Chapman and Hall.

Clausen, Bianca, Aart Kraay, and Peter Murrell. 2011. Does Respondent Reticence Affect the Results of Corruption Surveys? Evidence from the World Bank Enterprise Survey for Nigeria. In *International Handbook on the Economics of Corruption*, ed. Susan Rose-Ackerman and Tina Søreide, vol. 2. Cheltenham: Edward Elgar.

Coutts, Elisabeth, and Ben Jann. 2011. Sensitive Questions in Online Surveys: Experimental Results for the Randomized Response Technique (RRT) and the Unmatched Count Technique (UCT). *Sociological Methods & Research* 40: 169–193.

Funk, Patricia. 2016. How Accurate are Surveyed Preferences for Public Policies? Evidence from a Unique Institutional Setup. *Review of Economics and Statistics* 98: 442–454.

Gong, Erick. 2015. HIV Testing and Risky Sexual Behavior. *Economic Journal* 125: 32–60.

Holbrook, Allyson L., and Jon A. Krosnick. 2010. Measuring Voter Turnout by Using the Randomized Response Technique: Evidence Calling into Question the Method's Validity. *Public Opinion Quarterly* 74: 328–343.

Kraay, Aart, and Peter Murrell. 2016a. Misunderestimating Corruption. *Review of Economics and Statistics* 98: 455–466.

———. 2016b. *Comment on "The Use of Random Response Questions." Rosenfeld, Imai and Shapiro.* Working Paper, University of Maryland.

Lensvelt-Mulders, Gerty J.L.M., and Hennie R. Boeije. 2007. Evaluating Compliance with a Computer Assisted Randomized Response Technique: A Qualitative Study into the Origins of Lying and Cheating. *Computers in Human Behavior* 23: 591–608.

Lensvelt-Mulders, Gerty J.L.M., Joop J. Hox, Peter G.M. van der Heijden, and Cora J.M. Maas. 2005. Meta-Analysis of Randomized Response Research: Thirty-five Years of Validation. *Sociological Methods & Research* 33: 319–348.

Locander, William, Seymour Sudman, and Norman Bradburn. 1976. An Investigation of Interview Method, Threat and Response Distortion. *Journal of the American Statistical Association* 71: 269–275.

OECD. 2015. *The ABC of Gender Equality in Education: Aptitude, Behaviour, Confidence.* Paris: PISA, OECD Publishing.

Olken, Benjamin. 2009. Corruption Perceptions vs. Corruption Reality. *Journal of Public Economics* 93: 950–964.

Reinikka, Ritva, and Jakob Svensson. 2004. Local Capture: Evidence from a Central Government Transfer Program in Uganda. *Quarterly Journal of Economics*: 679–705.

Rose, Richard, and Caryn Peiffer. 2015. *Paying Bribes for Public Services.* Basingstoke, UK: Palgrave Macmillan.

Rosenfeld, Bryn, Kosuke Imai, and Jacob N. Shapiro. 2016. An Empirical Validation Study of Popular Survey Methodologies for Sensitive Questions. *American Journal of Political Science* 60: 783–802.

Shipton, D., D.M. Tappin, T. Vadiveloo, J.A. Crossley, D. Airken, and J. Chalmers. 2009. Reliability of Self Reported Smoking Status by Pregnant Women for Estimating Smoking Prevalence: A Retrospective, Cross Sectional Study. *British Medical Journal* 339: b4347.

Tourangeau, Roger, and Ting Yan. 2007. Sensitive Questions in Surveys. *Psychological Bulletin* 133: 859–833.

Trappmann, Mark, Ivar Krumpal, Antje Kirchner, and Ben Jann. 2014. Item Sum: A New Technique for Asking Quantitative Sensitive Questions. *Journal of Survey Statistics and Methodology* 2: 58–77.

Vuong, Quang H. 1989. Likelihood Ratio Tests for Model Selection and Nonnested Hypotheses. *Econometrica* 57: 307–333.

Warner, Stanley L. 1965. Randomized Response: A Survey Technique for Eliminating Evasive Answer Bias. *Journal of the American Statistical Association* 60: 63–69.

Wojcik, Sean P., Arpine Hovasapian, Jesse Graham, Matt Motyl, and Peter H. Ditto. 2015. Conservatives Report, But Liberals Display, Greater Happiness. *Science* 347: 1243–1247.

Wolter, Felix, and Peter Preisendörfer. 2013. Asking Sensitive Questions: An Evaluation of the Randomized Response Technique Versus Direct Questioning Using Individual Validation Data. *Sociological Methods & Research* 42: 321–353.

World Bank. 2015. Enterprise Surveys (WBES). http://www.enterprisesurveys.org/

Index

Note: Page numbers followed by "n" refers to notes.

© The Author(s) 2018
K. Basu, T. Cordella (eds.), *Institutions, Governance and the Control of Corruption*, International Economic Association Series,
https://doi.org/10.1007/978-3-319-65684-7

Printed in the United States
By Bookmasters